A FIELD GUIDE TO

PLANTS
—of—
ARIZONA

BY ANNE ORTH EPPLE
PHOTOGRAPHY BY LEWIS E. EPPLE

FALCON®

GUILFORD, CONNECTICUT
AN IMPRINT OF THE GLOBE PEQUOT PRESS

Published by The Globe Pequot Press
Previously published by Falcon Publishing, Inc.

ISBN 1-56044-563-7

Library of Congress Catalog Number 94-78616

All photos by Lewis E. Epple

Manufactured in Korea
First edition/Ninth printing

CONTENTS

Dedication

*To my husband, Lew, who inspired me to write this plant guide
and who traipsed all over Arizona with camera equipment
while we searched for plant subjects. His endless help, support,
and encouragement made this book possible.*

ACKNOWLEDGMENTS

The author wishes to thank the following for their invaluable assistance in identifying the more difficult plant subjects, and also for providing genus pronunciations where needed:

Dick Anderson, Chiricahua National Monument
Arizona-Sonora Desert Museum Botany Department, Tucson
Michael Bencic, Wupatki National Monument
Dr. Susann Biddulph
Jane Cole, Desert Botanical Garden, Phoenix
Dr. Carol Crosswhite, Boyce Thompson Southwestern Arboretum
Robert Dyson, Alpine Ranger District
Karen Foster, Saguaro National Monument West
Peggy Lu Gladhill, Alpine Ranger District
Wendy Hodgson, Desert Botanical Garden, Phoenix
Philip D. Jenkins, The University of Arizona, Tucson
Ron Kearns, Kofa Mountain Wildlife Refuge
Les Landrum, Arizona State University, Tempe
Dr. Charles Mason, The University of Arizona, Tucson
Sandy McMahan, Saguaro National Monument West
Vince Ordonez, Apache-Sitgreaves National Forest
Barbara Phillips, Coconino National Forest
Dr. Donald J. Pinkava, Arizona State University, Tempe
Patrick Quirk, Desert Botanical Garden, Phoenix
Roy Simpson, Chiricahua National Monument
Kathy Warren, Grand Canyon National Park

INTRODUCTION

After retiring to Arizona ten years ago my husband and I searched for a comprehensive field guide to Arizona plants—wildflowers, cacti, trees, shrubs, vines, and ferns. When we found none, we decided to write our own. And so, we planned this compact guide for hikers, campers, rangers, and other amateur botanists who are interested in recognizing, as well as learning more about, Arizona's plants.

During the past four years we traveled throughout the state photographing and carefully recording the measurements, elevations, and habitats of our plant subjects. These statistics were compared with the numerous references used to compile this guide. Where references proved inadequate, we queried plant experts. We are grateful for their interest in our extensive project, and for sharing their wealth of knowledge with us.

Arizona boasts over 3,000 species of plants—850 of which are pictured in this field guide. Grasses and most weeds are not included. It is impossible, too, for a book of this size to picture all of the species within a given genus. For this reason the miscellaneous section under each plant indicates the number of species found in Arizona for that particular genus.

The plants in any genus usually resemble each other; however, each species differs in some respect. Where a genus contains a large number of species, the amateur often finds it impossible to name the specific plant. In these instances, using a general name such as goldenrod, or thistle, or evening primrose will often suffice. On the other hand, dedicated botanists frequently spend years deliberating over a species, often changing the genus or species name several times before agreeing. These professionals deserve our greatest respect.

The ferns, the most primitive plants included in this guide, appear first in the color plates, arranged by genera. The trees appear next. They are grouped together by leaf shapes: needle-leaved, scale-leaved, fan-shaped, simple-untoothed, simple-toothed, simple-lobed, and finally, compound.

Next are the cacti, arranged as follows: tree or shrublike, cylindrical or round, jointed stems, and pad stems. The Agave Family, which includes agaves, dasylirion, nolinas, and yuccas, is represented next.

For the convenience of the amateur botanist, the remaining subjects with conspicuous flowers are arranged by flower color into the following eight groups:

    White or Whitish
    Cream to Yellow
    Orange
    Red
    Pink to Reddish Pink
    Blue to Purple (including Lavender)
    Green
    Brown

(Remember, there are color variations among flowers of the same species.)

In many instances, the flowers in each color group are divided again. Regular flowers (those with petals or petallike segments that are alike or nearly alike in size, shape, and color) are separated into the following groups: regular flowers with 3 segments, 4 segments, 5 segments (unclustered), 5 segments (clustered), and finally, 6 segments. Other categories are: daisylike (rays and disks), dandelionlike (only rays), rayless (only disks), umbels, and inconspicuous flowers.

Irregular flowers (those with petals or petallike segments differing in size, shape, or color) are also grouped together. Finally, shrubs and vines without conspicuous flowers are shown.

To use the guide, find the appropriate section in the color plates. Within that section, locate the characteristics of the plant you wish to identify. When you find the plant, or one very similar, proceed to the page of text to check description, sizes, blooming period, elevation, and habitat.

Each species is listed by its common name (e.g., QUAKING ASPEN), alternate common name(s) (e.g., "golden aspen," "quaking asp"), and its scientific name (e.g., *Populus tremuloides*)—in that order. Common names, while fun to use, vary from place to place. Scientific names, on the other hand, are standard throughout the world. The scientific names in this guide, as well as the order of the families, are based on *A Catalogue of the Flora of Arizona* by J. Harry Lehr, Curator of the Herbarium, Desert Botanical Garden. This catalogue supersedes *Arizona Flora* by Thomas H. Kearney and Robert H. Peebles, written in 1951 (with supplement in 1960). Of course, changes are ongoing and authorities often disagree on names.

We have tried to keep the scientific jargon to a minimum in the text. A glossary is included for easy reference. To help you further, the pronunciation of the genus is given in the "miscellaneous" section for each plant (the pronunciations are from numerous sources).

A majority of the photographs were taken during the period 1990–1994. The appearance of any plant varies according to the time of year and the elevation (not to mention natural factors such as the amount of rainfall). Therefore, as an aid to the reader, we indicate the location as well as the specific day of the month that the photo was taken.

With each succeeding generation more and more of our desert, woodland, and forest plants are destroyed. Many of the rarest species in our state are becoming extinct. We must protect Arizona's flora for future generations to enjoy by staying on established trails when hiking and by not picking or vandalizing our plant life.

Through the photographs and text in this guide, we hope the plants of Arizona—the common as well as the uncommon—take on a new meaning for you.

ARIZONA'S LIFE ZONES

The diversity of plant life in Arizona spans six main life zones, from a low point of 70 feet near Yuma to a high point of 12,670 feet in the San Francisco Peaks near Flagstaff. Although certain species characterize specific zones, others frequently overlap several zones. The contour of the land—canyons or mountain slopes—also influences the variety of flora within a zone. Rainfall, too, greatly affects life within a given environment. Thus, life zones are merely guides, rather than well-defined territories. Climbing 1,000 feet approximates traveling northward about 300 miles and results in a temperature drop of about five degrees.

The **Lower Sonoran Zone** is situated below 4,500 feet. Here, creosote, jojoba, paloverde, mesquite, ironwood, saltbush, bursage, and cacti abound. The plants in this zone endure high temperatures and low precipitation. Spring annuals survive as seeds, some for decades. When temperatures are just right and rainfall in the fall and winter (January and February) is sufficient, the seeds germinate. These so-called *ephemerals* ("of very short duration") develop quickly, burst into blossom, then soon go to seed. In contrast, paloverde, mesquite, ironwood, and bursage survive desert conditions because of their reduced leaf area. Others, such as jojoba and creosote, have specialized leaves for desert survival, while the ocotillo and brittlebush shed their leaves entirely during drought conditions. Still others, such as the cacti and certain bushes, have vestigial leaves or have modified their leaves to spines over evolutionary time.

The **Upper Sonoran Zone** ranges from 4,500 to 6,500 feet. At these elevations rainfall is more plentiful. Here, grasslands and sagebrush, as well as woodlands of oak, juniper, and pinyon pine are found. Here, too, lie large areas of chaparral with thickets of manzanita.

Between 6,500 and 8,000 feet lies the **Transition Zone.** Abundant rainfall at these altitudes produces huge stands of ponderosa pines. Scattered among these pines grow junipers, Gambel oaks, and Douglas firs.

The **Canadian Zone**, at 8,000 to 9,500 feet, is the province of cool, moist, fir forests. Douglas fir dominates this zone, with a mixture of blue and Engelmann spruce, quaking aspen, and white or subalpine fir.

Within the **Hudsonian Zone** (9,500 to 11,500 feet) grow spruce, fir, and bristlecone pines. These trees are usually stunted due to a short growing season; often they are twisted from the windy conditions found at these higher elevations.

The **Alpine Zone,** at above 11,500 feet, is represented on the San Francisco Peaks by sedges, lichens, grasses, and alpine wildflowers. It is above the timberline.

Each of the above zones is rich in wildflowers—some species are unique to a certain zone, others are present in several zones.

1 Forked Spleenwort, p. 7

2 Maidenhair Spleenwort, p. 7

3A Lady Fern, p. 7

3B Lady Fern, p. 7

4 Lindheimer's Lip Fern, p. 7

5 Fragile Bladder Fern, p. 8

6 *Male Fern, p. 8*   7 *Cloak Fern, p. 9*

8 *California Cloak Fern, p. 8*

9 *Narrow Cloak Fern, p. 8*

10 *Wavy Cloak Fern, p. 9*   11 *Star Cloak Fern, p. 9*

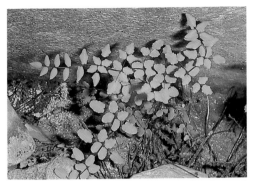

12 Wright's Cliff Brake, p. 9

13 Spiny Cliff Brake, p. 9

14 Western Polypody, p. 10

15 Bracken, p. 10

16 Flower Cup Fern, p. 10

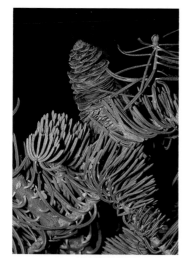

17 White Fir, p. 10

18 Subalpine Fir, p. 11

19 Engelmann Spruce, p. 11

21 Bristlecone Pine, p. 12

20 Blue Spruce, p. 12

22 Mexican Pinyon Pine, p. 12

23 Pinyon Pine, p. 13

24 Apache Pine, p. 13

25 Limber Pine, p. 14

26 Chihuahua Pine, p. 14

27 Ponderosa Pine, p. 14

29 *Douglas Fir, p. 15*

28 *Southwestern White Pine, p. 15*

TREES
Scale-Leaved

30 *Smooth-Bark Arizona Cypress, p. 16*

31 *Alligator Juniper, p. 17*

32A One-Seed Juniper, p. 17

32B One-Seed Juniper, p. 17

33A Utah Juniper, p. 17

33B Utah Juniper, p. 17

35 Salt Cedar, p. 154

34 Rocky Mountain Juniper, p. 18

TREES
Scale-Leaved

36 *Horsetail Casuarina, p. 37*

TREES
Fan-Shaped

37 *Desert Palm, p. 20*

TREES
SIMPLE-UNTOOTHED

38 *Bebb Willow, p. 39*

39 *Coyote Willow, p. 39*

40 Scouler Willow, p. 40

41A Yew Leaf Willow, p. 41

42 Silverleaf Oak, p. 44

41B Yew Leaf Willow, p. 41

43 Mexican Blue Oak, p. 45

44 Smoketree, p. 110

45 Sugar Sumac, p. 138

46 Canotia, p. 140

47 Bitter Condalia, p. 145

48 Russian Olive, p. 168

49 Quinine Bush, p. 180

50 Wright Silk Tassel, p. 180

51 Arizona Madrone, p. 181

52 Gum Bumelia, p. 186

53 Desert Olive, p. 187

54 Southern Catalpa, p. 237

55 Desert Willow, p. 238

56 Narrowleaf Cottonwood, p. 37   *57 Fremont Cottonwood, p. 38*

59 Arizona Alder, p. 42

58 Quaking Aspen, p. 38

60 Thinleaf Alder, p. 42

61 Bonpland Willow, p. 39

62 Goodding Willow, p. 40

63 Arizona White Oak, p. 43

64 Palmer Oak, p. 43

66 Netleaf Oak, p. 45

65 Emory Oak, p. 44

67 Shrub Live Oak, p. 46

68 Wavyleaf Oak, p. 46

69 Desert Hackberry, p. 47

71 White Mulberry, p. 48

70 Netleaf Hackberry, p. 47

72 Texas Mulberry, p. 49

74A *Utah Serviceberry, p. 91*

73 *Siberian Elm, p. 47*

74B *Utah Serviceberry, p. 91*

75 *Common Chokecherry, p. 100*

76 *Arizona Rosewood, p. 102*

77 *New Mexican Forestiera, p. 187*

78 *Gambel Oak, p. 44*

80 *Cerro Hawthorn, p. 95*

79 *Arizona Sycamore, p. 90*

81 *Rocky Mountain Maple, p. 141*

82 *Bigtooth Maple, p. 141*

83 White-Thorn Acacia, p. 103

84 Catclaw Acacia, p. 104

85 Desert Acacia, p. 104

86 Feather Bush, p. 115

87 Western Honey Mesquite, p. 121

88 Honey Mesquite, p. 121

89 *Screwbean Mesquite, p. 121*

90 *Velvet Mesquite, p. 121*

91 *Blue Paloverde, p. 107*

92 *Yellow Paloverde, p. 107*

94 *Arizona Walnut, p. 41*

93 *Mexican Paloverde, p. 119*

95 *Coursetia, p. 108*

96 *Ironwood, p. 118*

97 *New Mexico Locust, p. 123*

98 *Narrowleaf Hoptree, p. 132*

99 *Ailanthus, p. 133*

100 *Elephant Tree, p. 134*

101A Smooth Sumac, p. 138 *101B Smooth Sumac, p. 138*

102 Boxelder, p. 142 *103 Western Soapberry, p. 143*

104 Chinaberry, p. 143

105 Lowell Ash, p. 187 *106 Velvet Ash, p. 188*

107 Blueberry Elder, p. 248 *108 Mexican Elder, p. 248*

109A Saguaro, p. 157　　*109B Saguaro, p. 157*

109C Saguaro, p. 157

110 Senita Cactus, p. 158

111A Organ Pipe Cactus, p. 158

111B Organ Pipe Cactus, p. 158

112A Desert Night-Blooming Cereus, p. 168

112B Desert Night-Blooming Cereus, p. 168

113 Buckhorn Cholla, p. 162

114 Pencil Cholla, p. 162

115A *Teddy Bear Cholla, p. 163*

115B *Teddy Bear Cholla, p. 163*

116A *Chain Fruit Cholla, p. 164*

116B *Chain Fruit Cholla, p. 164*

117 *Cane Cholla, p. 166*

118 *Staghorn Cholla, p. 167*

119 Beehive Cactus, p. 159

120 Turk's Head, p. 159

121 Echinocactus, p. 159

122 Strawberry Hedgehog, p. 160

124 Claret Cup Cactus, p. 161

123 Rainbow Cactus, p. 160

125 *Barrel Cactus, p. 161*

126 *Pincushion Cactus, p. 161*

127 *Devil Cholla, p. 166*

CACTI
Jointed Stems

128 *Silver Cholla, p. 163*

129 *Desert Christmas Cactus, p. 165*

130 Diamond Cholla, p. 166   *131 Whipple Cholla, p. 167*

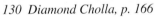

132 Beavertail Cactus, p. 162

133 Mohave Prickly Pear, p. 164

134 Grizzly Bear Cactus, p. 164

135A Engelmann's Prickly Pear, p. 165

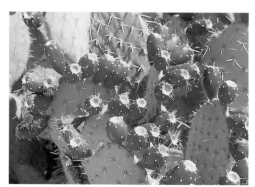

135B Engelmann's Prickly Pear, p. 165

136 Purple Prickly Pear, p. 167

137 Golden-Flowered Agave, p. 27

138 Parry's Agave, p. 27

139A Schott Agave, p. 27

139B Schott Agave, p. 27

140 Agave toumeyana, p. 28

141 Sotol, p. 28   *142 Bigelow Nolina, p. 29*

143 Beargrass, p. 29   *144 Banana Yucca, p. 29*

145A Joshua Tree, p. 30

145B Joshua Tree, p. 30

146 Soaptree Yucca, p. 30

147 Schott's Yucca, p. 31

148 Water-Plantain, p. 20

149 Texas Virgin Bower, p. 68   *150 White Virgin's Bower, p. 69*

151 Rocky Mountain Clematis, p. 69   *152 Bluestem Pricklepoppy (4 to 6 segments), p. 74*

153 *Heartleaved Bittercress, p. 77*

154 *Spectacle Pod, p. 77*

155 *Dryopetalon, p. 78*

156 *Western Pepperweed, p. 79*

157 *Thurber's Peppergrass, p. 79*

158 *Purple Bladderpod, p. 80*

159 White Watercress, p. 81

160 Arizona Jewel Flower, p. 82

161 Wild Candytuft, p. 83

162 Roughseed Clammyweed, p. 84

163 Cliff Fendlerbush, p. 86

164 Mockorange, p. 87

165 Woody Bottle-Washer, p. 170

166 Prairie Evening Primrose, p. 173

167 Stemless Primrose, p. 173

168 White Primrose, p. 173

169 Dune Primrose, p. 174

170 Red-Osier Dogwood, p. 179

171 Buttonbush, p. 244   *172 Common Bedstraw, p. 244*

173 Northern Bedstraw, p. 245   *174 Desert Bedstraw, p. 245*

175 Bastard Toadflax, p. 51

176 Red Maids, p. 61

177 Miner's Lettuce, p. 62

178 Spring Beauty, p. 62

180 Fendler's Sandwort, p. 64

179 Chamisso's Montia, p. 63

181 Sandwort, p. 64

182 Mouse-Ear Chickweed, p. 64

183 Starwort, p. 66

184 Chickweed, p. 66

185 Water Buttercup, p. 71

186 Bigelow Ragged Rock Flower, p. 91

187 Apache-Plume, p. 95

188 Bracted Strawberry, p. 95

189 Wild Strawberry, p. 96

190 New Mexican Raspberry, p. 101

191 Thimbleberry, p. 101

192 Red Raspberry, p. 102

193 Richardson's Geranium, p. 128

194 Desert Cotton, p. 150

195 White-Bracted Stick Leaf, p. 156

196 Wood Nymph, p. 183   *197 Rock Jasmine, p. 184*

198 Amsonia, p. 192   *199 Amsonia, p. 192*

200 Field Bindweed, p. 197   *201 Silver Morning Glory, p. 198*

202 Linanthus, p. 201   *203 Nuttall's Linanthus, p. 202*

205 Brittle Phacelia, p. 206

204 Desert Phlox, p. 202

207 Small Groundcherry, p. 218

206 Sweet-Scented Heliotrope, p. 208

208 Sacred Datura, p. 219

209 Desert Tobacco, p. 221

210 Wild Potato, p. 222   *211 Wild Cucumber, p. 252*

212 *Western Bistort, p. 54*   213 *Redfuzz Saxifrage, p. 89*

214 *Diamondleaf Saxifrage, p. 90*   215 *Fernbush, p. 93*

216 *Mountain Ninebark, p. 97*

217 Mountain Spray, p. 97   *218 Rock Mat, p. 97*

219 Arizona Mountain-Ash, p. 102

220A Desert Sumac, p. 138   *220B Desert Sumac, p. 138*

221 Fendler Ceanothus, p. 144

222A Gregg Ceanothus, p. 144

223 Deerbrush, p. 145   *222B Gregg Ceanothus, p. 144*

224 Pine-Needle Milkweed, p. 194   *225 Poison Milkweed, p. 195*

226 Climbing Milkweed, p. 196

227 Yerba Santa, p. 204

229 Narrow-Leaved Popcorn Flower, p. 207

228 Varileaf Phacelia, p. 206

231 Salt Heliotrope, p. 208

230 Bristly Hiddenflower, p. 207

232 White Nightshade, p. 223

233A Redberried Elder, p. 249

233B Redberried Elder, p. 249

234 Guardiola (1 to 5 segments), p. 274

235 Crowded Rayweed, p. 284

236 Stevia, p. 296

237 Funnel Lily, p. 23

238A Ajo Lily, p. 24

239 False Solomon's Seal, p. 25

240 Star Solomon's Seal, p. 25

238B Ajo Lily, p. 24

241 False Hellebore, p. 26

242 White Camas, p. 26

244 Marsh Marigold (5 to 12 segments), p. 68

243 Death Camas, p. 26

245 Western Yarrow (4 to 6 segments), p. 254

246 Desert Anemone, p. 67

247 Yerba Mansa, p. 36

248 White Aster, p. 258

249 Oxeye Daisy, p. 265

250 Fleabane, p. 272

251 Woolly Daisy, p. 272

252 Tidytips, p. 280

253 Baby Aster, p. 281

254 Blackfoot Daisy, p. 283

255 Mohave Desert Star, p. 284

257 Wild Zinnia, p. 301

256 Emory's Rock Daisy, p. 285

259 Stemless Daisy, p. 297

258 Tower Daisy, p. 297   *260 White Tackstem, p. 262*

261 Desert-Chicory, p. 288

262 *Ageratina, p. 255*

263 *Yerba-de-Pasmo, p. 259*

264 *Seep Willow, p. 259*

265 *Desert Broom, p. 260*

266 *Large-Flowered Brickellbush, p. 262*   267 *Brickellia, p. 262*

269 Esteve's Pincushion, p. 264

268 Fremont's Pincushion, p. 264

270 Water Parsnip, p. 175   *271 Water Hemlock, p. 176*

272 Hemlock-Parsley, p. 176   *273 Poison Hemlock, p. 176*

274 American Carrot, p. 177   *275 Osha, p. 177*

276 Hog Fennel, p. 178   *277 Parish's Yampah, p. 178*

278 Tall White Nettle, p. 49   *279 Russian Thistle, p. 56*

280 Redroot Eriogonum, p. 53   *281 Antelope-Sage, p. 53*

282 Alum-Root, p. 86   *283 Rattlesnake Weed, p. 135*

284 Pursh Plantain, p. 243   *285 Desert Holly, p. 254*

286 Pearly Everlasting, p. 257

287 Rocky Mountain Pussytoes, p. 257

288 Pussytoes, p. 257

289 Sand Sagebrush, p. 258

290 Ragweed Sagebrush, p. 258

291 Arizona Cudweed, p. 273

292A *Giant Rattlesnake Plantain, p. 34*   292B *Giant Rattlesnake Plantain, p. 34*

293A *Dwarf Rattlesnake Plantain, p. 34*   293B *Dwarf Rattlesnake Plantain, p. 34*

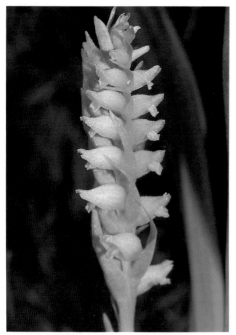

294 *Hooded Ladies' Tresses, p. 36*

295 *White-Ball Acacia, p. 103*

296 *False Mesquite, p. 106*

297B *Wait-A-Minute Bush, p. 117*

297A *Wait-A-Minute Bush, p. 117*

298 Graham Mimosa, p. 118

299 Astragalus, p. 105

300 Scruffy Prairie Clover, p. 108

301 Arizona Pea, p. 112

303 White Sweet Clover, p. 117

302 Peavine, p. 112

304 *White Prairie Clover, p. 119*   305 *Lemon Weed, p. 122*

306 *White Clover, p. 124*   307 *Sweet-Clover Vetch, p. 125*

308 White Milkwort, p. 135

309 Canada Violet, p. 155

310 Texas Frog Fruit, p. 211

311 Horse-Mint, p. 213

312 Horehound, p. 215

313 Spotted Horsemint, p. 216

314 Maiden Blue-Eyed Mary, p. 225

315 Mabrya, p. 227

317 Parry Pedicularis, p. 231

316 Twotone Owl's Clover, p. 230

318 Siphonoglossa, p. 242

319 Desert Mariposa, p. 24

320 Little Gold Poppy, p. 75

321 Brassica, p. 76   *322 Tansy Mustard, p. 77*

324 Golden Draba, p. 78

323 Draba, p. 78

325 *Western Wallflower, p. 79*

326 *Arizona Bladderpod, p. 79*

327 *Bladderpod Mustard, p. 80*

328 *Tumble Mustard, p. 81*

329 *London Rocket, p. 81*

330A Prince's Plume, p. 82

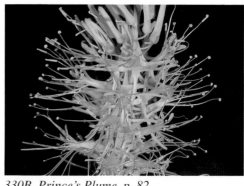

330B Prince's Plume, p. 82

332 Jackass Clover, p. 84

331 Yellow Bee Plant, p. 83

333 Hartweg Evening Primrose, p. 170

334 Yellow Cups, p. 170

335 Mustard Evening Primrose, p. 171

336 Camissonia, p. 171

337 Hooker's Evening Primrose, p. 174

338 Bottle Evening Primrose, p. 174

339 Yellow Primrose, p. 175

340 Spur Gentian, p. 191

341 Common Purslane, p. 63

343 Heartleaf Buttercup, p. 71

342 Yellow Columbine, p. 68

344 Aquatic Buttercup, p. 71

345 Macoun's Buttercup, p. 72

346 Cliff-Rose, p. 94

347 Big-Leaf Avens, p. 96

348 Creeping Wood Sorrel, p. 129

349 Varileaf Cinquefoil, p. 98

350 Shrubby Cinquefoil, p. 99

351 Clubleaf Cinquefoil, p. 99

352 Common Silverweed, p. 98

354 *Creosote Bush, p. 131*

353 *New Mexican Yellow Flax, p. 130*

356 *Janusia, p. 134*

355 *Puncture Vine, p. 131*

358 *Desert Rose Mallow, p. 150*

357 *Herissantia, p. 150*

359 Sida, p. 152 360 Tinker's Penny, p. 153

361 Southwestern St. John's Wort, p. 153 362 Venus Blazing Star, p. 156

363 Desert Blazing Star, p. 156 364 Yellow Menodora, p. 188

365 *Yellow Linanthus, p. 201*   366 *Whispering Bells, p. 204*

367 *Dingy Chamaesaracha, p. 218*   368 *Thick-Leaved Ground Cherry, p. 221*

369 *Buffalo-Bur, p. 223*

370A Utah Honeysuckle, p. 247   *370B Utah Honeysuckle, p. 247*

371 Finger-Leaved Gourd, p. 251   *372 Buffalo Gourd, p. 251*

373 Rock Echeveria, p. 85   *374 Agrimonia, p. 91*

375 Cinquefoil, p. 98   *376 Fringed Loosestrife, p. 185*

377 Corn-Kernel Milkweed, p. 194   *378 Leafless Milkweed, p. 195*

379 Butterfly Weed, p. 196   *380 Fiddleneck, p. 207*

382 Fringed Gromwell, p. 209

381 Mountain Gromwell, p. 209

383 Manyflower Puccoon, p. 209 *384 Green-Flowered Macromeria, p. 209*

385 Tree Tobacco, p. 221

386 Lemmon's Star, p. 25

387 Yellow-Eyed Grass, p. 32

388 Cream Cups, p. 75

389 Fremont Barberry, p. 72

391 Kofa Mountain Barberry, p. 73

390 Red Barberry, p. 73

392 *Creeping Barberry, p. 74*

393 *Holly Leaf Grape, p. 74*

394 *Meadow Arnica, p. 258*   395 *Bahia, p. 260*

396 Wild Chrysanthemum, p. 260

397 Desert Marigold, p. 261

398 Greeneyes, p. 261

399 Calliopsis, p. 268

400A Western Sneezeweed, p. 268

400B Western Sneezeweed, p. 268

401 Needleleaf Dogweed, p. 269

402 Five-Needle Fetid Marigold, p. 269

403 Brittlebush, p. 270

404 Engelmann's Daisy, p. 270

405 Slender Gaillardia, p. 273

406 Blanketflower, p. 273

407 Desert Sunflower, p. 273

408 Curlycup Gumweed, p. 274

409 Broom Snakeweed, p. 275

410 Arizona Sneezeweed, p. 275

411 Aspen Sunflower, p. 276

412 Common Sunflower, p. 276

413 *Prairie Sunflower, p. 276*

414A *Camphorweed, p. 277*

415 *Hairy Golden Aster, p. 277*

414B *Camphorweed, p. 277*

416 *Bitterweed, p. 279*

417 *Cooper's Goldflower, p. 279*

418 Goldfields, p. 280   *419 Yellow Spiny Daisy, p. 281*

420 Fetid-Marigold, p. 284   *421 Cooper's Paperflower, p. 287*

422 Paperflower, p. 287

423 Pyrrocoma, p. 287

424 Mexican Hat, p. 288

425 Cutleaf Coneflower, p. 288

426 Sand Wash Groundsel, p. 289

427 Threadleaf Groundsel, p. 289

428 Groundsel, p. 289

429 Senecio franciscanus, p. 290

430 Lemmon's Butterweed, p. 290

431 Axhead Butterweed, p. 291

432 Groundsel, p. 290

434 Senecio quercetorum, p. 291

433 New Mexico Butterweed, p. 291

435 Ragwort, p. 292

436 Broom Groundsel, p. 292

437 Wooton's Butterweed, p. 292

438 Golden Crownbeard, p. 298

439 Annual Goldeneye, p. 299

440 Parish Viguiera, p. 299

441 Goldeneye, p. 299

442 Many-Flowered Viguiera, p. 299

443 Arizona Mules Ears, p. 300

444 Sandpaper Mules Ears, p. 300

445 Prairie Zinnia, p. 301

446 Pale Agoseris, p. 255

447 Yellow Tackstem, p. 263

449 Prickly Lettuce, p. 280

448 Fendler's Hawkweed, p. 277

451 Fendler's Dandelion, p. 282

450 Desert Dandelion, p. 282

452 Microseris, p. 283

453 Silver Puffs, p. 283

454 Common Sowthistle, p. 295

455 Common Dandelion, p. 296

456A Yellow Salsify, p. 298

456B Yellow Salsify, p. 298

457 Chuckwalla's Delight, p. 261

458 Coulter's Brickellia, p. 262

459 Yellow Star Thistle, p. 264

460 Golden Rabbit Brush, p. 265

461 Parry's Thistle, p. 267

462 Rayless Encelia, p. 270

463 Rayless Gumweed, p. 274

464 Fineleaf Woollywhite, p. 278

465 Mexican Woollywhite, p. 278

466 Tailleaf Pericome, p. 285

467 Perityle, p. 285

468 Desert Fir, p. 286

469 Nodding Groundsel, p. 288

470 Gray Felt Thorn, p. 296

471 Hopi-Tea Greenthread, p. 297

472 Trixis, p. 298

473 Mountain Parsley, p. 179

474 Tall Goldenrod, p. 293   *475 Canada Goldenrod, p. 293*

476 Dwarf Goldenrod, p. 293

477 Missouri Goldenrod, p. 294

478 Alpine Goldenrod, p. 294

479 Sparse-Flowered Goldenrod, p. 294

480 San Felipe Dyssodia, p. 269   *481 Turpentine Brush, p. 271*

482 Jimmyweed, p. 279

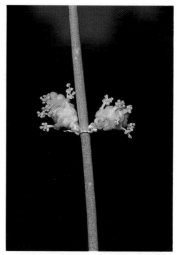

483A Longleaf Ephedra, p. 18   *483B Longleaf Ephedra, p. 18*

484A Hop, p. 48

484B Hop, p. 48

485 Rigid Spiny-Herb, p. 51

486 Winged Eriogonum, p. 52

487A Desert Trumpet, p. 52

487B Desert Trumpet, p. 52

488 Wild Buckwheat, p. 52

489 Yellow-Flowered Eriogonum, p. 53

490 Four-Wing Saltbush, p. 55

491 Woolly Tidestromia, p. 57

492A Alum-Root, p. 86

492B Alum-Root, p. 86

494 Lomatium, p. 177

493 Euphorbia, p. 136

496 Pringle's Woollyleaf, p. 272

495 Pretty Dodder, p. 197

497 Gymnosperma, p. 275

498 Yellow Lady's Slipper, p. 34

499 Golden Corydalis, p. 76

500 Yellow Bird-of-Paradise, p. 105

501 Desert Senna, p. 106

502 Birdsfoot Lotus, p. 112

503 Green's Lotus, p. 113

504 Wiry Lotus, p. 113

505 Hairy Lotus, p. 113

506 Wright's Deervetch, p. 114

507 *Bur Clover, p. 116*   508 *Black Medick, p. 116*

509 *Yellow Sweet Clover, p. 117*   510 *Rosary Bean, p. 122*

511 *Pine Thermopsis, p. 123*   512 *Mogollon Indian Paintbrush, p. 225*

513 *Wright's Birdbeak, p. 226*

514 *Bush Penstemon, p. 226*

516 *Common Monkey Flower, p. 229*

515 *Butter and Eggs, p. 227*

517 *Ghost Flower, p. 229*

518 *Yellow Owl's Clover, p. 229*   519 *Gray's Lousewort, p. 231*

520 *Yellow Rattle, p. 236*

521A *Common Mullein, p. 236*   521B *Common Mullein, p. 236*

523 *Yellow Trumpet Bush, p. 238*

522 *Moth Mullein, p. 236*

524 Squawroot, p. 239   *525 Clustered Broomrape, p. 240*

526 Common Bladderwort, p. 240   *527 Chaparral Honeysuckle, p. 247*

528 *Torrey's Crag Lily, p. 23*

529 *Desert Mariposa, p. 24*

531 *Wallflower, p. 79*

530 *Mexican Gold Poppy, p. 75*

532 *Plains Flax, p. 130*

533 Arizona Caltrop, p. 131

534 Indian Mallow, p. 149

535 Palmer's Abutilon, p. 149

536 Desert Globemallow, p. 152

537 Littleleaf Globemallow, p. 153

539 *Desert Honeysuckle, p. 241*

238 *Butterfly Weed, p. 196*

541 *Orange Skyflower, p. 287*   540 *Orange Agoseris, p. 255*

542 Scarlet Four O'Clock, p. 60

543 Mexican Silene, p. 65

544 Red Columbine, p. 68

545 Red Cinquefoil, p. 99

546 Southwestern Coral Bean, p. 111

547 Trifolium, p. 123

548 Cow Clover, p. 124

549 Crameria, p. 126

550A White Ratany, p. 126

550B White Ratany, p. 126

551 Hummingbird Trumpet, p. 175

552 Mountain Parsley, p. 179

553B Ocotillo, p. 186

553A Ocotillo, p. 186

554 Scarlet Creeper, p. 198   *555 Skyrocket, p. 200*

556 Arizona Gilia, p. 200

557A Texas Betony, p. 217

557B Texas Betony, p. 217

558 Desert Paintbrush, p. 224

559 Woolly Paintbrush, p. 225

560 Crimson Monkey Flower, p. 228

561 *Golden-Beard Penstemon, p. 232*

562 *Eatoni Penstemon, p. 233*

563 *Scarlet Bugler, p. 235*

565 *Jacobinia, p. 242*

564 *Chuparosa, p. 241*

567 Arizona Honeysuckle, p. 246

566 Smooth Bouvardia, p. 244

568 Cardinal Flower, p. 253   *569 Arizona Thistle, p. 266*

570 Mexican Hat, p. 288

571 Western Spiderwort, p. 21

572 Nodding Onion, p. 22

573 Geyer's Onion, p. 22

575 Desert Onion, p. 23

574 Red Onion, p. 22

576 Stiffarm Rock Cress, p. 76

577 Newberry's Twinpod (in pod), p. 80

579 Fireweed, p. 171

578 Rocky Mountain Bee Plant, p. 83

580 Epilobium, p. 172

581 *Scarlet Gaura (slightly irregular)*, p. 172

583 *Wright's Bluets*, p. 245

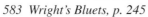

582 *Lizard-Tail (slightly irregular)*, p. 172

584 *Houstonia*, p. 246

585 Red Maids, p. 61

586 Clubleaf Flameflower, p. 63

588 Scouler's Catchfly, p. 65

587 Sleepy Catchfly, p. 65

589 Arizona Rose, p. 100

590 Fendler Rose, p. 100

591 *Prairie Smoke, p. 96*

592 *Himalaya-Berry, p. 101*

593 *Filaree, p. 127*

594 *Wild Geranium, p. 127*

595 *Carolina Geranium, p. 128*

596 *Wood Sorrel, p. 129*

597 Fagonia, p. 130   *598 Rock Hibiscus, p. 151*

599 Common Mallow, p. 151   *600 Cheeseweed, p. 151*

602 Buckley's Centaury, p. 189

601 Desert Globemallow, p. 152

603 *Northern Gentian, p. 190*   604 *Hoary Bindweed, p. 197*

605 *Bird's Foot Morning Glory, p. 199*   606 *Broad-Leaved Gilia, p. 200*

607 *Slender Phlox, p. 202*   608 *Spreading Phlox, p. 202*

609 *Woodhouse's Phlox, p. 203*

610 Purple Mat, p. 204   *611 Shrubby Coldenia, p. 210*

613 Long-Flowered Snowberry, p. 249

612 Twinflower, p. 246

615 Roundleaf Snowberry, p. 250

614 Mountain Snowberry, p. 249

616 Sand Verbena, p. 58

617 Coulter Spiderling, p. 59

618 Desert Wishbone Bush, p. 59

619 Ribbon Four O'Clock, p. 59

620 Colorado Four O'Clock, p. 59

621 Spreading Four O'Clock, p. 60

622 Tufted Four O'Clock, p. 60

623 Cockerell's Sedum, p. 85

624 Queen's Crown, p. 85

625 Coral Bells, p. 87

626B Desert Five Spot, p. 149

626A Desert Five Spot, p. 149

627 New Mexican Checkermallow, p. 152

628 Pringlei Manzanita, p. 181

629A Pointleaf Manzanita, p. 181

629B Pointleaf Manzanita, p. 181

630 Common Pipsissewa, p. 182

631 Parry's Primrose, p. 185

632 Spreading Dogbane, p. 192

633 Indian Hemp, p. 193

634A Showy Milkweed, p. 195

634B Showy Milkweed, p. 195

635 Rambling Milkweed, p. 196

636 Goodding's Verbena, p. 211

637 Mexican Vervain, p. 212

638 Dakota Verbena, p. 211

639 Arizona Valerian, p. 250

640 Bristlehead, p. 263

641 Southwestern Lewisia, p. 62   *642 Dwarf Lewisia, p. 63*

644 Nodding Thistle, p. 263

643 Cosmos, p. 268

645 New Mexico Thistle, p. 266

646 Wavyleaf Thistle, p. 267

647 Spanish Needles, p. 284

648 Flat-Top Buckwheat, p. 52   *650 Lady's Thumb, p. 54*

649 Water Smartweed, p. 54

652 Trailing Four O'Clock, p. 58

651 Calypso, p. 32

653 Fairy Duster, p. 106   *654 Bushy Tick Clover, p. 111*

655 Graham's Tick Clover, p. 111   *656 Arizona Lupine, p. 114*

657 Slimleaf Limabean, p. 120

658 Gray's Limabean, p. 120

660 American Vetch, p. 125

659 Wright's Limabean, p. 120

661 American Vetch, p. 125

662 Range Ratany, p. 126

663 *Bergamot, p. 215*   664 *Plains Beebalm, p. 216*

665 *Foothill Kittentails, p. 224*   666 *Club-Flower, p. 226*

667 Twining Snapdragon, p. 228

668 Bigelow Mimulus, p. 228

669B Owl Clover, p. 230

669A Owl Clover, p. 230

670 Bush Penstemon, p. 232

671 Pink Penstemon, p. 232   *672 Palmer's Penstemon, p. 233*

673 Parry's Penstemon, p. 234   *674 Arizona Penstemon, p. 234*

676B Devil's Claw, p. 239

675 Wandbloom Penstemon, p. 235

677 Perezia, p. 254

678 Wright Beeflower, p. 278

676A Devil's Claw, p. 239

679 Sego Lily, p. 24

680 Blue Dicks, p. 24

681 Rocky Mountain Iris, p. 31

682 Blue-Eyed Grass, p. 32

683 Pink Windmills, p. 82

684 Turpentine Broom, p. 132   *685 Parched Fireweed, p. 172*

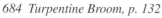

686 Rocky Mountain Columbine, p. 67   *687 Western Blue Flax, p. 129*

688 Western Shooting Star, p. 184

689 Parry Gentian, p. 190

690 Myrtle, p. 193

691 Arizona Blue Eyes, p. 198

692 Woolly Morning Glory, p. 199

693 Miniature Wool Star, p. 199

694 Blue Gila, p. 200

695 Towering Polemonium, p. 203

696 Small-Flowered Eucrypta, p. 204

697 Desert Bell, p. 205

698 Crinkle Mats, p. 210

699A *Anderson Thornbush, p. 219*

699B *Anderson Thornbush, p. 219*

700 *Berlandier Wolfberry*
(4- or 5-lobed), p. 219

701A *Fremont Thornbush, p. 220*

702 *Purple Ground Cherry, p. 222*

701B *Fremont Thornbush, p. 220*

703 Silverleaf Nightshade, p. 222

704 Purple Nightshade, p. 223

705A Harebell, p. 252

705B Harebell, p. 252

706 *Catchfly Gentian, p. 189*   707 *Pleated Gentian, p. 189*

708 *Gentianella, p. 190*   709 *Felwort, p. 191*

710 Many-Flowered Gilia, p. 201

711 Phacelia, p. 205

712 Scorpionweed, p. 205

713 Wild Heliotrope, p. 206

714 Many-Flowered Stickseed, p. 207

715 Franciscan Bluebells, p. 210

716 *Prostrate Vervain, p. 212*

717 *Lilac Chaste-Tree, p. 213*

718 *Leafybract Aster, p. 259*

720 *Aspen Fleabane, p. 271*

719 *Princely Daisy, p. 271*

721 *Machaeranthera* (var. *asteroides*), p. 281   722 *Machaeranthera* (var. *glandulosa*), p. 281

723 *Tansyleaf Spine Aster, p. 282*   724 *Mohave Aster, p. 282*

725 *Common Chicory, p. 265*

726 *Desert Straw, p. 295*   727 *Thurber's Stephanomeria, p. 295*

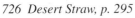

728 *Russian Knapweed, p. 263*   729 *Bull Thistle, p. 267*

730 Yellow Spine Thistle, p. 266

731 Wheeler Thistle, p. 268

732 Marsh Fleabane, p. 286

733 Odora, p. 286

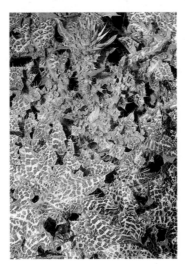

734 Milk Thistle, p. 292

735 *Desert Holly, p. 56*   736 *Red Spiderling, p. 58*

Purple Berries

737 *Pokeberry, p. 61*   738 *Rocky Mountain Blueberry, p. 182*

739 *Bearberry Honeysuckle, p. 247*   740 *Common Baneberry, p. 67*

741 Western Dayflower, p. 21

742A Cologania, p. 108

743 Emory Dalea, p. 109

742B Cologania, p. 108

744 Feather Dalea, p. 109

745 Trailing Smoke Bush, p. 109

747 *Alfalfa, p. 116*

746 *Dalea, p. 110*

748 *Red Clover, p. 124*   749 *Whitetop Clover, p. 124*

750 *Teasel, p. 253*

751A Western Dog Violet, p. 154

751B Western Dog Violet, p. 154

752 Meadow Violet, p. 155

753 Heal All, p. 216

754 Wood Betony, p. 230

755 Purple Scaly Stem, p. 242

756 Columbia Monkshood, p. 66

757 Nelson's Larkspur, p. 70

758 Paleface Delphinium, p. 70

759 Barestem Larkspur, p. 70

760 Towering Delphinium, p. 71

761A False Indigo, p. 105

761B False Indigo, p. 105

762 Foxtail Dalea, p. 109

763 Parry Dalea, p. 110

764 Silverstem Lupine, p. 114

765 *Bajada Lupine, p. 114*   766 *Hill's Lupine, p. 115*

767 *Coulter's Lupine, p. 115*   768 *Purple Loco, p. 119*

769 *New Mexico Vervain, p. 212*   770 *Hillside Vervain, p. 213*

771 *Sweet Scent, p. 214*   772 *Mock-Pennyroyal, p. 214*

773 Desert Lavender, p. 214

774 Field Mint, p. 215

776 Marsh Skullcap, p. 217

775 Chia, p. 217

777 Hedge Nettle, p. 218

778 Nuttall's Snapdragon, p. 224   *779 Blue Toadflax, p. 227*

780 Narrowleaf Penstemon, p. 233   *781 Penstemon linarioides*
(var. viridis), p. 233

782 *Porch Penstemon, p. 234* 783 *Whipple's Penstemon, p. 235*

784 *American Brooklime, p. 237* 785 *Thyme Speedwell, p. 237*

786 *Burro Weed Strangler, p. 240*   787 *Mountain Lobelia, p. 252*

788A *Whitevein Wintergreen, p. 183*

789 *Side-Bells Pyrola, p. 183*

788B *Whitevein Wintergreen, p. 183*

790 *Green Pyrola, p. 184*

791 *Deers Ears, p. 191*

793 *Antelope Horns, p. 194*

792 *Utah Swertia, p. 192*

795 *Rabbit Thorn, p. 220*

794 *Desert Thorn, p. 220*

796 Fendler's Meadow Rue, p. 72

797 Adder's Mouth, p. 36

798 Dwarf Mistletoe, p. 50

799 Desert Mistletoe, p. 50

800 Juniper Mistletoe, p. 50

801 Curly Dock, p. 55   *802 Canaigre, p. 55*

803 Desert Poinsettia, p. 136

804 Sweet Cicely, p. 178

805 Buckhorn Plantain, p. 243   *806A Canyon Ragweed, p. 256*

807 Triangle Bursage, p. 256   *806B Canyon Ragweed, p. 256*

808 *White Bursage, p. 256*   809 *Giant Ragweed, p. 256*

810 *Common Cocklebur, p. 300*

811A Slender Bog Orchid, p. 35   *811B Slender Bog Orchid, p. 35*

812 Sparsely-Flowered Bog Orchid, p. 35   *813 Long-Bracted Habenaria, p. 35*

814 *Narrowleaf Cattail, p. 19*   815 *Common Cattail, p. 19*

816 *Spotted Coral Root, p. 33*   817 *Striped Coral Root, p. 33*

818 Spring Coral Root, p. 33   *820 Woodland Pinedrops, p. 182*

819 Mountain Lover, p. 140

821 Common Juniper, p. 16

822 Black Greasewood, p. 57

823 Wax Currant, p. 87

824 Squaw Currant, p. 88

825 White-Stem Gooseberry, p. 88

826 Trumpet Gooseberry, p. 88

827A Orange Gooseberry, p. 89

827B Orange Gooseberry, p. 89

828 Wolf Currant, p. 89

829 Birchleaf Mountain Mahogany, p. 92

830 Curlleaf Mountain Mahogany, p. 92

831 True Mountain Mahogany, p. 93

832 Hairy Mountain Mahogany, p. 93

833 Blackbrush, p. 94

834 Crucifixion Thorn, p. 133

835 Limber Bush, p. 136

836A Jojoba, p. 137

836B Jojoba, p. 137

837 Mearns Sumac, p. 137

838 Poison Ivy, p. 139

839 Skunk Bush, p. 139

840 Sandpaper Bush, p. 140

841 Hopbush, p. 142

842 California Snake Bush, p. 145

843 Warnock Condalia, p. 146   *844 Birchleaf Buckthorn, p. 146*

845 California Buckthorn, p. 146

846A Hollyleaf Buckthorn, p. 147

847 Sageretia, p. 147

846B Hollyleaf Buckthorn, p. 147

848 Gray Thorn, p. 148   *849 Virginia Creeper, p. 148*

851 Russet Buffalo Berry, p. 169

850 Canyon Grape, p. 148

852 Roundleaf Buffalo Berry, p. 169   *853 Burro Brush, p. 278*

FERN FAMILY

Polypodiaceae (Pol-i-poh-di-AY-see-ee)

Non-flowering plants that reproduce by spores located in spore sacs, or *sori*, on undersides of fertile fronds. Each frond, or fern leaf, consists of a stem called a *rachis*—the section bearing leaflets. If the frond is compound, the leaflets are called *pinnae* (*pinna*, singular). When the leaf is divided again (*bipinnate*), the subleaflets are called *pinnules*. The lower part of the rachis (below the leafy section) is known as the *stipe* or *stalk*.

FORKED SPLEENWORT   1

Asplenium septentrionale
Fern Family (Polypodiaceae)

Description: Dark green, shiny, grasslike leaves, grows to 6" long, 1/8" wide.
Elevation: 7,700 to 9,000'.
Habitat: Crevices in rocks.
Comments: Evergreen. Eight species of *Asplenium* (as-PLEE-nee-uhm) in Arizona. Photograph taken near Willow Springs Lake, September 9.

MAIDENHAIR SPLEENWORT   2

Asplenium trichomanes
Fern Family (Polypodiaceae)

Description: Dark green, evergreen, dainty, rounded. Pinnae: 1/4" long, toothed at tips. Stipe and rachis: dark purplish brown and brittle. Grows to 7" tall, 1/2" wide. Sori: few, elongated, often overlapping each other.
Elevation: 6,000 to 9,000'.
Habitat: Moist cracks under overhanging rock ledges.
Comments: A tiny fern. Eight species of *Asplenium* (as-PLEE-nee-uhm) in Arizona. Photograph taken at Woods Canyon Lake, July 7.

LADY FERN   3A and B

Athyrium felix-femina
Fern Family (Polypodiaceae)

Description: Green, not evergreen; delicate, pinnately cleft. Pinnae with pointed tips, cleft, and toothed. Lower pinnae project forward. Rachis: smooth and slightly grooved. Grows to 3' tall, 8" wide at widest section. Sori: dark brown, curved, in 2 rows on underside of each pinnule.
Elevation: 7,000 to 9,500'.
Habitat: Shaded areas along streams and springs in rich soil.
Comments: Fronds form a vase-shaped, circular cluster.
One species of *Athyrium* (a-THIR-i-uhm) in Arizona. Photographs taken at Lee Valley Reservoir in mountains above Greer, July 2.

LINDHEIMER'S LIP FERN   4

Fairy sword
Cheilanthes lindheimeri
Fern Family (Polypodiaceae)

Description: Silvery green above, thick cinnamon brown scales beneath, tripinnate, beadlike segments. Stipe: dark brown, scaly, woolly haired. Grows to 6" at lower elevations,

11" in mountains.

Elevation: 2,000 to 8,000'.

Habitat: Dry slopes among rocks.

Comments: Grows in long rows. Thirteen species of *Cheilanthes* (ky-LAN-theez) in Arizona. Photograph taken on Mount Graham, April 21.

FRAGILE BLADDER FERN   5

Brittle fern, bottle fern, fragile fern
Cystopteris fragilis
Fern Family (Polypodiaceae)

Description: Bright green to dark green; stalk very brittle, pinnules fan-shaped and very variable in toothing. Stipe: black to dark brown. Rachis: smooth, green or straw-colored. Grows to 10" tall, 3" wide. Sori: brown.

Elevation: 5,000 to 12,000'.

Habitat: Rich, moist soil among rock ledges and springs, in shade.

Comments: Two species of *Cystopteris* (sis-TOP-ter-iss) in Arizona. Photograph taken at Woods Canyon Lake, August 9.

MALE FERN   6

Shield fern
Dryopteris filix-mas
Fern Family (Polypodiaceae)

Description: Dark green above, lighter green beneath, semi-evergreen, leathery; pinnules parallel-sided and blunt-tipped. Grows to 18" tall, 8" wide; widest at center of frond. Sori: large, whitish, located toward midvein.

Elevation: 6,500 to 10,000'.

Habitat: Rock crevices in rich soil, cool forests and along streams.

Comments: The drug aspidium is derived from this fern. Three species of *Dryopteris* (dry-OP-ter-is) in Arizona. Photograph taken on San Francisco Peaks, June 4.

CALIFORNIA CLOAK FERN   8

Notholaena californica (*Cheilanthes deserti*)
Fern Family (Polypodiaceae)

Description: Dull green and very glandular above, yellowish beneath; rough, star-shaped fronds. Frond to 1 1/2" wide, 1 1/2" long. Stipe: round, chestnut brown. Grows to 5" tall.

Elevation: 1,000 to 3,000'

Habitat: Crevices on dry, rocky slopes; in canyons.

Comments: Thirteen species of *Notholaena* (no-thoh-LAY-nah) in Arizona. Photograph taken in Superstition Mountains, January 28.

NARROW CLOAK FERN   9

Notholaena cochisensis (*Cheilanthes cochisensis*)
Fern Family (Polypodiaceae)

Description: Olive green above, brownish scales beneath; tall narrow fronds. Stipe: round, brownish. Rachis: reddish brown, very hairy, to 8" long. Pinnae: 1 or 2 pairs of lobes, roundish to oval, hairy, to 1/4" long, 3/16" wide. Frond and stem to 1/2" wide, 9" long.

Elevation: 1,000 to 7,000'.

Habitat: Dry, rocky slopes and canyons.
Comments: Poisonous to livestock. Thirteen species of *Notholaena* (no-thoh-LAY-nah) in Arizona. Photograph taken at Saguaro National Monument West, April 17.

WAVY CLOAK FERN 10
Notholaena sinuata (Cheilanthes sinuata)
Fern Family (Polypodiaceae)

Description: Olive green above, brownish scales beneath; tall narrow fronds. Stipe: round, brown with whitish scales, to 4" long. Rachis: very scaly, to 16" long. Pinnae: 3 to 6 pairs of lobes, wavy-edged, to 3/4" long. Frond and stem to 1 1/4" wide, 2' long.
Elevation: 1,000 to 7,000'.
Habitat: Dry, rocky slopes.
Comments: Often found in limestone areas. Thirteen species of *Notholaena* (no-thoh-LAY-nah) in Arizona. Photograph taken at Tortilla Flat, December 10. Another species, *Notholaena aurea,* is found in rock crevices in the oak woodlands of the Santa Rita Mountains. Photograph (**PLATE 7**) taken May 11.

STAR CLOAK FERN 11
Standley's cloak fern
Notholaena standleyi
Fern Family (Polypodiaceae)

Description: Dark green and shiny above, covered with golden wax beneath; symmetrical, star-shaped fronds. Stipe: round, reddish brown. Frond to 4" wide. Grows to 8" high.
Elevation: 1,000 to 6,500'.
Habitat: Dry banks and rock ledges.
Comments: Loses more than 50 percent of its water content during drought, forming a dusty-brown curl. Thirteen species of *Notholaena* (no-thoh-LAY-nah) in Arizona. Photograph taken at Tortilla Flat, December 10.

WRIGHT'S CLIFF BRAKE 12
Pellaea ternifolia var. *wrightiana*
Fern Family (Polypodiaceae)

Description: Bluish green. Stipe: round, grooved, shiny, very dark chestnut brown to almost black. Blade: narrowly triangular, bipinnate. Pinnae: slightly wavy-edged with margins rolled under. Grows to 15" tall.
Elevation: 4,000 to 8,000'.
Habitat: Rocky hillsides and crevices.
Comments: Evergreen rock fern. Five species of *Pellaea* (pell-EE-ah) in Arizona. Photograph taken on Mount Graham, April 21.

SPINY CLIFF BRAKE 13
Pellaea truncata (Pellaea longimucronata)
Fern Family (Polypodiaceae)

Description: Bluish green, triangular-shaped frond; bipinnate, up to 10 pairs of oval leaflets. Stipe: shiny, chestnut brown, hairless, grooved, stiff. Grows to 15" high.
Elevation: 2,000 to 6,000'.
Habitat: Rocky crevices and cliffs.
Comments: Five species of *Pellaea* (pell-EE-ah) in Arizona. Photograph taken in Superstition Mountains, February 4.

WESTERN POLYPODY 14

Polypodium hesperium (*Polypodium vulgare*)
Fern Family (Polypodiaceae)

Description: Dark green above, lighter green beneath, evergreen; pinnately cleft, 4 to 14 pairs of pinnae with rounded tips. Grows from 4 to 15" tall, 1 3/4" wide. Sori: brown, round, in 2 rows on underside of each pinnule.
Elevation: 7,000 to 9,000'.
Habitat: Moist slopes in canyons and conifer forests.
Comments: Creeping, scaly rhizomes. Two species of *Polypodium* (pol-i-POH-di-uhm) in Arizona. Photograph taken at Woods Canyon Lake, July 7.

BRACKEN 15

Brake
Pteridium aquilinum
Fern Family (Polypodiaceae)

Description: Dark green, very coarse texture, thick; bipinnate to tripinnate; broadly triangular, edges of segments turned under. Stipe: smooth, stiff, about same length as leafy part; green at first, turning dark brown with age. Frond to 3' long, 3' wide. Grows to 4' high.
Elevation: 5,000 to 8,500'.
Habitat: Meadows, open woodlands, pine forests, and burned-over areas.
Comments: The commonest fern; weedy. Often found in large colonies. Killed by first frost. One species of *Pteridium* (ter-RID-ee-um) in Arizona. Photograph taken at Black Canyon Lake, June 4.

FLOWER CUP FERN 16

Woodsia plummerae
Fern Family (Polypodiaceae)

Description: Light green, thin; pinnules fringed and wavy-edged. Stipe: dark reddish brown; undersides of fertile fronds have large dark brown patches covering the sori. Pinnae to 1" long. Grows to 7" long, 2" wide.
Elevation: 2,000 to 9,000'.
Habitat: In the shade of cliffs and rock ledges.
Comments: Mostly rock-inhabiting ferns. Four species of *Woodsia* (WOOD-zi-ah) in Arizona. Photograph taken at Woods Canyon Lake, August 3.

PINE FAMILY

Pinaceae (py-NAY-see-ee)
Represented in Arizona by evergreen trees.

Flowers: Male flowers in naked catkinlike clusters; female flowers consist of naked ovules between bases of woody scales (at maturity, the cone).
Fruit: Woody cone.
Leaves: Alternate or whorled; needlelike; borne mostly in bundles of 2, 3, or 5.

WHITE FIR 17

Silver fir, concolor fir, balsam fir, white balsam
Abies concolor
Pine Family (Pinaceae)

Height:	To 150'.
Trunk:	To 3 1/2' in diameter.
Bark:	Dark gray, thick, deeply furrowed.
Cones:	Grayish green, to 5" long; upright in top part of tree; do not fall after shedding seeds.
Needles:	Pale blue-green or silvery; spreading and curved upward; flat, to 3" long.
Elevation:	5,500 to 9,000'.
Habitat:	Ponderosa and spruce-fir forests.
Comments:	Evergreen. When young, forms a perfect pyramid if growing in open. Pollen-producing cones appear on lower branches in spring and early summer. These soon die after wind currents send the pollen upward to female cones forming near top of tree. Birds and mammals eat seeds; porcupines chew on bark. Two species of *Abies* (AY-beez) in Arizona. Photograph taken at Black Canyon Lake area, June 5.

SUBALPINE FIR   18

White balsam, alpine fir, pino real, balsam fir, Rocky Mountain fir
Abies lasiocarpa
Pine Family (Pinaceae)

Height:	To 90'.
Trunk:	To 2' in diameter.
Bark:	Grayish brown, smooth, becoming fissured and scaly with age.
Cones:	Dark purplish to almost black, covered with beads of pitch; cylindrical, to 4" long; stand upright in top part of tree, disintegrate at maturity, leaving behind a vertical core in tree.
Needles:	Dark bluish green with 2 silvery lines on surfaces; spreading or in 2 rows, curve upward; flexible, soft, flat, with rounded or notched tip; to 1" long.
Elevation:	8,000 to 12,000'.
Habitat:	Cool, moist spruce-fir forests.
Comments:	Evergreen; smallest of true firs. Crown is long, narrow, and comes to sharp point. Branches extend almost to base of tree. Browsed by deer and sheep. Seeds eaten by birds and small mammals. Two species of *Abies* (AY-beez) in Arizona. Photograph taken at Hannagan Meadow, August 17. (Mature cone in photograph dropped on us by a careless red squirrel.)

ENGELMANN SPRUCE   19

White spruce, mountain spruce, silver spruce
Picea engelmannii
Pine Family (Pinaceae)

Height:	To 100' (rarely this height in Arizona).
Trunk:	To 3' in diameter (rarely in Arizona).
Bark:	Purplish to reddish brown; thin and scaly.
Cones:	Chestnut brown with papery scales; stiff, rounded and thinner at tip; pendent, to 2 1/2" long.
Needles:	Dark green or pale blue-green; slightly curved, flexible, 4-sided in cross section; to 1 1/4" long.
Elevation:	8,000 to 12,000'.
Habitat:	Moist spruce-fir forests.
Comments:	Twigs are minutely hairy. Narrow, pointed, conical crown; horizontal to drooping branches nearly to ground. Shallow root system easily uprooted in winds. Wood

weak and knotty, used by Native Americans for bows and hoops. Two species of *Picea* (PYE-see-uh) in Arizona. Photograph taken near Mexican Hay Lake, July 2. Mainly distinguished from **BLUE SPRUCE** (*Picea pungens*) by its shorter cones with scales thinner at tips; brownish, scaly bark; and flexible needles. If you squeeze a spruce branch without hurting your hand, it's this species.

BLUE SPRUCE   20

Colorado spruce, silver spruce, Colorado blue spruce
Picea pungens
Pine Family (Pinaceae)

Height:	To 80'.
Trunk:	To 2' in diameter.
Bark:	Dark gray or brown; thick, rough, furrowed into ridges.
Cones:	Chestnut brown; scales more or less straight across, and are not thinner at tip; to 4" long.
Needles:	Silvery blue and stiff; protrude in all directions from branch; diamond-shaped in cross section; to 1 1/2" long.
Elevation:	7,000 to 11,000'.
Habitat:	Mixed conifer forests.
Comments:	Twigs not hairy. Conical crown of bluish foliage on young trees. State tree of Colorado and Utah. Smaller than Engelmann spruce, and less widely distributed than Engelmann spruce in Arizona. Two species of *Picea* (PYE-see-uh) in Arizona. Photograph taken in mountains above Greer, July 2. Mainly distinguished from **ENGELMANN SPRUCE** (*Picea engelmannii*) by its longer cones with scales of even thickness, dark grayish, furrowed bark, and stiff needles. If you squeeze a spruce branch and say "OUCH," it's more than likely this species.

BRISTLECONE PINE   21

Foxtail pine, hickory pine, Rocky Mountain bristlecone pine
Pinus aristata
Pine Family (Pinaceae)

Height:	To 40'.
Trunk:	To 2 1/2' in diameter.
Bark:	Whitish and smooth on young trees; reddish brown, scaly, fissured on mature trees.
Cones:	Dark purplish brown, hanging; each scale tipped with a stiff, 1/4" long, incurved prickle; to 4" long.
Needles:	Dark green, curved, to 1 1/2" long; 5 in bundle, crowded, forming brushlike groupings along branch ends. Remain on tree up to 30 years before being shed.
Elevation:	9,500 to 12,000'. (Found only on San Francisco Peaks in Arizona.)
Habitat:	Spruce-fir forests up to timberline.
Comments:	Resembles a bushy, twisted shrub at timberline. Some bristlecone pines in California are over 4,000 years old. A tree ring expert dated one on Arizona's San Francisco Peaks at more than 1,400 years old. Nine species of *Pinus* (PY-nus) in Arizona. Photograph taken at Great Basin National Park, Nevada, July 21.

MEXICAN PINYON PINE   22

Mexican pinyon, nut pine, pinyon pine, three-leaved pinyon, stoneseed pinyon
Pinus cembroides
Pine Family (Pinaceae)

Height:	To 20'.
Trunk:	To 1' in diameter.
Bark:	Light gray, smooth when young; reddish brown and scaly on older trees.
Cones:	Dull reddish brown, round or egg-shaped with thick scales; to 2" wide, 2" long; open to reveal hard, dark brown seeds to 3/4" long (known as "pinyon nuts").
Needles:	Blue-green with silvery lines; 3 in bundle, fine, flexible; to 2 1/2" long.
Elevation:	5,000 to 7,500'.
Habitat:	Dry, rocky slopes with juniper and oaks.
Comments:	Slow grower. Can reach age of 350 years. Cones fall the winter after seeds disperse. Seeds or nuts under cone scales are hard-shelled and flavorful. Pinyon nuts food for Native Americans; also consumed by birds and rodents. Pinyon pitch used as jewelry cement and for waterproofing baskets. Nine species of *Pinus* (PY-nus) in Arizona. Photograph taken at Chiricahua National Monument, April 25. This pinyon pine recognizable by bundle of 3 needles.

PINYON PINE   23
Nut pine, pinyon, Colorado pinyon pine, two-leaf pinyon.
Pinus edulis
Pine Family (Pinaceae)

Height:	To 35'.
Trunk:	To 30" in diameter.
Bark:	Gray to reddish brown, furrowed into scaly ridges.
Cones:	Light brown to yellowish brown; egg-shaped; thick, blunt scales; to 2" long.
Needles:	Dark green, slightly curved; usually 2 per bundle; to 2" long.
Elevation:	4,000 to 7,000'.
Habitat:	Mesas, plateaus, and lower mountain slopes.
Comments:	Compact, rounded crown; often with short, crooked trunk. Slow grower. Large, 1/2"-long brown seeds from cones are oily and edible; known variously as pinones, pinyon nuts, pine nuts, Christmas nuts, and Indian nuts. They are eaten by wild turkeys, pinyon jays, and mammals, and are used commercially (raw and roasted) and in candies. Most drought-resistant of all pines in Arizona. Wood used for fence posts and fuel. Nine species of *Pinus* (PY-nus) in Arizona. Photograph taken near Sunset Crater National Monument, September 8. This pinyon pine recognizable by bundle of 2 needles. **SINGLELEAF PINYON** (*Pinus monophylla*) is very similar, but its needles occur singly.

APACHE PINE   24
Arizona longleaf pine, Engelmann pine
Pinus engelmannii (*Pinus latifolia*)
Pine Family (Pinaceae)

Height:	To 75'.
Trunk:	To 30" in diameter.
Bark:	Dark brown and lighter brown; deeply furrowed with age.
Cones:	Light brown; asymmetrical at base; scales tipped with prickles; conical or egg-shaped; to 5 1/2" long.
Needles:	Dark green; usually 3 in bundle; spreading or drooping; to 15" long.
Elevation:	5,000 to 8,200'.
Habitat:	Dry, sandy soil in southeastern Arizona.
Comments:	Has mostly taproots. Seeds eaten by wildlife. Not a common pine in Arizona. Can

live up to 500 years. Nine species of *Pinus* (PY-nus) in Arizona. Photograph taken near Cave Creek, Portal, April 23. Recognized by very long, widely spreading or drooping needles.

LIMBER PINE   25

Rocky Mountain white pine, white pine limbertwig
Pinus flexilis
Pine Family (Pinaceae)

Height:	To 50'.
Trunk:	To 3' in diameter.
Bark:	Young trees: smooth, whitish gray. Mature trees: dark brown to black, split by deep furrows.
Cones:	Yellowish brown; columnar, without prickles; thickened, rounded scales, blunt-pointed tip; to 6" long.
Needles:	Dark green, long-pointed, with silvery white lines on all surfaces; not toothed; 5 in a bundle; to 3 1/2" long.
Elevation:	7,500 to 10,000'.
Habitat:	Spruce-fir forests and ponderosa forests (to a lesser degree).
Comments:	Short trunk, widely branched crown with drooping, plumelike, flexible branches. Squirrels feed on seeds. Foliage browsed by elk and deer. Nine species of *Pinus* (PY-nus) in Arizona. Photograph taken near Willow Springs Lake, September 14. Distinguished from **SOUTHWESTERN WHITE PINE** (*Pinus strobiformis*) by its wider cones ending in blunt tips, needles with silvery white lines on all surfaces, and drooping ends of branches.

CHIHUAHUA PINE   26

Yellow pine, white pitch pine, rough-barked pitch pine, pino real
Pinus leiophylla var. *chihuahuana* (*Pinus chihuahuana*)
Pine Family (Pinaceae)

Height:	To 60'.
Trunk:	To 2' in diameter.
Bark:	Dark reddish brown to black; very thick, broad ridges, deep furrows.
Cones:	Light brown and shiny; scales tipped with shedding prickles; to 3" long; 3 years to mature.
Needles:	Pale green to dull gray with white lines; to 4 1/2" long; 3 in bundle, sheaths around bundles soon shed. Needles often appear randomly in clusters on trunk.
Elevation:	5,000 to 7,800'.
Habitat:	Dry, rocky slopes. Scattered in pine forests in mountains of southeastern Arizona.
Comments:	Cones stay on tree a long time. Nine species of *Pinus* (PY-nus) in Arizona. Photograph taken at Cave Creek, Portal, April 22. Similar to **PONDEROSA PINE** (*Pinus ponderosa*) but has shorter needles, smaller cones, and much darker bark.

PONDEROSA PINE   27

Western yellow pine, yellow pine, bull pine, blackjack pine, pinabete
Pinus ponderosa
Pine Family (Pinaceae)

Height:	To 125'.
Trunk:	To 4' in diameter.
Bark:	Young trees: dark brown to almost black (hence called "blackjack" pine); older

	trees: cinnamon brown to orangish yellow with irregular fissures.
Cones:	Light reddish brown, tipped with prickly scales; conical or egg-shaped; to 5" long.
Needles:	Dark green, to 7" long; usually 3 in a bundle, at times 2 (5 in Arizona pine, a variety of ponderosa found in southeastern Arizona).
Elevation:	5,000 to 9,500' (6,000 to 9,000' for Arizona pine, a variety of ponderosa pine).
Habitat:	Mountains and higher plateaus.
Comments:	The most abundant species of pine in Arizona. Lumber valuable for construction, furniture, and many other uses. Seeds in cones provide food for wildlife. The ponderosa forest extending about 300 miles on Mogollon Plateau is largest forest of ponderosa in West. With mainly surface roots, tree is easily blown down in open areas. The wood beneath the bark is twisted, which protects many of these trees from wind damage. Some large trees are 400 to 500 years old. Nine species of *Pinus* (PY-nus) in Arizona. Photograph taken at Sunset Crater National Monument, May 31. Mature trees recognizable by large, straight, orangish brown, fissured trunk free of lower branches; existing branches turn upward.

SOUTHWESTERN WHITE PINE 28

Border white pine
Pinus strobiformis
Pine Family (Pinaceae)

Height:	To 80'.
Trunk:	To 3' in diameter.
Bark:	Dark gray or dull reddish brown, becoming deeply furrowed and narrowly ridged.
Cones:	Yellowish brown, cylindrical; long and slightly thickened cone scales; tip narrow, spreading, and bent back; to 9" long.
Needles:	Bluish green, silvery white lines on inner surface only, to 3 1/2" long; 5 in bundle, slender, finely toothed near tip.
Elevation:	6,500 to 10,000'.
Habitat:	Dry, rocky slopes and canyons.
Comments:	Closely related to limber pine. Seeds eaten by wildlife. Nine species of *Pinus* (PY-nus) in Arizona. Photograph taken at Greer, August 10. Unlike similar **LIMBER PINE** (*Pinus flexilis*), cones are slimmer and have narrow, bent-back tips, and needles have white lines only on inner surfaces.

DOUGLAS FIR 29

Oregon pine, Douglas spruce, red fir, yellow fir, false spruce, Douglastree
Pseudotsuga menziesii
Pine Family (Pinaceae)

Height:	To 200' in Pacific Northwest; 100 to 130' in Arizona.
Trunk:	To 6' in diameter in Pacific Northwest, but less in Arizona.
Bark:	Dark reddish brown, very thick, deeply furrowed.
Cones:	Reddish brown, thin with rounded scales; long, distinctive three-pointed papery bracts extending from between scales; to 3" long, hanging from branches.
Needles:	Dark bluish green; protrude in all directions from branch; narrow, flat, and soft, rounded at apex; to 1 1/8" long.
Elevation:	6,500 to 10,000', down to 5,000' in canyons.
Habitat:	Mixed with ponderosa pines or with spruce-firs.
Comments:	Not a true fir. The largest tree in Arizona. Valuable for its timber. Compact, conical crown with drooping side branches. Seeds and foliage eaten by wildlife. One

species of *Pseudotsuga* (soo-doh-TSOO-guh) in Arizona. Photograph taken in Willow Springs Lake area, September 15. The cones' three-pointed, papery bracts are unique to this species.

CYPRESS FAMILY

Cupressaceae (kew-press-AY-see-ee)
Evergreen trees and shrubs.

Leaves: Opposite or whorled, short, scalelike.
Fruit: Cones. Roundish, dry, scaly; or fleshy and berrylike.

SMOOTH-BARK ARIZONA CYPRESS   30

Cupressus glabra
Cypress Family (Cupressaceae)

Height: To 40' (90' maximum).
Trunk: To 2' in diameter (5 1/2' maximum).
Bark: Variable. After shedding, smooth, dark reddish inner bark is exposed.
Cones: Reddish brown, short-stalked, hard, woody; wedge-shaped scales with a point in center of each; to 1" in diameter.
Leaves: Pale, bluish green, scalelike; thick, pointed, resinous; to 1/16" long.
Elevation: 3,500 to 5,500'.
Habitat: Canyons and slopes.
Comments: Evergreen. Cones open when mature and remain attached to tree for a number of years. Crown either conical or rounded. Two species of *Cupressus* (kew-PRESS-suss) in Arizona. Photograph taken north of Payson, September 2. A very similar species, **ARIZONA CYPRESS** (*Cupressus arizonica*), has rough bark and is found in southern and southeastern Arizona.

COMMON JUNIPER   821

Dwarf juniper, ground-cedar
Juniperus communis
Cypress Family (Cupressaceae)

Height: Shrub to 3'.
Bark: Reddish brown, scaly.
Cones: Bluish, berrylike; to 5/16" in diameter, grow at junction of leaves and branchlets.
Needles: Broad, white band above, shiny, dark green beneath; needle-shaped and concave, sharp-pointed and stiff; to 1/2" long; in whorls of three, spreading at right angles to branchlets.
Elevation: 7,500 to 11,500'.
Habitat: Rocky soils from spruce-fir forests to timberline.
Comments: Prostrate evergreen shrub growing to 10' in diameter. A valuable erosion fighter. Cones take 3 seasons to mature. "Berries" of all junipers consist of cone scales that have thickened and grown together—actually cones that never open. "Berries" are eaten by birds and other wildlife, and are used commercially to add flavor to gin. Six species of *Juniperus* (joo-NIH-peh-russ) in Arizona. Photograph taken in mountains above Greer, August 14. This juniper is recognizable by its dwarf size and shrubbiness.

ALLIGATOR JUNIPER   31

Western juniper, checkered-bark juniper, cedro chino
Juniperus deppeana
Cypress Family (Cupressaceae)

Height:	To 50'.
Trunk:	To 4' in diameter.
Bark:	On older trees the bark's deep fissures are divided into 1 to 2" squares that resemble an alligator's hide.
Cones:	Reddish brown beneath a grayish, waxy coating; hard, 4-seeded; to 1/2" in diameter.
Leaves:	Bluish green, scalelike, pointed; to 1/16" long; dense on branches.
Elevation:	4,500 to 8,000'.
Habitat:	In oak and pinyon-juniper woodlands, and lower elevation ponderosa pine.
Comments:	Evergreen; largest juniper species in Arizona. Rounded or pyramidal crown. Cones do not mature until second year. "Berries" eaten by wildlife. Cut stumps send forth new shoots. Slow grower; lives 500 to 800 years, with records of 1,100 and 1,400 years. Six species of *Juniperus* (joo-NIH-peh-russ) in Arizona. Photograph taken on Mount Graham, April 21. Mature trees recognized by alligatorlike bark.

ONE-SEED JUNIPER   32A and B

Cherrystone, sabina, redberry juniper
Juniperus monosperma
Cypress Family (Cupressaceae)

Height:	To 25'.
Trunk:	To 1 1/2' in diameter. Has several limbs arising from ground.
Bark:	Gray, shreddy, fibrous.
Cones:	Coppery (red at maturity), covered with a bluish, waxy substance; to 1/4" in diameter; usually only 1-seeded.
Leaves:	Yellowish green, scalelike; about 1/16" long.
Elevation:	3,000 to 7,000'.
Habitat:	Plateaus, plains, foothills, and pinyon-juniper woodlands.
Comments:	Evergreen shrub or small tree with very aromatic wood. Usually shrubby and limbs normally well-hidden by lower branches. Cones mature in 1 year. Seeds smaller than Utah juniper. Male and female flowers borne on different trees: pollen on male trees and "berries" on female trees. Wood used for fuel and fence posts. Cones eaten by wildlife. Native Americans had many uses for bark and seeds. Six species of *Juniperus* (joo-NIH-peh-russ) in Arizona. Photographs taken in Ashurst Lake area, September 6. This juniper recognizable by its many limbs arising from ground level; limbs are usually hidden by lower branches.

UTAH JUNIPER   33A and B

Shaggy bark juniper, cedro, western juniper, sabina
Juniperus osteosperma
Cypress Family (Cupressaceae)

Height:	To 20'.
Trunk:	To 1 1/2' in diameter. Has clearly defined trunk.
Bark:	Gray, shreddy in long strips, fibrous.
Cones:	Reddish brown covered with grayish, waxy coating; 1- to 2-seeded; to 3/4" in diameter.
Leaves:	Yellowish green, scalelike; about 1/16" long.

Elevation:	3,000 to 7,500'.
Habitat:	Dry hills, plains, plateaus, and mountains in pinyon-juniper woodlands.
Comments:	Commonest juniper in Arizona. Has broad, rounded crown. Seeds larger than one-seed juniper. Male and female flowers on same tree. Cones mature in two seasons. Native Americans use berries for beads and medicine, and wood for firewood, posts, and hogans. Cones eaten by wildlife. Mistletoe often grows in these trees. Six species of *Juniperus* (joo-NIH-peh-russ) in Arizona. Photographs taken at Ashurst Lake area, September 6. This juniper recognizable by its definite trunk.

ROCKY MOUNTAIN JUNIPER   34

Colorado juniper, Rocky Mountain red cedar, western red cedar, Colorado red cedar, weeping juniper
Juniperus scopulorum
Cypress Family (Cupressaceae)

Height:	To 40', but usually about 20'.
Trunk:	To 1 1/2' in diameter.
Bark:	Reddish brown or gray, shreddy, fibrous.
Cones:	Blue, covered with a grayish, waxy coating; 1/4" in diameter; usually 2-seeded.
Leaves:	Grayish green, scalelike, 1/8" long; young twigs on immature trees have needlelike leaves.
Elevation:	5,000 to 9,000'.
Habitat:	Mesas and rocky mountain slopes.
Comments:	Wood and leaves have pencil smell when crushed. Branches often droop at ends. Cones mature in two seasons; provide food for wildlife. Wood used for cedar chests, fuel, fence posts, and lumber. Six species of *Juniperus* (joo-NIH-peh-russ) in Arizona. Photograph taken at Oak Creek Canyon, June 8. This juniper recognizable by its upright growth and drooping branch tips.

JOINT-FIR FAMILY

Ephedraceae (eh-feh-DRAY-see-ee)
Shrubs.

Flowers:	Conelike, primitive.
Fruit:	1 to 3 hard seeds.
Leaves:	Reduced to scales.

LONGLEAF EPHEDRA   483A and B

Desert jointfir, desert ephedra, Mormon tea, popotilla, teposote, canatilla, long-leaved jointfir
Ephedra trifurca
Joint-Fir Family (Ephedraceae)

Height:	Usually 3' to 4'.
Flowers:	Tiny, pale yellow, in dense conelike clusters. Male and female flowers on separate plants.
Leaves:	Reduced to scales when present; to 1/2" long.
Blooms:	February–March.
Elevation:	Below 4,500'.
Habitat:	Desert and grassland.
Comments:	Yellow-green stemmed perennial shrub. Valuable soil binder whose scalelike leaves

help conserve moisture. Mormon settlers made tea from dried stems. Native Americans used plant medicinally for treatment of certain diseases. Eight species of *Ephedra* (eh-FEH-druh) in Arizona. Photographs taken in Superstition Mountains, February 6 (flower closeup taken March 1).

CATTAIL FAMILY
Typhaceae (ty-FAY-see-ee)
Semiaquatic perennial herbs.

Flowers:　Tiny, very dense terminal, cylindrical, brown, sausage-shaped spike of pistillate (female) flowers. Above are paler staminate (male) flowers on narrower spike.
Leaves:　Long, narrow, erect, stiff.

NARROWLEAF CATTAIL　814
Typha angustifolia (Typha domingensis)
Cattail Family (Typhaceae)

Height:　To 6'.
Flowers:　Male: topmost, yellowish and minute, grow on clublike spike; to 5" long (after pollen shed, spike is bare). Female: beneath male flowers, minute, in brownish cylinder; grow to 4" long. A definite bare space between male (staminate) and female (pistillate) flowers in this species.
Leaves:　Dark green, erect, straplike; to 6' long, 1/2" wide.
Blooms:　June–September.
Elevation:　1,000 to 5,500'.
Habitat:　Marshy areas in shallow water and at marshy areas at lake edges.
Comments:　Perennial herb. Prefers alkaline water. Three species of *Typha* (TY-fah) in Arizona. Photograph taken at Lynx Lake, September 11.

COMMON CATTAIL　815
Broadleaf cattail, flag mace, reed mace
Typha latifolia
Cattail Family (Typhaceae)

Height:　To 9'.
Flowers:　Male: topmost; yellowish and minute, grow on clublike spike; to 6" long (after pollen shed, spike is bare). Female: beneath male flowers, minute, in brownish cylinder; grow to 6" long. No space between male (staminate) and female (pistillate) flowers in this species.
Leaves:　Dark green, flat, reedlike, erect, straplike; to 9' long, 2" wide.
Blooms:　June–August.
Elevation:　3,500 to 7,500'.
Habitat:　Marshy areas in shallow water, ponds, and edges of lakes.
Comments:　Perennial herb. Leaves are used to weave mats. Pioneers used cattail fluff for bedding. Native Americans used rootstocks for food. Muskrats feed on rootstocks. Red-winged blackbirds, marsh wrens, and other birds make their nests among cattails. Three species of *Typha* (TY-fah) in Arizona. Photograph taken at McNary, August 10.

WATER-PLANTAIN FAMILY

Alismataceae (ah-liz-mah-TAY-see-ee)
Aquatic or semi-aquatic herbs.

Flowers:	Regular, white, 3 petals, 3 sepals, 6 or more stamens, 6 or more pistils. Ovary 1-celled, usually 1-seeded.
Fruit:	Achenelike, compressed.
Leaves:	Mostly basal, with bases of leaves sheathing stems.

WATER-PLANTAIN   148

Mud-plantain
Alisma triviale
Water-Plantain Family (Alismataceae)

Height:	To 3'.
Flowers:	White, 3 rounded, notched petals; 3 green sepals showing between petals; 6 green-tipped stamens; flower to 3/8" wide, in large, loose cluster.
Leaves:	Dark green, leathery, broadly elliptical; basal, to 9" long with stem, to 4" long without stem; to 2" wide.
Blooms:	June–August.
Elevation:	4,000 to 8,000'.
Habitat:	Shallow water and muddy areas.
Comments:	Many-branched. Branches and branchlets arranged in whorls around stem. Two species of *Alisma* (ah-LIZ-mah) in Arizona. Photograph taken at Woodland Lake near Lakeside, July 6.

PALM FAMILY

Palmae (palm-EE)
Arizona's only native species belongs to the fan palm group.

Flowers:	Small, in large, drooping clusters; 6 perianth segments; usually 6 stamens, 1 style, 1 stigma. Superior ovary, 3-celled.
Fruit:	Small drupe.
Leaves:	Palmate; leaf segments radiate outward from a single point.

DESERT PALM   37

California-palm, California Washingtonia, California fan palm, California Washington palm, desert fan palm, petticoat palm
Washingtonia filifera
Palm Family (Palmae)

Height:	To 60' (to 30' in Kofa Mountains).
Trunk:	To 2' in diameter.
Bark:	Grayish brown, checkered, rough.
Flowers:	White, fragrant, 3/8" long; in branched, drooping clusters to 12' long, followed by black, 1/2"-long oval fruits.
Leaves:	Light green, leathery, fan-shaped, to 6' long; 3 to 6' broad with outer part consisting of narrowly folded segments, the edges of which have threadlike fibers. Leafstalks: thick, to 3" wide, with hooked spines along edges.
Blooms:	May–June.
Elevation:	2,500'.

Habitat: Canyons of desert mountains (only Kofa and Hieroglyphic Mountains in Arizona).
Comments: Largest native palm in this country. Dead brown leaves hang on tree, forming skirt covering trunk. Provides roosting sites for birds and bats. Fruits were eaten by Native Americans, who ground seeds for meal. One species of *Washingtonia* (wash-ing-TOH-ni-ah) in Arizona. Photograph taken of an introduced specimen at Hassayampa Preserve, Wickenburg, February 27.

SPIDERWORT FAMILY
Commelinaceae (kom-mel-lye-NAY-see-ee)
Herbs.

Flowers: Regular or irregular, 3 colored petals, 3 green sepals, 6 stamens, single style (2- or 3-lobed). Superior ovary, 3-celled.
Fruit: 3-celled capsule.
Leaves: Alternate, thick, linear; parallel-veined, leaf base clasps stem.

WESTERN DAYFLOWER   741
Birdbill dayflower
Commelina dianthifolia
Spiderwort Family (Commelinaceae)
Height: To 15".
Flowers: Blue, to 1" wide; 3 petals, lower petal a bit smaller; yellow stamens; hairless; boat-shaped bract beneath flower cluster. Flower opens early in the day, wilts by midday.
Leaves: Green, narrow, to 6" long, 1/4" wide.
Blooms: August–September.
Elevation: 3,500 to 9,500'.
Habitat: Pine woods and mixed conifer forests.
Comments: Two species of *Commelina* (kom-mel-LYE-nah) in Arizona. Photograph taken in Woods Canyon Lake area, August 3. A similar species, **WHITEMOUTH DAY-FLOWER** (*Commelina erecta*), has 2 blue petals instead of 3; the third or lower petal is very small and white.

WESTERN SPIDERWORT   571
Prairie spiderwort
Tradescantia occidentalis
Spiderwort Family (Commelinaceae)
Height: To 30"
Flowers: Pink to rose or purple; 3 (rarely 4) equal-sized petals; to 1" wide, in clusters at tip of stems.
Leaves: Bluish green, long, narrow, folded lengthwise; drooping, clasping stems at base; to 3/8" wide, to 12" long.
Blooms: April–September.
Elevation: 2,500 to 7,000'.
Habitat: Rocky slopes, mesas, and clearings in pine forests.
Comments: Perennial herb. Stems contain slimy sap. Used by Native Americans as potherbs. Pollenized by bees. Two species of *Tradescantia* (tray-des-KAN-ti-ah) in Arizona. Photograph taken at Oak Creek Canyon, June 18. (Notice that instead of the normal 3 petals, one of the flowers in the photograph has 4.)

LILY FAMILY

Liliaceae (lih-lih-AY-see-ee)
Represented by herbs in Arizona.

Flowers:	Regular or near regular. Typically a flower cup with 6 sections; 3 petals, 3 sepals, 6 stamens (3 frequently without anthers); most commonly with a long pistil with 3-lobed stigma. Superior ovary, 3-celled.
Fruit:	3-celled capsule or berry.
Leaves:	Usually alternate, occasionally whorled or in a basal rosette; straight-veined, stalkless; generally simple.

NODDING ONION   572

Nodding wild onion
Allium cernuum
Lily Family (Liliaceae)

Height:	To 20".
Flowers:	Pink to white with long stamens, bell-shaped; to 1/4" long; in clustered, nodding umbel at top of leafless stem; to 1 3/4" wide.
Leaves:	Dark green, basal, grasslike; to 14" long.
Blooms:	July–October.
Elevation:	5,000 to 8,500'.
Habitat:	Cool, moist ponderosa forests.
Comments:	No other species has a nodding umbel. Crushed leaves have onion smell. Twelve species of *Allium* (AL-ee-uhm) in Arizona. Photograph taken in vicinity of Ashurst Lake, September 5.

GEYER'S ONION   573

Wild onion
Allium geyeri
Lily Family (Liliaceae)

Height:	To 1'.
Flowers:	Pink, 1/4" long, in 1 1/2" erect umbel at top of leafless stalk; thick rib on back of each petal.
Leaves:	Grasslike, shorter than flower stem; to 8" long; have onion odor.
Blooms:	June–August.
Elevation:	5,000 to 10,000'.
Habitat:	Moist pine forests and clearings.
Comments:	In certain sections of Arizona flowers replaced by small bulblets. Twelve species of *Allium* (AL-ee-uhm) in Arizona. Photograph taken in vicinity of Willow Springs Lake, August 5.

RED ONION   574

Allium geyeri var. *tenerum* (*Allium rubrum*)
Lily Family (Liliaceae)

Height:	Flower stems to 16".
Flowers:	Pink (when present), to 5/16" long, in erect umbel; sterile; replaced by small pinkish bulblets.
Leaves:	Dark green, few, onionlike; flat or curved; to 8" long.
Blooms:	July–August.

Elevation:	7,000 to 9,500'.
Habitat:	Moist mountain meadows.
Comments:	Perennial herb. Solitary, fibrous-coated bulb. Twelve species of *Allium* (AL-ee-uhm) in Arizona. Photograph taken in mountains above Greer, July 8.

DESERT ONION   575
Arizona onion
Allium macropetalum
Lily Family (Liliaceae)

Height:	To 8".
Flowers:	Pale pink, 6 petals; each petal with reddish brown, vertical stripe; to 3/4" wide.
Leaves:	Yellowish green, grasslike; to 4" long.
Blooms:	March–June.
Elevation:	1,000 to 7,000'.
Habitat:	Desert flats.
Comments:	Crushed leaves smell like onion. Grows from bulb down to 12" below soil surface. Twelve species of *Allium* (AL-ee-uhm) in Arizona. Photograph taken south of Globe, April 20.

FUNNEL LILY   237
Androstephium breviflorum
Lily Family (Liliaceae)

Height:	Flower stalk to 1'.
Flowers:	Whitish to light pink, with darker central stripe on petals; 6 petals, black anthers, petals and sepals partly joined; stamen filaments are partly united to form a tube in the center. Flower to 5/8" wide, in loose, terminal cluster of up to 12 flowers.
Leaves:	Grayish green, grasslike, narrow; few, grooved on upper surface, basal; to 8" long.
Blooms:	March–April.
Elevation:	2,000 to 7,000'.
Habitat:	Dry, sandy soil of slopes and plains.
Comments:	Leafless stem arises from a bulb. Lacks onion odor. One species of *Androstephium* (an-dro-STEE-fi-uhm) in Arizona. Photograph taken south of Parker, March 7.

TORREY'S CRAG LILY   528
Crag-lily, amber lily
Anthericum torreyi
Lily Family (Liliaceae)

Height:	To 16".
Flowers:	Yellowish orange, starlike, with 3 wide petals, 3 narrower sepals; petals and sepals have greenish to brownish vertical veins; to 1" wide; along slender flower stalk, followed by an oblong capsule.
Leaves:	Dark green, basal, pointing upward; grasslike, margins curved inward; to 1/8" wide, to 8" long.
Blooms:	August.
Elevation:	6,000 to 9,000'.
Habitat:	Coniferous forests and canyons.
Comments:	Leafless stem. One species of *Anthericum* (an-THER-i-kum) in Arizona. Photograph taken at Woods Canyon Lake, August 3.

DESERT MARIPOSA   319 and 529
Mariposa lily, desert mariposa tulip
Calochortus kennedyi
Lily Family (Liliaceae)
Height: To 2'.
Flowers: Bright orange or yellow petals with purple to black markings; membranes at base;
short-stemmed when growing in open, long-stemmed among shrubs; to 3" wide.
Leaves: Grayish green, narrow, grasslike, few; to 8" long.
Blooms: March–May, but usually April.
Elevation: Below 5,000'.
Habitat: Open or shrubby areas in dry soil.
Comments: Perennial herb. *Mariposa* means "butterfly" in Spanish. Five species of *Calochortus*
(kal-oh-KOR-tuhs) in Arizona. Yellow flower photograph taken at Patagonia Lake
State Park, April 26. Orange flower photograph taken near Superior, April 12.

SEGO LILY (SEE-go)   679
Star tulip, butterfly tulip, butterfly lily, mariposa lily
Calochortus nuttallii
Lily Family (Liliaceae)
Height: To 20".
Flowers: Tuliplike, with 3 creamy white to lavender petals; yellow petal base is marked with
a crescent-shaped purple band; dense, slender hairs near base of petals; to 2" wide,
to 5 flowers per stalk.
Leaves: Grayish green, narrow, grasslike; margins rolled upward; to 4" long.
Blooms: May–July.
Elevation: 5,000 to 8,000'.
Habitat: Dry mesas, open pine forests, and hillsides.
Comments: State flower of Utah. Bulbous root once used for food by Native Americans and
Mormon settlers. Five species of *Calochortus* (kal-oh-KOR-tuhs) in Arizona.
Photograph taken near Willow Springs Lake, June 10.

BLUE DICKS   680
Desert hyacinth, bluedicks, Papago lily, purplehead, grassnuts, covena, coveria
Dichelostemma pulchellum (*Brodiaea pulchella*)
Lily Family (Liliaceae)
Height: To 30", but usually much less.
Flowers: Lavender, 6 segments, in terminal cluster on slender stem; flower to 1" wide.
Leaves: Dark green, few, grasslike; rising from bulb; to 15".
Blooms: February–May.
Elevation: Below 5,000'.
Habitat: Mesas, open slopes, and plains.
Comments: Perennial lily. Has onionlike bulb used for food by pioneers and Native Americans.
One species of *Dichelostemma* (di-kel-oh-STEM-ah) in Arizona. Photograph taken
in Superstition Mountains, February 23.

AJO LILY (AH-hoe)   238A and B
Desert lily, ajo silvestre
Hesperocallis undulata
Lily Family (Liliaceae)

Height:	To 4'.
Flowers:	White, trumpet-shaped, fragrant; to 2 1/2" long; on long, clustered flower stalk.
Leaves:	Bluish green, narrow, wavy-margined; in basal rosette; to 20" long.
Blooms:	Mid-February–mid-April.
Elevation:	Below 2,000' in southwestern Arizona.
Habitat:	Dunes and sand-gravel flats.
Comments:	Perennial. Resembles Easter lily; called ajo lily because its big, edible bulb resembles garlic (*ajo* in Spanish). Bulbs sometimes grow as deep as 2' below surface of soil. Hawk moths pollinate flowers. One species of *Hesperocallis* (hes-per-oh-CAL-is) in Arizona. Photographs taken near Salome, March 28.

FALSE SOLOMON'S SEAL   239
Feather Solomon-plume, branched Solomon's seal, wild spikenard, treacleberry
Smilacina racemosa
Lily Family (Liliaceae)

Height:	To 3'.
Flowers:	White, starlike, with 6 petallike segments; flower to 1/8" long in branched, dense, terminal raceme on arching stem, followed by a cluster of reddish berries dotted with purple; each berry to 1/4" long.
Leaves:	Dark green, broadly lance-shaped to oval; clasping stem at base; to 6" long.
Blooms:	May–July.
Elevation:	6,000 to 10,000'.
Habitat:	Rich soil in coniferous forests.
Comments:	Perennial herb. Two species of *Smilacina* (smy-la-SEE-nah) in Arizona. Photograph taken at Greer, June 17.

STAR SOLOMON'S SEAL   240
Starry Solomon-plume, starflower
Smilacina stellata
Lily Family (Liliaceae)

Height:	To 2'.
Flowers:	White, starlike, with 6 petallike segments; to 1/4" wide; loosely spaced on a terminal, zigzag raceme, followed by green berries with dark blue, vertical stripes, berries turning black with maturity.
Leaves:	Dark green, lance-shaped; to 5" long.
Blooms:	May–June.
Elevation:	7,500 to 10,000'.
Habitat:	Moist, rich forests.
Comments:	Perennial herb. Two species of *Smilacina* (smy-la-SEE-nah) in Arizona. Photograph taken near Greer, June 22.

LEMMON'S STAR   386
Triteleia lemmonae
Lily Family (Liliaceae)

Height:	To 9".
Flowers:	Yellow, star-shaped, 6 segments, in terminal cluster on leafless stem; to 3/4" wide.
Leaves:	Dark green, 1 or 2, grasslike; to 6" long.
Blooms:	May–August.
Elevation:	5,000 to 7,700'.

Habitat: Partial shade among ponderosa pines.
Comments: This species is unique to Arizona. One species of *Triteleia* (trye-te-LAY-ah) in Arizona. Photograph taken near Willow Springs Lake, June 16.

FALSE HELLEBORE 241
Corn-lily, California corn-lily, cornhusk lily, skunk cabbage
Veratrum californicum
Lily Family (Liliaceae)
Height: To 8'.
Flowers: Whitish to greenish, star-shaped; V-shaped green gland at base; to 3/4" long, 1/2" wide; in branching, terminal cluster to 1' long.
Leaves: Yellowish green, oval, strongly veined; appear pleated; to 1' long.
Blooms: July–August.
Elevation: 7,500 to 9,500'.
Habitat: Wet meadows, around springs and bogs, and moist forests.
Comments: Perennial herb. Extremely poisonous to livestock as well as to bees and other insects. One species of *Veratrum* (ver-RAH-trum) in Arizona. Photograph taken at Greer, July 20.

WHITE CAMAS 242
Mountain death camas, wand lily, alkali grass, elegant camas
Zigadenus elegans
Lily Family (Liliaceae)
Height: To 3'.
Flowers: White to greenish white; 6 segments with green, heart-shaped gland at each base; to 3/4" wide; in elongated, terminal cluster.
Leaves: Bluish green, onionlike; to 1/4" wide, 12" long.
Blooms: July–September.
Elevation: 5,000 to 10,000'.
Habitat: Clearings in moist ponderosa pine and spruce-fir forests.
Comments: From a bulb similar to an onion. This species not as poisonous as **DEATH CAMAS** (*Z. virescens*). Three species of *Zigadenus* (zig-a-DEN-us) in Arizona. Photograph taken near Willow Springs Lake, September 15.

DEATH CAMAS 243
Wand lily, frillybell camas
Zigadenus virescens
Lily Family (Liliaceae)
Height: To 2'.
Flowers: White to greenish, bell-shaped; to 1/4" wide; widely spaced on long flower stalks that curve away from main stalk.
Leaves: Dark green, narrow, grasslike; to 12" long.
Blooms: July–September.
Elevation: 6,500 to 11,000'.
Habitat: Rich soil in moist coniferous forests.
Comments: From a bulb similar to an onion. All parts contain zygadenine, a heart depressant, and are poisonous. Three species of *Zigadenus* (zig-a-DEN-us) in Arizona. Sometimes spelled *Zygadenus*. Photograph taken south of Alpine, August 2.

AGAVE FAMILY
Agavaceae (ah-gah-VAY-see-ee)
Herbs or somewhat woody at base.

Flowers: Regular or nearly regular; 3 petals and 3 sepals, which look alike and are united below into a tube; 6 stamens. Inferior ovary, 3-celled.
Fruit: A capsule.
Leaves: Grasslike or succulent, narrow; forming basal rosette of rigid leaves.

GOLDEN-FLOWERED AGAVE   137
Golden-flowered century plant
Agave chrysantha (*Agave palmeri* var. *chrysantha*)
Agave Family (Agavaceae)

Height: Flower stalk to 20'.
Flowers: Golden yellow with no purplish tinge, in dense clusters of up to 300 flowers, on tall flower stalk.
Leaves: Bluish green, evergreen, thick; prickles on margins to 3/8" long; crowded in basal cluster to 40" wide, 32" high.
Blooms: June–August.
Elevation: 3,000 to 6,000'.
Habitat: Foothills, mountains, and canyons.
Comments: After several years, plant produces flower stalk and then dies. Native Americans roasted emerging flower stalk for food. Twelve species of *Agave* (ah-GAH-vee) in Arizona. Photograph taken at Superior, April 12, shows huge, asparaguslike flower stalk. Flowering clusters similar to Parry's agave, but lack purplish red tinge on buds.

PARRY'S AGAVE   138
Parry's century plant, mescal
Agave parryi
Agave Family (Agavaceae)

Height: Foliage to 20", flowering stalk to 18'.
Flowers: Buds reddish orange, after opening turn yellow; 6 petallike parts to 2 1/2" long; facing skyward, in large, flattened, terminal clusters.
Leaves: Grayish green, spatula-shaped, concave on upper surface; hooked spines on margins; sharp, terminal spine; leaf to 20" long, in large, basal rosette.
Blooms: June–August.
Elevation: 4,500 to 8,000'.
Habitat: Dry, rocky slopes.
Comments: After approximately 25 years plant sends up flowering stalk; after blooming, it dies. New plants already formed on root system take over. Pollinated by insects and hummingbirds. The juice of this species can be irritating to the skin. Native Americans use plant for food, fiber, soap, beverages, and medicines. Twelve species of *Agave* (ah-GAH-vee) in Arizona. Photograph taken near Payson, June 27.

SCHOTT AGAVE   139A and B
Amole, Schott century plant
Agave schottii
Agave Family (Agavaceae)

Height: Unbranched flower stalk to 9'.

Flowers:	Light yellow, waxy; 6 flower segments, long yellow stamens; flower to 2 1/2" long, 1" wide; in crowded, narrow, elongated cluster to 40" long; followed by woody fruit capsule to 3/4" long, 3/8" in diameter.
Leaves:	Dark green to yellowish green (depending on variety); linear, frequently curved; margins have fine, curved fibers, spine-tipped, concave or flat on upper surface (depending on variety); without marginal spines; to 16" long, in crowded, basal rosette.
Blooms:	May–October.
Elevation:	4,000 to 7,000'.
Habitat:	Dry, exposed slopes.
Comments:	Perennial. Resembles a yucca. Plants grow crowded together forming large mats which cover good-sized areas. Twelve species of *Agave* (ah-GAH-vee) in Arizona. Photographs taken at Molino Canyon, Mount Lemmon, May 13.

AGAVE TOUMEYANA var. BELLA   140

Agave toumeyana var. bella
Agave Family (Agavaceae)

Height:	Flower stalk to 6'.
Flowers:	Green to pale yellow, sac-shaped perianth with large anthers extended; flower to 1" long; in elongated terminal cluster on long spike, followed by oblong, thin-walled capsule to 1/2" long.
Leaves:	Light green with grayish white slashings; whitish threads along leaf margins; reddish tips; linear, concave on upper surface; to 8" long, 1" wide; in compact, circular rosette of 100 or more leaves at maturity.
Blooms:	May–July.
Elevation:	4,000 to 5,000' in south-central Arizona.
Habitat:	Rocky slopes in chaparral.
Comments:	Native to higher elevations in south-central Arizona. Some authorities rank this variety as a subspecies. Twelve species of *Agave* (ah-GAH-vee) in Arizona. Photograph taken at the Arizona-Sonora Desert Museum, November 12.

SOTOL (SOH-tole)   141

Spoonplant, desert spoon, cactus spoon
Dasylirion wheeleri
Agave Family (Agavaceae)

Height:	To 3'; flower stem to 15'.
Flowers:	Greenish white with 6 petallike segments; tiny, thousands in narrow cluster to 8' long. Male and female flowers on different plants.
Leaves:	Green, ribbonlike; margins with forward-facing teeth, split ends; to 3' long, 1" wide; in rounded, basal cluster.
Blooms:	May–August.
Elevation:	4,000 to 6,000'.
Habitat:	Rocky slopes in desert grassland and oak woodlands.
Comments:	Produces a flower stalk yearly. Desert Native Americans eat heart and young stalks, and use stalks for building material and leaves for thatching, baskets, mats, and cordage. Spaniards called plant "desert spoon" because when pulled from the plant the dried leaf and its base resemble a *cuchara* or "spoon." Dried "desert spoons" were once sold for flower arrangements, but this practice is now discouraged by conservation-minded groups. Bighorn sheep browse sotols. Heads contain a sugary sap that, when fermented, is used to produce a potent beverage called *sotol*. One

species of *Dasylirion* (das-i-LIR-i-on) in Arizona. Photograph taken at Madera Canyon, June 10. Unlike sharply pointed yucca leaves, sotol leaves have split ends; its flowers, unlike the large bell-shaped flowers of the yucca, are small.

BIGELOW NOLINA 142
Nolina bigelovii
Agave Family (Agavaceae)

Height: (Usually with a flower stalk) to 8'.
Flowers: White, tinged with green; to 1/8" long; very numerous. On upright flower stalk to 8' long: flowering upper half or two-thirds is branched, followed by thin, 3-lobed seed capsule; to 1/2" in diameter.
Leaves: Dark green, stiff and leathery; evergreen, rough-margined, narrow; to 4 1/2' long, 3/4" wide; in dense, basal cluster.
Blooms: June–July.
Elevation: 500 to 3,500'.
Habitat: Hillsides and canyons.
Comments: Erect, unbranched trunk. Occasionally poisonous to livestock. Four species of *Nolina* (no-LYE-nah) in Arizona. Photograph taken near Burro Creek and Wikieup, July 15. A very similar species, **PARRY NOLINA** (*Nolina parryi*), has sharply toothed leaf margins and slightly larger flowers and seed capsules.

BEARGRASS 143
Sacahuista, basketgrass, nolina
Nolina microcarpa
Agave Family (Agavaceae)

Height: Flower stalk to 8'.
Flowers: Creamy white, 1/8" wide, in dense plumelike, often bending or crooked, flowering cluster; to 3' long, followed by papery fruit capsule to 3/8" in diameter.
Leaves: Green, tough, grasslike; no marginal spines; loose fibers on margins at tips; to 1/2" wide, 4' long; in large, basal rosette.
Blooms: May–June.
Elevation: 3,000 to 6,500'.
Habitat: Rocky slopes and exposed areas on mountainsides.
Comments: Resembles a large, coarse grass. During drought, leaves are browsed by wildlife, but sheep and goats are occasionally poisoned. Mexicans use leaves for basketry. Native Americans used bud stalks for food. Four species of *Nolina* (no-LYE-nah) in Arizona. Photograph taken at Sedona, June 18.

BANANA YUCCA 144
Datil, blue yucca, Indian banana, broadleaf yucca
Yucca baccata
Agave Family (Agavaceae)

Height: Flower stalk to 5'.
Flowers: White, waxy, bell-shaped, with 6 yellow anthers and 6 petallike segments; to 3" long; on a stalk in long cluster; reddish buds, followed by large, fleshy, bananalike fruits, which grow to 5" long.
Leaves: Green, broad, stiff, spine-tipped; white fibers on margins; to 3' long, 2" wide; in a basal rosette.
Blooms: April–July.

Elevation:	3,000 to 8,000'.
Habitat:	Dry plains and slopes.
Comments:	Has short flower stem scarcely taller than leaves. Dried roots are soaked in water to produce a soapy lather. Native Americans used leaves for making baskets, sandals, and mats, and ate the fruits. Yuccas are pollinated by the female yucca moth. After mating, the female collects pollen from several flowers and rolls it into a ball. She moves to another flower, lays several eggs in its pistil, then presses pollen onto the stigma, thus ensuring fertilization. When her eggs hatch, each larva feeds on some of the developing yucca seeds before dropping to the ground where it buries itself and spins a cocoon. During fall and winter it transforms into a moth, ready to renew the cycle in spring. Nine species of *Yucca* (YUKK-kuh) in Arizona. Photograph taken near Willcox, April 22.

JOSHUA TREE   145A and B
Tree yucca, giant Joshua, Joshua tree yucca, yucca-palm
Yucca brevifolia
Agave Family (Agavaceae)

Height:	To 30'.
Trunk:	To 3' in diameter. Brown or gray, corky, and rough, deeply furrowed. Young trunks covered with dead leaves.
Flowers:	Greenish white, waxy, bell-shaped; to 2 1/2" long; in tight clusters on stalks to 1 1/2' long at ends of branches; flowers do not open fully; followed by egg-shaped, greenish fruit about 4" long.
Leaves:	Dark green, long and narrow, with pointed tip and toothed margins; to 14" long; clustered in dense rosettes at ends of branches.
Blooms:	March–April.
Elevation:	2,000 to 3,500'.
Habitat:	Rocky plains and hillsides.
Comments:	Symbol of the Mojave Desert and the largest yucca, the Joshua tree was named by Mormon pioneers who likened its grotesque shape to the biblical Joshua lifting his arms in prayer. An evergreen, this narrow-leaved yucca can live between 100 and 300 years. It does not bloom every year, as flowering is governed by temperature and rainfall. Birds, woodrats, and a small species of night lizard make their homes in the Joshua tree. A healthy Joshua tree needs periods of low temperatures to go into dormancy. Wood is used for splints and veneering. Nine species of *Yucca* (YUKK-kuh) in Arizona. The Joshua Tree Parkway northwest of Wickenburg is a good example of a Joshua "forest." Photographs taken on Joshua Tree Parkway, May 29 (tree) and March 11 (flowers).

SOAPTREE YUCCA   146
Palmilla, soapweed, Whipple yucca, Spanish bayonet
Yucca elata
Agave Family (Agavaceae)

Height:	Flower stalk to 30'.
Flowers:	Creamy white, bell-shaped; to 2" long; in dense cluster on upright branch, followed by light brown, 3-celled, cylindrical seed capsule.
Leaves:	Yellowish green, long and narrow, evergreen; with threadlike margins and a sharp spine at terminal end; to 2 1/2' long.
Blooms:	May–July.

Elevation:	1,500 to 6,000'.
Habitat:	Mesas, desert washes, sandy plains, and grasslands.
Comments:	This yucca forms clumps. Arrangement of leaves channels moisture to plant's center. Native Americans use leaves for basket weaving. Flowers and buds were used as food. Roots, known as *amole*, used as substitute for soap. Nine species of *Yucca* (YUKK-kuh) in Arizona. Photograph taken in Sedona area, June 18.

SCHOTT'S YUCCA 147
Spanish dagger, mountain yucca, Spanish bayonet, hoary yucca
Yucca schottii
Agave Family (Agavaceae)

Height:	Flower stalk to 18'.
Flowers:	White, waxy, bell-shaped, with 6 broad, pointed sepals; to 1 1/2" long; in short-stalked, upright cluster, followed by green, fleshy, bananalike fruit growing to 5" long, to 2" in diameter; falling before winter.
Leaves:	Bluish green; edges are reddish without teeth or threads; lance-shaped, flat, flexible, and leathery; sharp-pointed; to 2 1/2' long, 2" wide.
Blooms:	April–August.
Elevation:	4,000 to 7,000'.
Habitat:	Hillsides and canyons.
Comments:	Evergreen. Grows new asparaguslike flower stalk yearly. Native Americans eat buds, flowers, and young flower stalks. Leaf fibers made into mats, baskets, cloth, rope, and sandals. Prepared roots used as soap substitute. Nine species of *Yucca* (YUKK-kuh) in Arizona. Photograph taken in Madera Canyon, April 28.

IRIS FAMILY
Iridaceae (eye-rih-DAY-see-ee)
Herbs.

Flowers:	Regular or nearly regular, flower parts in 3s; either 3 petallike sepals stand out or down and 3 petals stand up, or all 6 parts are of same size and color and form a flat circle; 2 bracts, 3 stamens, single, 3-cleft style. Inferior ovary, 3-celled.
Fruit:	3-celled, many-seeded capsule.
Leaves:	Long, narrow, toothless, sword-shaped.

ROCKY MOUNTAIN IRIS 681
Snake lily, water flag, fleur-de-lis, western blue flag
Iris missouriensis
Iris Family (Iridaceae)

Height:	Flower stem to 3'.
Flowers:	Pale blue to violet, streaked with white; 3 narrow, erect petals, 3 wider sepals curved downward; to 4" wide; at top of stout, leafless stem, followed by a thin-walled, oblong capsule with 6 ribs; to 1 1/2" long, 3/4" wide.
Leaves:	Dark green, sword-shaped; to 20" long, 1/2" wide.
Blooms:	May–September.
Elevation:	6,000 to 9,500'.
Habitat:	Wet meadows and moist forest clearings.
Comments:	Perennial. Grows in clumps. Rootstalks and leaves are poisonous if eaten. One species of *Iris* (EYE-ris) in Arizona. Photograph taken at Ashurst Lake area, June 1.

YELLOW-EYED GRASS 387
Sisyrinchium arizonicum
Iris Family (Iridaceae)

Height: To 2' tall.

Flowers: Orange to yellowish orange; 6 pointed segments, all alike; 3 yellow stamens tipped with black; 3-branched style; flower to 1 1/2" wide, followed by an oblong capsule to 1/2" long.

Leaves: Dark green, linear, prominently veined; grasslike, flattened; to 10" long, 1/4" wide, basal and up along stem.

Blooms: July–August.

Elevation: 6,000 to 9,500'.

Habitat: Coniferous forests.

Comments: Perennial herb. Stems erect and branching. Four species of *Sisyrinchium* (sis-i-RINK-i-uhm) in Arizona. Photograph taken at Woods Canyon Lake, August 3.

BLUE-EYED GRASS 682
Blue star grass
Sisyrinchium demissum
Iris Family (Iridaceae)

Height: To 1'.

Flowers: Dark purple or deep blue with yellow stamens; 6 segments with fine point at tips; striped on undersides; to 3/4" wide; terminal on long, flat stem.

Leaves: Dark bluish green, narrow, sword-shaped; mainly basal; to 6" long.

Blooms: June–September.

Elevation: 5,000 to 9,500'.

Habitat: Moist meadows and along streams.

Comments: Perennial herb. Wiry stem. Four species of *Sisyrinchium* (sis-i-RINK-i-uhm) in Arizona. Photograph taken in mountain meadow above Greer, August 10.

ORCHID FAMILY
Orchidaceae (or-kid-DAY-see-ee)
Herbs.

Flowers: Irregular, with 3 outer sepals, 3 inner petals (2 are alike; the third forms a lip or large sac). Stamens and pistil joined together to form a column with anther at tip, stigma below. Inferior ovary, 1- to 3-celled.

Fruit: 3-valved capsule.

Leaves: Usually alternate, toothless, parallel-veined, simple.

CALYPSO 651
Fairy slipper
Calypso bulbosa
Orchid Family (Orchidaceae)

Height: Flower stalk to 8".

Flowers: Rose-pink, orchidlike, bearded with yellow hairs; to 2" long, 1 1/2" wide; single on leafless stalk.

Leaves: Dark green, single, oval to egg-shaped; to 2 1/2" long; at base of tall, pinkish flower stalk.

Blooms: May–July.

Elevation:	8,000 to 10,000'.
Habitat:	Cool, moist spruce-fir forests.
Comments:	Flower hangs at tip of tall pink stem that grows from perennial bulbous root. One species of *Calypso* (kah-LIHP-soh) in Arizona. Photograph taken in vicinity of Hannagan Meadow, May 28.

SPOTTED CORAL ROOT   816
Large coral root
Corallorhiza maculata
Orchid Family (Orchidaceae)

Height:	To 20".
Flowers:	Brown to purplish red, orchidlike flowers along a purplish, leafless flower stem; lip cream-colored to white with purple spots; to 3/4" long.
Leaves:	Scalelike, tubular sheaths on stem.
Blooms:	June–July.
Elevation:	6,000 to 10,000'.
Habitat:	Coniferous forests.
Comments:	Saprophytic orchid lacking chlorophyll. Has corallike underground stem. Receives nourishment from a fungus that decomposes dead plant material. Three species of *Corallorhiza* (kor-al-loh-RIZ-ah) in Arizona. Photograph taken near Greer, June 16.

STRIPED CORAL ROOT   817
Corallorhiza striata
Orchid Family (Orchidaceae)

Height:	To 20".
Flowers:	Pale brownish, yellowish, or whitish, striped with purplish to brownish, tiny orchids to 1" wide; oval lip to 1/2" long is bent downward; in racemes on erect, reddish purple stems.
Leaves:	Nearly leafless, with only a few scalelike vestiges of leaves on lower stems.
Blooms:	June–July.
Elevation:	7,000 to 9,000'.
Habitat:	Ponderosa pine and spruce-fir forests.
Comments:	Saprophytic orchid lacking chlorophyll. Receives nourishment from a fungus that decomposes dead plant material. Has corallike underground stem. Three species of *Corallorhiza* (kor-al-loh-RIZ-ah) in Arizona. Photograph taken in vicinity of Forest Lakes, June 13.

SPRING CORAL ROOT   818
Wister's coral root
Corallorhiza wisteriana
Orchid Family (Orchidaceae)

Height:	To 1'.
Flowers:	Brown upper lobes and backward pointing spur; white lower lip petal with faint pink markings; unlobed lower lip projects noticeably forward and downward; flower to 1/8" wide, 1/2" long, in slender raceme.
Leaves:	Leafless; reduced to scales.
Blooms:	April–May.
Elevation:	6,000 to 8,000'.
Habitat:	Hillsides and clearings in ponderosa pine forests.

Comments: A saprophyte lacking chlorophyll. Pinkish brown stem. Three species of *Corallorhiza* (kor-al-loh-RIZ-ah) in Arizona. Photograph taken in Sharp Creek area northeast of Christopher Creek, April 22.

YELLOW LADY'S SLIPPER   498
Yellow moccasin flower
Cypripedium calceolus var. *pubescens*
Orchid Family (Orchidaceae)

Height: To 2'.
Flowers: Golden yellow, inflated slipperlike lip petal to 2" long; 2 spirally twisted side petals ranging in color from yellow to yellowish brown with reddish markings. Two greenish yellow, lance-shaped sepals with reddish markings, one above and one below lip petal; usually one bloom but sometimes twin blooms per stem.
Leaves: Dark green, clasping stem; hairy, oval to elliptical, deeply veined; usually 3 to 5 per stem; to 8" long.
Blooms: June–July.
Elevation: 6,000 to 9,000'.
Habitat: Rich soil in well-shaded locations of moist coniferous forests.
Comments: Perennial herb. Extremely rare in Arizona. One species of *Cypripedium* (sip-pri-PEE-di-um) in Arizona. [Because of its rarity we have never seen this orchid growing in Arizona. We are, however, very familiar with the species and include here a photograph taken in 1982 in our wildflower garden in the Northeast where our plant multiplied year after year.]

GIANT RATTLESNAKE PLANTAIN   292A and B
Green-leaved rattlesnake plantain, Menzies's rattlesnake orchid
Goodyera oblongifolia
Orchid Family (Orchidaceae)

Height: To 18".
Flowers: White to pinkish, hairy; to 5/8" long, 3/4" wide; upper sepal and petals united in hood over lip; on long, densely flowered, hairy, naked stem; flowering section of stem to 4" long.
Leaves: Dark green, with mottled, white central line; oblong; to 4" long; in basal rosette.
Blooms: July–September.
Elevation: 8,000 to 9,500'.
Habitat: Rich, moist coniferous forests.
Comments: The giant rattlesnake plantain is named for its mottled leaves, which resemble rattlesnake skin. Two species of *Goodyera* (GOOD-yerah) in Arizona. Photograph (full view) taken south of Alpine, August 2. Closeup taken at Greer, August 10.

DWARF RATTLESNAKE PLANTAIN   293A and B
Dwarf rattlesnake orchid, creeping rattlesnake plantain
Goodyera repens
Orchid Family (Orchidaceae)

Height: Flower stem to 1'.
Flowers: White to greenish, occasionally pink-tinged; upper sepal and petals united in hood over lip; to 1/8" long; along one side of slender flower spike.
Leaves: Dark green, shiny, fleshy, mostly basal; faint network, broadly oval; to 1 1/2" long.
Blooms: July–August.

Elevation: 9,000 to 10,000'.
Habitat: Moist mountain slopes in coniferous forests.
Comments: Two species of *Goodyera* (GOOD-yerah) in Arizona. Photographs taken in mountains above Greer, August 8.

SLENDER BOG ORCHID   811A and B
Rein orchid, male orchid
Habenaria saccata
Orchid Family (Orchidaceae)

Height: To 3'.
Flowers: Light green, with 3 petals and 3 sepals; orchidlike, lower petal (called the "lip") is long and curved upward; flower to 3/8" long, in long, narrow, loosely flowered spike.
Leaves: Dark green, sunken midvein; alternate, lance-shaped; clasping stem; to 10" long, 1 1/2" wide.
Blooms: July–September.
Elevation: 8,500 to 9,500'.
Habitat: Moist spruce-fir forests and along mountain streams in coniferous forests.
Comments: Five species of *Habenaria* (ha-be-NAY-ri-ah) in Arizona. Photographs taken in mountains above Greer, August 9.

SPARSELY-FLOWERED BOG ORCHID   812
Northern rein orchid, sparse rein orchid
Habenaria sparsiflora
Orchid Family (Orchidaceae)

Height: To 30".
Flowers: Greenish to yellowish, slender spur as long as or longer than lip petal; to 1/4" wide, 3/4" long, in elongated and loosely flowered flower spike.
Leaves: Light green, fleshy, clasping stem; straplike to lance-shaped; alternate; to 7 1/2" long, at intervals on flower stalk.
Blooms: June–October.
Elevation: 5,000 to 9,000'.
Habitat: Wet, boggy areas and moist ledges in coniferous forests.
Comments: Five species of *Habenaria* (ha-be-NAY-ri-ah) in Arizona. Photograph taken in Oak Creek Canyon, Sedona, June 8.

LONG-BRACTED HABENARIA   813
Satyr orchid, frog orchid
Habenaria viridis var. *bracteata*
Orchid Family (Orchidaceae)

Height: To 2'.
Flowers: Greenish; flowers borne in narrow, elongated cluster. Upper sepal and 2 erect, pointed, lateral petals forming hood; rectangular-shaped, greenish yellow, 2- or 3-lobed lip pointing downward to 1/2" long; flower to 1/2" long; floral bract much longer than flower.
Leaves: Dark green, lance-shaped; alternate; clasping stem; to 6" long, 1" wide.
Blooms: July–August.
Elevation: Not available. Photograph taken at 8,700'.
Habitat: Moist spruce-fir forests.

Comments: Five species of *Habenaria* (ha-be-NAY-ri-ah) in Arizona. Photograph taken in mountains above Greer, July 8. This species recognizable by its very long flower bracts and rectangular lip with 2 or 3 lobes.

ADDER'S MOUTH 797
Rattail, mountain malaxis
Malaxis soulei
Orchid Family (Orchidaceae)

Height: To 6".
Flowers: Yellowish green, less than 1/8" long, clustered on single flower spike to 4" long.
Leaves: Dark green, single, oval; clasping stem; to 3" long.
Blooms: July–September.
Elevation: 6,000 to 9,500'.
Habitat: Mixed conifer forests.
Comments: Grows from a corm. Four species of *Malaxis* (MAL-ax-is) in Arizona. Photograph taken south of Alpine, August 2.

HOODED LADIES' TRESSES 294
Pearl twist, lady's tresses
Spiranthes romanzoffiana
Orchid Family (Orchidaceae)

Height: Flower stem to 16".
Flowers: White, 3 sepals, 3 petals; 2 upper petals form a hood; lip petal curved downward and pinched in on each margin near tip; flower to 1/2" long, 1/8" wide; flowers densely arranged in 3-spiraled rows on a slender spike.
Leaves: Light green, shiny, smooth, lanced-shaped; succulent, basal; to 8" long, 1/2" wide.
Blooms: August–September.
Elevation: 8,500 to 9,500'.
Habitat: Wet meadows, bogs, streamsides.
Comments: Often several stems in a clump. Four species of *Spiranthes* (spy-RAN-theez) in Arizona. Photograph taken in Mount Baldy Wilderness, August 13.

LIZARD TAIL FAMILY
Saururaceae (saur-ur-AY-see-ee)
Represented in Arizona by 1 herb.

Flowers: Regular; calyx and corolla absent; white petallike bracts; in dense spike; 3, 6, or 8 stamens, 3 or 4 pistils. Ovary 1-celled.
Fruit: Succulent capsule.
Leaves: Alternate, mostly basal, simple.

YERBA MANSA 247
Anemopsis californica
Lizard Tail Family (Saururaceae)

Height: To 16".
Flowers: Very tiny, numerous and dense; on conical spike to 2" long; with 7 or 8 one-inch-long, white, petallike bracts surrounding base of cone.
Leaves: Grayish green, leathery, oblong; mostly basal; to 6" long; smaller leaves erect on flower stem.

Blooms:	May–August.
Elevation:	2,000 to 5,500'.
Habitat:	Moist, saline soil.
Comments:	Perennial herb. Root used medicinally by Native Americans and Spaniards. One species of *Anemopsis* (ane-MOP-sis) in Arizona. Photograph taken at Hassayampa River Preserve, Wickenburg, May 7.

CASUARINA FAMILY
Casuarinaceae (cas-you-a-rye-NAY-see-ee)
An Australian tree, not native to Arizona.

Flowers:	Tiny, petalless, 1 pistil. Superior ovary.
Fruit:	Conelike, hard, woody.
Leaves:	Scalelike.

HORSETAIL CASUARINA 36
Australian-pine, beefwood, she-oak
Casuarina equisetifolia
Casuarina Family (Casuarinaceae)

Height:	To 100'.
Trunk:	To 30" in diameter.
Bark:	Reddish brown, deeply furrowed on mature trees.
Flowers:	Tiny, male and female on separate trees. Female flowers followed by brownish, hard, warty, conelike fruit which grow to 1/2" in diameter.
Leaves:	Grayish green, scalelike; in whorls on drooping stems.
Blooms:	Spring.
Habitat:	Floodplains and moist areas.
Comments:	Native to Australia. Fast-growing and long-lived. Branchlets are wirelike and jointed. Although not listed in *A Catalogue of the Flora of Arizona*, *Casuarina* (cas-you-a-RYE-nah) is included here because of its massiveness and frequency in certain areas of Arizona. Photograph taken at Catalina State Park, April 15.

WILLOW FAMILY
Salicaceae (say-li-KAY-see-ee)
Trees or large shrubs.

Flowers:	Minute, without sepals or petals; in catkins. Male and female on separate trees, appearing with or before the leaves. Ovary 1-celled.
Fruit:	Small, 2- to 4-valved splitting capsule; seeds surrounded by silky hairs.
Leaves:	Simple, alternate, deciduous. Identifying a particular species of willow is very difficult. Leaves within a species vary, and some species hybridize.

NARROWLEAF COTTONWOOD 56
Mountain cottonwood, black cottonwood, narrowleaf poplar, alamo
Populus angustifolia
Willow Family (Salicaceae)

Height:	To 50'.
Trunk:	To 1 1/2' in diameter.
Bark:	Yellowish green and smooth when young, brownish to grayish brown and deeply

furrowed on large trunks.

Flowers:	Narrow, reddish catkins to 3" long, with male and female on separate trees.
Leaves:	Shiny, yellowish green above, paler beneath; lance-shaped, finely saw-toothed; leathery; yellowish midvein; tapering and long-pointed; to 5" long, 1" wide.
Blooms:	Early spring.
Elevation:	5,000 to 7,000'.
Habitat:	Along mountain streams.
Comments:	Pointed, very resinous leaf buds. Wood used for fence posts and fuel. Six species of *Populus* (POP-pew-luss) in Arizona. Photograph taken at Eager, August 18.

FREMONT COTTONWOOD   57

Rio Grande cottonwood, Fremont poplar, alamo, meseta cottonwood,
valley cottonwood
Populus fremontii
Willow Family (Salicaceae)

Height:	To 100', but usually less.
Trunk:	To 4' in diameter, but usually less.
Bark:	Branches on young trees are gray-brown, thin, and smooth; on old trees, dark reddish brown, thick, and deeply furrowed.
Flowers:	Greenish yellow, tiny, male and female on separate trees (female forms long, slender catkins); to 4" long; followed by fuzzy white, cottony seeds.
Leaves:	Yellow-green, shiny, broadly triangular and pointed; nearly straight across base; coarsely toothed margins; to 2 1/2" long, 3" wide.
Blooms:	Early spring before leaves form.
Elevation:	150 to 6,000'.
Habitat:	Along streams and moist areas.
Comments:	In autumn, leaves turn golden yellow before falling. Wood used as fuel. Hopi Indians use roots for kachina dolls, wood for drums. A favorite of beavers for food and for dam building. Six species of *Populus* (POP-pew-luss) in Arizona. Photograph taken at Saguaro Lake, October 18.

QUAKING ASPEN   58

Golden aspen, aspen, trembling poplar, quaking asp, trembling aspen, alamillo,
mountain aspen
Populus tremuloides
Willow Family (Salicaceae)

Height:	Usually to 40', rarely to 80'.
Trunk:	Usually to 1' in diameter, rarely to 30".
Bark:	Whitish or yellowish, waxy-appearing, smooth, thin. Older trees are dark gray, thick, furrowed.
Flowers:	Tiny, inconspicuous, in catkins; male and female on separate trees; followed by cottony seeds on female trees.
Leaves:	Almost round, short-pointed, finely saw-toothed; shiny green above, dull green beneath; leaf stalk longer than leaf blade and flattened lengthwise at right angles to leaf; to 3" long.
Blooms:	Early spring before leaves form.
Elevation:	6,500 to 10,000'.
Habitat:	Ponderosa pine and spruce-fir forests.
Comments:	Every breeze causes slender, flattened leaf stalks to tremble. In autumn, leaves turn

golden yellow or orange before falling. Browsed by livestock, deer, and elk, a favorite of beavers. Bark used medicinally by pioneers and Native Americans. Early growth in burned or logged areas, later replaced by conifers. Wood used mainly for paper pulp. Six species of *Populus* (POP-pew-luss) in Arizona. Photograph taken near Willow Springs Lake, September 13.

BEBB WILLOW   38
Sauz, diamond willow, sauce, beaked willow
Salix bebbiana
Willow Family (Salicaceae)

Height:	Usually much-branched shrub or small tree to 15'.
Trunk:	To 6" in diameter.
Bark:	Grayish, with reddish orange twigs. Smooth when young; rough and furrowed with age.
Flowers:	Catkins on short, leafy twigs; to 1 1/2" long.
Leaves:	Dull green and finely haired above; whitish, finely haired and strongly net-veined beneath. Untoothed; elliptical or oblong; to 3 1/2" long, 1" wide.
Blooms:	Spring.
Elevation:	7,000 to 11,000'.
Habitat:	Coniferous forests along streams, springs, and lakes.
Comments:	Often forming clusters. Broad, rounded crown. Browsed by elk and deer, and used by beavers for food and dam building. Twigs used in basket- and furniture-making. Extract from bark used medicinally. More than a dozen species of *Salix* (SAY-liks) in Arizona. Photograph taken in Mormon Lake area, June 2.

BONPLAND WILLOW   61
Toumey willow, polished willow, red willow
Salix bonplandiana
Willow Family (Salicaceae)

Height:	To 50', usually to 25'.
Trunk:	To 2' in diameter.
Bark:	Dark gray to black; ridged and fissured. Twigs are reddish purple.
Flowers:	Tiny, in catkins, to 1 1/2" long.
Leaves:	Yellowish green above, shiny, whitish beneath; yellowish midrib; narrowly lance-shaped, long-pointed, broadest in middle; very finely toothed; to 6" long, 3/4" wide.
Blooms:	April.
Elevation:	3,000 to 5,000'.
Habitat:	Wet soils along lakes and streams in southeastern and central Arizona.
Comments:	Has broad, rounded crown. Branches droop at ends. Semi-evergreen; leaves shed irregularly during winter, rather than in fall like other willows. Browsed by deer and livestock; bark is eaten by beavers, rabbits, and small rodents. More than a dozen species of *Salix* (SAY-liks) in Arizona. Photograph taken at Patagonia Lake State Park, April 27.

COYOTE WILLOW   39
Basket willow, sandbar willow, acequia willow, narrowleaf willow, gray willow
Salix exigua
Willow Family (Salicaceae)

Height:	Shrub to 15'.

Trunk:	To 5" in diameter.
Bark:	Greenish; smooth when young, grayish brown with age.
Flowers:	In catkins; hairy, with yellow scales; to 2 1/2" long.
Leaves:	Silvery-hairy on unfolding, later becoming dull grayish green and less hairy; very long and narrow, untoothed or with a few teeth; leaf to 4" long, to 1/4" wide.
Blooms:	Spring.
Elevation:	To 9,500'.
Habitat:	Along streams, silt flats, and riverbanks.
Comments:	Rarely treelike. Often forms thickets of clustered stems. Prevents erosion. Browsed by livestock and wildlife. Twigs and bark used by Native Americans for basketmaking. More than a dozen species of *Salix* (SAY-liks) in Arizona. Photograph taken at Lynx Creek, Prescott, May 27.

GOODDING WILLOW   62
Western black willow, Dudley willow
Salix gooddingii
Willow Family (Salicaceae)

Height:	To 45'.
Trunk:	To 30" in diameter.
Bark:	Gray, thick, rough, deeply furrowed with narrow ridges. Twigs are yellow.
Flowers:	Tiny; in catkins to 3 1/2" long; followed by cottony seeds.
Leaves:	Shiny green or yellowish green, narrowly lance-shaped, long-pointed; slightly curved to one side, finely toothed; to 5" long, 3/4" wide.
Blooms:	March.
Elevation:	Below 7,000'.
Habitat:	Along streams.
Comments:	Largest willow in Arizona. Has broad, rounded crown. Prevents stream erosion with its deep root system. More than a dozen species of *Salix* (SAY-liks) in Arizona. Photograph taken near Granite Reef Dam, March 1.

SCOULER WILLOW   40
Mountain willow, fire willow, black willow, river willow
Salix scouleriana
Willow Family (Salicaceae)

Height:	Large shrub to small tree, rarely a tree to 30' tall.
Trunk:	To 4" in diameter.
Bark:	Grayish, smooth, and thin when young; dark brown and fissured with age.
Flowers:	In catkins; nearly stalkless; stout; catkin to 2" long.
Leaves:	Dark green, shiny above, whitish with grayish to reddish hairs beneath; midvein yellow; untoothed; elliptical but variable in shape; to 4" long, 1 1/2" wide.
Blooms:	April–May.
Elevation:	7,000 to 10,000'.
Habitat:	Coniferous forests and clearings in moist or dry conditions.
Comments:	Form clusters with rounded crown. Among the first trees to appear after a fire, stopping erosion and providing protection for developing conifers. Browsed by livestock and deer. More than a dozen species of *Salix* (SAY-liks) in Arizona. Photograph taken at River Reservoir, Greer, July 5.

YEW LEAF WILLOW   41A and B
Yew willow
Salix taxifolia
Willow Family (Salicaceae)

Height:	Shrub, or tree to 40', but smaller in Arizona.
Trunk:	To 18" in diameter.
Bark:	Grayish brown, rough, and fissured.
Flowers:	In catkins with yellowish, hairy scales; catkin to 3/4" long.
Leaves:	Grayish green, linear, needlelike; crowded along stems; to 2" long, 1/8" wide.
Blooms:	March and occasionally again in fall.
Elevation:	3,500 to 6,000'.
Habitat:	In oak woodlands and along streams and washes in mountains and foothills.
Comments:	Compact, rounded crown. Browsed by livestock. Slow grower. Branches droop at tips. A soil binder. More than a dozen species of *Salix* (SAY-liks) in Arizona. Photograph taken at Catalina State Park, November 10. Photograph showing conelike, woolly insect galls taken at Springerville, August 10.

WALNUT FAMILY
Juglandaceae (joo-glan-DAY-see-ee)
Represented in Arizona by 1 species of tree.

Flowers:	Male flowers have several stamens in drooping catkins; female flowers have 3- to 5-lobed calyx, solitary or in small clusters. Inferior ovary, 1-celled.
Fruit:	Round, hard-shelled nut.
Leaves:	Alternate, pinnately compound.

ARIZONA WALNUT   94
Nogal, Arizona black walnut
Juglans major
Walnut Family (Juglandaceae)

Height:	To 50', but usually less.
Trunk:	To 3' in diameter.
Bark:	Grayish brown, furrowed on mature trees.
Flowers:	Greenish, male and female separate on same tree, male flowers are hanging catkin; female flowers in erect cluster; no petals; followed by round, brown-haired husks, to 1 1/2" in diameter within each which lies a deeply grooved shell.
Leaves:	Yellowish green, pinnately compound; 9 to 13 coarsely toothed, lance-shaped leaflets, each to 4" long, 1 1/2" wide; leaf to 14" long.
Blooms:	Before or during leaf development.
Elevation:	3,500 to 7,000'.
Habitat:	Along streams and in canyons in upper desert, grasslands, and oak woodlands.
Comments:	Deciduous. Rounded crown of widely spreading branches. Favorite of squirrels. Only species of *Juglans* (JOO-glanz) in Arizona. Photograph taken at Mormon Lake, September 3.

BIRCH FAMILY

Betulaceae (bet-you-LAY-see-ee)
Represented in Arizona by trees and shrubs.

Flowers: Male flowers in long, slender catkins; female flowers in short spikes or conelike clusters; petalless, 1 pistil. Inferior ovary, 2-celled.
Fruit: 1-seeded nutlet, often winged or conelike.
Leaves: Alternate, simple.

ARIZONA ALDER   59

New Mexican alder, Mexican alder
Alnus oblongifolia
Birch Family (Betulaceae)

Height: To 60'.
Trunk: To 3' in diameter.
Bark: Dark gray, thin, and smooth; scaly with age.
Flowers: Minute, male and female flowers on separate catkins on same tree; female flowers followed by small cones to 1/2" long.
Leaves: Dark green above, paler and slightly hairy beneath; elliptical, narrowed at base, with doubly toothed margins; to 3" long, 2" wide.
Blooms: March.
Elevation: 4,500 to 7,500'.
Habitat: Along streams and canyons in ponderosa pine forests and oak woodlands.
Comments: Rounded crown. Alders add nitrogen to soil thus improving it. Two species of *Alnus* (AL-nuss) in Arizona. Photograph taken at Lynx Creek, Prescott, September 11. This alder recognizable by more elliptical leaves, which gradually narrow at base.

THINLEAF ALDER   60

Mountain alder, river alder, black alder, barana, aliso
Alnus tenuifolia
Birch Family (Betulaceae)

Height: Large shrub, or small tree to 25'.
Trunk: Several trunks to 6" in diameter.
Bark: Grayish, reddish brown, and scaly with age.
Flowers: Minute, male and female flowers in separate catkins on same tree; female flowers followed by small cones 3/8" to 1/2" long.
Leaves: Dark green above, yellowish and slightly hairy beneath; egg-shaped to oblong, rounded at base; doubly toothed margins, bent stem; to 4" long, to 2 1/2" wide.
Blooms: Early spring.
Elevation: 7,000 to 9,000'.
Habitat: Along streams and in moist meadows in ponderosa pine and spruce-fir forests.
Comments: Rounded crown. Thick and woody alder cones remain on trees. The Navajo used powdered bark to make red dye for wool. Deer, rabbits, and beaver eat alder bark; birds eat the seeds. Two species of *Alnus* (AL-nuss) in Arizona. Photograph taken south of Alpine, August 8. This alder recognizable by its oval to oblong leaves, which are rounded or heart-shaped at base.

BEECH FAMILY

Fagaceae (fay-GAY-see-ee)

Represented in Arizona by oak trees.

Flowers: Male flowers in catkins; 5-lobed perianth; 5 to 10 stamens. Female flowers solitary or in small clusters; 6-lobed perianth, 3 styles. Inferior ovary, 1-celled.

Fruit: Acorns on oak trees.

Leaves: Alternate, simple, lobed or toothed; deciduous or evergreen.

ARIZONA WHITE OAK   63

Arizona oak, roble

Quercus arizonica

Beech Family (Fagaceae)

Height: To 60'.

Trunk: To 3' in diameter.

Bark: Light gray, fissured into thick plates.

Flowers: Tiny; male and female on same tree. Male: drooping catkin; female in short spike, followed by light brown, to 1"-long acorn, with lower half partly covered by hairy-scaled, shallow, bowllike cup.

Leaves: Dull blue green, with sunken veins above; lighter color, densely haired with brownish fuzz and raised veins beneath. Broadly oval, thick, and stiff; margins slightly wavy and toothed toward apex; to 3" long.

Blooms: Spring.

Elevation: 5,000 to 7,500'.

Habitat: Oak woodlands, foothills, mountains, and canyons.

Comments: Evergreen; among the largest southwestern oaks. New leaves emerge when old leaves drop in May. Rounded crown. Wood is hard and difficult to split. More than a dozen species of *Quercus* (KWUR-kuss) in Arizona. Photograph taken at Harshaw, April 27. The broadly oval, bluish green leaves with brownish, fuzzy undersides are characteristic of this oak.

PALMER OAK   64

Quercus dunnii (*Quercus chrysolopis* var. *palmeri*)

Beech (Fagaceae)

Height: Shrub, or small tree to 20'.

Trunk: To 4" in diameter.

Bark: Grayish or brown, smooth or scaly.

Flowers: Tiny; males in drooping clusters, females in short spikes; followed by a narrow or broad acorn to 1 1/2" long with an oversized cup, coated with golden hairs, variable.

Leaves: Yellowish green; shiny above, yellowish beneath; elliptical to oval; stiff, leathery, spiny-toothed (hollylike) or untoothed and short-pointed; to 1 1/2" long.

Blooms: April–May.

Elevation: 3,500 to 7,000'.

Habitat: Mountainsides, canyons, and oak woodlands.

Comments: Has broad crown. Acorns take 2 years to mature. More than a dozen species of *Quercus* (KWUR-kuss) in Arizona. Photograph taken along East Verde River north of Payson, September 2.

EMORY OAK   65

Black oak, blackjack oak, bellota

Quercus emoryi

Beech Family (Fagaceae)

Height:	Shrub, small or large tree to 50'.
Trunk:	To 2 1/2' in diameter.
Bark:	Black and thick, in rectangular plates.
Flowers:	Tiny; male and female on same tree. Male in drooping catkin, female in short spike; followed by brownish, oblong, 3/4"-long acorn, with lower third covered by a hairy cup.
Leaves:	Yellowish green on both sides; shiny, thick, stiff, and leathery; broadly lance-shaped, with spiny tip, some spiny teeth on margins; base of leaf blade is fuzzy where it joins stem on over half-mature leaves; to 2 1/2" long.
Blooms:	Spring.
Elevation:	4,000 to 7,000'.
Habitat:	Moist canyons and dry foothills.
Comments:	Evergreen; found from southeastern to central Arizona. An important source of firewood in southern Arizona. Acorns (*bellota* in Spanish) mature in first year. Sweet and tasty, they are eaten by wildlife as well as by people, in particular Native Americans and Hispanics of the region. More than a dozen species of *Quercus* (KWUR-kuss) in Arizona. Photograph taken at Harshaw, April 27. The shiny yellow-green, hairless, spiny-toothed leaves are distinguishing features of this oak.

GAMBEL OAK   78

Rocky Mountain white oak, Utah white oak, scrub

Quercus gambelii

Beech Family (Fagaceae)

Height:	Shrub to 6 1/2', tree to 50'.
Trunk:	To 2 1/2' in diameter.
Bark:	Gray, thick, deeply furrowed or scaly.
Flowers:	Very tiny; male and female on same tree. Male in drooping catkin, female in short spike; followed by brownish, broadly oval, 3/4"-long acorn, with lower half covered by hairy scales, bowllike cup.
Leaves:	Dark green and smooth above, lighter green and with soft hairs beneath; oblong, with 7 to 11 rounded lobes; to 6" long.
Blooms:	Spring.
Elevation:	5,000 to 8,000'.
Habitat:	Mountains and plateaus in ponderosa forests.
Comments:	Deciduous; with rounded crown. Turns yellow and reddish in autumn before leaves fall. Wood used for fuel and fence posts. Browsed by livestock and deer. Acorns eaten by birds and mammals, and also used by Native Americans. More than a dozen species of *Quercus* (KWUR-kuss) in Arizona. Photograph taken near Ashurst Lake, September 5. Has a distinctive, lobed leaf for an Arizona oak.

SILVERLEAF OAK   42

White-leaf oak

Quercus hypoleucoides

Beech Family (Fagaceae)

Height:	Tree to 60'.

Trunk:	To 2 1/2' in diameter.
Bark:	Blackish, deeply furrowed into plates and ridges.
Flowers:	Tiny; males in drooping clusters, females in short spikes; followed by egg-shaped acorn with thick, scaly cup; to 5/8" long.
Leaves:	Yellow-green and shiny above, silvery white and woolly beneath; lance-shaped, leathery, with edges rolled under; evergreen; to 4" long, 1" wide.
Blooms:	April–May.
Elevation:	5,000 to 7,000'.
Habitat:	Mountain slopes and canyons in oak woodlands.
Comments:	Acorns mature in 1 or 2 years. Found in southern Arizona. More than a dozen species of *Quercus* (KWUR-kuss) in Arizona. Photograph taken at Chiricahua National Monument, April 25. An easily recognizable oak by its narrow, yellow-green leaves with silvery undersides.

MEXICAN BLUE OAK   43
Quercus oblongifolia
Beech Family (Fagaceae)

Height:	To 30'.
Trunk:	To 18" in diameter.
Bark:	Gray, fissured in square plates.
Flowers:	Tiny; males in drooping clusters, females in short spikes; followed by egg-shaped acorn, 3/4" long, 1/3 enclosed by scaly cup; 1 to a stalk (sometimes stalkless).
Leaves:	Blue-green above, paler beneath; evergreen, stiff, hairless, and toothless; rounded at both ends; short-stalked; to 2" long.
Blooms:	April–May.
Elevation:	4,500 to 6,000'.
Habitat:	Oak woodlands at upper edge of desert; foothills and canyons.
Comments:	Has spreading, rounded crown. Acorns mature first year. Leaves fall in spring when new leaves appear. Browsed by deer. More than a dozen species of *Quercus* (KWUR-kuss) in Arizona; *Q. oblongifolia* found in southern Arizona. Photograph taken in vicinity of Mount Lemmon, April 30. Identifiable by blue-green, rounded, toothless, hairless leaves.

NETLEAF OAK   66
Quercus rugosa (Quercus reticulata)
Beech Family (Fagaceae)

Height:	Tree to 40'.
Trunk:	To 1' in diameter.
Bark:	Gray, fissured, scaly.
Flowers:	Tiny; males in narrow, drooping clusters, females in leaf axils; followed by two or three 3/4"-long oblong acorns, 1/4 of each enclosed in scaly cup on long, slender stalk.
Leaves:	Dark green; finely haired, with sunken veins above, yellow-haired with raised veins beneath; stiff, thick, broad, variable in size and shape; a few spiny teeth toward rounded tip; notched at base; to 2 3/4" long.
Blooms:	April–May.
Elevation:	4,000 to 8,000'.
Habitat:	Canyons, mountain slopes, and oak woodlands.
Comments:	Has broad, rounded crown. Acorns mature first year; are eaten by wildlife. More

than a dozen species of *Quercus* (KWUR-kuss) in Arizona. Photograph taken at Chiricahua National Monument, April 25. Recognizable by broadness of leaf at tip end and by prominent network of leaf veins.

SHRUB LIVE OAK   67
Scrub oak, California scrub oak, turbinella oak
Quercus turbinella
Beech Family (Fagaceae)

Height:	Many-branched shrub or small tree to 13'.
Bark:	Gray, scaly, fissured.
Flowers:	Tiny; male and female on same tree. Male in drooping catkin, female in short spike; followed by brownish, narrow, pointed, 3/4"-long acorn in shallow, scaly cup.
Leaves:	Bluish green with a bloom (delicate powdery coating); nearly hairless above, yellowish green and finely haired beneath; elliptical to oblong, thick, stiff; margins have small, spinelike teeth; evergreen; to 1 1/4" long.
Blooms:	Spring.
Elevation:	4,500 to 8,000'.
Habitat:	Lower ponderosa forests, hillsides, and chaparral.
Comments:	Characteristic tree of Arizona chaparral. Often forms dense thickets. Retards soil erosion. Provides browse for livestock, acorns for wildlife. More than a dozen species of *Quercus* (KWUR-kuss) in Arizona. Photograph taken at Oak Creek Canyon, September 9. Identifiable by spiny-toothed, thick, stiff leaves with whitish bloom.

WAVYLEAF OAK   68
Rocky Mountain shin oak, shinnery, scrub oak
Quercus undulata
Beech Family (Fagaceae)

Height:	Shrub to 6', tree to 15'.
Trunk:	To 4" in diameter.
Bark:	Light gray and scaly.
Flowers:	Tiny; male in drooping cluster, female in short spike, followed by oblong acorn to 7/8" long with deep cup.
Leaves:	Grayish green, pinkish velvety cast when young; evergreen, wavy-margined; variable in shape, elliptical or oblong; wavy-lobed or toothed; to 2 1/2" long.
Blooms:	April–May.
Elevation:	6,000 to 9,000'.
Habitat:	Mountainsides and canyons.
Comments:	Often found in burned areas. Over a dozen species of *Quercus* (KWUR-kuss) in Arizona. Photograph taken on Mount Lemmon, April 30. Recognizable by shallow, wavy lobes of leaf.

ELM FAMILY
Ulmaceae (ull-MAY-see-ee)

Flowers:	Inconspicuous, petalless, 4 or 5 sepals, generally 4 to 5 stamens. Superior ovary, 1-celled.
Fruit:	Flat, winged, waferlike fruit, or a drupe.
Leaves:	Alternate, simple, lopsided at base.

DESERT HACKBERRY 69
Granjeno
Celtis pallida
Elm Family (Ulmaceae)

Height:	To 20'.
Flowers:	Whitish, tiny, to 1/16" wide; single or in small clusters on new growth; followed by twinned or single green, egg-shaped berry, to 1/4" long, which ripens to yellowish or orange in fall.
Leaves:	Dark green, elliptical to oval, alternate, toothed or untoothed; smooth when young, rough when older; to 1 1/2" long, 3/4" wide.
Blooms:	Summer.
Elevation:	1,500 to 3,500'.
Habitat:	Washes, canyons, and open desert.
Comments:	Spiny, evergreen shrub. Spines on new branches to 5/8" long; on older branches to 1" long. Fruits provide food for wildlife; cover for many species of birds. Native Americans use fruits for food. Wood occasionally used for fence posts. Two species of *Celtis* (SELL-tiss) in Arizona. Photograph taken at Usery Mountain Recreation Area, September 3.

NETLEAF HACKBERRY 70
Sugarberry, western hackberry, false elm, palo blanco
Celtis reticulata
Elm Family (Ulmaceae)

Height:	Large shrub, or small tree to 30'.
Trunk:	To 1' in diameter.
Bark:	Gray, smooth; fissured and warty in older trees.
Flowers:	Greenish, protrude from base of immature leaf, to 1/8" wide; followed by orange-red, sweet berry to 3/8" in diameter, on long stem at each leaf axil.
Leaves:	Dark green and rough above, yellow-green and slightly hairy with prominent veins beneath; growing in 2 rows; margins can be coarsely saw-toothed; thick, lopsided, usually oval, but variable; to 2 1/2" long, 1 1/2" wide.
Blooms:	March–April.
Elevation:	1,500 to 6,000'.
Habitat:	Moist soils along streams, in canyons, and on hillsides from upper desert to oak woodlands.
Comments:	This is the common hackberry of the West. Deciduous; in autumn, leaves turn yellow before falling. Fruits eaten by birds and other wildlife; also consumed by Native Americans. Wood is used for fence posts and fuel. Mites and fungi often cause deformed, bushy growths called "witches'-brooms" in branches. At times plant lice cause galls to form on leaves. Two species of *Celtis* (SELL-tiss) in Arizona. Photograph taken at Patagonia Lake State Park, April 26.

SIBERIAN ELM 73
Asiatic elm, dwarf elm
Ulmus pumila
Elm Family (Ulmaceae)

Height:	To 60', but smaller in Arizona.
Trunk:	To 1 1/2' in diameter; less in Arizona.
Bark:	Grayish or brown, rough, and furrowed.

Flowers:	Greenish, petalless, to 1/8" wide; in clusters, appearing before leaves unfold; followed by a roundish, flat, waferlike, notched fruit, to 1/2" wide, in small clusters on branches.
Leaves:	Dark green with toothed margins; lopsided at base, narrowly elliptical; to 2 1/2" long.
Blooms:	Early spring.
Elevation:	1,000 to 5,000'.
Habitat:	Dry or moist soils in woodlands and parks.
Comments:	Introduced from northern China and eastern Siberia. Grown for shade and wind-breaks, they seed prolifically and could be considered naturalized in some areas. Browsed by deer. No native species of *Ulmus* (UHL-mus) grow in Arizona. Photograph taken at Lynx Creek, near Prescott, May 27.

MULBERRY FAMILY

Moraceae (moh-RAY-see-ee)

Represented by 2 tree species and a twining herb in Arizona.

Flowers:	Regular, tiny, inconspicuous; in catkins or in loose clusters. Superior ovary, 1- to 2-celled.
Fruit:	Fleshy or surrounded by bracts.
Leaves:	Alternate or opposite, simple, often palmately lobed.

HOP   484A and B

Humulus americanus

Mulberry Family (Moraceae)

Height:	Long, twining vine that climbs over rocks and up into trees.
Flowers:	Cream-colored, small, to 1/8" wide, in loose clusters in leaf axils; followed by drooping cluster of overlapping bracts, to 1 1/4" long, 1" wide.
Leaves:	Dark green above, lighter with prickly veins beneath; 3- to 7-lobed, very rough, sharply toothed; to 10" long, 7" wide.
Blooms:	July–August.
Elevation:	5,500 to 9,500'.
Habitat:	Coniferous forests, rocky slopes, and streambanks.
Comments:	Perennial. Stems are rough; main stem is candy-cane–striped. One species of *Humulus* (HEW-mew-luss) in Arizona. Photograph in flower taken at Luna Lake, August 5. Photograph in fruit taken at Greer, August 15.

WHITE MULBERRY   71

Russian mulberry, silkworm mulberry

Morus alba

Mulberry Family (Moraceae)

Height:	To 40'.
Trunk:	To 1' in diameter.
Bark:	Tan, smooth; on older trees furrowed into scaly ridges.
Flowers:	Green, tiny, in short clusters; followed by pinkish white fruits, to 3/4" long, maturing to dark purple.
Leaves:	Dark green, broadly oval, toothed, long-stalked; often 3- to 5-lobed; to 7" long, 5" wide.
Blooms:	Spring.

Elevation:	Not available. Photograph taken at 2,100'.
Habitat:	Cities and lots.
Comments:	This species of *Morus* (MOH-rus) was introduced from China; now naturalized throughout eastern and western U.S. Birds relish the fruits; also a main food source for silkworms. The Texas mulberry, below, is the only native mulberry found in Arizona. Photograph taken at Hassayampa River Preserve, Wickenburg, May 7.

TEXAS MULBERRY 72
Mexican mulberry, mountain mulberry, western mulberry, dwarf mulberry, small-leaved mulberry
Morus microphylla
Mulberry Family (Moraceae)

Height:	Shrub, or small tree to 20'.
Trunk:	To 8" in diameter.
Bark:	Pale gray, smooth, becoming scaly and fissured.
Flowers:	Green, tiny, in dense catkins to 3/4" long; male and female on separate trees; followed by red to black, 1/2"-long cylindrical fruits.
Leaves:	Dark green above, paler and hairy beneath; variable in shape from oval to 3- to 5-lobed; coarsely saw-toothed; to 2 1/2" long.
Blooms:	March–April.
Elevation:	2,000 to 6,000'.
Habitat:	Moist areas in upper desert; grasslands, and woodlands among streams, washes, and in canyons.
Comments:	Fruits are juicy, acidic, and edible; eaten by humans as well as by wildlife. The Texas mulberry is the only native species of *Morus* (MOH-rus) in Arizona. Photograph taken at Catalina State Park, November 9.

NETTLE FAMILY
Urticaceae (ur-ti-KAY-see-ee)
Represented by herbs in Arizona.

Flowers:	Petalless; male flowers with 4- to 5-parted calyx, female flowers tubular or with 3- to 5-parted calyx; 4 to 5 stamens. Superior ovary, 1-celled.
Fruit:	Dry, 1-seeded achene.
Leaves:	Alternate or opposite; simple.

TALL WHITE NETTLE 278
Urtica gracilis
Nettle Family (Urticaceae)

Height:	To 5'.
Flowers:	Whitish, tiny, petalless, to 1/8" wide; in threadlike, drooping clusters in leaf axils.
Leaves:	Dark green, opposite, lance-shaped, with prominent, spiny veins; triangular-toothed; to 7" long.
Blooms:	July–August.
Elevation:	To 9,000'.
Habitat:	Along streams and springs.
Comments:	Has spiny stems. Four species of *Urtica* (UR-ti-kah) in Arizona. Photograph taken at Greer, July 5.

MISTLETOE FAMILY

Viscaceae (viss-CAY-see-ee)

Parasites on shrubs and trees.

Flowers: Perianth is calyxlike; small, 2- to 4-lobed or toothed. Inferior ovary, 1-celled.
Fruit: Berry.
Leaves: Opposite. Jointed stems.

DESERT MISTLETOE   799

American mistletoe, "the slow killer"
Phoradendron californicum
Mistletoe Family (Viscaceae)

Dimension: A mass in tree branches to 2' in diameter.
Flowers: Yellowish green, inconspicuous, male and female on separate plants. Fruits, pinkish berries, grow to 1/8" in diameter.
Leaves: Scalelike, with brownish yellow stems; dense clustered, on branches of host tree.
Blooms: Spring.
Elevation: Below 4,000'.
Habitat: Deserts and foothills.
Comments: Evergreen. A partial parasite, mainly on leguminous trees and shrubs such as paloverde, mesquite, ironwood, and acacia. Over time, often kills host plant by invading bark and sap with its roots, draining moisture and nutrients from host. Fragrant flowers attract bees and other insects. Phainopepla birds especially like its berries, and help to spread this species from tree to tree. Verdin often nest in mass of stems. Six species of *Phoradendron* (for-ah-DEN-dron) in Arizona. Photograph taken in Superstition Mountains, February 4. *Phoradendron flavescens*, a mistletoe of higher elevations, has bright green, 2"-long, rounded leaves, and white berries, and resembles the "kissing" mistletoe of Christmas season. It parasitizes cotton-wood, sycamore, oak, and willow trees.

JUNIPER MISTLETOE   800

Phoradendron juniperinum
Mistletoe Family (Viscaceae)

Dimension: A mass in juniper branches growing to 2' in diameter.
Flowers: Greenish, inconspicuous; male and female on separate plants; white to pinkish berries.
Leaves: Triangular and scalelike with yellowish green stems; jointed, shiny, growing in dense clusters on branches of juniper trees.
Blooms: July–August.
Elevation: 4,000 to 7,000'.
Habitat: Juniper woodlands.
Comments: Evergreen. A parasite on several species of juniper, sapping nutrients from host plant with its modified roots, sometimes killing host plant. Birds feed on berries, carrying sticky seeds from tree to tree, thus spreading this parasite. This species used medicinally by Hopi Indians. Six species of *Phoradendron* (for-ah-DEN-dron) in Arizona. Photograph taken east of Camp Verde, September 30. A variety of **DWARF MISTLETOE** (*Arceuthobium microcarpum*) is found at higher elevations and is parasitic on spruce. Photograph (**PLATE 798**) taken in mountains above Greer, August 7.

SANDALWOOD FAMILY

Santalaceae (san-tah-LAY-see-ee)

Represented by a root parasite in Arizona.

Flowers: Petalless, 4- to 5-lobed, with bell-shaped calyx, 5 stamens. Inferior ovary.
Fruit: Nutlike.
Leaves: Alternate, simple.

BASTARD TOADFLAX 175

False toadflax
Comandra pallida
Sandalwood Family (Santalaceae)

Height: To 14".
Flowers: White to pinkish white, starlike, petalless; 5 to 6 pointed lobes surround greenish center, 5 greenish white stamens; to 3/8" wide; in terminal cluster.
Leaves: Green, narrow, lance-shaped; to 1 1/2" long.
Blooms: April–August.
Elevation: 4,000 to 9,500'.
Habitat: Mountainsides, oak woodlands, and ponderosa pine forests.
Comments: A root parasite on many different plants. One species of *Comandra* (koh-MAN-drah) in Arizona. Photograph taken on mountainside at Madera Canyon, April 29.

BUCKWHEAT FAMILY

Polygonaceae (pol-lig-oh-NAY-see-ee)

Represented in Arizona by herbs and woody plants.

Flowers: Regular, tiny, petalless; 2 to 6 petallike sepals, 2 to 9 stamens; 2 to 3 styles, 4- to 5-lobed calyx. One pistil with 2 to 4 stigmas. Superior ovary, usually 1-celled.
Fruit: Usually 3-sided nutlet or achene.
Leaves: Usually alternate or in rosettes; simple.

RIGID SPINY-HERB 485

Devil's spiny-herb, Turk's rug
Chorizanthe rigida
Buckwheat Family (Polygonaceae)

Height: To 4".
Flowers: Yellowish, surrounded by 3 long spines.
Leaves: Dark green, basal, broadly oval, long-stemmed; to 1 1/2" long. Stem leaves are bractlike.
Blooms: March–May.
Elevation: Below 2,500'.
Habitat: Hot, coarse gravels of lower deserts.
Comments: Annual; sprouts up by the thousands after wet winter, then dies. Dried, blackened plants remain in desert soil for a year or more like spiny tufts. Five species of *Chorizanthe* (kor-i-ZAN-thee) in Arizona. Photograph taken south of Gila Bend, March 30.

WINGED ERIOGONUM 486

Winged buckwheat, wing eriogonum
Eriogonum alatum
Buckwheat Family (Polygonaceae)

Height: To 5'.
Flowers: Yellowish green to yellowish brown; tubular, petalless, small (to 3/16" wide); in numerous loose clusters on upper branches, followed by small, hard, winged, triangular seeds.
Leaves: Grayish green, spatula-shaped, very hairy; mainly basal; to 7" long.
Blooms: July–September.
Elevation: 5,500 to 9,500'.
Habitat: Roadsides and forest clearings.
Comments: Erect and many-branched, with hairy stems. Navajo and Hopi Indians used plant medicinally to ease pain. Fifty-three species of *Eriogonum* (eh-rih-AW-guh-num) in Arizona. Photograph taken in vicinity of Woods Canyon Lake, August 2.

WILD BUCKWHEAT 488

Eriogonum corymbosum (*Eriogonum aureum*)
Buckwheat Family (Polygonaceae)

Height: To 2'.
Flowers: Grayish white to yellowish, tiny, and numerous; in rounded clusters to 3/4" wide; on many-stemmed branches.
Leaves: Light green, oval; to 1 3/4" long, 1 1/8" wide.
Blooms: July–October.
Elevation: 4,500 to 8,000'.
Habitat: Clearings in ponderosa pine forests.
Comments: Fifty-three species of *Eriogonum* (eh-rih-AW-guh-num) in Arizona. Photograph taken at Sunset Crater National Monument, September 6.

FLAT-TOP BUCKWHEAT 648

Wild buckwheat
Eriogonum fasciculatum var. *polifolium*
Buckwheat Family (Polygonaceae)

Height: Shrub to 2'.
Flowers: White to pink, slightly fragrant; to 1/8" wide, in slightly flat, terminal clusters.
Leaves: Grayish green, finely haired, leathery, and narrow; to 3/8" long.
Blooms: February–June.
Elevation: 1,000 to 4,500'.
Habitat: Rocky slopes, flats, and along washes.
Comments: Attractive to bees; a source of honey. Fifty-three species of *Eriogonum* (eh-rih-AW-guh-num) in Arizona. Photograph taken at Usery Mountain Recreation Area, February 14.

DESERT TRUMPET 487A and B

Bladderstem, Indian pipe-weed
Eriogonum inflatum
Buckwheat Family (Polygonaceae)

Height: To 3'.
Flowers: Yellow, tiny; on threadlike stalks at stem divisions.

Leaves:	Dark green, oval, long-stemmed; to 2" long; in basal rosette.
Blooms:	February–October.
Elevation:	Below 3,500'.
Habitat:	Rocky or sandy desert slopes.
Comments:	Perennial herb. Stems above nodes are inflated. Some species of wasps drill holes in the hollow stems, fill the hollows with captured insect larvae, then lay their eggs within the stems, thus ensuring food for their young. Fifty-three species of *Eriogonum* (eh-rih-AW-guh-num) in Arizona. Photographs taken at Cattail Cove State Park, February 24. The inflated stems are common to numerous species of *Eriogonum*.

ANTELOPE-SAGE   281
Eriogonum jamesii
Buckwheat Family (Polygonaceae)

Height:	To 14".
Flowers:	White to cream-colored with long, whitish stamens; to 1/4" wide, 3/8" long, in tight or loose cluster above whorl of small leaves.
Leaves:	Grayish green above, very white and hairy beneath; lance-shaped; to 2" long; in basal rosette.
Blooms:	July–October.
Elevation:	5,000 to 9,000'.
Habitat:	Rocky areas and cliffs in clearings in oak woodlands and pine forests.
Comments:	Fifty-three species of *Eriogonum* (eh-rih-AW-guh-num) in Arizona. Photograph taken in Heber vicinity, August 4.

REDROOT ERIOGONUM   280
Wild buckwheat, red root buckwheat
Eriogonum racemosum
Buckwheat Family (Polygonaceae)

Height:	Flowering stem to 1 1/2'.
Flowers:	White to pinkish, with dark pink ribs on back of petals; to 1/8" wide, 1/4" long; in loose, spikelike clusters along upper half of gray, leafless flowering stems.
Leaves:	Grayish green, on long leaf stem; basal cluster, erect, broadly oval, and feltlike; to 1 1/4" long, 3/4" wide.
Blooms:	June–October.
Elevation:	5,000 to 9,000'.
Habitat:	Clearings in pine forests.
Comments:	Fifty-three species of *Eriogonum* (eh-rih-AW-guh-num) in Arizona. Photograph taken in vicinity of Upper Lake Mary, September 2.

YELLOW-FLOWERED ERIOGONUM   489
Eriogonum sp.
Buckwheat Family (Polygonaceae)

Height:	To 1 1/2'.
Flowers:	Bright yellow, with 3 petals, 3 sepals, to 3/16" wide; in flattish, terminal cluster to 3" wide.
Leaves:	Grayish green, hairy, lance-shaped; mainly basal; to 6" long.
Blooms:	May–September.
Elevation:	5,000 to 9,000'.

Habitat: Clearings in ponderosa pine forests and pinyon-juniper woodlands.
Comments: A variable species with over 20 varieties. Has a leafless flower stem, and grows in clumps. Almost all species of *Eriogonum* are difficult to identify, even for the expert botanist. For the amateur, simply recognizing wild buckwheat as such is an accomplishment. Fifty-three species of *Eriogonum* (eh-rih-AW-guh-num) in Arizona. Photograph taken at Walnut Canyon National Monument, September 7.

WATER SMARTWEED 649
Swamp smartweed, knotweed
Polygonum amphibium
Buckwheat Family (Polygonaceae)

Height: Flower stalk to 6".
Flowers: Deep pink; to 1/16" wide, 3/16" long; petalless and in a slender, spikelike cluster, to 2" long.
Leaves: Dark green, shiny, and leathery; alternate, mainly floating, lance-shaped to oval; to 6" long.
Blooms: July–September.
Elevation: 5,000 to 9,000'.
Habitat: Marshes, ponds, and lakes.
Comments: Some authorities now consider this species a variety of *Polygonum coccineum*. Twenty-one species of *Polygonum* (pol-LIG-oh-num) in Arizona. Photograph taken at Nelson Reservoir, August 3.

WESTERN BISTORT 212
Smokeweed
Polygonum bistortoides
Buckwheat Family (Polygonaceae)

Height: To 2'.
Flowers: Snow white to pale pink with 5 petallike segments; to 3/16" long; in dense, spikelike, terminal cluster to 2" long, 3/4" wide; on long, erect, nearly leafless stem.
Leaves: Dark green, with prominent, yellowish midvein; lance-shaped to elliptical, mainly basal; to 7" long.
Blooms: June–September.
Elevation: 8,500 to 11,000'.
Habitat: Wet meadows and along mountain streams.
Comments: Stem is reddish near the ground. Roots are starchy and edible, raw or boiled. Twenty-one species of *Polygonum* (pol-LIG-oh-num) in Arizona. Photograph taken in Hannagan Meadow area, June 30.

LADY'S THUMB 650
Smartweed, knotweed
Polygonum persicaria
Buckwheat Family (Polygonaceae)

Height: To 32".
Flowers: Pinkish, 1/16" long; in dense spikes; to 2" long, some erect, others arched from weight of flowers.
Leaves: Dark green, lance-shaped; to 6" long; stems swollen and streaked with reddish brown at joint where leaf base clasps stem.
Blooms: July–September.

Elevation:	5,000 to 7,000'.
Habitat:	Along ditches and in moist pastures and marshy areas.
Comments:	Of European origin; now naturalized. Twenty-one species of *Polygonum* (pol-LIG-oh-num) in Arizona. Photograph taken at Nelson Reservoir, August 3.

CURLY DOCK   801
Curlyleaf dock
Rumex crispus
Buckwheat Family (Polygonaceae)

Height:	To 4'.
Flowers:	Small, yellowish green, with 6 sepals in 2 circles (inner 3 enlarge to become the fruit), later becoming rosy-colored; in long, loose clusters on upper branches, followed by small, reddish brown fruits to 1/4" long.
Leaves:	Dark green to bluish green, lance-shaped, wavy-curled margins; alternate on stem, mostly basal; to 1' long.
Blooms:	May–October.
Elevation:	100 to 8,000'.
Habitat:	Moist soil along streams, roadsides, ditches, and in pastures.
Comments:	A perennial herb and a weed, occasionally used as a potherb. Native to Eurasia, it is now naturalized. Has deep taproot and reddish stems. Fifteen species of *Rumex* (ROO-mecks) in Arizona. Photograph taken in vicinity of Prescott, June 7.

CANAIGRE (can-IH-gray)   802
Dock, desert rhubarb, wild rhubarb, sorrel
Rumex hymenosepalus
Buckwheat Family (Polygonaceae)

Height:	To 2 1/2'.
Flowers:	Pinkish green; to 3/4" wide; in erect, crowded, terminal raceme to 1' long; followed by clusters of pinkish, heart-shaped, 3-sided, winged seed capsules.
Leaves:	Dark green, broadly lance-shaped, and thick; to 1' long.
Blooms:	Mid-February–April.
Elevation:	1,000 to 6,000'.
Habitat:	Fields, sandy washes, and roadsides.
Comments:	A perennial herb. Tubers are a source of tannin. Fifteen species of *Rumex* (ROO-mecks) in Arizona. Photograph taken at Alamo Lake, February 26.

GOOSEFOOT FAMILY
Chenopodiaceae (ken-oh-poh-di-AY-see-ee)
Herbs and shrubs.

Flowers:	Small, inconspicuous, when present; 1 to 5 perianth segments, stamens same number or fewer than perianth segments, 2 or 3 styles. Superior ovary, 1-celled.
Fruit:	Achene or a small, often bladdery, 1-seeded fruit that does not split.
Leaves:	Mostly alternate, simple.

FOUR-WING SALTBUSH   490
Cenizo, chamiza, shadscale, chamiso, orache
Atriplex canescens
Goosefoot Family (Chenopodiaceae)

Height:	To 8', but more commonly to 4'.
Flowers:	Pale yellow, tiny, inconspicuous, in clusters along the stems; male and female on different plants; followed on the female plant by bunches of small, burlike seeds encased in 4 papery, light green, winglike bracts; to 1/2" wide; bracts dry to pale brown.
Leaves:	Gray-green, narrow; to 2" long.
Blooms:	July–August.
Elevation:	2,000 to 8,000'.
Habitat:	Sandy, sometimes saline soil, from creosote bush to pinyon to ponderosa belts.
Comments:	This salt-tolerant shrub is the most widely spread species of *Atriplex* in the U.S. Its deep roots help control erosion. Its foliage tastes salty. Some female bushes become a mass of fruits. A browse shrub for livestock, deer, and antelope, its seeds provide food for birds and small rodents. Native Americans used seeds for meal, and leaves and new shoots for greens and a yellow dye. The Hopi used this plant as a leavening agent for making bread. Eighteen species of *Atriplex* (AT-ri-plex) in Arizona. Photograph taken at Wupatki National Monument, September 8. **LITTLELEAF SALTBUSH** (*Atriplex polycarpa*) resembles the four-wing saltbush but its leaves are small and it lacks the prominent, four-winged fruits.

DESERT HOLLY   735
Salt bush
Atriplex hymenelytra
Goosefoot Family (Chenopodiaceae)

Height:	To 3'.
Flowers:	Pinkish tube with 2 dark pink stamens, in terminal clusters of small silvery leaves; followed by large, light green, fan-shaped, compressed, fruiting bractlets.
Leaves:	Silvery, succulent, evergreen, and hollylike; rubbery, thick, crinkly; fan-shaped with pointed lobes or teeth; to 1 1/2" wide, 1 3/4" long (including stem).
Blooms:	March.
Elevation:	Below 1,000'.
Habitat:	Dry, sandy soil of washes, hillsides, and plains.
Comments:	A rounded shrub whose foliage is often sold as Christmas decorations. Eighteen species of *Atriplex* (AT-ri-plex) in Arizona. Photograph taken in Kofa Mountains, March 6.

RUSSIAN THISTLE   279
Tumbleweed, wind witch
Salsola iberica (*Salsola kali*)
Goosefoot Family (Chenopodiaceae)

Height:	To 4'.
Flowers:	Whitish, minute, without petals; growing at base of leaves on upper branches; followed by the drying and enlargement of the 5 flower parts that cover tiny fruit.
Leaves:	Grayish green, fleshy on young plants; to 2" long; replaced by bractlike, small, awl-shaped leaves ending in spines.
Blooms:	May–October.
Elevation:	150 to 7,000'.
Habitat:	Roadsides, overgrazed range, and disturbed soil.
Comments:	Not a true thistle. This annual, a native of Russia, was accidentally brought to South Dakota in the 1870s in a shipment of flax seed. Multiple-branching, the often

reddish stems form a large, prickly, bushy ball. When dry, the plant breaks off at ground level, allowing winds to roll tumbleweed, scattering thousands of seeds as it moves along. Two species of *Salsola* (sal-SO-lah) in Arizona. Photograph taken at Wupatki National Monument, September 8.

BLACK GREASEWOOD   822
Chicobush, chico, greasewood
Sarcobatus vermiculatus
Goosefoot Family (Chenopodiaceae)

Height:	To 8'.
Flowers:	Inconspicuous female flowers are borne in axils of leaves, followed by a green to tan, winglike, membranous disk surrounding the seeds. Male flowers are in conelike spikes at branch ends.
Leaves:	Grayish green, fleshy, narrow; to 1 1/4" long, 1/16" wide; dense along branches.
Blooms:	June–September.
Elevation:	1,000 to 6,000'.
Habitat:	Alkaline soil.
Comments:	Creosote bush is often incorrectly called greasewood, but this is actually the only true greasewood. It has white or tannish bark, many rigid branches, and salty tasting leaves. Browsed by cattle and sheep, but overeating causes bloating; also a favorite of jackrabbits. Native Americans use wood to make digging sticks for planting corn, and for dice and knitting needles. One species of *Sarcobatus* (sar-koh-BAY-tuss) in Arizona. Photograph taken at Canyon de Chelly National Monument, June 27.

AMARANTH FAMILY
Amaranthaceae (am-a-ran-THAY-see-ee)
Weedy herbs.

Flowers:	Small, inconspicuous, petalless; 3 to 5 sepals, 3 to 5 stamens opposite the sepals; in spikes or in dense clusters. Superior ovary, 1-celled.
Fruit:	Small, dry, 1-seeded.
Leaves:	Alternate or opposite, simple.

WOOLLY TIDESTROMIA   491
Tidestromia lanuginosa
Amaranth Family (Amaranthaceae)

Height:	Prostrate; but occasionally up to 1 1/2' high, to a mound of 5' wide.
Flowers:	Yellowish green, petalless; 5 pointed sepals, 5 yellow-tipped stamens; flower to 1/8" wide, in clusters in leaf axils.
Leaves:	Grayish green, very downy, in pairs; heart-shaped to oval to roundish, in clusters; to 2" long (including stem), 1" wide.
Blooms:	June–October.
Elevation:	100 to 5,500'.
Habitat:	Fields, dry plains, and roadsides.
Comments:	Annual; pinkish, with very hairy stems. Host plant of beet leafhopper. Collects blowing sand. Two species of *Tidestromia* (tide-e-STROH-mi-ah) in Arizona. Photograph taken in Mesa, June 16.

FOUR O'CLOCK FAMILY

Nyctaginaceae (nik-tah-ji-NAY-see-ee)
Represented in Arizona by herbs.

Flowers:	Regular or near regular, petalless, colorful, and tubular; calyx flares into 4 to 5 lobes, usually 5 stamens but varies from 3 to 10, 1 pistil with long style and buttonlike stigma. Superior ovary, 1-celled.
Fruit:	1-seeded, nutlike achene.
Leaves:	Mostly opposite, simple.

SAND VERBENA   616

Wild lantana, desert sand verbena, hairy sand verbena
Abronia villosa
Four O'Clock Family (Nyctaginaceae)

Height:	Trailing plant to 3' long; upright flower stalks to 12" high.
Flowers:	Pink-purple, to 3"-wide heads or clusters of individual tubular flowers.
Leaves:	Dark green, oval, sticky, and finely haired; to 1 1/2" long.
Blooms:	February–May.
Elevation:	Below 1,500'.
Habitat:	Roadsides, sandy flats, and dunes.
Comments:	Annual. Flowers have delicate fragrance, principally at night. Soft hairs on leaves restrict water loss through evaporation. Five species of *Abronia* (ah-BRO-nee-ah) in Arizona. Photograph taken at Painted Rocks State Park, March 29.

TRAILING FOUR O'CLOCK   652

Windmills, pink three-flower, allionia
Allionia incarnata
Four O'Clock Family (Nyctaginaceae)

Height:	Trailing to 10' long.
Flowers:	Pinkish purple; 3 irregular flowers close together appear as one regular flower in cluster of 3; to 1" wide; in leaf axils.
Leaves:	Dirty green above, silvery beneath; sticky, hairy, oval; to 2" long.
Blooms:	March–October.
Elevation:	Below 6,000'.
Habitat:	Roadsides, open sandy plains, and mesas.
Comments:	Perennial herb. Characterized by sticky stems. Three species of *Allionia* (al-ee-OHN-ee-ah) in Arizona. Photograph taken in Patagonia area, April 27.

RED SPIDERLING   736

Indian boerhaavia, wine-flower, scarlet spiderling
Boerhaavia coccinea
Four O'Clock Family (Nyctaginaceae)

Height:	Trailing to 3' long.
Flowers:	Purplish red, short tube, with 5 spreading lobes; to 1/8" wide; in tight clusters to 1/4" wide, on stems at leaf axils.
Leaves:	Dark green, some pink along margins; lighter green beneath; sticky, wavy-margined; oval to elliptical; to 2" long.
Blooms:	April–November.
Elevation:	Below 5,500'.

Habitat:	Deserts, roadsides, and fields.
Comments:	Perennial herb. Pinkish, with sticky stems. Twelve species of *Boerhaavia* (boor-HAH-vi-ah) in Arizona. Photograph taken near Granite Reef Dam, May 14.

COULTER SPIDERLING   617
Boerhaavia coulteri
Four O'Clock Family (Nyctaginaceae)

Height:	To 3'.
Flowers:	Pink with darker pink toward center, or white; tubular with 5 flaring lobes, each notched at tips; long stamens; to 3/8" wide, in raceme to 1 1/4" long.
Leaves:	Dark green above, lighter green beneath, very hairy on both surfaces; triangular; to 3 1/2" long. Leaves variable.
Blooms:	August–November.
Elevation:	500 to 5,000'.
Habitat:	Roadsides and dry plains.
Comments:	Pinkish stems. Twelve species of *Boerhaavia* (boor-HAH-vi-ah) in Arizona. Photograph taken in vicinity of Pinnacle Peak, Scottsdale, August 25.

DESERT WISHBONE BUSH   618
Wishbone bush
Mirabilis bigelovii
Four O'Clock Family (Nyctaginaceae)

Height:	To 2'.
Flowers:	White to pale pink, funnel-shaped, broad, petallike calyx (no true petals); to 3/4" wide.
Leaves:	Dark green, hairy, oval to kidney-shaped; to 1 1/4" long.
Blooms:	March–October.
Elevation:	Below 3,000'.
Habitat:	Lower desert flats, slopes, and canyons.
Comments:	Perennial herb. Weak-stemmed, straggling; with sticky stems. Branches form "wishbones." Six species of *Mirabilis* (mi-RAB-i-liss or my-RAB-i-liss) in Arizona. Photograph taken in Superstition Mountains, March 26.

RIBBON FOUR O'CLOCK   619
Mirabilis linearis (*Oxybaphus linearis*)
Four O'Clock Family (Nyctaginaceae)

Height:	To 3'.
Flowers:	Reddish purple, 5-lobed, trumpet-shaped, with long stamens; flower to 3/4" wide, 1" long.
Leaves:	Grayish green, linear, to 3" long.
Blooms:	April–September.
Elevation:	4,500 to 9,500'.
Habitat:	Oak woodlands and pine forests.
Comments:	Has sticky stem. Six species of *Mirabilis* (mi-RAB-i-liss or my-RAB-i-liss) in Arizona. Photograph taken in Santa Rita Mountains, April 28.

COLORADO FOUR O'CLOCK   620
Desert four o'clock, wild four o'clock, maravilla, showy four o'clock
Mirabilis multiflora
Four O'Clock Family (Nyctaginaceae)

Height:	To 2'.
Flowers:	Magenta-purple, funnel-shaped, petallike calyx (no true petals), to 1" wide; in groups of 3 to 6 bell-shaped cups in leaf axils, followed by a smooth, dark brown, 1/2"-long fruit.
Leaves:	Dark green, smooth, oval to heart-shaped; to 4" long.
Blooms:	April–September.
Elevation:	2,500 to 6,500'.
Habitat:	Roadsides, open sandy areas, and mesas.
Comments:	Perennial. Forms a rounded clump, appearing almost shrublike. Flowers open in late afternoon, wither the next morning. The root is used for various remedies. Six species of *Mirabilis* (mi-RAB-i-liss or my-RAB-i-liss) in Arizona. Photograph taken near Nutrioso, August 3.

SPREADING FOUR O'CLOCK   621
Wild four o'clock
Mirabilis oxybaphoides
Four O'Clock Family (Nyctaginaceae)

Height:	To 2'.
Flowers:	Purplish red, funnel-shaped, with notched lobes; 3 flowers within the hairy bracts, 3 or 4 yellow-tipped stamens; flowers to 3/8" long, 3-flower cluster to 3/4" wide.
Leaves:	Dark green, wavy margins with sharp hairs, long-stalked, elliptical to oval but variable in shape; to 3 1/2" long; few, opposite.
Blooms:	August–September.
Elevation:	6,000 to 8,000'.
Habitat:	Clearings and roadsides.
Comments:	Spreading or erect plant, with many branches and hairy stems and buds. Six species of *Mirabilis* (mi-RAB-i-liss or my-RAB-i-liss) in Arizona. Photograph taken at Nelson Reservoir, August 18.

SCARLET FOUR O'CLOCK   542
Red four o'clock
Oxybaphus coccineus (*Mirabilis coccinea*)
Four O'Clock Family (Nyctaginaceae)

Height:	To 3 1/2'.
Flowers:	Deep carmine-red, tubular, with very long stamens; bright purple on tip of longest stamen; to 1 3/4" including stamens; in long-stemmed clusters of 3.
Leaves:	Grayish green, very narrow, almost threadlike; to 4" long; no basal leaves, few leaves on stalk.
Blooms:	May–August.
Elevation:	4,000 to 6,500'.
Habitat:	Grassy slopes and clearings in ponderosa pine forests.
Comments:	Produces a brilliant flower that opens only at night. Five species of *Oxybaphus* (oks-ee-BAY-fuss) in Arizona. Photograph taken at Lynx Lake, May 27.

TUFTED FOUR O'CLOCK   622
Oxybaphus comatus (*Mirabilis comata*)
Four O'Clock Family (Nyctaginaceae)

Height:	To 2'.
Flowers:	Purplish red to rose, flaring tube; long stamens extend way beyond tube; to 3/4"

wide; in terminal clusters.

Leaves:	Grayish green, triangular, finely haired; to 2 3/4" long, 1 3/4" wide at widest point.
Blooms:	May–October.
Elevation:	3,500 to 9,000'.
Habitat:	Meadows and clearings in ponderosa pine forests.
Comments:	The plant's many branches spring from the ground. Five species of *Oxybaphus* (oks-ee-BAY-fuss) in Arizona. Photograph taken at Lynx Lake, September 11.

POKEBERRY FAMILY

Phytolaccaceae (fye-to-lak-KAY-see-ee)
Represented in Arizona by herbs.

Flowers:	Regular, small, petalless; 4 or 5 perianth segments, 4 to 12 stamens, 1 or several styles. Superior ovary.
Fruit:	Juicy berry.
Leaves:	Alternate, simple.

POKEBERRY   737

Pokeweed, scoke, inkberry
Phytolacca americana
Pokeberry Family (Phytolaccaceae)

Height:	To 10', but usually to 6'.
Flowers:	Greenish white to pinkish, petals absent, 5 sepals; to 1/4" wide, in terminal raceme, followed at maturity by dark purplish to black 1/4" berries in drooping cluster.
Leaves:	Dark green, oval to lance-shaped, smooth; to 9" long.
Blooms:	August.
Elevation:	4,000 to 6,000' in Chiricahua Mountains.
Habitat:	Clearings, roadsides, and open woods.
Comments:	A branched, perennial herb. Likely introduced to Arizona from eastern U.S. Root is used medicinally. Stems become reddish in fall. Berries are poisonous, and leave a purple stain when overly ripened. One species of *Phytolacca* (fye-to-LAK-kah) in Arizona. Photograph taken in northeastern U.S. where this same species is found.

PORTULACA FAMILY

Portulacaceae (por-tew-lah-KAY-see-ee)
Herbs.

Flowers:	Regular or near regular, 4 or 5 or more petals; generally 2 sepals; usually 5 stamens, but occasionally 10; 1 pistil, several styles. Mostly superior ovary, 1-celled.
Fruit:	Dry, 3-valved pod (capsule).
Leaves:	Alternate or opposite; simple, toothless, thick, and succulent.

RED MAIDS   176 and 585

Rock purslane
Calandrinia ciliata
Portulaca Family (Portulacaceae)

Height:	Prostrate or semi-prostrate stems to 16" long.
Flowers:	Reddish pink or very white, usually with 5 petals with rounded tips; hairy sepals; to 1/2" wide; on short stalks in leaf axils.

Leaves:	Green, narrow, and thick; hairy, succulent; to 3" long.
Blooms:	February–April.
Elevation:	1,500 to 4,000'.
Habitat:	Washes, foothills, and plains.
Comments:	Two species of *Calandrinia* (kal-an-DRIN-i-ah) in Arizona. Photograph of red-flowered plant taken at Usery Mountain Recreation Area, February 14. Photograph of white-flowered plant taken in Superstition Mountains, February 23.

MINER'S LETTUCE   177
Indian lettuce
Claytonia perfoliata (*Montia perfoliata*)
Portulaca Family (Portulacaceae)

Height:	To 14".
Flowers:	White to pinkish; to 1/4" wide, in tiny raceme rising above center of circular leaf.
Leaves:	Dark green, fleshy, circular, flower-bearing leaf; to 2" wide. Other leaves lance-shaped on narrow stalks.
Blooms:	February–May.
Elevation:	2,500 to 7,500'.
Habitat:	Moist places in shade, along brooks, and around springs.
Comments:	Annual. Used by pioneers and Native Americans as a potherb and for salads. Two species of *Claytonia* (clay-TOE-ni-ah) in Arizona. Photograph taken at Saguaro Lake area, February 6.

SPRING BEAUTY   178
Mayflower
Claytonia rosea (*Claytonia lanceolata*)
Portulaca Family (Portulacaceae)

Height:	To 4".
Flowers:	White to pinkish, 5 petals, 5 pink-tipped stamens; to 5/8" wide; in loose raceme.
Leaves:	Dark green above, pinkish beneath, narrow, and smooth; succulent, lance-shaped; 1 pair, opposite; to 1 3/4" long.
Blooms:	February–May.
Elevation:	5,500 to 8,000'.
Habitat:	Moist coniferous forests.
Comments:	Perennial. Two species of *Claytonia* (clay-TOE-ni-ah) in Arizona. Photograph taken at Willow Springs Lake, April 22.

SOUTHWESTERN LEWISIA   641
Southern lewisia
Lewisia brachycalyx
Portulaca Family (Portulacaceae)

Height:	To 2 1/2".
Flowers:	Very pale pink, 5 to 9 petals arranged singly on short stem; to 2" wide.
Leaves:	Green, flat, smooth; broadly linear and succulent; to 4" long, in basal rosette.
Blooms:	April–June.
Elevation:	5,000 to 8,000'.
Habitat:	Oak-juniper woodlands and ponderosa pine forests.
Comments:	A perennial herb with thick, starchy roots. Three species of *Lewisia* (lew-IS-i-ah) in Arizona. Photograph taken near Willow Springs Lake, May 9.

DWARF LEWISIA 642
Pygmy lewisia
Lewisia pygmaea
Portulaca Family (Portulacaceae)

Height: To 3".
Flowers: Deep pink to white, 5 to 9 petals with faint stripes radiating outward; to 3/4" wide.
Leaves: Dark green, fleshy, rounded, and linear; to 3" long; in basal tuft.
Blooms: June–August.
Elevation: 8,000 to 9,000'.
Habitat: Moist mountain meadows.
Comments: Perennial herb. Three species of *Lewisia* (lew-IS-i-ah) in Arizona. Photograph taken at Crescent Lake, June 17.

CHAMISSO'S MONTIA 179
Montia chamissoi
Portulaca Family (Portulacaceae)

Height: Creeping stems to 6" long.
Flowers: White or pink, 5 petals, 5 pink-tipped stamens; to 1/2" wide; in loose cluster of up to 8 flowers.
Leaves: Dark green, lance-shaped; very succulent; opposite; to 1 1/2" long.
Blooms: June–August.
Elevation: 6,000 to 9,500'.
Habitat: Springs and other wet areas in coniferous forests.
Comments: Perennial. Runner branches end in bulblets. One species of *Montia* (MON-ti-ah) in Arizona. Photograph taken at Lee Valley Reservoir, August 11.

COMMON PURSLANE 341
Pursley, wild portulaca
Portulaca oleracea
Portulaca Family (Portulacaceae)

Height: Normally prostrate to 2' long; occasionally erect to 6" high.
Flowers: Yellow, with 5 petals; to 1/4" wide; singly or in small clusters in leaf axils or at stem tips; followed by a small, round capsule.
Leaves: Bronze-green with reddish margins, succulent, thick, smooth, and shiny; wedge-shaped, rounded at tip; to 1 1/2" long.
Blooms: June–September.
Elevation: 1,000 to 8,500'.
Habitat: Clearings in ponderosa forests, overgrazed areas, meadows, and cultivated areas.
Comments: Annual. Reddish on stems. Joints produce roots when in contact with soil. Introduced from Europe; now naturalized. Its iron content is very high, so it is eaten as a salad green and as a potherb. Six species of *Portulaca* (por-tew-LAK-ah) in Arizona. Photograph taken in Pine, September 2.

CLUBLEAF FLAMEFLOWER 586
Pigmy talinum
Talinum brevifolium
Portulaca Family (Portulacaceae)

Height: To 4" tall.
Flowers: Lavender or rose, with 5 wide-separated petals; about 20 yellow stamens;

to 3/4" wide.

Leaves:	Grayish green, succulent, semi-rounded; to 1/2" long, crowded all along stem.
Blooms:	May–September.
Elevation:	5,000 to 8,000'.
Habitat:	Clearings in coniferous forests.
Comments:	Perennial herb. Sedumlike. Reddish, spreading stems. Seven species of *Talinum* (ta-LYE-num) in Arizona. Photograph taken in vicinity of Luna Lake, June 29.

PINK FAMILY
Caryophyllaceae (carry-oh-fill-AY-see-ee)
Represented in Arizona by herbs and slightly woody plants.

Flowers:	Regular, 4 to 5 petals, 4 to 5 sepals; 8 to 10 stamens, 1 pistil, 2 to 5 styles. Superior ovary, 1-celled.
Fruit:	Dry; many-seeded capsule or 1-seeded achene.
Leaves:	Opposite or whorled; simple.

FENDLER'S SANDWORT   180
Arenaria fendleri
Pink Family (Caryophyllaceae)

Height:	To 10".
Flowers:	White, starlike, light green filaments; 5 petals; bright pink anthers; to 3/8" wide; in open, branched cluster.
Leaves:	Dark green, threadlike, sharply pointed; to 2 1/2" long.
Blooms:	April–September.
Elevation:	4,000 to 12,000'.
Habitat:	Clearings in ponderosa pine and mixed conifer forests.
Comments:	Perennial herb. Ten species of *Arenaria* (a-re-NAY-ri-ah) in Arizona. Photograph taken at Upper Lake Mary, September 6.

SANDWORT   181
Arenaria lanuginosa ssp. *saxosa*
Pink Family (Caryophyllaceae)

Height:	To 5".
Flowers:	White and starlike, with pink anthers; to 1/2" wide.
Leaves:	Dark green, opposite, elliptical to lance-shaped; to 1/2" long.
Blooms:	May–September.
Elevation:	7,000 to 12,000'.
Habitat:	Coniferous forests.
Comments:	Grows in compact mounds. Ten species of *Arenaria* (a-re-NAY-ri-ah) in Arizona. Photograph taken near Greer, June 20.

MOUSE-EAR CHICKWEED   182
Large mouse-ear, perennial mouse-ear chickweed, powder-horn
Cerastium vulgatum
Pink Family (Caryophyllaceae)

Height:	To 16".
Flowers:	White, greenish in center, with 5 deeply notched, 2-lobed petals, 5 yellow stamens; to 1/2" wide; in small, loose cluster at top of stalk.

Leaves:	Yellowish green, very hairy, opposite, oval to oblong; stalkless; to 3/4" long.
Blooms:	May–September.
Elevation:	2,500 to 8,000'.
Habitat:	Fields and roadsides.
Comments:	Perennial herb; a common weed introduced from Europe. Sticky hairs on stem. Boiled leaves can be eaten. Seven species of *Cerastium* (see-RASS-tee-uhm) in Arizona. Photograph taken in Greer area, July 4.

SLEEPY CATCHFLY   587
Catchfly
Silene antirrhina
Pink Family (Caryophyllaceae)

Height:	To 3'.
Flowers:	Light pink petals notched at tips; to 1/4" wide.
Leaves:	Dark green and narrow; to 3" long.
Blooms:	March–August.
Elevation:	Below 6,000'.
Habitat:	Washes and waste areas.
Comments:	Sticky areas on stems. Eight species of *Silene* (sy-LEE-ne) in Arizona. Photograph taken in Superstition Mountains, March 26.

MEXICAN SILENE   543
Mexican campion, catchfly
Silene laciniata
Pink Family (Caryophyllaceae)

Height:	To 3'.
Flowers:	Cardinal red, with 5 petals, each cut at tips into 4 segments; flowerhead to 1 1/2" wide.
Leaves:	Dark green, narrowly lance-shaped, sticky, and finely haired; to 6" long.
Blooms:	July–October.
Elevation:	5,500 to 9,000'.
Habitat:	Coniferous forests.
Comments:	Perennial herb. "Pinked" petals give family its name. Eight species of *Silene* (sy-LEE-ne) in Arizona. Photograph taken at Greer, September 11.

SCOULER'S CATCHFLY   588
Silene scouleri
Pink Family (Caryophyllaceae)

Height:	To 3'.
Flowers:	Pinkish, with 5 deeply forked, very narrowly lobed petals in groups of 2; sticky; to 3/4" wide, 3/4" long. Sticky calyx distended and striped like a miniature watermelon.
Leaves:	Dark green, opposite, hairy, and sticky, with deep midvein; spoon-shaped at base; to 5" long; linear and gradually smaller along upper stem.
Blooms:	July–September.
Elevation:	5,000 to 9,500'.
Habitat:	Moist pine and spruce-fir forests and mountain meadows.
Comments:	Entire plant is sticky and hairy. Eight species of *Silene* (sy-LEE-ne) in Arizona. Photograph taken south of Alpine, August 6.

STARWORT   183
Chickweed, sticky starwort
Stellaria jamesiana
Pink Family (Caryophyllaceae)

Height: To 1'.

Flowers: White; 5 triangular petals, each with a V-shaped notch; to 1/2" wide; in loose clusters.

Leaves: Dark green, opposite, hairy, lance-shaped; deep center vein; clasping stem; to 4" long.

Blooms: April–July.

Elevation: 7,000 to 8,500'.

Habitat: Moist coniferous forests and mountain meadows.

Comments: Sticky, weak stems. Six species of *Stellaria* (stell-LAIR-i-ah) in Arizona. Photograph taken at North Rim of Grand Canyon National Park, June 25.

CHICKWEED   184
Starwort
Stellaria longipes
Pink Family (Caryophyllaceae)

Height: To 16".

Flowers: White, 5 deeply cleft, pointed petals longer than the 5 sepals; black-tipped stamens; flower to 1/2" wide; 1 to 3 on long, erect stalk in leaf axil.

Leaves: Dark green, opposite, shiny, ascending, and stemless; linear to lance-shaped; sharp-pointed at tip; to 3/4" long.

Blooms: May–August.

Elevation: 8,500 to 10,000'.

Habitat: Wet meadows and moist spruce-fir forests.

Comments: Perennial herb. Six species of *Stellaria* (stell-LAIR-i-ah) in Arizona. Photograph taken in mountains above Greer, July 8.

BUTTERCUP FAMILY
Ranunculaceae (ra-nun-kew-LAY-see-ee)
Represented in Arizona by herbs and slightly shrubby plants.

Flowers: Regular or irregular; generally 3 to 5 petals, but sometimes petalless; spurred or hooded; 3 to 15 sepals, often petallike; numerous stamens; 1 pistil or many. Superior ovary, 1-celled.

Fruit: 1-celled achene, pod, or berry.

Leaves: Alternate or opposite and occasionally basal; simple or compound.

COLUMBIA MONKSHOOD   756
Blue-weed, friar's cap, western monkshood, aconite, wolfbane
Aconitum columbianum
Buttercup Family (Ranunculaceae)

Height: To 7', but averaging to 3'.

Flowers: Dark blue to blue-violet, occasionally white; to 1 1/4" long; in raceme; 5 sepals resembling petals, upper sepal forming hood, 2 oval side sepals, 2 narrow bottom sepals; petals concealed under hood.

Leaves: Dark green, palmately lobed, jagged-margined; to 8" wide.

Blooms:	June–September.
Elevation:	5,000 to 9,500'.
Habitat:	Along mountain streams and in meadows and rich, moist forests.
Comments:	Very poisonous to livestock and humans if ingested. Two species of *Aconitum* (ak-oh-NEYE-tuhm) in Arizona. Photograph taken at Greer, July 21.

COMMON BANEBERRY   740
Red baneberry, snakeberry, chinaberry
Actaea rubra
Buttercup Family (Ranunculaceae)

Height:	To 3'.
Flowers:	White, with 4 to 10 small petals, many stamens; to 1/8" long; in elongated cluster to 5" long; followed by cluster of 1/2" purplish red berries.
Leaves:	Green, few but very large; pinnately divided into oval, sharply toothed leaflets, each to 3 1/2" long, with up to 2 dozen leaflets per triangular leaf.
Blooms:	May–July.
Elevation:	7,000 to 10,000'.
Habitat:	Moist mountain forests and streambanks.
Comments:	Perennial herb with poisonous berries. One species of *Actaea* (ak-TEE-ah) in Arizona. Photograph taken at Greer, July 21.

DESERT ANEMONE   246
Desert windflower
Anemone tuberosa
Buttercup Family (Ranunculaceae)

Height:	To 16".
Flowers:	White to pinkish purple, petalless, with petallike structures that are actually sepals; to 1 1/2" wide; at ends of erect stems.
Leaves:	Green, divided several times into sections; basal and in whorl midway on stem; to 4" long, 2" wide.
Blooms:	February–April.
Elevation:	2,500 to 5,000'.
Habitat:	Rocky desert slopes.
Comments:	Perennial herb. Three species of *Anemone* (a-NEM-oh-nee) in Arizona. Photograph taken in Superstition Mountains, February 4.

ROCKY MOUNTAIN COLUMBINE   686
Colorado columbine, blue columbine
Aquilegia caerulea (ssp. *pinetorum* is found in Arizona. It is paler in color and has longer, more slender spurs than the typical phase in the photograph).
Buttercup Family (Ranunculaceae)

Height:	To 30".
Flowers:	To 3" wide; 5 petallike, pale blue sepals; 5 paler blue to white petals with backward-pointing spurs to 2" long.
Leaves:	Bluish green, mostly basal, divided into several lobes; leaflets to 1 1/4" long, about as wide.
Blooms:	June–July.
Elevation:	8,000 to 11,000'.

| Habitat: | Coniferous forests in rich, moist soil. |
| Comments: | State flower of Colorado. Seven species of *Aquilegia* (ak-wih-LEE-jih-uh) in Arizona. Photograph taken Colorado, July 16. |

YELLOW COLUMBINE 342
Golden columbine
Aquilegia chrysantha
Buttercup Family (Ranunculaceae)

Height:	To 4'.
Flowers:	Canary yellow, with 5 yellow petals with 2"-long spurs projecting backwards; flower horizontal or upward pointing; to 3" wide.
Leaves:	Bluish green, mostly basal, divided into threes; leaflets to 1 1/2" long about as wide.
Blooms:	April–September.
Elevation:	3,000 to 11,000'.
Habitat:	Alongside streams and in rich, moist soil in shady forests.
Comments:	Perennial herb. Seven species of *Aquilegia* (ak-wih-LEE-jih-uh) in Arizona. Photograph taken at Willow Springs Lake, September 9.

RED COLUMBINE 544
Barrel columbine
Aquilegia triternata
Buttercup Family (Ranunculaceae)

Height:	To 1'.
Flowers:	5 reddish petals tipped with yellow; long spurs pointing backwards; 5 reddish sepals, stamens projecting and nodding; to 1 3/4" long.
Leaves:	Olive-green, divided into threes; leaflets to 1 1/2".
Blooms:	May–October.
Elevation:	4,000 to 10,000'.
Habitat:	Moist coniferous forests.
Comments:	Perennial herb. Seven species of *Aquilegia* (ak-wih-LEE-jih-uh) in Arizona. Photograph taken south of Alpine, August 2.

MARSH MARIGOLD 244
Elk's-lip, cowslip, meadowbright
Caltha leptosepala
Buttercup Family (Ranunculaceae)

Height:	To 8".
Flowers:	White, with 5 to 12 petallike sepals, not true petals; a center of numerous yellow stamens; to 1 1/2" wide.
Leaves:	Dark green, shiny; heart-shaped, minutely scalloped; basal; to 3" long.
Blooms:	May–September.
Elevation:	7,500 to 11,000'.
Habitat:	Wet, boggy meadows and along streams.
Comments:	Perennial. The name elk's-lip refers to the shape of plant's leaf. One species of *Caltha* (KAL-thah) in Arizona. Photograph taken at Hannagan Meadow, June 24.

TEXAS VIRGIN BOWER 149
Barbas de chivato, old man's beard
Clematis drummondii

	Buttercup Family (Ranunculaceae)
Height:	Woody vine to 20' or more.
Flowers:	White, petalless, with 4 white, petallike sepals, and numerous white stamens; to 1" wide; followed by fluffy, white plume.
Leaves:	Grayish green, downy-haired, thin; pinnately compound, cleft or lobed; to 2" long.
Blooms:	March–September.
Elevation:	Below 4,000'.
Habitat:	Open ground.
Comments:	Six species of *Clematis* (KLEM-uh-tiss) in Arizona. (Also pronounced klih-MAT-iss, klih-MAH-tiss, and klih-MATE-iss). Photograph taken at Patagonia Lake State Park, April 26.

WHITE VIRGIN'S BOWER   150

Western virgin's bower, traveler's joy, muermera, barba de chivo, old-man's-beard, yerba de chivato, pipestems, clematide, pepper vine
Clematis ligusticifolia
Buttercup Family (Ranunculaceae)

Height:	Woody vine to 20' or more.
Flowers:	White and petalless, with 4 white, petallike sepals, numerous white stamens; to 1" wide; followed by fluffy, white plume on female plant.
Leaves:	Green, thin, smooth, pinnately compound; 5 to 7 toothed or 3-lobed leaflets, each to 3" long.
Blooms:	May–September.
Elevation:	3,000 to 8,000'.
Habitat:	Along streams and in other moist places.
Comments:	Perennial vine; clings by twisting leaf stems that form tendrils. Weak stems climb over shrubs, up into trees, and over rocks. Chewed by Native Americans and pioneers as sore throat treatment. Infusion of leaves used for treating sores on horses. Leaves and stems taste like pepper; certain species of *Clematis*, however, are poisonous. Very fragrant; a favorite of bees. Six species of *Clematis* (KLEM-uh-tiss) in Arizona; this species hybridizes with *Clematis drummondii* and varies greatly in leaflet size, shape, and dentation. (*Clematis* is also pronounced klih-MAT-iss, klih-MAH-tiss, and klih-MATE-iss.) Photograph taken in vicinity of Nutrioso, August 18.

ROCKY MOUNTAIN CLEMATIS   151

Alpine clematis
Clematis pseudoalpina
Buttercup Family (Ranunculaceae)

Height:	Trailing or climbing woody vine to 5'.
Flowers:	White to violet or purple; 4 drooping, petallike sepals on leafless stem; to 2" long, followed by seeds in cluster of long silky plumes.
Leaves:	Dull green, compound, divided twice into threes; toothed; to 2" long.
Blooms:	June–July.
Elevation:	7,000 to 9,000'.
Habitat:	Rich soil in moist coniferous forests.
Comments:	Plumes aid in distribution of seeds by the wind. Six species of *Clematis* (KLEM-uh-tiss) in Arizona. (Other pronunciations include klih-MAT-iss, klih-MAH-tiss, and klih-MATE-iss.) Photograph taken at Greer, June 17.

NELSON'S LARKSPUR 757
Delphinium nelsoni
Buttercup Family (Ranunculaceae)

Height:	To 15".
Flowers:	Deep blue to bluish purple; upper petals in center of flower are white, notched, and with faint blue lines; 4 petals, 5 sepals, backward-projecting spur; flower including spur to 1 1/4" long, clustered on spikelike raceme; followed by 3-sectioned seed capsule.
Leaves:	Grayish green, finely haired, succulent, and palmate; 3- to 5-lobed, each lobe generally 3-cleft with well-rounded tips; basal; to 1 1/4" wide.
Blooms:	June.
Elevation:	6,000 to 8,500'.
Habitat:	Pine forests.
Comments:	Perennial herb. Contains delphinine and other toxic alkaloids. Ten species of *Delphinium* (dell-FIN-i-uhm) in Arizona. Photograph taken at Upper Lake Mary, June 1.

PALEFACE DELPHINIUM   758
Paleface larkspur
Delphinium parishii (*Delphinium amabile*)
Buttercup Family (Ranunculaceae)

Height:	To 4'.
Flowers:	Pale blue to lavender, with 4 petals in unequal pairs and backward-pointing spur; to 1" long; in elongated cluster.
Leaves:	Green, cleft into narrow lobes with sharp points; on long stalks, mainly at or near base of stem; to 3" long. Leaves often wither at blooming time.
Blooms:	February–May.
Elevation:	Below 5,000'.
Habitat:	Desert mesas and washes.
Comments:	Perennial herb. Ten species of *Delphinium* (dell-FIN-i-uhm) in Arizona. Photograph taken at Boyce Thompson Southwestern Arboretum, Superior, April 12.

BARESTEM LARKSPUR   759
Wild delphinium, espuelita, naked delphinium
Delphinium scaposum
Buttercup Family (Ranunculaceae)

Height:	To 30".
Flowers:	Royal blue with whitish center; backward-projecting spur, 4 petals, and 5 sepals; to 1" wide; clustered on spikelike raceme, followed by 3-sectioned seed capsule.
Leaves:	Dark green, basal, palmately divided into lobes with rounded tips; to 2 1/2" wide.
Blooms:	March–May.
Elevation:	Below 5,000'.
Habitat:	Gravelly mesas, hillsides, and open desert.
Comments:	Perennial herb with leafless stem. Contains delphinine and other toxins poisonous to humans and livestock. Hopi Indians use ground flowers in religious ceremonies. Ten species of *Delphinium* (dell-FIN-i-uhm) in Arizona. Photograph taken at Saguaro National Monument, March 31.

TOWERING DELPHINIUM 760
Towering larkspur
Delphinium tenuisectum
Buttercup Family (Ranunculaceae)

Height: To 3'.

Flowers: 4 dark blue to bluish purple petals; 5 colored, petallike sepals, one forming a long, backward-facing spur; flower to 1" long, 1" wide, in long, densely flowered spike.

Leaves: Dark green, smooth, finely dissected into wedge-shaped lobes that are again cleft into narrow lobes; leaf to 6" long, 4" wide.

Blooms: July–August.

Elevation: 8,500 to 9,000'.

Habitat: Mountain meadows and forest clearings.

Comments: Perennial herb, with very leafy stem and no hair. Plant contains a poisonous juice. Ten species of *Delphinium* (dell-FIN-i-uhm) in Arizona. Photograph taken above Greer, August 10.

WATER BUTTERCUP 185
Water crowfoot, white water buttercup
Ranunculus aquatilis
Buttercup Family (Ranunculaceae)

Height: Aquatic flower; projects about 1" above surface of water.

Flowers: White; 5 petals, yellow at base; to 3/4" wide.

Leaves: Submerged, cut into numerous forked, hairlike segments.

Blooms: May–August.

Elevation: 4,500 to 9,000'.

Habitat: Ponds and slow streams.

Comments: Aquatic perennial; forms dense beds in ponds. Food for ducks and geese. Nineteen species of *Ranunculus* (ra-NUN-kew-lus) in Arizona. Photograph taken at Nelson Reservoir, August 3.

HEARTLEAF BUTTERCUP 343
Heart-leaved buttercup
Ranunculus cardiophyllus
Buttercup Family (Ranunculaceae)

Height: To 16".

Flowers: Shiny yellow, with 5 waxy petals; to 1 1/2" wide.

Leaves: Dark green, heart-shaped, with scalloped margins; to 2" long.

Blooms: June–July.

Elevation: 7,000 to 9,500'.

Habitat: Moist meadows in pine and spruce-fir belts.

Comments: Buttercups contain a cardiac poison and are poisonous if eaten. Nineteen species of *Ranunculus* (ra-NUN-kew-lus) in Arizona. Photograph taken near Greer, June 21.

AQUATIC BUTTERCUP 344
Ranunculus hydrocharoides
Buttercup Family (Ranunculaceae)

Height: To 3".

Flowers: Golden yellow, with 5 petals; waxy-looking; to 1/4" wide; grow singly at end of stalk.

Leaves:	Green, shiny, oval to lance-shaped; to 1 1/2" long.
Blooms:	June–September.
Elevation:	7,000 to 9,500'.
Habitat:	Springs, marshes, streams, and wet meadows in mixed coniferous forests.
Comments:	Aquatic perennial. Nineteen species of *Ranunculus* (ra-NUN-kew-lus) in Arizona. Photograph taken near Hannagan Meadow, June 24.

MACOUN'S BUTTERCUP   345
Ranunculus macounii
Buttercup Family (Ranunculaceae)

Height:	To 3'.
Flowers:	Golden yellow, with 5 rounded petals; to 5/8" wide.
Leaves:	Dark green, finely haired above, lighter green beneath; triangular-shaped but divided and cleft; to 8" long, including stem; leaves smaller on upper stems.
Blooms:	July–August.
Elevation:	6,000 to 8,000'.
Habitat:	In mud along streams and in marshes in coniferous forests.
Comments:	Perennial. A sprawling plant with either hairy or smooth stems. Nineteen species of *Ranunculus* (ra-NUN-kew-lus) in Arizona. Photograph taken at Greer, July 5.

FENDLER'S MEADOW RUE   796
Fendler meadow rue
Thalictrum fendleri
Buttercup Family (Ranunculaceae)

Height:	To 3'.
Flowers:	Petalless; greenish to yellowish stamens on purplish, threadlike stalks; to 3/8" wide. Male and female flowers on separate plants; male flowers resemble miniature tassels, female flowers are tiny clusters.
Leaves:	Green, fernlike, delicate; thin, stalked, compound; divided several times into leaflets wider than long; to 1 1/2" long.
Blooms:	May–August.
Elevation:	5,000 to 9,500'.
Habitat:	Pine and spruce-fir forests.
Comments:	Perennial herb. Two species of *Thalictrum* (tha-LICK-trum) in Arizona. Photograph taken at Greer, July 5. A similar species, *Thalictrum dasycarpum* has thick, rigid leaflets that are longer than wide, and white stamens.

BARBERRY FAMILY
Berberidaceae (ber-beh-rih-DAY-see-ee)
Represented in Arizona by small, woody plants and shrubs.

Flowers:	Regular, usually tiny; 6 petals in 2 circles, 6 sepals in 2 circles; 6 stamens. Superior ovary, 1-celled.
Fruit:	Berry or capsule.
Leaves:	Alternate, simple, or compound, often spiny.

FREMONT BARBERRY   389
Holly-grape, barberry, berbero, palo amarillo, algerita, Fremont mahonia
Berberis fremontii

Barberry Family (Berberidaceae)

Height: Shrub to 10'.

Flowers: 6 yellow petals, flower to 1" wide, in clusters of 3 to 9; followed by loose cluster of dark blue, 1/2"-wide berries.

Leaves: Dark grayish green, leathery, pinnately compound, with 3 to 7 leaflets to 3" long; leaf to 5" long.

Blooms: April–July.

Elevation: 4,000 to 7,000'.

Habitat: Pinyon-juniper and pine woodlands.

Comments: Evergreen. Fragrant. Hopi Indians use wood for crafts and roots for yellow dye. Berries used for jams and jellies. Contains the drug berberine. Six species of *Berberis* (BER-ber-iss) in Arizona. Photograph taken at Vernon, June 13.

RED BARBERRY   390
Algerita
Berberis haematocarpa
Barberry Family (Berberidaceae)

Height: To 6'.

Flowers: Fragrant, to 1/2" wide, with 6 yellow petals and stamens; in loose few-flowered cluster; followed by red, juicy, berry to 3/8" in diameter.

Leaves: Bluish green covered with a whitish bloom, pinnate, 3 to 5 leaflets; leaflets unstalked, leathery, stiff, to 3/4" wide, each tapering to a sharp, terminal spine, terminal leaflet longest, pointed lobes on leaflets ending in sharp spines; leaf to 4" long.

Blooms: February–May.

Elevation: 3,000 to 5,000'.

Habitat: Desert grasslands and oak woodlands.

Comments: Red jelly made from fruits; root and bark used in making a yellow dye. Six species of *Berberis* (BER-ber-iss) in Arizona. Photograph taken at Desert Botanical Garden, Phoenix, March 3. Native to upper desert slopes and to chaparral in central Arizona.

KOFA MOUNTAIN BARBERRY   391
Kofa mahonia
Berberis harrisoniana
Barberry Family (Berberidaceae)

Height: Small shrub to 3'.

Flowers: Yellow, with 6 large petals and sepals; to 1/2" wide; in large, loose cluster; followed by bluish black, slightly oval fruits, to 1/4" in diameter.

Leaves: Grayish green, palmate, with 3 similar leaflets; thick, leathery, and stiff, ending in stout, sharp spines; leaf to 2" long.

Blooms: February–March.

Elevation: 2,500 to 3,500'.

Habitat: Rocky slopes in Ajo and Kofa Mountains.

Comments: Forms a sprawling bush. Six species of *Berberis* (BER-ber-iss) in Arizona. Photograph taken at Palm Canyon in Kofa Mountains, February 22.

CREEPING BARBERRY   392

Creeping Oregon grape, sangre de Cristo, mountain holly, Oregon grape, creeping mahonia, creeping holly-grape, yerba de la sangre
Berberis repens (Mahonia repens)
Barberry Family (Berberidaceae)

Height:	Low, creeping shrub to 1'.
Flowers:	Fragrant, to 3/4" wide; 6 yellow petals; in dense cluster, followed by cluster of 1/4" bluish purple berries.
Leaves:	Dark green, shiny, leathery, hollylike; to 10" long; pinnately compound; 3 to 7 wavy leaflets with spiny margins, leaflets to 3" long.
Blooms:	April–June.
Elevation:	5,000 to 10,000'.
Habitat:	Open coniferous forests and wooded slopes.
Comments:	Evergreen shrub. Excellent ground cover and erosion fighter. Stems root when they come in contact with soil. In fall, leaves turn shades of red, yellow, or purple. Berries are used for jelly and eaten by wildlife; twigs and leaves are used medicinally. Yellow dye is made from roots. Six species of *Berberis* (BER-ber-iss) in Arizona. Photograph taken at Sharp Creek northeast of Christopher Creek, April 22. A similar shrub, **HOLLY LEAF GRAPE** (*Berberis wilcoxii*), is taller and has fewer than 10 coarse teeth on each leaflet. Photograph (**PLATE 393**) taken at Cave Creek, Portal, April 23.

POPPY FAMILY

Papaveraceae (pap-pa-ver-RAY-see-ee)
Represented in Arizona by herbs.

Flowers:	Regular or irregular; 4 to 6 petals, often wrinkled; usually 2 sepals, 4 to 6 or more stamens; bulky pistil, style short or absent. Superior ovary, 1-celled.
Fruit:	Dry capsule.
Leaves:	Alternate or basal; simple or divided.

BLUESTEM PRICKLEPOPPY   152

Prickly poppy, thistle poppy, chicalote, cowboys' fried egg
Argemone pleiacantha
Poppy Family (Papaveraceae)

Height:	To 3'.
Flowers:	White, tissue-paper thin, with 4 to 6 crinkled petals, numerous bright orange stamens; to 5" wide; followed by oblong, prickly seed pod to 1 1/2" long.
Leaves:	Bluish green, deeply lobed; clasping stem; prickles on veins and margins; to 8" long.
Blooms:	April–November.
Elevation:	1,400 to 8,000'.
Habitat:	Fields, roadsides, mesas, and washes.
Comments:	Perennial herb; with very spiny stems, acrid yellow sap. All parts are poisonous; however, mourning doves feed on seeds. Large expanses of this species on rangeland indicate overgrazing. Six species of *Argemone* (ar-JEM-oh-nee) in Arizona. Photograph taken at Theodore Roosevelt Lake, April 29.

MEXICAN GOLD POPPY 530
Amapola del campo, desert gold poppy, gold poppy
Eschscholtzia mexicana
Poppy Family (Papaveraceae)

Height: To 16".

Flowers: Orange, with 4 petals forming a cup; to 1 1/2" wide on a single stalk, with numerous flowers per plant; followed by a slender seed capsule to 4" long.

Leaves: Fernlike, pale bluish green; to 2 1/2" long.

Blooms: Mid-February–May, starting earliest in warmer desert areas.

Elevation: Below 4,500'.

Habitat: Slopes, plains, foothills, and mesas.

Comments: Annual; remains open only in full sunlight. Whole areas of desert become a sea of gold from these poppies after abundant winter rainfalls. Dr. Eschscholtz, for whom genus is named, was a Russian surgeon, naturalist, and traveler. Three species of *Eschscholtzia* (esh-SHOLT-zi-ah) in Arizona. Photograph taken in Superstition Mountains, February 22. The **DESERT GOLD** or **MOHAVE POPPY** (*Eschscholtzia glyptosperma*) has orange-yellow flowers on long, naked stems, with all the leaves in a basal cluster.

LITTLE GOLD POPPY 320
Pygmy poppy
Eschscholtzia minutiflora
Poppy Family (Papaveraceae)

Height: To 20".

Flowers: Yellow-orange, 4 petals; to 3/4" wide; followed by a long, slender seed capsule.

Leaves: Bluish green, fernlike, divided into narrow segments; on long stalks at stem joints; to 2" near the ground, decreasing in size upward.

Blooms: February–May.

Elevation: Below 4,500'.

Habitat: Lower deserts in sandy soil.

Comments: A rather bushy plant. Three species of *Eschscholtzia* (esh-SHOLT-zi-ah) in Arizona. Photograph taken in Kofa Mountain area, March 29.

CREAM CUPS 388
Cream Cup
Platystemon californicus
Poppy Family (Papaveraceae)

Height: To 1'.

Flowers: Pale yellow or cream; normally 6 petals, occasionally more (as in photograph); terminal on stem; to 1" wide.

Leaves: Grayish green, softly haired, linear to narrowly lance-shaped; to 3" long; mainly on lower stems.

Blooms: March–May.

Elevation: 1,500 to 4,500'.

Habitat: Rocky slopes, hillsides, and along streams.

Comments: Annual. One species of *Platystemon* (plat-i-STEE-mon) in Arizona. Photograph taken in vicinity of Roosevelt Dam, March 23.

FUMITORY FAMILY

Fumariaceae (few-mare-i-AY-see-ee)
Represented in Arizona by herbs.

Flowers: Irregular; 4 petals (in 2 pairs) somewhat joined, with 1 or 2 petals often forming a spur or hood; 4 or 6 stamens, 2 tiny sepals, 1 pistil. Superior ovary.
Fruit: Mainly a long, dry, 1-celled capsule.
Leaves: Alternate; compoundly dissected.

GOLDEN CORYDALIS 499

Golden smoke, scrambled eggs.
Corydalis aurea
Fumitory Family (Fumariaceae)

Height: To 1 1/2', but, because it is weak-stemmed, often supported or prostrate.
Flowers: Golden yellow, irregularly shaped; to 3/4" long; in spikelike cluster; followed by a flat-sided, curved, narrow seed capsule to 1" long.
Leaves: Silvery bluish green, finely dissected, slightly succulent; to 6" long.
Blooms: February–June (sometimes late summer).
Elevation: 1,500 to 9,500'.
Habitat: Disturbed areas, washes, and pastures.
Comments: Short-lived perennial herb. Plant contains poisonous alkaloid. One species of *Corydalis* (kor-RID-a-liss) in Arizona. Photograph taken on Mount Graham, May 3.

MUSTARD FAMILY

Cruciferae (kroo-SIFF-er-ee)
Represented in Arizona by herbs and slightly woody plants.

Flowers: Regular, small; 4 petals arranged like a cross, 4 sepals; 6 stamens: 4 long, 2 shorter; and 1 pistil. Style with 1 or 2 stigmas. Superior ovary, 2-celled.
Fruit: Mostly a dry capsule with 2 cells.
Leaves: Alternate; simple or pinnately divided; bitter tasting.

STIFFARM ROCK CRESS 576

Arabis perennans
Mustard Family (Cruciferae)

Height: To 2'.
Flowers: Pink to purplish with darker veins; 4 petals; to 1/4" long, 1/2" wide; in loose terminal cluster; followed by widely spreading, horizontal seed pod to 2" long.
Leaves: Grayish green, toothed, spatula-shaped, and roughly haired; mainly basal, straplike leaves on lower stem; to 3" long.
Blooms: February–October.
Elevation: 2,000 to 8,000'.
Habitat: Hot canyons and lower mountain slopes.
Comments: Ten species of *Arabis* (AR-rah-bis) in Arizona. Photograph taken in Superstition Mountains, February 4.

BRASSICA 321

Brassica tournefortii
Mustard Family (Cruciferae)

Height:	To 3'.
Flowers:	Yellow, with 4 petals; to 1/4" wide; followed by cylindrical seed pod to 2 1/2" long on 1"-long stem.
Leaves:	Dark green to yellowish green, pinnately lobed, warty-looking; hairy, toothed, with clasping stem; to 10" long at base, smaller on upper stem.
Blooms:	Late winter to early spring.
Elevation:	Not available. Photograph taken at 1,700'.
Habitat:	Roadsides and fields.
Comments:	Hairy-stemmed. A native of Europe; rapidly taking over in some areas of Arizona. Six species of *Brassica* (BRASS-i-kah) in Arizona. Photograph taken in Mesa, February 22.

HEARTLEAVED BITTERCRESS   153
Cardamine cordifolia
Mustard Family (Cruciferae)

Height:	To 32".
Flowers:	White, with 4 notched petals; to 5/8" wide, 3/4" long; in cluster to 1 1/2" wide; followed by long-stalked, upright, slender, slightly flattened seed pod, to 1 1/2" long.
Leaves:	Light green, heart-shaped, and shiny, with scalloped margins with hardened, rounded teeth; to 4" long.
Blooms:	July–August.
Elevation:	9,000 to 11,000'.
Habitat:	Streambanks, mountain streams, and wet alpine meadows.
Comments:	Perennial. Two species of *Cardamine* (kar-DAM-i-nee) in Arizona. Photograph taken in Mount Baldy Wilderness, August 13.

TANSY MUSTARD   322
Mountain tansy mustard
Descurainia richardsonii
Mustard Family (Cruciferae)

Height:	To 40".
Flowers:	Bright yellow, with 4 petals; to 1/16" wide; in terminal raceme; followed by 1/2"-long slender seed capsule containing 1 row of seeds.
Leaves:	Grayish green, slightly hairy, pinnate; to 2 1/2" long.
Blooms:	July–August.
Elevation:	6,500 to 9,500'.
Habitat:	Roadsides and fields.
Comments:	Annual. Native Americans used seeds for making pinole, a ground meal. Five species of *Descurainia* (des-kyoo-RAIN-i-ah) in Arizona. Photograph taken near Nutrioso, August 3.

SPECTACLE POD   154
Dithyrea wislizeni
Mustard Family (Cruciferae)

Height:	To 2'.
Flowers:	White, with 4 petals; to 1/2" long; in dense raceme; followed by a flat green, 1/2"-wide double pod, 2 round lobes resembling spectacles.
Leaves:	Grayish, pinnately lobed; to 6" long (shorter on stem).

Blooms:	February–October.
Elevation:	1,000 to 6,000'.
Habitat:	Open areas of shady soil in deserts and grasslands.
Comments:	Two species of *Dithyrea* (dith-eh-REE-ah) in Arizona. Photograph taken near Gila Bend, March 29.

DRABA   323
Draba asprella
Mustard Family (Cruciferae)

Height:	To 5".
Flowers:	Yellow, with 4 petals; to 1/4" wide; in long, terminal cluster or raceme on leafless stem.
Leaves:	Green, very hairy, oval to elliptical; in basal rosette; to 1/2" long.
Blooms:	Starting in February.
Elevation:	5,000 to 8,000'.
Habitat:	Pine forests.
Comments:	Plants vary in hairiness of foliage. Eleven species of *Draba* (DRAH-bah) in Arizona. Photograph taken at Black Canyon Lake area, June 4.

GOLDEN DRABA   324
Willow whitlow, golden whitlow, whitlow grass
Draba aurea
Mustard Family (Cruciferae)

Height:	To 9".
Flowers:	Golden yellow, with 4 petals; hairy, tiny; to 1/4" long, 3/16" wide, in loose, terminal cluster; followed by small, hairy, flat, nearly erect seed pod to 1/2" long (including stem), ending in persistent style to 1/16" long.
Leaves:	Grayish green, covered with short, starlike hairs; elliptical-shaped on stem, spatula-shaped in basal rosette; faintly toothed; to 1 1/2" long.
Blooms:	July–August.
Elevation:	5,000 to 12,000'.
Habitat:	Clearings in coniferous forests.
Comments:	Perennial herb. Erect to sprawling stems are covered with short hairs. Eleven species of *Draba* (DRAH-bah) in Arizona. Photograph taken at Luna Lake, August 5.

DRYOPETALON   155
Dryopetalon runcinatum
Mustard Family (Cruciferae)

Height:	To 25".
Flowers:	Bright white, with 4 petals; pinnately cleft into 4 to 9 lobes; to 3/8" wide; in terminal cluster, followed by long, very narrow, erect seed pod to 2 1/2" long.
Leaves:	Dark green, pinnately divided or lobed; to 6" long at base, shorter on upper stems.
Blooms:	February–mid-May.
Elevation:	2,000 to 7,000'.
Habitat:	Moist rock crevices in canyons.
Comments:	Annual. One or more stems. One species of *Dryopetalon* (dry-oh-PET-ah-lon) in Arizona. Photograph taken in north-facing rock crevice in Chiricahua National Monument, May 7.

WESTERN WALLFLOWER   325
Desert wallflower, Douglas's wallflower
Erysimum capitatum
Mustard Family (Cruciferae)

Height:	To 32".
Flowers:	Bright yellow, with 4 petals; to 3/4" wide; in cluster on rounded, terminal raceme; followed by very slender, erect 4-sided pod to 4" long.
Leaves:	Grayish green, lance-shaped, toothed margins; in basal rosette; to 5" long. Stem leaves are narrow with small teeth.
Blooms:	March–September.
Elevation:	2,500 to 9,500'.
Habitat:	Roadsides, open flats, slopes, and dry, stony banks.
Comments:	Biennial or perennial. Four species of *Erysimum* (e-RISS-i-mum) in Arizona. Photograph taken near Globe, March 29. Another species, *Erysimum wheeleri*, has dark orange to maroon flowers and is found above 7,000' in coniferous forests. Photograph (**PLATE 531**) taken south of Alpine, July 23.

WESTERN PEPPERWEED   156
Western pepper-grass
Lepidium montanum
Mustard Family (Cruciferae)

Height:	To 2'.
Flowers:	White and minute, with 4 petals; to 1/8" wide; in short, dense raceme; on slender branch, followed by oval pod with tiny notch at tip.
Leaves:	Green, pinnately lobed at base; to 3" long; narrow on stem, to 1/2" long.
Blooms:	April–September.
Elevation:	3,000 to 7,500'.
Habitat:	Roadsides, fields, and other open areas.
Comments:	Many-branched and shrublike; often grows in loose mounds. Nine species of *Lepidium* (lep-ID-ee-uhm) in Arizona. Photograph taken at Heber, August 4.

THURBER'S PEPPERGRASS   157
Thurber's pepperweed
Lepidium thurberi
Mustard Family (Cruciferae)

Height:	To 2'.
Flowers:	Pure white, with 4 petals, 6 stamens; 1/8" wide; in long, dense, terminal cluster; followed by elliptical or roundish pod with small notch.
Leaves:	Light green, slightly haired or nearly hairless, pinnately divided into narrow lobes; to 2 1/2" long.
Blooms:	February–November.
Elevation:	Below 5,000'.
Habitat:	Roadsides and fields.
Comments:	A conspicuous white roadside flower. Nine species of *Lepidium* (lep-ID-ee-uhm) in Arizona. Photograph taken near Portal, April 22.

ARIZONA BLADDERPOD   326
Lesquerella arizonica (crossbreeds with *Lesquerella intermedia*)
Mustard Family (Cruciferae)

Height:	To 6".
Flowers:	Bright yellow, with 4 petals; to 1/2" wide; in short flower cluster; followed by a thick, oval fruit to 1/4" in diameter.
Leaves:	Silvery gray, woolly, linear; to 2" long.
Blooms:	April–May.
Elevation:	3,500 to 7,000'.
Habitat:	Rocky slopes and mesas.
Comments:	Has unbranched, erect stem. Eleven species of *Lesquerella* (les-kwe-REL-lah) in Arizona. Photograph taken on San Carlos Indian Reservation, April 20.

BLADDERPOD MUSTARD   327

Gordon's bladderpod, bead-pod
Lesquerella gordoni
Mustard Family (Cruciferae)

Height:	To 16".
Flowers:	Bright yellow, with 4 petals; to 1/3" wide; in terminal, loose raceme; followed by 1/8" diameter spherical pod tipped with slender point.
Leaves:	Green, but often appearing silvery because of hairs; narrow, lance- or spatula-shaped; basal leaves often lobed; to 2" long.
Blooms:	February–May.
Elevation:	100 to 5,000'.
Habitat:	Desert flats, dry plains, and among desert shrubs on mesas.
Comments:	An annual; erect or spreading. Forage for cattle. Eleven species of *Lesquerella* (les-kwe-REL-lah) in Arizona. Photograph taken at Alamo Lake, February 26.

PURPLE BLADDERPOD   158

Lesquerella purpurea
Mustard Family (Cruciferae)

Height:	To 20".
Flowers:	White, streaked with purple, and fading to purplish; to 3/8" wide; in loose, open cluster; followed by globular fruit to 1/4" long on 1/2"-long stem.
Leaves:	Silvery green, hairy, narrowing toward base; slightly toothed; to 3" long; graduating upward on stem.
Blooms:	January–May.
Elevation:	1,500 to 5,000'.
Habitat:	Along washes, desert flats, and in the shade of bushes on mesas.
Comments:	Eleven species of *Lesquerella* (les-kwe-REL-lah) in Arizona. Photograph taken in Superstition Mountains, February 4.

NEWBERRY'S TWINPOD   577

Physaria newberryi
Mustard Family (Cruciferae)

Height:	To 4" in circular tuft.
Flowers:	Yellow, with 4 petals; to 1/2" wide; in terminal raceme; followed by pale pinkish, twin, bladderlike seed capsules deeply notched between the 2 cells; twin pods to 1" wide, in cluster above leaves.
Leaves:	Silvery gray, roundish to squarish, and downy; with upwardly curved margins; toothed; basal; to 2" long.
Blooms:	May.

Elevation:	5,000 to 7,000'.
Habitat:	Dry, rocky slopes; often in volcanic cinders.
Comments:	At first glance the pink bladders resemble flowers. Two species of *Physaria* (FISS-air-ee-ah) in Arizona. Photograph in pod taken at Sunset Crater National Monument, June 5.

WHITE WATERCRESS   159

True watercress, pepperleaf
Rorippa nasturtium-aquaticum (Nasturtium officinale)
Mustard Family (Cruciferae)

Height:	To 16", but usually grows horizontally.
Flowers:	White, with 4 rounded petals; yellowish at base; to 1/4" wide; in rounded, terminal cluster; followed by slender, curved, upward-pointing, smooth, shiny pod to 1/2" long, on 1/2"-long stem.
Leaves:	Dark green, succulent; pinnately compound, alternate; to 6" long; 3 to 11 smooth, wavy leaflets, each to 1/2" long (terminal leaflet is the longest).
Blooms:	April–August.
Elevation:	1,500 to 8,500'.
Habitat:	Cool water of ponds, brooks, springs, and along mountain streams.
Comments:	Perennial herb; native of Europe, now naturalized in North America. Floats or lies in water or mud. Succulent, reddish stems which root at nodes. Leaves have a peppery taste. Eight species of *Rorippa* (ROR-ri-pah) in Arizona. Photograph taken near Greer, July 7.

TUMBLE MUSTARD   328

Tall sisymbrium, tall hedge mustard
Sisymbrium altissimum
Mustard Family (Cruciferae)

Height:	To 4'.
Flowers:	Pale yellow, with 4 petals; to 1/2" wide; in loose, terminal cluster on branch; followed by slender, 4"-long seed capsule that spreads from stem.
Leaves:	Dark green, hairy, deeply lobed; to 11" long; upper leaves are pinnately lobed to linear, to 4" long.
Blooms:	April–September.
Elevation:	5,000 to 7,000'.
Habitat:	Roadsides, fields, and waste places.
Comments:	Many branched and spreading. Introduced from Europe. Six species of *Sisymbrium* (si-SIM-bri-uhm) in Arizona. Photograph taken at Dead Horse Ranch State Park, May 30.

LONDON ROCKET   329

Sisymbrium irio
Mustard Family (Cruciferae)

Height:	To 3'.
Flowers:	Yellow, with 4 petals; to 1/8" long; on slender stalk, in small, terminal cluster on stem; followed by long, slender seed pod thicker than flower stalk, to 2" long.
Leaves:	Dark green, fleshy, large, and pointed; with terminal lobe, 1 to 4 pairs of smaller lobes below; to 8" long.
Blooms:	December–April.

Elevation:	100 to 4,500'.
Habitat:	Irrigated fields, roadsides, and waste places.
Comments:	Annual. Introduced from Europe. The flower stem gradually elongates as the seed pods mature. Six species of *Sisymbrium* (si-SIM-bri-uhm) in Arizona. Photograph taken near Granite Reef Dam, February 6.

PRINCE'S PLUME   330A and B

Desert plume, golden prince's plume
Stanleya pinnata
Mustard Family (Cruciferae)

Height:	To 6'.
Flowers:	Yellow, with long stamens and pistil, 4 narrow petals, and 4 sepals; to 1 1/4" long; in dense, terminal spike to 2' long; blooming first at base and progressing up spike; followed by slender, drooping seed pods to 2" long.
Leaves:	Grayish green, narrow; to 7" long at base, shorter on upper stem; some pinnately divided at base and on stem.
Blooms:	May–September.
Elevation:	2,500 to 7,000'.
Habitat:	Mesas, dry plains, and sagebrush areas.
Comments:	Perennial herb. Native Americans used seeds for mush and plant as a potherb. Three species of *Stanleya* (STAN-lee-ah) in Arizona. Photographs taken at Sunset Crater National Monument, September 8.

ARIZONA JEWEL FLOWER   160

Arizona twist flower
Streptanthus arizonicus
Mustard Family (Cruciferae)

Height:	To 3 1/2' tall.
Flowers:	White to cream, goblet-shaped, on short stems along erect branches; 4 petals; to 1/2" long; followed by slender, flat, seed pod to 3" long.
Leaves:	Grayish green, rubbery, elongated, and triangular-shaped; base lobes projecting beyond stem; to 8" long.
Blooms:	January–April.
Elevation:	1,500 to 4,500'.
Habitat:	Desert washes or flats to open juniper-pinyon woodlands.
Comments:	Four species of *Streptanthus* (strep-TAN-thus) in Arizona. Photograph taken in Tucson area, March 31.

PINK WINDMILLS   683

Windmills
Thelypodiopsis linearifolia (*Sisymbrium linearifolium*)
Mustard Family (Cruciferae)

Height:	To 4'.
Flowers:	Lavender, with 6 stamens, and 4 separated petals narrower at bases; to 1" long; in terminal cluster, followed by long, narrow, upright seed pod.
Leaves:	Light green, smooth, and narrow; linear to lance-shaped; to 1 3/4" long.
Blooms:	May–September.
Elevation:	2,500 to 9,500'.

Habitat:	Fields, woodlands, chaparral, and ponderosa pine forests.
Comments:	One species of *Thelypodiopsis* (the-ly-poh-dee-OP-sis) in Arizona. Photograph taken at Oak Creek Canyon, September 9.

WILD CANDYTUFT 161
White candytuft
Thlaspi montanum
Mustard Family (Cruciferae)

Height:	To 1', but usually much less.
Flowers:	White, 4-petaled, with yellow-tipped stamens; to 3/8" long, 3/8" wide; in terminal cluster to 1 1/4" wide.
Leaves:	Green, arrow-shaped, succulent; alternate, clasping stem; to 1/2" long; basal leaves are oval-shaped, toothed; to 3/4" long.
Blooms:	February–August.
Elevation:	4,000 to 12,000'.
Habitat:	Mainly coniferous forests.
Comments:	Perennial. Unbranched stem. Two species of *Thlaspi* (THLAS-pee or THLAS-pye) in Arizona. Photograph taken in vicinity of Willow Springs Lake, April 22.

CLEOME FAMILY
Cleomaceae (klee-oh-MAY-see-ee)
Represented in Arizona by herbaceous or woody plants.

Flowers:	Regular or nearly regular, 4 petals, 4 sepals, 6 or more stamens. Superior ovary, 1-celled.
Fruit:	Mostly a 2-valved capsule.
Leaves:	Alternate, simple, or palmately compound.

YELLOW BEE PLANT 331
Spiderflower, yellow spiderwort
Cleome lutea
Cleome Family (Cleomaceae)

Height:	To 2 1/2'.
Flowers:	Yellow, 6 long stamens, 4 petals; to 3/8" wide, 1/4" long, in cluster at top of stem; followed by slender seed pod to 1 1/2" long, hanging downward on long stalk.
Leaves:	Green, palmately compound; usually 5 lance-shaped leaflets, each to 3" long.
Blooms:	May–September.
Elevation:	2,000 to 6,000'.
Habitat:	Along streams and in other moist areas.
Comments:	The Hopi Indians use immature plants as potherbs. Four species of *Cleome* (klee-OH-me) in Arizona. Photograph taken in Kayenta area, June 27.

ROCKY MOUNTAIN BEE PLANT 578
Stinking clover, skunkweed, bee spiderflower, pink cleome
Cleome serrulata
Cleome Family (Cleomaceae)

Height:	To 4'.
Flowers:	Pink to purple, 4-petaled; 1/2" long; long stamens tipped with green anthers; raceme 2 to 3" long (sometimes up to 10" long) and 2 to 3" wide; followed by thin,

bananalike seed pod, to 2 1/2" long.

Leaves:	Bluish green, palmately compound; leaflets to 3" long.
Blooms:	June–September.
Elevation:	4,500 to 7,000'.
Habitat:	Roadsides, plains, foothills, and fields.
Comments:	Annual. Seeds eaten by doves. Attracts bees and hummingbirds, and is an excellent source for honey. Boiling the leaves produces a thick, black substance which is dried and later softened to use as a black pottery paint. Four species of *Cleome* (klee-OH-me) in Arizona. Photograph taken in vicinity of Nutrioso, August 3.

ROUGHSEED CLAMMYWEED   162

Western clammyweed
Polanisia dodecandra (*Polanisia trachysperma*)
Cleome Family (Cleomaceae)

Height:	To 3'.
Flowers:	White to cream, with 4 petals and 6 to 20 long, pink to purple stamens of varying lengths; to 3/4" wide; in terminal clusters on many branches, followed by erect, cylindrical pod, to 3" long. Flowers and fruits are present at the same time.
Leaves:	Dark green, clammy-feeling, finely haired; 3 elliptical or broadly lance-shaped leaflets, each to 1 1/2" long.
Blooms:	May–October.
Elevation:	1,000 to 6,500'.
Habitat:	Sandy washes.
Comments:	Annual. Foliage gives off objectionable odor, especially when handled. Stems are sticky and hairy. A favorite of bees and butterflies. One species of *Polanisia* (pol-an-ISS-i-ah) in Arizona. Photograph taken at Saguaro Lake, May 20.

JACKASS CLOVER   332

Wislizenia refracta
Cleome Family (Cleomaceae)

Height:	To 4'.
Flowers:	Tiny and yellow, with 4 petals; 1/8" long; in dense, terminal raceme, followed by 1/8" pod on a sharply bent stalk.
Leaves:	Light green, with 3 segments, elliptical leaflets; to 1 1/4" long.
Blooms:	April–November.
Elevation:	1,000 to 6,500'.
Habitat:	Roadsides, dry streambeds, and other sandy areas.
Comments:	Annual. One species of *Wislizenia* (wis-li-ZEN-i-ah) in Arizona. Photograph taken at Organ Pipe Cactus National Monument, November 14.

ORPINE FAMILY

Crassulaceae (krass-yew-LAY-see-ee)
Represented in Arizona by herbs.

Flowers:	Regular, usually starlike; 4, 5, or no petals (when present, petals sometimes unite into a tube); 4 to 5 sepals, 4 or 5 stamens or twice as many; 3 or more pistils. Superior ovary.
Fruit:	Dry, 1-celled capsule.
Leaves:	Alternate, opposite, or basal, simple; succulent.

ROCK ECHEVERIA   373
Live-forever
Dudleya saxosa
Orpine Family (Crassulaceae)

Height: Flower stalk to 1 1/2'.

Flowers: 5 yellow petals, reddish sepals; to 1/2" long, spaced at end of curved flower stem.

Leaves: Grayish green, succulent; flat on upper surface, rounded beneath; linear, tapering to reddish-tipped point; to 6" long, 3/4" wide, 1/8" thick; in basal rosette.

Blooms: April–June.

Elevation: 3,000 to 5,000'.

Habitat: Dry, rocky, desert slopes.

Comments: Reddish stems. Two species of *Dudleya* (DUD-li-ah) in Arizona. Photograph taken in vicinity of Roosevelt Lake, April 29.

COCKERELL'S SEDUM   623
Stonecrop
Sedum cockerellii
Orpine Family (Crassulaceae)

Height: To 8".

Flowers: White to pale pink, stamens with darker pink or purplish tips; 5-petaled, starlike; to 1/4" wide; in small, loose cluster at branch end.

Leaves: Light green (reddish in sunny locations) and succulent; flattened in cross-section; to 1/2" long; in compact, basal rosette and up flowering stem.

Blooms: June–October.

Elevation: 5,000 to 11,500'.

Habitat: Rocky areas, often among mosses and usually in shady locations.

Comments: Five species of *Sedum* (SEE-dum) in Arizona. Photograph taken in Greer area, July 29.

QUEEN'S CROWN   624
Rose crown, red orpine, stonecrop
Sedum rhodanthum
Orpine Family (Crassulaceae)

Height: To 16".

Flowers: Pink to white, with 5 pointed petals forming partly closed, tulip-shaped cup; bright red-tipped stamens; to 3/8" long, 1/8" wide; in rounded, terminal cluster.

Leaves: Light green, rubbery, and succulent; flat, elliptical; alternate, spiraling up stem; to 1" long.

Blooms: July–August.

Elevation: 9,000 to 12,000'.

Habitat: Along mountain streams.

Comments: Plant forms a cluster of stiff, upright stems. Five species of *Sedum* (SEE-dum) in Arizona. Photograph taken in Mount Baldy Wilderness, August 12.

SAXIFRAGE FAMILY

Saxifragaceae (sacks-ih-fra-GAY-see-ee)

Represented in Arizona by herbs and shrubs.

Flowers: Regular, with 4 or 5 petals, 4 or 5 sepals, 4 to 10 (or more) stamens, and 1 pistil. Inferior ovary, 2-celled.

Fruit: Capsule or berry.

Leaves: Alternate, opposite, or basal, mostly simple.

CLIFF FENDLERBUSH   163

False mockorange

Fendlera rupicola

Saxifrage Family (Saxifragaceae)

Height: Straggling shrub to 6'.

Flowers: White and fragrant; 4 spoon-shaped petals, fringed, hairy, and faintly edged in pink; 8 stamens; to 2" wide; pinkish buds, single or in small clusters, each followed by 4-chambered, woody, grayish green, acornlike capsule to 1/2" long.

Leaves: Shiny, rough, dark green above, dull green beneath; 3 prominent sunken veins; thick, elongated, opposite; to 1 3/4" long.

Blooms: March–June.

Elevation: 3,000 to 7,000'.

Habitat: Dry, rocky, and gravelly slopes.

Comments: New shoots have reddish stems. Browsed by bighorn sheep, deer, and goats. The Navajo Indians use parts of the bush for ceremonial food and to smoke. One species of *Fendlera* (FEND-lurr-uh) in Arizona. Photograph taken at Cave Creek, Portal, April 23. Unlike the similar **UTAH SERVICEBERRY** (*Amelanchier utahensis*), cliff fendlerbush has narrow, pointed leaves and 4-petaled flowers followed by 4-chambered, woody capsules. **MOCKORANGE** (*Philadelphus microphyllus*) also resembles cliff fendlerbush, but its 4 petals are not spoon-shaped and it has many more than 8 stamens.

ALUM-ROOT   492A and B

Heuchera eastwoodiae

Saxifrage Family (Saxifragaceae)

Height: Flower stalk to 20".

Flowers: Yellowish green, without petals; pointed sepals, 6 short, yellow stamens; to 3/16" wide; in loose, terminal raceme on weak, leafless stalk.

Leaves: Dark green, roundish, finely haired, and scalloped; to 3 1/2" wide; basal, on long leaf stalks.

Blooms: May–August.

Elevation: 5,000 to 8,000'.

Habitat: Moist slopes in ponderosa pine forests and canyons.

Comments: Perennial herb; found in central Arizona. Seven species of *Heuchera* (HEW-ker-ah) in Arizona. Photographs taken at Black Canyon Lake, June 4.

ALUM-ROOT   282

Heuchera novomexicana

Saxifrage Family (Saxifragaceae)

Height: Flower stalk to 2'.

Flowers:	White and small, in small cluster on weak, 2'-long flower stalk.
Leaves:	Dark green above, lighter beneath; roundish and scalloped; hairy, basal; on 4"-long stalks; to 2" wide, 2" long.
Blooms:	May–June.
Elevation:	8,000 to 9,000'.
Habitat:	Mixed coniferous forests.
Comments:	Hairy plant. Seven species of *Heuchera* (HEW-ker-ah) in Arizona. Photograph taken south of Hannagan Meadow, June 30.

CORAL BELLS   625
Alum root
Heuchera sanguinea
Saxifrage Family (Saxifragaceae)

Height:	To 2'.
Flowers:	Pinkish to coral-red, bell-shaped; with 5 petals; to 1/2" long; in loose clusters on leafless stalk.
Leaves:	Dark green, roundish, with pointed lobes; basal; on long stalk; to 3" wide;
Blooms:	March–October.
Elevation:	4,000 to 8,500'.
Habitat:	Shaded hillsides and moist, rocky areas in shade.
Comments:	Perennial herb with woolly stems. Used as an ornamental. Seven species of *Heuchera* (HEW-ker-ah) in Arizona. Photograph taken in Santa Rita Mountains, June 18.

MOCKORANGE   164
Syringa, jeringuilla
Philadelphus microphyllus
Saxifrage Family (Saxifragaceae)

Height:	To 4'.
Flowers:	White and fragrant, with 4 broad and rounded petals, numerous yellow stamens; to 1/2" wide.
Leaves:	Dark green, shiny; faintly lined in lighter green above, paler green beneath; oval to elliptical; to 1/2" long.
Blooms:	June–July.
Elevation:	5,000 to 9,000'.
Habitat:	Rocky slopes and canyons.
Comments:	Erect shrub with shreddy bark. To some, its flowers smell like orange blossoms. Browsed by bighorn sheep. Native Americans used stems for bows, arrows, and pipe stems. Eight species of *Philadelphus* (fih-luh-DELL-fuss) in Arizona. Photograph taken at the North Rim of Grand Canyon National Park, June 25. A similar plant, **CLIFF FENDLERBUSH** (*Fendlera rupicola*) has spoon-shaped petals and only 8 stamens.

WAX CURRANT   823
Ribes cereum
Saxifrage Family (Saxifragaceae)

Height:	To 6' tall and 8' wide.
Flowers:	White or pink, tubular, and sticky; to 3/8" long; in groups of 1 to 4; followed by red to yellowish red, sticky fruits to 1/4" in diameter.

Leaves:	Light green with tiny white dots; sticky, 3- to 5-lobed, glandular-haired; to 1" wide.
Blooms:	May–July.
Elevation:	5,500 to 9,000'.
Habitat:	Clearings in pine forests.
Comments:	Fruits lack spines. Browsed by elk and deer; fruits eaten by wildlife. Hopi Indians ate berries and used plant medicinally. Eleven species of *Ribes* (RYE-beez) in Arizona. Photograph taken at Nelson Reservoir, August 3.

SQUAW CURRANT   824
Grosellero
Ribes inebrians
Saxifrage Family (Saxifragaceae)

Height:	To 4'.
Flowers:	White to pinkish, tubular; to 3/8" long; followed by round, red, 3/8" diameter fruit.
Leaves:	Light green, fan-shaped, lobed, and glandular; to 1 1/2" wide.
Blooms:	May–August.
Elevation:	5,000 to 9,000'.
Habitat:	Dry, sunny slopes and ridges.
Comments:	Lacks spines. Currants eaten by birds and animals; shrubs browsed by deer. Cross-breeds with **WAX CURRANT** (*Ribes cereum*). Eleven species of *Ribes* (RYE-beez) in Arizona. Photograph taken at North Rim of Grand Canyon National Park, June 25.

WHITE-STEM GOOSEBERRY   825
Ribes inerme
Saxifrage Family (Saxifragaceae)

Height:	To 5'.
Flowers:	Greenish to purplish sepals, with hidden petals; bell-shaped; up to 3 flowers on stems in leaf axils; followed by round, striped, smooth berry, to 1/4" in diameter; turning purplish red when mature.
Leaves:	Dark green above and beneath, 3- to 5-lobed, toothed; to 1 1/2" wide.
Blooms:	April–May.
Elevation:	7,000 to 8,500'.
Habitat:	Clearings in pine forests.
Comments:	Deciduous plant, with whitish stems; greenish spines on stems to 1/2" long. Eleven species of *Ribes* (RYE-beez) in Arizona. Photograph taken at North Rim of Grand Canyon National Park, June 25.

TRUMPET GOOSEBERRY   826
Ribes leptanthum
Saxifrage Family (Saxifragaceae)

Height:	Shrub to 5'.
Flowers:	White to cream-colored, trumpet-shaped; to 1/4" long; in cluster; followed by dark red to black berry, to 5/16" in diameter.
Leaves:	Light green, alternate, broad, rounded; 5-lobed, toothed; to 1" wide.
Blooms:	May–June.
Elevation:	6,000 to 9,500'.
Habitat:	Along streams and mountain meadows.
Comments:	Deciduous. Browsed by livestock and deer. Its tart berries are eaten by birds, and were used (both fresh and dried) by Native Americans. This genus of plant serves as

an alternate host to white pine blister rust, which kills 5-needled pines (these pines are not common in Arizona). Eleven species of *Ribes* (RYE-beez) in Arizona. Photograph taken near Greer, June 22.

ORANGE GOOSEBERRY   827A and B
Ribes pinetorum
Saxifrage Family (Saxifragaceae)

Height:	Sprawling to 6'.
Flowers:	Reddish orange, with 5 petals; hairy; to 3/4" long; on short branchlet; followed by very spiny, 1/2" round berry, maturing to dark reddish purple.
Leaves:	Dark green, alternate, roundish; 5-lobed, toothed, glandular-hairy; to 2 1/2" long, 2" wide; in clusters on branches.
Blooms:	April–September.
Elevation:	7,000 to 10,000'.
Habitat:	Coniferous forests.
Comments:	The most abundant species of gooseberry in mountains of southern Arizona. Tan spines, to 3/8" long, with 1 to 3 at nodes, curve downward from branches. Eleven species of *Ribes* (RYE-beez) in Arizona. Photograph of flower taken on Mount Lemmon, May 13. Photograph of berry taken in Greer area, July 21.

WOLF CURRANT   828
Black currant
Ribes wolfii
Saxifrage Family (Saxifragaceae)

Height:	Straggly shrub to 15'.
Flowers:	Yellowish white, small, and bell-shaped, in small cluster. Followed by round currant with soft hairs tipped with brown, to 1/4" in diameter; in clusters, blackish with a whitish bloom when mature.
Leaves:	Green, maplelike, 3-lobed; toothed, deeply veined; to 3" long, 2 1/2" wide.
Blooms:	May–August.
Elevation:	8,500 to 11,500'.
Habitat:	Moist coniferous forests and areas of springs.
Comments:	Often sends shoots up into nearby trees. Browsed by elk. Birds and small mammals feed on fruits. Though tart, fruits are used for baking and for jelly. Eleven species of *Ribes* (RYE-beez) in Arizona. Photograph taken at Greer, August 10.

REDFUZZ SAXIFRAGE   213
Saxifraga eriophora
Saxifrage Family (Saxifragaceae)

Height:	To 6", but usually less.
Flowers:	White, with 5 petals, reddish hairs on calyx lobes; to 3/16" wide; in loose, terminal cluster.
Leaves:	Dark green above, reddish hairs beneath; succulent, somewhat thick; oval to elliptical, with scalloped or toothed margins; to 1" long, 1/2" wide; in basal rosette.
Blooms:	March–mid-May.
Elevation:	5,000 to 8,500'.
Habitat:	Moist mountain slopes in coniferous forests, often in very mossy areas.
Comments:	Reddish hairs on stems. Six species of *Saxifraga* (sacks-IFF-ra-gah) in Arizona. Photograph taken on Mount Graham, May 3.

DIAMONDLEAF SAXIFRAGE   214
Rockfoil
Saxifraga rhomboidea
Saxifrage Family (Saxifragaceae)

Height: Flower stem to 1'.
Flowers: White, 5-petaled, greenish in center with light yellow anthers; to 1/4" wide; in terminal cluster to 3/4" wide on erect, sticky, hairy stem.
Leaves: Dark green to light green, basal, diamond-shaped; toothed or scalloped, succulent, sparsely haired on margins; to 2" long, 1 1/4" wide.
Blooms: April–July.
Elevation: 5,500 to 11,000'.
Habitat: Moist meadows.
Comments: Perennial. Six species of *Saxifraga* (sacks-IFF-ra-gah) in Arizona. Photograph taken at Willow Springs Lake, April 22.

PLANE TREE FAMILY
Platanaceae (pla-ta-NAY-see-ee)
Trees.

Flowers: Minute sepals and petals in a dense ball-like cluster; 3 to 7 stamens, 5 to 9 pistils.
Fruit: 4-angled nutlet crowded in ball.
Leaves: Alternate, simple, palmately lobed.

ARIZONA SYCAMORE   79
Plane tree, button-wood
Platanus wrightii
Plane Tree Family (Platanaceae)

Height: To 80'.
Trunk: To 4' or more in diameter.
Bark: On branches, whitish, smooth, and thin; on trunk and very large branches, whitish and peeling in brownish flakes; on very large old trunks, dark gray with odd-shaped, thick plates that hang loose.
Flowers: Inconspicuous; male and female flowers in separate, dense, round clusters of 2 to 4. The female cluster matures into light brown, hairy, globular, seed head; to 1" in diameter; with 2 to 4 along a raceme to 8" long.
Leaves: Light green above, paler beneath, with small hairs; palmately lobed, divided into 3, 5, or 7 narrow, pointed lobes; to 10" long and wide.
Blooms: March–April.
Elevation: 2,000 to 6,000'.
Habitat: Along streams and in rocky canyons.
Comments: Deciduous. Tree has large, spreading branches and broad, open crown. Its roots help slow down soil erosion along streambanks. Small owls and other birds nest in the hollows of old branches. One species of *Platanus* (PLA-ta-nus or PLAT-a-nus) in Arizona. Photograph taken north of Payson, June 3.

CROSSOSOMA FAMILY

Crossosomataceae (kro-so-so-mah-TAY-see-ee)
Represented in Arizona by shrubs.

Flowers:	5 petals, 5 sepals, numerous stamens, 2 to 5 pistils.
Fruit:	Several-seeded follicle.
Leaves:	Alternate, simple.

BIGELOW RAGGED ROCK FLOWER   186

Crossosoma bigelovii
Crossosoma Family (Crossosomataceae)

Height:	Straggly shrub to 6'.
Flowers:	White, with 5 petals, numerous stamens; very fragrant; to 2" wide.
Leaves:	Bluish green, alternate, thick, smooth; somewhat oval; to 3/4" long, 3/8" wide.
Blooms:	February–May.
Elevation:	1,500 to 4,000'.
Habitat:	Dry, rocky slopes and canyons.
Comments:	A rough-barked shrub. Two species of *Crossosoma* (kro-so-SO-mah) in Arizona. Photograph taken in Superstition Mountains, February 4.

ROSE FAMILY

Rosaceae (roh-ZAY-see-ee)
Represented in Arizona by herbs, shrubs, and trees.

Flowers:	Regular, with 4 to 5 petals, 4 to 5 sepals, 10 or more stamens; in clusters or solitary; 1 to many pistils. Superior or inferior ovary, 1- to 5-celled.
Fruit:	Pod, achene, drupe, or pome.
Leaves:	Alternate; simple or compound, or basal.

AGRIMONIA   374

Agrimonia striata
Rose Family (Rosaceae)

Height:	To 6'.
Flowers:	Yellow, with 5 petals, yellow stamens; to 5/16" wide; on long, slender spike.
Leaves:	Dark green and hairy above, pale green and hairy beneath; pinnate, divided into large and small leaflets to 2" long, with pointed tips, toothed; up to 11 leaflets per leaf.
Blooms:	July–September.
Elevation:	6,500 to 8,500'.
Habitat:	Rich soil in pine forests and along streams.
Comments:	Perennial herb with very hairy stem. Two species of *Agrimonia* (ag-ri-MO-nee-ah) in Arizona. Photograph taken at Greer, July 5.

UTAH SERVICEBERRY   74A and B

Juneberry, shadberry, shadbush, shadblow
Amelanchier utahensis
Rose Family (Rosaceae)

Height:	Shrub or small tree to 15'.
Bark:	Smooth, gray.

Flowers:	White, with 5 long, narrow petals; to 1/2" wide; 3 to 6 in a cluster; followed by small, applelike fruits to 3/8" in diameter, maturing to bluish purple.
Leaves:	Dark green, nearly round to elliptical; toothed on margins from midleaf to tip; to 1 1/2" long, 1" wide.
Blooms:	April–May.
Elevation:	2,000 to 7,500'.
Habitat:	Rocky slopes in pinyon-juniper woodlands and ponderosa pine forests.
Comments:	Browsed by livestock and deer. Fruits are eaten by birds and rodents. Berries are used for wine, jelly, and jam. Two species of *Amelanchier* (a-meh-LAN-kih-err) in Arizona. Photograph in fruit taken at Ashurst Lake, June 1. Photograph in flower taken at Double Springs, in vicinity of Mormon Lake, June 1. Unlike the similar **CLIFF FENDLERBUSH** (*Fendlera rupicola*), Utah serviceberry has rounded, toothed leaves and 5-petaled flowers, followed by small, fleshy, applelike fruits.

BIRCHLEAF MOUNTAIN MAHOGANY   829

Hardtack, birchleaf cercocarpus, sweetbrush
Cercocarpus betuloides
Rose Family (Rosaceae)

Height:	Shrub to 8', or small tree to 20'.
Trunk:	To 6" in diameter.
Bark:	Gray or brown, smooth, becoming scaly.
Flowers:	Yellowish, petalless, funnel-shaped, 5-lobed; nearly stalkless; to 3/8" wide; 1 to 3 at leaf base, followed by narrow 3/8"-long fruit, with hairy, twisted tail, to 3 1/4" long.
Leaves:	Evergreen; dark green above, paler and hairy beneath; elliptical, finely pointed, tapering toward base, toothed beyond middle; prominent sunken veins; short-stalked; to 1 1/4" long.
Blooms:	March–July.
Elevation:	3,500 to 6,500'.
Habitat:	Dry, rocky mountain slopes in oak and chaparral areas.
Comments:	Crossbreeds with **HAIRY CERCOCARPUS** (*Cercocarpus breviflorus*). Browsed by livestock, pronghorn, elk, and deer. Sharp end and twisted tail of hard fruit aid in penetration into soil. Four species of *Cercocarpus* (sur-koh-KAR-pus) in Arizona. Photograph taken north of Superior, April 20.

CURLLEAF MOUNTAIN MAHOGANY   830

Curlleaf cercocarpus
Cercocarpus ledifolius
Rose Family (Rosaceae)

Height:	Shrub or small tree to 25'.
Trunk:	To 1' in diameter.
Bark:	Reddish brown, deeply furrowed, and scaly.
Flowers:	Yellowish, petalless, funnel-shaped; 5-lobed, stalkless; to 3/8" wide; growing at leaf bases; followed by reddish brown, narrow, 1/4"-long fruit with twisted, 3"-long, hairy tail.
Leaves:	Evergreen. Dark green above, hairy beneath; shiny, elliptical, thick, leathery; edges rolled under; almost stalkless; aromatic; grooved midvein; to 1 1/4" long, usually in clusters.
Blooms:	April–June.
Elevation:	5,000 to 9,000'.

Habitat:	Dry, rocky mountain slopes.
Comments:	Evergreen, with very hard wood. Unrelated to true mahogany. Browsed by elk, deer, and livestock. Native Americans concoct a red dye from roots. Four species of *Cercocarpus* (sur-koh-KAR-pus) in Arizona. Photograph taken at Madera Canyon, April 29.

TRUE MOUNTAIN MAHOGANY   831
Alderleaf mountain-mahogany, deerbrowse, featherbush, hardtack, palo duro
Cercocarpus montanus
Rose Family (Rosaceae)

Height:	To 10'.
Flowers:	Greenish, petalless, with green sepals forming a tube with pinkish, flared lobes; followed by 1/2"-long seed attached to fuzzy, spirally twisted tail to 3" long.
Leaves:	Grayish green, paler green beneath; wedge-shaped, toothed on upper margins; deeply veined; to 1" long, 1/2" wide.
Blooms:	Spring.
Elevation:	4,500 to 7,000'.
Habitat:	Canyons and hillsides in pinyon-juniper and pine belts.
Comments:	Hardwood shrub. Browsed by livestock, bighorns, and deer. Navajo Indians use shrub to make a red dye for wool. Four species of *Cercocarpus* (sur-koh-KAR-pus) in Arizona. Some authorities reduce all Arizona *Cercocarpus* to varieties of this species and *Cercocarpus ledifolius*. Photograph taken at Canyon de Chelly National Monument, June 27.

HAIRY MOUNTAIN MAHOGANY   832
Hairy cercocarpus
Cercocarpus montanus var. *paucidentatus* (*Cercocarpus breviflorus*)
Rose Family (Rosaceae)

Height:	Shrub or small tree to 15'.
Trunk :	To 6" in diameter.
Bark:	Gray to reddish brown and smooth, becoming fissured and scaly with age.
Flowers:	Yellowish, funnel-shaped, and petalless; 5-lobed; to 1/4" wide, 1/2" long; 1 to 3 in leaf axils; followed by reddish brown, hairy, 1/4"-long fruit with twisted tail of whitish hairs, to 1 1/2" long.
Leaves:	Evergreen, dark green and slightly hairy above, paler green and hairy beneath; elliptical, tapering to base; edges turned under, rounded teeth near tip; to 1" long, 1/2" wide.
Blooms:	March–November.
Elevation:	5,000 to 8,000'.
Habitat:	Dry slopes in chaparral and oak woodlands.
Comments:	Has open crown. Browsed by deer and livestock. Four species of *Cercocarpus* (sur-koh-KAR-pus) in Arizona. Photograph taken at Lynx Lake, May 27.

FERNBUSH   215
Desert-sweet, tansy-bush
Chamaebatiaria millefolium
Rose Family (Rosaceae)

Height:	To 6'.
Flowers:	White, sticky, with 5 crinkly petals, yellow stamens; to 3/8" wide; in elongated

cluster to 4" long at end of branch; followed by small, dry pod.

Leaves:	Grayish green, much-divided, fernlike; fragrant, scaly, sticky; to 1 1/2" long.
Blooms:	July–November.
Elevation:	4,500 to 8,000'.
Habitat:	Pinyon-juniper-sagebrush areas.
Comments:	Evergreen. Bark is tinged red and shrubby. Browsed by deer, sheep, and goats. One species of *Chamaebatiaria* (kah-mee-bah-tih-AY-rih-uh) in Arizona. Photograph taken at Walnut Canyon National Monument, September 7.

BLACKBRUSH 833
Coleogyne ramosissima
Rose Family (Rosaceae)

Height:	To 5'.
Flowers:	Four yellowish green sepals, petalless, numerous stamens; to 3/8" long; short-lived; solitary, at ends of short branchlets; followed by small, brown fruit capsule, to 1/2" long, which, when dried, reveal white hairs in center.
Leaves:	Grayish green, hairy, narrow; somewhat thick, club-shaped; to 3/8" long, 1/16" wide; in clusters all along branchlets.
Blooms:	March–May.
Elevation:	3,000 to 6,500'.
Habitat:	Dry, gravelly or sandy open plains and mesas.
Comments:	A rigid, many-branched shrub, often with spiny-tipped ends. Its dark gray bark turns blackish with age and very black when wet. Gives a blackish appearance to the landscape when found in dense stands devoid of other shrubs. Browsed mainly by sheep, goats, and deer. Wrongly called burro-brush. One species of *Coleogyne* (koh-lee-AH-jih-nee) in Arizona. Photograph taken in Page area, June 26.

CLIFF-ROSE 346
Quinine bush, buckbrush, Stansbury cliffrose
Cowania mexicana var. *stansburiana*
Rose Family (Rosaceae)

Height:	Shrub to 8', or small tree to 20'.
Trunk:	To 8" in diameter for a tree.
Bark:	Reddish brown, shredding.
Flowers:	Creamy white to pale yellow, 5-petaled with gold centers, very fragrant; to 1" wide; each flower followed by 5 to 10, 1/4"-long fruits, each with a 2"-long feathery plume attached.
Leaves:	Dark green above, white, woolly hairs beneath; leathery, glandular-dotted, wedge-shaped; divided into 3 to 5 narrow lobes; edges rolled under; to 1" long.
Blooms:	April–September.
Elevation:	3,500 to 8,000'.
Habitat:	Dry, rocky hillsides and plateaus in upper desert, grasslands, and oak-pinyon-juniper areas.
Comments:	Evergreen. Excellent winter browse for deer, sheep, and cattle despite its bitter taste. Native Americans used stringy bark for mats and clothing and wood for arrows. Two species of *Cowania* (kow-WAY-nih-uh) in Arizona. Photograph taken at North Rim of Grand Canyon National Park, June 25. Unlike the **APACHE PLUME** (*Fallugia paradoxa*), cliff-rose is treelike, with a single trunk, and has waxy,

hairless leaves, cream-colored flowers, and sparser plumes. Another similar shrub, **ANTELOPEBRUSH** (*Purshia tridentata*), has wider leaves and smaller, yellowish flowers.

CERRO HAWTHORN   80
Manzana de puya larga, thornapple, shinyleaf hawthorn
Crataegus erythropoda
Rose Family (Rosaceae)

Height:	Spiny shrub to 9', or small tree to 20'.
Trunk:	To 4" in diameter.
Bark:	Reddish brown or gray, and scaly.
Flowers:	White, with 5 petals; to 3/4" wide; in up to 2 1/2" compact cluster of 5 to 10 flowers; followed by orange-red, 3/8" roundish fruits.
Leaves:	Dark green and shiny above, paler beneath; broadly oval, coarsely toothed; prominently veined, often shallowly lobed; to 2 1/2" long, 1 3/4" wide.
Blooms:	April–May.
Elevation:	4,500 to 8,000'.
Habitat:	Along streams and in moist canyons.
Comments:	Has widely spreading branches, with reddish brown, zigzag twigs. Has numerous 2"-long, nearly straight, shiny, dark reddish spines on branches. Fruits are called *haws*. Birds and other animals feed on fruits. Two species of *Crataegus* (kra-TEE-gus) in Arizona. Photograph taken in Oak Creek Canyon, Sedona, September 9. The similar **RIVER HAWTHORN** (*Crataegus rivularis*) has fewer spines, which are blackish, curved, and only 1" long, and leaves that are double-toothed.

APACHE-PLUME   187
Ponil, feather rose, feather duster bush
Fallugia paradoxa
Rose Family (Rosaceae)

Height:	Shrub to 6'.
Flowers:	Pure white, 5-petaled, roselike, and yellow-centered; to 2" wide; followed by seeds on long, white-to-pinkish long-lasting plumes.
Leaves:	Grayish green, slightly downy, pinnately divided into 3 to 7 linear lobes; to 3/4" long.
Blooms:	April–October.
Elevation:	4,000 to 8,000'.
Habitat:	Roadsides, dry washes, dry hillsides, and chaparral.
Comments:	Evergreen shrub. An erosion deterrent along banks of washes. Native Americans used stems for arrowshafts. Good browse for sheep, cattle, goats, and deer. One species of *Fallugia* (fal-LEW-jih-uh) in Arizona. Photograph taken at Sunset Crater National Monument, September 7. Differs from the similar **CLIFF-ROSE** (*Cowania mexicana* var. *stansburiana*), by its numerous branches at base, more shrublike appearance, short-haired leaves, white flowers, and fuller plumes.

BRACTED STRAWBERRY   188
Wood strawberry
Fragaria bracteata
Rose Family (Rosaceae)

Height:	Creeper, with flower stalks to 2".

Flowers:	White with yellow center, 5 petals, to 1" wide; followed by 3/4"-long, red, cone-shaped berry with seeds barely attached to berry's surface.
Leaves:	Dark green, thin, compound, with 3 leaflets, each to 3/4" long; toothed on margins.
Blooms:	May–September.
Elevation:	7,000 to 9,500'.
Habitat:	Coniferous forests.
Comments:	Perennial herb. Hairs on stem spread out. Fruits are eaten by birds and mammals, including humans. Two species of *Fragaria* (fra-GAIR-i-ah) in Arizona. Photograph taken at Greer, June 18. This species recognizable by its dark green, toothed leaflets and by berries with seeds barely attached.

WILD STRAWBERRY 189
Fragaria ovalis
Rose Family (Rosaceae)

Height:	Creeper, with flower stalk to 2".
Flowers:	White with fuzzy, yellow center; 5 petals; to 1" wide; followed by 3/4"-long, red, cone-shaped berry with seeds partly buried in flesh.
Leaves:	Light green, slightly covered with whitish bloom; haired on margins; thick, compound, with 3 leaflets, each to 3/4" long; toothed on margins mainly from center to tip.
Blooms:	May–October.
Elevation:	7,000 to 11,000'.
Habitat:	Coniferous forests.
Comments:	Perennial herb, with somewhat flattened hairs on stem. Plant spreads by runners. Fruits relished by wildlife. Two species of *Fragaria* (fra-GAIR-i-ah) in Arizona. Photograph taken in mountains above Greer, July 3. This species identifiable by its partially toothed leaflets, which whiten slightly, and its strawberries with seeds partly buried in flesh.

BIG-LEAF AVENS 347
Largeleaf avens, large-leaved geum
Geum macrophyllum
Rose Family (Rosaceae)

Height:	To 4'.
Flowers:	Yellow, waxy, with 5 petals as long or longer than sepals; numerous stamens and pistils; flower to 1/2" wide, in loose cluster on upper branches.
Leaves:	Dark green, pinnately compound; bristly haired, toothed, and large; roundish segment at tip with small segments toward main stem; basal leaf to 18" long, progressively shorter toward flowers.
Blooms:	July–September.
Elevation:	7,000 to 9,800'.
Habitat:	Mountain streambanks and clearings in moist coniferous forests.
Comments:	Perennial herb, with bristly, hairy stems. Four species of *Geum* (JEE-um) in Arizona. Photograph taken in Mount Baldy Wilderness, August 13.

PRAIRIE SMOKE 591
Purple avens, old man's whiskers, grandfather's-beard, Johnny smokers
Geum triflorum
Rose Family (Rosaceae)

Height:	Flower stalk to 20".
Flowers:	Reddish sepals hide pinkish to yellowish petals; bell-shaped, nodding; on long stalks; to 1/2" long; followed by reddish, seed-carrying, silky plumes, to 2" long.
Leaves:	Green, hairy, fernlike, pinnately divided, mostly basal; to 7" long.
Blooms:	May–August.
Elevation:	6,000 to 9,500'.
Habitat:	Ponderosa pine and mixed conifer forests.
Comments:	Perennial herb. Good forage for sheep. After fertilization, flowers turn upward. Four species of *Geum* (JEE-um) in Arizona. Photograph taken near Mormon Lake, June 2.

MOUNTAIN SPRAY   217
Rock spiraea, creambush, foam-bush, ocean spray
Holodiscus dumosus
Rose Family (Rosaceae)

Height:	To 8'.
Flowers:	Creamy white to pinkish, with yellow center; 3/16" wide; in spikelike, terminal cluster to 2" long; followed by small, dry, brown seed case.
Leaves:	Green above, lighter green and velvety beneath; oval to wedge-shaped; sawtooth-notched on margins of broad outer end; to 1 1/2" long.
Blooms:	June–September.
Elevation:	5,500 to 10,000'.
Habitat:	Rocky slopes, ponderosa pine and spruce clearings, and often in lava flows.
Comments:	Deciduous. Young twigs are hairy, older branches are gray and shreddy. Buds are pink. Dried blooms remain into fall and winter. Plant is browsed by deer. One species of *Holodiscus* (hah-loh-DISS-kuss) in Arizona. Photograph taken at Sunset Crater National Monument, June 22.

ROCK MAT   218
Rockrose, Rocky Mountain rockmat
Petrophytum caespitosum
Rose Family (Rosaceae)

Height:	To 8".
Flowers:	White to light pink, with 5 petals, long stamens; to 1/8" long; in dense, spikelike raceme.
Leaves:	Grayish green and spatula-shaped, with silky hairs; to 1/4" long; basal rosettes form dense mats.
Blooms:	June–October.
Elevation:	5,000 to 8,000'.
Habitat:	Rock crevices and ledges.
Comments:	A well-named plant; in Greek *petra* means "rock" and *phyton* means "plant." One species of *Petrophytum* (pe-tre-FYE-tum) in Arizona. Photograph taken at Walnut Canyon National Monument, September 7.

MOUNTAIN NINEBARK   216
Low ninebark
Physocarpus monogynus
Rose Family (Rosaceae)

Height:	Small shrub to 4'.

Flowers:	White, with 5 petals, 5 sepals, and yellow stamens; to 5/8" wide; in rounded, terminal cluster.
Leaves:	Dull, dark green above, paler green and powdery beneath; palmately lobed, toothed, prominent network; to 3" long.
Blooms:	June–July.
Elevation:	8,000 to 9,500'.
Habitat:	Pine and mixed conifer forests.
Comments:	Old bark of the shrub continually shreds. Native Americans used boiled roots as poultice. One species of *Physocarpus* (fye-soh-KAR-puss) in Arizona. Photograph taken south of Alpine, June 30.

COMMON SILVERWEED   352

Feather silverweed, fivefingers, goosegrass
Potentilla anserina
Rose Family (Rosaceae)

Height:	Strawberrylike runners, with flower stalk to 12".
Flowers:	Yellow, with 5 petals; to 3/4" wide.
Leaves:	Silvery green, featherlike; upper surface is silky-haired, lower surface woolly haired; pinnately compound, with 9 to 31 lancelike, sharply toothed leaflets; to 10" long.
Blooms:	May–August.
Elevation:	5,600 to 9,500'.
Habitat:	Open, moist ground in ponderosa pine and spruce-fir forests.
Comments:	Perennial herb, introduced from Eurasia. At joints on runners, roots form and enter soil; leaves then develop and new plants form. Twenty-one species of *Potentilla* (poh-ten-TILL-luh) in Arizona. Photograph taken at Luna Lake, July 23.

CINQUEFOIL   375

Potentilla
Potentilla arguta
Rose Family (Rosaceae)

Height:	To 40".
Flowers:	Pale yellow, with 5 rounded petals; 5 long sepals visible between petals; yellow-centered stamens; to 3/4" wide.
Leaves:	Dark green, very hairy, pinnate; 5 to 9 broadly oval, toothed leaflets; unequally divided leaf to 8" long.
Blooms:	June–July.
Elevation:	5,000 to 8,000'.
Habitat:	Meadows and hillsides.
Comments:	Stems are reddish, hairy, and sticky. Twenty-one species of *Potentilla* (poh-ten-TILL-luh) in Arizona. Photograph taken at Black Canyon Lake, June 4.

VARILEAF CINQUEFOIL   349

Meadow cinquefoil, fivefingers
Potentilla diversifolia
Rose Family (Rosaceae)

Height:	To 20".
Flowers:	Golden yellow and buttercuplike, with 5 notched petals; 5 sepals showing between petals; orangish stamens; to 3/4" wide; in loose, terminal cluster.

Leaves:	Dark green and silky-haired above, whitish beneath; palmate, to 7 leaflets; sharply toothed, with hairs extending beyond teeth; to 2 3/4" wide, 2" long.
Blooms:	June–September.
Elevation:	8,000 to 12,000'.
Habitat:	Roadsides and moist, rocky areas.
Comments:	*Cinquefoil* means "five leaves" in French. Twenty-one species of *Potentilla* (poh-ten-TILL-luh) in Arizona. Photograph taken south of Alpine, June 30.

SHRUBBY CINQUEFOIL   350
Bush cinquefoil, fivefinger
Potentilla fruticosa
Rose Family (Rosaceae)

Height:	To 3'.
Flowers:	Bright golden yellow, with 5 broad petals, up to 30 stamens; to 1 1/4" wide.
Leaves:	Grayish green above, paler beneath; very hairy, pinnately divided into 3 to 7 leaflets (normally 5) tipped with a red dot and with margins rolled under; leaflet to 3/4" long, leaf to 1 1/8" long; cover entire shrub.
Blooms:	June–August.
Elevation:	7,000 to 9,500'.
Habitat:	Moist meadows, pine forest clearings, streamsides, and plains.
Comments:	Only shrubby *Potentilla* growing in Arizona. This erosion fighter has reddish brown, shreddy bark. Browsed by livestock and deer. Twenty-one species of *Potentilla* (poh-ten-TILL-luh) in Arizona. Photograph taken in Greer area, July 3.

CLUBLEAF CINQUEFOIL   351
Potentilla subviscosa
Rose Family (Rosaceae)

Height:	To 4" tall in leafy, rather flat rosette at higher elevations.
Flowers:	Bright yellow, with 5 slightly notched petals; sepals shorter than petals; tack-shaped, glandular hairs on sepals and buds; to 5/8" wide.
Leaves:	Dark green, very hairy; toothed; 3 large segments with 2 smaller segments; to 3/4" wide, 1 3/4" long, including stem.
Blooms:	April–June.
Elevation:	6,500 to 12,000'.
Habitat:	Mountain meadows and coniferous forests; often blooming at edges of snowbanks.
Comments:	Hairy-stemmed. Twenty-one species of *Potentilla* (poh-ten-TILL-luh) in Arizona. Photograph taken on Mount Graham at 8,300', May 3.

RED CINQUEFOIL   545
Five-finger
Potentilla thurberi
Rose Family (Rosaceae)

Height:	To 16".
Flowers:	Dark red, with 5 petals; in loose cluster; to 1" wide.
Leaves:	Dark green, basal leaves with silky hairs on underside and 5 to 7 finely toothed leaflets, each to 2" long; smaller leaves on stem.
Blooms:	July–October.
Elevation:	6,000 to 9,000'.

Habitat:	Rich soil in coniferous forests.
Comments:	Perennial herb. Twenty-one species of *Potentilla* (poh-ten-TILL-luh) in Arizona. Photograph taken south of Alpine, July 23.

COMMON CHOKECHERRY   75

Western chokecherry, black chokecherry, wild black cherry, capulin
Prunus virginiana
Rose Family (Rosaceae)

Height:	To 25'.
Trunk:	To 8" in diameter.
Bark:	Shiny and reddish brown, darker and scaly as plant ages.
Flowers:	White, with 5 rounded petals; to 1/2" wide; in cylindrical cluster to 4" long; followed by shiny, dark red or black, juicy, bitter cherry, to 3/8" in diameter.
Leaves:	Shiny green above, lighter green beneath (occasionally slightly hairy); elliptical, with finely, sharply saw-toothed margins; to 4" long, 2" wide.
Blooms:	April–June.
Elevation:	4,500 to 8,000'.
Habitat:	Roadsides, along streams, and in forests and woodland clearings.
Comments:	Cherries are very bitter, with poisonous pits. Bears are fond of them. Cherries are used for making syrup, jelly, and wine. There are 2 varieties of this species: *demissa* and *melanocarpa*. Four species of *Prunus* (PREW-nuss) in Arizona. Photograph taken at Chiricahua National Monument, April 25.

ARIZONA ROSE   589

Wild rose
Rosa arizonica
Rose Family (Rosaceae)

Height:	To 3'.
Flowers:	Pink, with 5 wavy petals, which are uneven in size; yellow stamens; fragrant; to 1 3/4" wide; followed by berrylike fruit called a *hip*, which turns red when mature.
Leaves:	Dark green above, lighter beneath; pinnate, 3- to 9-toothed; to 2 1/2" long; oval to elliptical leaflets, each to 3/4" long.
Blooms:	May–July.
Elevation:	4,000 to 9,000'.
Habitat:	Along streams and small clearings in ponderosa pine forests.
Comments:	The most abundant rose in Arizona. Thorns, to 1/4" long, are hooked; stems are grayish, brownish on twigs. Browsed by wildlife. Fruits, or *hips*, used for making wines, jams, and jellies. Four species of *Rosa* (ROH-zuh) in Arizona. Photograph taken at Woods Canyon Lake, July 7. This species is shorter than the related **FENDLER ROSE** (*Rosa fendleri*), and has smaller flowers and larger, stout, curved thorns.

FENDLER ROSE   590

Wild rose, Wood's rose, Fendler's rose
Rosa fendleri (*Rosa woodsii*)
Rose Family (Rosaceae)

Height:	To 7'.
Flowers:	Fragrant, with 5 broad, pink petals and yellow stamens; to 2 1/4" wide; followed by berrylike fruit called a *hip*, which turns red when mature.

Leaves:	Dark green, pinnate, 3- to 7-toothed; oval to elliptical leaflets to 1" long; leaf to 3" long.
Blooms:	June–August.
Elevation:	5,500 to 9,000'.
Habitat:	Roadsides, slopes, and clearings in ponderosa forests.
Comments:	Thorns are short, red, slender, and nearly straight; stems are reddish. Browsed by wildlife. Fruits, or *hips*, used in vitamin supplements and for making wine, jams, and jellies; also eaten by Native Americans as well as by birds and small mammals. Four species of *Rosa* (ROH-zuh) in Arizona. Photograph taken near Prescott, May 26. This species is taller than the **ARIZONA ROSE** (*Rosa arizonica*), has larger flowers, and slender, nearly straight thorns.

NEW MEXICAN RASPBERRY 190
Thimbleberry
Rubus neomexicanus
Rose Family (Rosaceae)

Height:	To 5', rarely to 9'.
Flowers:	White, with 5 rounded petals and bright yellow stamens; to 3" wide; followed by red, juicy raspberry.
Leaves:	Green, finely haired above, velvety beneath; toothed, 3- to 5-lobed; to 3" wide.
Blooms:	May–September.
Elevation:	5,000 to 9,000'.
Habitat:	Moist slopes and woods.
Comments:	Young shrubs have brownish bark with vertical stripes. Browsed by deer. Fruits eaten by humans and by birds and other wildlife. Six species of *Rubus* (REW-buss) in Arizona. Photograph taken on Mount Graham, April 21.

THIMBLEBERRY 191
Salmonberry, western thimbleberry, thimble raspberry, white-flowering raspberry
Rubus parviflorus var. *parvifolius*
Rose Family (Rosaceae)

Height:	To 6', usually closer to 3'.
Flowers:	White, with 5 rounded petals, numerous yellowish tan stamens, and 5 sharply pointed sepals; to 2" wide; in terminal cluster of 3 or more; followed by a very seedy, red, raspberrylike fruit.
Leaves:	Dark green, 5-lobed, toothed, hairy above, deeply veined; to 8" wide.
Blooms:	July–September.
Elevation:	8,000 to 9,500'.
Habitat:	On slopes in ponderosa pine and spruce-fir forests.
Comments:	A thornless, sprawling shrub. Berries eaten by birds and other wildlife. Six species of *Rubus* (REW-buss) in Arizona. Photograph taken in mountains above Greer, July 8.

HIMALAYA-BERRY 592
Blackberry, Arizona blackberry
Rubus procerus
Rose Family (Rosaceae)

Height:	Creeping or clambering stems to 6' long.
Flowers:	Pinkish white, with 5 petals, numerous yellowish stamens; to 1 1/4" wide; followed by a blackberry, which when ripened is thimble-shaped.

Leaves:	Dark green above, white-felty beneath; pinnate, 3 to 5 toothed leaflets; to 9" long with stem.
Blooms:	June.
Elevation:	Not available. Photograph taken at 6,000'.
Habitat:	Mainly Oak Creek Canyon and Grand Canyon National Park.
Comments:	An introduced species thriving in limited areas. Stem is grooved, very prickly, and white-spined. Six species of *Rubus* (REW-buss) in Arizona. Photograph taken at Oak Creek Canyon, June 18.

RED RASPBERRY   192
Western red raspberry, wild red raspberry
Rubus strigosus (Rubus idaeus)
Rose Family (Rosaceae)

Height:	To 5'.
Flowers:	White, with 5 petals, 5 prominent sepals which are longer than petals and have spiny undersides; to 1" wide; followed by bright red fruits when mature.
Leaves:	Dark green above, grayish green beneath; pinnate, 3 to 7 toothed leaflets; to 8" long.
Blooms:	June–July.
Elevation:	7,000 to 11,000'.
Habitat:	Ponderosa pine and spruce forests.
Comments:	Pinkish stems are prickly. Fruits eaten by birds and other wildlife. People eat them raw or use for making jams and jellies; leaves and twigs are used for tea. Six species of *Rubus* (REW-buss) in Arizona. Photograph taken near Woods Canyon Lake, June 5.

ARIZONA MOUNTAIN-ASH   219
Serbal de cazadores, serbo
Sorbus dumosa
Rose Family (Rosaceae)

Height:	To 10'.
Bark:	Young growth is pinkish and hairy; mature bark is smooth and gray.
Flowers:	White, with 5 petals, numerous stamens; to 1/4" wide; in flat-topped cluster; followed by orange-red berry at maturity.
Leaves:	Dark green, paler green beneath; pinnate, sharp-toothed; to 7" long; 5 to 13 elliptical leaflets to 2" long.
Blooms:	June–July.
Elevation:	7,500 to 10,000'.
Habitat:	Moist soil in coniferous forests.
Comments:	Not a true ash. Berries eaten by birds and small mammals. One species of *Sorbus* (SOR-buss) in Arizona. Photograph taken at Black Canyon Lake area, June 4.

ARIZONA ROSEWOOD   76
Torrey vauquelinia
Vauquelinia californica
Rose Family (Rosaceae)

Height:	Shrub, or small tree to 25'.
Trunk:	To 8" in diameter.
Bark:	Gray to reddish brown, thin; shaggy or divided into small, square scales.
Flowers:	White, with 5 rounded petals; to 1/4" wide; in dense, flat-topped, terminal cluster to

3" wide; followed by hard, woody seed capsules, each to 1/4" wide, splitting into 5 sections and remaining all winter.

Leaves: Yellowish green and smooth above, with yellowish, sunken midvein; white, finely haired beneath; narrow, lance-shaped, thick, and stiff; leathery, spiny saw-toothed; to 4" long, 1/2" wide.

Blooms: May–June.

Elevation: 2,500 to 5,000'.

Habitat: Canyons and mountains in upper desert and oak woodlands.

Comments: Evergreen; slow growing. Wood is hard and heavy. One species of *Vauquelinia* (vaw-kah-LIN-ee-ah) in Arizona. Photograph taken on Peralta Trail in Superstition Mountains, May 20.

PEA FAMILY

Leguminosae (leh-gew-mih-NOH-see)
Represented in Arizona by herbs, shrubs, and small trees.

Flowers: Variable, mostly irregular. Many are pealike, with upper petal, or *standard*, 2 side petals called *wings*, and 2 lower petals which form the *keel*. Some are in dense balls with numerous prominent stamens. Others are in spikes or long, hanging clusters. Few or many stamens; 1 pistil. Superior ovary, 1-celled.

Fruit: 2-valved pod called a *legume*.

Leaves: Alternate, compound (twice or three times compound), 3-leaved, rarely single.

WHITE-BALL ACACIA   295

Fern acacia
Acacia angustissima
Pea Family (Leguminosae)

Height: To 3'.

Flowers: White, at times tinged with pink, with numerous stamens crowded into a ball-shaped head, to 1/2" in diameter; in clusters on stems in leaf axils and in elongated, terminal cluster; followed by brown, flattened pod (at maturity); to 3" long.

Leaves: Green to bluish green, bipinnate; first leaflets to 14 pairs, secondary leaflets to 33 pairs; linear-oblong, leaflet to 1/8" long, 1/16" wide.

Blooms: May–September.

Elevation: 3,000 to 6,500'.

Habitat: Roadsides and dry slopes commonly in chaparral areas.

Comments: No prickles or spines on branches; stems are deeply grooved and very hairy. Roots are perennial, but plant dies back to ground after hard frost. Browsed by horses and cattle; flowers attract butterflies, bees, and other insects. Inhibits soil erosion. There are numerous varieties of this species. Six species of *Acacia* (ah-KAY-shah) in Arizona. Photograph taken near Superior, September 2.

WHITE-THORN ACACIA   83

Mescat acacia, white-thorn
Acacia constricta
Pea Family (Leguminosae)

Height: Shrub to 10'.

Flowers: Yellowish orange, very fragrant, crowded into 1/2" balls; followed by curved, reddish brown pod to 5" long, to 1/4" wide.

Leaves: Light green, bipinnately compound; to 2" long, 1" wide.
Blooms: May–August.
Elevation: 2,500 to 5,000'.
Habitat: Mesas, dry slopes, washes, shallow caliche soil, and desert grassland.
Comments: Semi-deciduous; leafless during winter months. Branches armed with pairs of white spines to 2" long. Golden stamens (up to 40 per ball) give ball its color. Jackrabbits feed on young growth. Six species of *Acacia* (ah-KAY-shah) in Arizona. Photograph taken near Saguaro Lake, August 26.

CATCLAW ACACIA   84
Cat's claw, tearblanket, devil's claw, una de gato, wait-a-minute, Gregg catclaw
Acacia greggii
Pea Family (Leguminosae)

Height: Shrub, or small tree to 23'.
Trunk: To 8" in diameter.
Bark: Gray to brown; scaly.
Flowers: Pale yellow, dense, fragrant, cylindrical spike, to 2 1/2" long; followed by flattened, twisted pod to 6" long, 1/2" wide.
Leaves: Grayish green, bipinnately compound; to 3" long.
Blooms: April–October, with heaviest blooms in April and May.
Elevation: Below 5,000'.
Habitat: Slopes, canyons, desert grasslands, and along washes and streams.
Comments: Deciduous. Branches have short, sharp, 1/4"-long, recurved spines that resemble cats' claws and can rip clothing and flesh if brushed against. Wax-coated seeds delay germination for several years. Flowers attract bees and other insects. Stringbeanlike fruits are ground into meal by Native Americans. Wood used for tool handles and fuel. Six species of *Acacia* (ah-KAY-shah) in Arizona. Photograph taken near Saguaro Lake, August 26.

DESERT ACACIA   85
Huisache, sponge tree, cassie, sweet acacia
Acacia smallii (*Acacia farnesiana*)
Pea Family (Leguminosae)

Height: Spiny shrub, or small tree to 20'.
Trunk: To 1' in diameter.
Bark: Reddish brown, ridged, scaly, and thin.
Flowers: Golden yellow, ball-shaped, very fragrant; to 3/8" in diameter; followed by a purplish pod to 3" long.
Leaves: Bright green, bipinnately compound; to 4" long; leaflets to 1/4" long.
Blooms: November–May.
Elevation: 2,500 to 4,000'.
Habitat: Rarely grows in the wild.
Comments: Deciduous to semi-deciduous. Has white, straight, inch-long spines at base of leaves. Foliage and pods eaten by livestock. When mature has round, widely spreading crown. Six species of *Acacia* (ah-KAY-shah) in Arizona. Photograph taken at Tortilla Flat, November 11.

FALSE INDIGO   761A and B

Bastard indigo, indigobush, spice-bush
Amorpha fruticosa var. *occidentalis*
Pea Family (Leguminosae)

Height:	To 10'.
Flowers:	Deep violet-purple, 1-petaled; stamens tipped with bright orange anthers; to 3/8" long, 1/8" wide; dense; on long, slender flower spike (spike to 7" long) in leaf axil, often 2 or 3 spikes per axil.
Leaves:	Dark green above, lighter green beneath; compound; to 10 pairs of oblong leaflets, each to 2" long.
Blooms:	May–July.
Elevation:	2,500 to 7,000'.
Habitat:	Streamsides, canyons, and other moist locations.
Comments:	Deciduous. Two species of *Amorpha* (uh-MOR-fuh) in Arizona. Photographs taken at Cave Creek, Portal, May 5.

ASTRAGALUS   299

Astragalus praelongus
Pea Family (Leguminosae)

Height:	Sprawling to 4'.
Flowers:	Cream-colored, pealike, and drooping; to 7/8" long; in raceme to 3" long; followed by whitish, inflated, warty pod to 1/2" wide, 1 1/2" long.
Leaves:	Grayish green, to 6" long; with 11 to 27 elliptical leaflets, each to 3/4" long and slightly curved upward lengthwise.
Blooms:	May–August.
Elevation:	3,000 to 6,500'.
Habitat:	Sandy soil.
Comments:	Coarse, malodorous plant; toxic to sheep. Its largest stems are reddish. The species of *Astragalus* (as-TRAG-a-luss), a very large genus, are difficult to identify. There are more than 6 dozen species of *Astragalus* in Arizona. Identifying them as either a milk vetch or a locoweed is in most cases as far as one can go. Photograph taken at Concho Lake, August 4.

YELLOW BIRD-OF-PARADISE   500

Bird-of-paradise flower, Mexican bird-of-paradise
Caesalpinia gilliesii (*Poinciana gilliesii*)
Pea Family (Leguminosae)

Height:	Shrub to 10'.
Flowers:	Yellow petals, 10 red stamens; to 3" long; in terminal raceme; followed by a flattened bean, to 5" long, splitting and curling when mature.
Leaves:	Grayish green, twice pinnately compound; to 14 primary leaflets, up to 10 pairs of oval secondary leaflets; leaf to 6" long, 3" wide.
Blooms:	April–September.
Habitat:	Roadsides and waste areas in warmer counties of Arizona.
Comments:	Open, deciduous shrub to 6' wide. Native of South America and Mexico, now naturalized in the Southwest and grown as a landscape shrub. Flowers and foliage have an unpleasant odor. Seed pods are poisonous. One naturalized species of *Caesalpinia* (sez-al-PIN-i-ah) in Arizona. Photograph taken in vicinity of Scottsdale, May 7.

FAIRY DUSTER   653
Calliandra, false mesquite, hairy-leaved calliandra, mesquitilla
Calliandra eriophylla
Pea Family (Leguminosae)

Height:	To 4'.
Flowers:	Each pink powder puff contains several flowers. Long stamens, white at base and tipped with pink, make up the 2"-wide puff; followed by flat, brown, 2"-long seed pod covered with short, velvety hairs. Upon ripening, the pod splits and its halves stand widely apart for a long period.
Leaves:	Dark green, twice-compound, acacialike; to 3" long.
Blooms:	At any time of year, but mostly October–May.
Elevation:	Below 5,000'.
Habitat:	Open hillsides, washes, and arid grasslands.
Comments:	Thornless, perennial shrub and soil-binding plant. Many desert animals feed on foliage, and insects and hummingbirds frequent its flowers. During dry spells leaves wilt, but soon revive after rain. Three species of *Calliandra* (kal-i-AN-drah) in Arizona. Photograph taken in vicinity of Apache Lake, March 29.

FALSE MESQUITE (mess-KEET)   296
Calliandra humilis
Pea Family (Leguminosae)

Height:	To 2" tall, sprawling to 8".
Flowers:	White, numerous, with long, conspicuous stamens; flowerhead to 5/8" in diameter; followed by narrow, flat pod with thick, riblike margins. Reddish buds.
Leaves:	Grayish green edged in red; hairy; leaf segments to 1/8" long, leaf to 2 1/2" long. On some plants leaf segments close when touched and stay closed for several minutes.
Blooms:	June–August.
Elevation:	4,000 to 9,000'.
Habitat:	Dry soil in oak or pine woodlands.
Comments:	Stems are reddish and very hairy. Three species of *Calliandra* (kal-i-AN-drah) in Arizona. Photograph taken in vicinity of Prescott, June 7.

DESERT SENNA   501
Rattlebox, senna, dais, rosemaria, rattleweed, cove senna
Cassia covesii
Pea Family (Leguminosae)

Height:	To 2'.
Flowers:	Rusty yellow, with 5 petals; to 1" wide; in terminal cluster; followed by slightly curving, woody seed pod, to 1 1/4" long.
Leaves:	Grayish green, with fine, white hairs; pinnate; 3 pairs of elliptical leaflets; to 2" long.
Blooms:	April–October.
Elevation:	1,000 to 3,000'.
Habitat:	Dry, rocky slopes, mesas, and roadsides.
Comments:	A bushy perennial. Nine species of *Cassia* (KASH-i-ah or KAS-i-ah) in Arizona. Photograph taken at Usery Mountain Recreation Area, March 1.

BLUE PALOVERDE (PAH-low-VEHR-dee) 91
Paloverde
Cercidium floridum
Pea Family (Leguminosae)

Height:	To 30'.
Trunk:	To 1 1/2' in diameter.
Bark:	Blue-green, smooth, and thin, becoming brown and scaly on large, older trunks.
Flowers:	Bright yellow, 5-petaled (all petals yellow); to 1" wide; 4 or 5 in 2"-long cluster; followed by flat, yellowish brown pod, short-pointed at ends; to 3" long.
Leaves:	Dull bluish green when present; to 1 1/2" long; bipinnately compound with oblong leaflets to 3/16" long.
Blooms:	April–May.
Elevation:	500 to 4,000'.
Habitat:	Along washes, valleys, flood plains, desert slopes, and desert grasslands.
Comments:	Blue paloverde is widely spreading, with a very open crown. Photosynthesis takes place in the bark, in addition to the leaves, which are drought-deciduous. Twigs bear a 1/4" spine at each node. Branches and pods are browsed by wildlife; seeds provide food for birds and mammals, and are ground by Native Americans for meal. Two species of *Cercidium* (ser-SID-ee-yum) in Arizona; both are official state trees. Blue paloverde is distinguished from **YELLOW PALOVERDE** (*Cercidium microphyllum*) by its larger leaves, 5 yellow petals, bluish bark, and 1/4"-long spines at the nodes. Photograph taken at Usery Mountain Recreation Area, May 3.

YELLOW PALOVERDE (PAH-low-VEHR-dee) 92
Foothill paloverde, littleleaf paloverde, hillside paloverde, littleleaf horsebean
Cercidium microphyllum
Pea Family (Leguminosae)

Height:	To 25'.
Trunk:	To 1' in diameter.
Bark:	Yellow-green and smooth.
Flowers:	Pale yellow, with 5 petals (the largest petal is creamy white); 1/2" wide; in 1" cluster; followed by cylindrical pod with long, narrow points; pod to 3" long, 1/4" in diameter.
Leaves:	Yellowish green, bipinnately compound; 5 to 7 pairs of elliptical leaflets, each to 1/16" long; leaf to 3/4" long.
Blooms:	March–May.
Elevation:	500 to 4,000'.
Habitat:	Dry, rocky hillsides and mesas, plains, and deserts.
Comments:	*Paloverde* is Spanish for "green stick" (or "pole" or "tree") and refers to the tree's smooth, green bark. During the dry season, when leaves are dropped, photosynthesis is carried on by the chlorophyll in the bark. Both yellow and blue paloverde are Arizona's official state trees; yellow is the more common species. The tree has a widely spreading, open crown. Twigs end in stout, stiff spines, to 2" long. Flowers are attractive to bees and other insects. Seeds are eaten by animals; Native Americans ground them into meal. The wood is soft and makes poor fuel. Two species of *Cercidium* in Arizona. Distinguished from **BLUE PALOVERDE** (*Cercidium floridum*) by its smaller leaves, one whitish petal, yellowish bark, and spine-tipped branchlets. Photograph taken at Usery Mountain Recreation Area, May 3.

COLOGANIA 742A and B
Narrowleaf tick clover
Cologania angustifolia (Cologania longifolia)
Pea Family (Leguminosae)

Height: Trailing or nearly erect to 4' long.

Flowers: Reddish purple, pealike, notched; to 1" long, 3/4" wide on 1/8"-long stem; erect upper petal to 5/8" wide; lower petals curve forward; occurs singly or 2 to 3 in leaf axils, followed by a downy or smooth, flat pod.

Leaves: Dark green, pinnate; to 6" long on long stem; usually 3 but sometimes 5 very narrow leaflets, often folded in half lengthwise, hairy on margins and beneath, to 2 1/2" long. Leaflets very variable.

Blooms: July–September.

Elevation: 4,000 to 9,000'.

Habitat: Coniferous forests.

Comments: Perennial herb. A highly variable species, as photographs show. Two species of *Cologania* (kol-oh-GAN-i-ah) in Arizona. Photograph A taken near Willow Springs Lake, September 13; photograph B taken in vicinity of Lakeside, July 6.

COURSETIA 95
Coursetia microphylla
Pea Family (Leguminosae)

Height: To 20'; usually less.

Flowers: Cream-colored upper petals, yellow lower petals, pealike; to 1/2" long, 1/4" wide; in short, glandular raceme; followed by a brown, thick-walled seed pod, to 2" long, constricted between seeds.

Leaves: Grayish green, hairy, pinnately compound; to 1" long, singly or in clusters. Elliptical to oblong leaflets to 1/4" long, and in pairs; no terminal leaflet.

Blooms: March–April.

Elevation: Below 4,000'.

Habitat: Canyons and dry, rocky slopes.

Comments: Plant has grayish bark; no spines, and hairy stems. One species of *Coursetia* (koor-SET-i-ah) in Arizona. Photograph taken at Saguaro National Monument West, April 17.

SCRUFFY PRAIRIE CLOVER 300
White dalea
Dalea albiflora
Pea Family (Leguminosae)

Height: To 2'.

Flowers: Whitish, tiny, and pealike; in dense, elongated, terminal spike to 1 1/2" long, 1/2" wide.

Leaves: Grayish green, pinnate, with linear lobes; covered with short, whitish hairs; to 1 1/2" long.

Blooms: April–October.

Elevation: 3,500 to 7,500'.

Habitat: Clearings in ponderosa forests and roadsides.

Comments: Has hairy stems. Thirty-six species of *Dalea* (DAY-leh-uh) in Arizona. Photograph taken near Camp Verde, September 30. This species resembles **WHITE PRAIRIE CLOVER** (*Petalostemum candidum*); however, it has 10 stamens instead of the 5 found in species of *Petalostemum*.

EMORY DALEA   743
White dalea
Dalea emoryi
Pea Family (Leguminosae)

Height:	To 3', but straggly.
Flowers:	Purple, pealike; to 1/4" long; in roundish flower cluster to 1" wide.
Leaves:	Grayish white, felty, covered with spreading white hairs and sunken black glands; pinnate; to 2" long; 1 to 13 narrow leaflets; terminal leaflet to 1" long, side leaflets to 1/4" long.
Blooms:	March–April; occasionally in the fall.
Elevation:	Below 500'.
Habitat:	Sandy mesas.
Comments:	Entire plant is very felty. Thirty-six species of *Dalea* (DAY-leh-uh) in Arizona. Photograph taken near Yuma, March 29.

FEATHER DALEA   744
Indigo bush, pea bush, feather plume
Dalea formosa
Pea Family (Leguminosae)

Height:	To 16".
Flowers:	Purplish, pealike, largest petal cream-colored, to 1/2" long; 2 to 6 in feathery cluster.
Leaves:	Dark green, pinnate; 7 to 15 narrow leaflets dotted with very dark glands; to 3/8" long.
Blooms:	March–June.
Elevation:	2,000 to 6,500'.
Habitat:	Rocky hillsides, mountains, and dry plains.
Comments:	Many-branched. Browsed by deer; pollinated by bees. Thirty-six species of *Dalea* (DAY-leh-uh) in Arizona. Photograph taken north of Safford, April 20.

TRAILING SMOKE BUSH   745
Gregg dalea
Dalea greggii
Pea Family (Leguminosae)

Height:	To 18".
Flowers:	Rose-purple, pea-shaped; to 3/16" long; many in a globular flowerhead to 3/4" wide.
Leaves:	Grayish green, hairy; to 1" long; 5 to 7 leaflets, which are 1/4" long.
Blooms:	February–May.
Elevation:	2,500 to 5,000'.
Habitat:	Rocky hillsides, gravelly slopes, and canyons.
Comments:	Thirty-six species of *Dalea* (DAY-leh-uh) in Arizona. Photograph taken at Desert Botanical Garden, Phoenix, March 23. This species native to southern Arizona.

FOXTAIL DALEA   762
Dalea leporina
Pea Family (Leguminosae)

Height:	To 3'.
Flowers:	Bluish or purplish with white bases; to 3/16" long; flower spike to 4" long.
Leaves:	Dark green, smooth, glandular-dotted; to 3" long, with 19 to 35 leaf segments.
Blooms:	June–October.
Elevation:	5,500 to 8,000'.
Habitat:	Roadsides and at borders of ponderosa forests.
Comments:	Many smooth stems and branches. Thirty-six species of *Dalea* (DAY-leh-uh) in Arizona. Photograph taken in vicinity of McNary, August 10.

PARRY DALEA 763
Dalea parryi
Pea Family (Leguminosae)

Height:	Sprawling, to 2 1/2'.
Flowers:	Deep purple upper petals, white lower petals, pealike; to 3/8" long, 3/16" wide; in terminal, many-flowered, spikelike cluster.
Leaves:	Grayish green, hairy, pinnate; leaflets to 1/8" long, leaf to 1" long.
Blooms:	March–June.
Elevation:	Below 4,000'.
Habitat:	Desert flats and washes.
Comments:	Perennial. Has very open growth and branches freely. Slender-branched and glandular. Thirty-six species of *Dalea* (DAY-leh-uh) in Arizona. Photograph taken at Saguaro National Monument West, April 17.

DALEA 746
Dalea pulchra
Pea Family (Leguminosae)

Height:	To 4'.
Flowers:	Rose-purple above, whitish below, pealike; to 1/4" wide, in round head.
Leaves:	Grayish green to silvery, velvety-haired, with 3 to 9 segments, each to 1/4" long; leaf to 1/2" long.
Blooms:	February–May.
Elevation:	2,500 to 5,000'.
Habitat:	Rocky hills and mountainsides.
Comments:	Thirty-six species of *Dalea* (DAY-leh-uh) in Arizona. Photograph taken at Saguaro National Monument East, April 15.

SMOKETREE 44
Smokethorn, smokethorn dalea, indigo bush
Dalea spinosa
Pea Family (Leguminosae)

Height:	Shrub, or small tree to 20'.
Trunk:	To 1' in diameter.
Bark:	Dark, grayish brown, scaly, fissured.
Flowers:	Bluish purple, pealike; 1/2" long; in cluster to 1 1/2" long; followed by egg-shaped, brown, 3/8"-long, gland-dotted seed pod.
Leaves:	When present, wedge-shaped, hairy, dotted with glands; to 1" long.
Blooms:	May–June.
Elevation:	250 to 1,000'.
Habitat:	Sandy washes in frost-free areas.

Comments: Spiny shrub or tree which is smoky gray all over and leafless most of the year. Twigs produce food by performing photosynthesis. Thirty-six species of *Dalea* (DAY-leh-uh) in Arizona. Photograph taken in Kofa Mountains, February 21.

BUSHY TICK CLOVER   654

Beggar's ticks, sticktights
Desmodium batocaulon
Pea Family (Leguminosae)

Height: Climbing or prostrate, to 5'.
Flowers: Rose to purplish, pealike, with large upper petal; lower petals folded lengthwise; column of stamens projecting upward; to 1/2" wide, 3/4" long; followed by seed pods formed by 1-seeded segments covered with barbed hairs; up to 7 segments per pod.
Leaves: Dark green with silvery white, irregularly shaped central markings; pinnately divided into 3 narrow, lancelike segments; prickly haired, leaflets to 2" long, leaf to 3 1/2" long.
Blooms: June–September.
Elevation: 3,500 to 6,500'.
Habitat: Roadsides and pine forests.
Comments: Barbed hairs cause individual seed pods to break off and cling to anything that touches them. Stems are prickly and sticky. Fourteen species of *Desmodium* (des-MOH-di-uhm) in Arizona. Photograph taken in vicinity of Christopher Creek, August 2.

GRAHAM'S TICK CLOVER   655

Desmodium grahami
Pea Family (Leguminosae)

Height: Sprawling, to 2'. Flower stem to 15" tall.
Flowers: Light pink on outer lobes, darker pink on inner lobes; pea-shaped; stamens project forward. Flower to 3/8" long, in upright raceme in leaf axils and terminal, followed by beadlike seed pod with 3 to 5 joints.
Leaves: Grayish green, very hairy on both surfaces, with 3 broadly oval leaflets, slightly curved upward; to 2" long.
Blooms: June–September.
Elevation: 4,500 to 8,000'.
Habitat: Clearings in pine woods and hillsides.
Comments: Stems are reddish and very hairy. Fourteen species of *Desmodium* (des-MOH-di-uhm) in Arizona. Photograph taken in vicinity of Prescott, June 7.

SOUTHWESTERN CORAL BEAN   546

Coral tree, Indian bean, chilicote, western coral bean
Erythrina flabelliformis
Pea Family (Leguminosae)

Height: Shrub, or small tree to 15', usually shorter.
Flowers: Bright red or reddish orange, with whitish, waxy calyx, and long, narrow corolla; pealike; to 3" long, 1/4" wide; several in terminal cluster, followed by large, thick-walled pod, to 10" long, 3/4" wide; seeds to 1/2" long.
Leaves: (When present) grayish green, pinnate, with 3 triangular leaflets, each to 3" long, 4" wide.

Blooms:	May–July (sometimes in late summer).
Elevation:	3,000 to 5,000'.
Habitat:	Dry, rocky hillsides.
Comments:	Has short, hooked spines on stems and leafstalks. Flowers appear before leaves. Bright red seeds are very poisonous; used in Mexican jewelry. One species of *Erythrina* (eh-rith-REEN-ah) in Arizona. Photograph taken in Tucson area, May 12.

ARIZONA PEA   301
Arizona sweet pea, wild sweetpea, Arizona peavine
Lathyrus arizonicus
Pea Family (Leguminosae)

Height:	Sprawling to 16".
Flowers:	White, pealike, with wide upper petal with pinkish veins; to 5/8" wide, 1/2" long; 2 to 5 flowers in cluster.
Leaves:	Dark green, thin, pinnate, with 2 to 6 broadly linear leaflets, each to 1 3/4" long; tendrils small, bristlelike, and not prehensile.
Blooms:	May–October.
Elevation:	8,000 to 11,000'.
Habitat:	Coniferous forests.
Comments:	Not favored as browse by livestock, as are vetches. Seven species of *Lathyrus* (LATH-i-russ) in Arizona. Photograph taken on San Francisco Peaks, June 4.

PEAVINE   302
Lathyrus leucanthus
Pea Family (Leguminosae)

Height:	Twining to 2'.
Flowers:	Whitish with pale pink veins; pealike; to 3/8" wide, 3/4" long; 2 to 5 on long stem arising from leaf axil, followed by flat seed pod to 1/4" wide, 2" long.
Leaves:	Dark green, pinnately divided into 10 leaflets, each with tiny bristle at tip; leaflet to 3/8" wide, 2" long; leaf to 4" long and tipped with well-defined tendril. Stipules in leaf axils.
Blooms:	May–August.
Elevation:	6,000 to 7,000'.
Habitat:	Pine forests.
Comments:	Seven species of *Lathyrus* (LATH-i-russ) in Arizona. Photograph taken in vicinity of Mormon Lake, June 1.

BIRDSFOOT LOTUS   502
Bird's foot trefoil, ground honeysuckle, baby's slippers, bloom-fell
Lotus corniculatus
Pea Family (Leguminosae)

Height:	Sprawling stems, tips upright to 18".
Flowers:	Bright yellow, pealike, with upright upper hood; 5-petaled; to 5/8" long, 3/8" wide; on axil stem, in flat-topped, loose cluster of up to 12 flowers; cluster to 1 1/4" wide; followed by 1"-long, narrow pod with a hair at tip; pods radiating outward in half-circle.
Leaves:	Dark green, pinnate, with 3 oblong leaflets, each to 3/4" long.
Blooms:	June–September.
Elevation:	Not available. Photograph taken at 5,600'.

Habitat:	Roadsides and meadows.
Comments:	Perennial. Introduced from Eurasia. Configuration of pods suggests a bird's foot. Fifteen species of *Lotus* (LOH-tus) in Arizona. Photograph taken in vicinity of Christopher Creek, August 11.

GREEN'S LOTUS   503
Lotus greenei
Pea Family (Leguminosae)

Height:	Creeper to 6" high.
Flowers:	Yellow, with orangish backs; pealike; banner (upper) petal very large; to 3/8" wide, on long flower stem.
Leaves:	Grayish green, densely haired, pinnate, 4 to 5 spatula-shaped leaflets in fanlike cluster, to 1/4" long.
Blooms:	March–May.
Elevation:	3,000 to 5,000' in southern Arizona.
Habitat:	Roadsides, rocky hillsides, and mesas.
Comments:	Fifteen species of *Lotus* (LOH-tus) in Arizona. Photograph taken at Sonoita, April 26.

WIRY LOTUS   504
Desert rock-pea
Lotus rigidus
Pea Family (Leguminosae)

Height:	To 3'.
Flowers:	Yellow-tinged with orange; pealike, banner (upper) petal flares backward; on long flower stem; flower to 1" long; followed by long, narrow seed pod to 1 1/2" long.
Leaves:	Grayish green, pinnate, widely spaced on stem; 3 to 5 narrow leaflets; leaf to 1 1/8" long.
Blooms:	February–May.
Elevation:	Below 5,000'.
Habitat:	Dry, rocky slopes, in canyons and in deserts.
Comments:	The most drought-resistant lotus in Arizona. Several erect, wiry, gray stems. Fifteen species of *Lotus* (LOH-tus) in Arizona. Photograph taken near Superior, April 3. Recognizable by wide spacing on stems between leaves, and by its very gray stems and foliage.

HAIRY LOTUS   505
Desert lotus
Lotus tomentellus
Pea Family (Leguminosae)

Height:	Prostrate to 10".
Flowers:	Yellow and pealike; to 1/8" wide; 1 to 2 on long flower stem.
Leaves:	Grayish, hairy, and pinnate, with 5 to 6 blunt leaflets; to 1" long.
Blooms:	March–May.
Elevation:	Below 3,000'.
Habitat:	Sandy deserts.
Comments:	Fifteen species of *Lotus* (LOH-tus) in Arizona. Photograph taken in Superstition Mountains, March 15.

WRIGHT'S DEERVETCH 506
Lotus, deer clover, red and yellow pea
Lotus wrightii
Pea Family (Leguminosae)

Height:	To 16".
Flowers:	Yellow, tinged with orange or red with age; pealike; to 1/2" long; in leaf axils; followed by a slender pod to 1" long.
Leaves:	Dark green; pinnately compound with 3 to 5 leaflets, each to 1/2" long.
Blooms:	May–September.
Elevation:	4,500 to 9,000'.
Habitat:	Roadsides and dry, open pine forests and juniper woods.
Comments:	Fifteen species of *Lotus* (LOH-tus) in Arizona. Photograph taken in Willow Springs Lake area, August 9.

SILVERSTEM LUPINE 764
Silvery lupine
Lupinus argenteus
Pea Family (Leguminosae)

Height:	To 2'.
Flowers:	Bluish to lilac, pealike; banner (upper) petal wide and hairy on back; flowers to 1/2" long, in long, terminal cluster; followed by hairy pod, to 1" long.
Leaves:	Dark green above with short hairs, lighter green and hairy beneath; troughlike; to 3" wide, 3" long; palmately divided, with 7 to 9 leaflets.
Blooms:	June–October.
Elevation:	7,000 to 10,000'.
Habitat:	Clearings in coniferous forests.
Comments:	A perennial herb, with silvery-haired stems. Seeds are eaten by birds. *Lupus* is Latin for wolf; it was believed these plants robbed the soil of nutrients. Actually their root nodules, with the aid of certain bacteria, allow lupines and other legumes to absorb free nitrogen from the air, thus enriching the soil. Twenty-three species of *Lupinus* (loo-PINE-us) in Arizona. Photograph taken south of Alpine, August 6. Its elevation, leaf shape, and silvery-haired stem help to identify this variable species.

ARIZONA LUPINE 656
Lupinus arizonicus
Pea Family (Leguminosae)

Height:	To 2'.
Flowers:	Pinkish, with a yellow center; pealike; to 1/2" long; in long, terminal cluster.
Leaves:	Bright green above, hairy beneath; palmately divided, with up to 9 leaflets; to 1 1/2" long.
Blooms:	January–May.
Elevation:	Below 3,000'.
Habitat:	Roadsides and sandy washes in desert.
Comments:	Twenty-three species of *Lupinus* (loo-PINE-us) in Arizona. Photograph taken near Hope, March 28.

BAJADA LUPINE 765
Elegant lupine
Lupinus concinnus

Pea Family (Leguminosae)
Height: To 6".
Flowers: Pale purple, edged with deeper purple; pealike, in flower cluster among leaves.
Leaves: Grayish green, densely haired; palmate, rounded at tips; to 1" wide.
Blooms: March–May.
Elevation: Below 5,000'.
Habitat: Sandy desert flats and bajadas.
Comments: Low, prostrate stems. Twenty-three species of *Lupinus* (loo-PINE-us) in Arizona. Photograph taken at Usery Mountain Recreation Area, March 10.

HILL'S LUPINE   766
Lupinus hillii
Pea Family (Leguminosae)
Height: To 8".
Flowers: Bluish to purple and pealike; to 1/4" long, in an elongated cluster.
Leaves: Grayish green, very hairy; palmate, with 8 to 10 leaflets; to 2 1/2" wide.
Blooms: May–August.
Elevation: 6,000 to 9,000'.
Habitat: Ponderosa pine forests.
Comments: Perennial. Less erect than other lupines. Twenty-three species of *Lupinus* (loo-PINE-us) in Arizona. Photograph taken at North Rim of Grand Canyon National Park, June 25.

COULTER'S LUPINE   767
Desert lupine
Lupinus sparsiflorus
Pea (Leguminosae)
Height: To 16".
Flowers: Pale blue to violet; pealike, banner (upper) petal has yellow spot that changes to purplish red when bees contact it; keel (lower) petals are short, wide, and curve upward; flowers to 1/2" long, in elongated cluster; followed by flattened pod to 1 1/2" long.
Leaves: Dark green, palmately divided; to 3" long; 5 to 9 linear leaflets, each to 1 1/2" long, 1/8" wide.
Blooms: January–May.
Elevation: Below 3,000'.
Habitat: Desert roadsides, slopes, and mesas.
Comments: Perennial herb; a favorite of bees. Like other legumes, it improves the soil. Lupines adjust their leaflets during the day to absorb maximum sunlight. When rains of fall and winter are sufficient, these plants carpet roadsides during the blooming period. Twenty-three species of *Lupinus* (loo-PINE-us) in Arizona. Photograph taken in Superstition Mountains, March 22.

FEATHER BUSH   86
Feather tree, fern-of-the-desert
Lysiloma microphylla var. *thornberi*
Pea Family (Leguminosae)
Height: To 15'.
Trunk: To 5" in diameter.

Bark:	Brownish gray, fissured and scaly.
Flowers:	Creamy to white, in a dense ball; with numerous stamens; to 1/2" in diameter; followed by a large, dark brown, flat, broad pod to 9" long, 1" wide.
Leaves:	Bright green, bipinnately compound, alternate; oval leaflets to 1/4" long, 1/8" wide; leaf to 7" long, 4" wide.
Blooms:	April–June.
Elevation:	2,800 to 4,000'.
Habitat:	Rocky hillsides in upper desert.
Comments:	A very localized species in southern Arizona. Dies back in hard winters. One species of *Lysiloma* (lie-suh-LOW-mah) in Arizona. Photograph taken at Desert Botanical Garden, Phoenix, April 30.

BUR CLOVER   507
Medicago hispida
Pea Family (Leguminosae)

Height:	Prostrate to semi-erect, to 2'.
Flowers:	Yellow and pealike; to 1/8" wide; 3 to 5 in a cluster on short stalk; followed by coiled, burlike seed pod with curved prickles on the sharp edge of a spiral; to 5/16" in diameter.
Leaves:	Bright green, divided into 3 wedge-shaped, toothed leaflets with slightly indented tips; to 1" wide.
Blooms:	March–May; a longer period of time under moist conditions.
Elevation:	100 to 5,500'.
Habitat:	Fields, lots, and disturbed areas.
Comments:	Annual. Introduced from Europe; now naturalized in the U.S. Four species of *Medicago* (med-i-KAY-go) in Arizona. Photograph taken on Apache Trail, March 19.

BLACK MEDICK   508
Nonesuch, hop medic
Medicago lupulina
Pea Family (Leguminosae)

Height:	Trailing to 2' long.
Flowers:	Bright yellow and pealike; to 1/8" long; clustered together on short, dense spike; followed by tiny, 1-seeded, kidney-shaped pod, to 1/8" long.
Leaves:	Dark green, divided into 3 leaflets with rounded tips; to 1" long including stalk.
Blooms:	April–September.
Elevation:	2,500 to 9,000'.
Habitat:	Roadsides, fields, lawns, and waste areas.
Comments:	Annual; a forage plant. Native of Eurasia; now naturalized in U.S. Four species of *Medicago* (med-i-KAY-go) in Arizona. Photograph taken at Black Canyon Lake, September 29.

ALFALFA   747
Lucerne, purple medic, burgundy trefoil
Medicago sativa
Pea Family (Leguminosae)

Height:	To 3'.
Flowers:	Violet to purplish, pealike; in short, terminal cluster from leaf axils; followed by downy, spirally coiled seed pod.

Leaves:	Dark green, pinnately divided into 3 segments; sharply toothed on margins near tips; to 2" long.
Blooms:	April–October.
Elevation:	Not available. Photograph taken at approximately 7,500'.
Habitat:	Roadsides and old fields.
Comments:	Perennial herb; native of southwestern Asia. Grown as a forage plant; occasionally escapes from cultivation. Has long taproot and enriches soil by adding nitrogen. A favorite of bees and butterflies. Four species of *Medicago* (med-i-KAY-go) in Arizona. Photograph taken at Nelson Reservoir, August 3.

WHITE SWEET CLOVER   303
Tree clover, white melilot, bokhara clover
Melilotus albus
Pea Family (Leguminosae)

Height:	To 6' or more.
Flowers:	White and pealike; to 1/4" long; in long, spikelike raceme of 30 to 80 flowers; spike to 8" long.
Leaves:	Light green, pinnately divided into 3 lance-shaped, toothed leaflets, each to 1" long.
Blooms:	July–October.
Elevation:	100 to 7,500'.
Habitat:	Roadsides and fields.
Comments:	A native of Eurasia; now naturalized in the U.S. Forage plant; enriches soil with nitrogen. Smells like newly mown hay. Excellent honey producer. Three species of *Melilotus* (mel-li-LOH-tus) in Arizona. Photograph taken near Nutrioso, July 23.

YELLOW SWEET CLOVER   509
Honey clover, yellow melilot, king's clover
Melilotus officinalis
Pea Family (Leguminosae)

Height:	To 5'.
Flowers:	Yellow and pealike; to 1/4" long; in long, spikelike raceme to 6" long.
Leaves:	Light green, pinnately divided into 3 lance-shaped, toothed leaflets, each to 1" long.
Blooms:	June–August.
Elevation:	To 8,000'.
Habitat:	Roadsides and fields.
Comments:	From Eurasia; now naturalized in the U.S. Biennial. Roots bind soil and enrich it with nitrogen. An excellent honey producer; browsed by deer. Three species of *Melilotus* (mel-li-LOH-tus) in Arizona. Photograph taken near Greer, June 18.

WAIT-A-MINUTE BUSH   297A and B
Wait-a-bit, cat claw
Mimosa biuncifera
Pea Family (Leguminosae)

Height:	To 8'.
Flowers:	White to pinkish, with a ball-like head; to 5/8" in diameter; on long flower stalks in leaf axils; followed by a cluster of slightly curved, flat pods, brown to reddish brown on upper surface, greenish beneath; to 2" long, 1/8" wide; with a few marginal prickles.

Leaves:	Dark green, bipinnate, with primary leaflets to 7 pairs, secondary leaflets to 13 pairs; haired; leaf to 2" long.
Blooms:	May–August.
Elevation:	3,000 to 6,000'.
Habitat:	Mesas, hillsides, desert grassland, and chaparral.
Comments:	Nodes of stems armed with clawlike spines to 1/4" long. Brown bark; honey plant; occasionally browsed by livestock. Forms thickets which prevent soil erosion and provide cover for wildlife. Four species of *Mimosa* (mih-MO-sah or my-MO-sah) in Arizona. Photograph in flower taken near Lake Pleasant, May 7. Photograph in fruit taken at Dead Horse Ranch State Park, October 3.

GRAHAM MIMOSA   298
Mimosa grahamii
Pea Family (Leguminosae)

Height:	To 2'.
Flowers:	Creamy white, ball-shaped; to 3/4" wide; with purplish red tinged corolla, creamy white filaments tipped with pale yellow anthers; each ball on 1"-long stem in leaf axil; followed by pod to 1 1/2" long, 5/16" wide with prickles on margins.
Leaves:	Grayish green, very hairy, bipinnate; oblong leaflet to 1/4" long; leaf to 6 1/2" long; midrib beneath is lined with short, curved spines.
Blooms:	April–August.
Elevation:	4,000 to 6,000'.
Habitat:	Hillsides and dry slopes in canyons in southern Arizona.
Comments:	An uncommon species. Stems have irregularly spaced spines to 1/16" long. Four species of *Mimosa* (mih-MO-sah or my-MO-sah) in Arizona. Photograph taken at Cave Creek Canyon near Portal, May 4.

IRONWOOD   96
Desert ironwood, palo-de-hierro, tesota, palo fierro, Arizona ironwood
Olneya tesota
Pea Family (Leguminosae)

Height:	To 30'.
Trunk:	To 1 1/2' in diameter.
Bark:	Gray and smooth on young trees; fissured and dark gray with age.
Flowers:	Pink and purplish to white; pealike; 5 unequal petals; to 1/2" wide in short cluster; followed by brown, hairy, beanlike pod, to 2 1/2" long.
Leaves:	Bluish green, finely haired, pinnately compound; to 2" long; 2 to 10 oblong leaflets to 3/4" long.
Blooms:	May–June.
Elevation:	Below 2,500'
Habitat:	Along desert washes and in sandy canyons.
Comments:	Evergreen, with widely spreading crown that can extend up to 30' across. At base of each leaf is pair of 1/2"-long, brown-tipped, slightly curved spines. To germinate, the hard coating on seeds must pass through digestive system of deer or cattle. Mistletoe is often found growing in branches. A frost-sensitive tree, therefore useful as a gauge for citrus grove selection. Browsed by bighorn sheep. Seeds provide food to birds and other animals and were also an important part of the Native American diet. Ironwood is one of the heaviest woods in the world; one cubic foot weighs 66 pounds. It makes excellent firewood, producing intense heat and lasting coals. Wood

was used by Native Americans for arrowheads and tool handles. Today the polished wood is used for curios. One species of *Olneya* (OLE-nee-ah) in Arizona. Photograph taken at Usery Mountain Recreation Area, May 20.

PURPLE LOCO 768
Lambert's loco, Lambert's crazyweed, Colorado loco, Rocky Mountain locoweed
Oxytropis lambertii
Pea Family (Leguminosae)

Height:	To 16".
Flowers:	Reddish purple or white, pealike; 2 keel (lower) petals are pointed; to 1" long; in raceme held above leaves; followed by leathery, beaked pod to 1 1/4" long.
Leaves:	Silvery, silky-haired, basal; to 12" long; pinnately compound, 7 to 17 leaflets, each to 1 1/2" long.
Blooms:	June–September.
Elevation:	5,000 to 8,000'.
Habitat:	Plains and clearings in ponderosa forests.
Comments:	Perennial herb. A dangerous locoweed toxic to livestock. Addictive. Often fatal. Taproot can descend 8'. Two species of *Oxytropis* (ox-IT-ro-pis) in Arizona. Photograph taken at Sunset Crater National Monument, September 7.

MEXICAN PALOVERDE 93
Jerusalem-thorn, horse bean
Parkinsonia aculeata
Pea Family (Leguminosae)

Height:	To 40'.
Trunk:	To 1' in diameter.
Bark:	Yellowish green, smooth, scaly at base, and brown when larger.
Flowers:	Golden yellow; 5 petals, the largest orange or yellow with orange spots; to 1" wide, in cluster to 7" long; followed by dark brown pod narrowing between seeds, to 4" long.
Leaves:	Bright green, twice pinnately compound; to 20" long; up to 30 pairs of leaflets, each to 3/16" long. Leaves fall off during drought or cold conditions.
Blooms:	April–May.
Elevation:	To 4,500'.
Habitat:	Desert valleys.
Comments:	Gradually becoming naturalized in Arizona. Foliage and seeds eaten by wildlife. A favorite of bees. One species of *Parkinsonia* (par-kin-SOH-ni-ah) in Arizona. Photograph taken in Mesa, May 3. Easily recognizable by its branches of long streamers; spines on branches grouped in threes.

WHITE PRAIRIE CLOVER 304
White tassel-flower
Petalostemum occidentale (*Petalostemum candidum*)
Pea Family (Leguminosae)

Height:	To 2 1/2'.
Flowers:	White, pealike; to 1/4" long; with yellow-tipped stamens; growing in axils of bracts on dense, terminal spike.
Leaves:	Dark green, gland-dotted, hairless; pinnate, with 3 to 9 leaflets, very narrow to lance-shaped; leaf to 1" long.

Blooms:	May–September.
Elevation:	3,000 to 7,000'.
Habitat:	Roadsides, plains, and mesas.
Comments:	Perennial herb, with gland-dotted flower stems. Genus often spelled *Petalostemon*. Five species of *Petalostemum* (pet-a-los-TEE-mum) in Arizona. Photograph taken in vicinity of Christopher Creek, September 14.

SLIMLEAF LIMABEAN 657
Phaseolus angustissimus
Pea Family (Leguminosae)

Height:	Trailing vine to 10" high.
Flowers:	Rose-pink, pealike; to 1/2" wide; followed by limabeanlike pea pod.
Leaves:	Dark green, pinnately compound; to 3" long; long, narrow, leaflets to 1 1/4" long. There is a wide range of leaf shapes and sizes within this species.
Blooms:	May–October.
Elevation:	3,500 to 7,000'.
Habitat:	Mesas, clearings in ponderosa forests, and hillsides.
Comments:	Ten species of *Phaseolus* (fah-SEE-oh-luss) in Arizona. Photograph taken at Sunset Crater National Monument, September 7.

GRAY'S LIMABEAN 658
Phaseolus grayanus
Pea Family (Leguminosae)

Height:	Trailing vine.
Flowers:	Deep pink and pealike, rounded upper lobe with shallow cleft; to 1/2" long, 3/8" wide; in terminal cluster on stem to 3" long; followed by pealike, curved seed pod to 2" long.
Leaves:	Grayish green, pinnately compound; 3 leaflets with 3 pointed lobes; silvery central blotches; to 3" long, 3" wide. Center leaflet to 1 3/4" long; 2 side leaflets to 1 1/2" long; terminal leaflet may fold back between 2 side leaflets.
Blooms:	July–September.
Elevation:	5,000 to 8,500'.
Habitat:	Clearings in ponderosa pine forests.
Comments:	Ten species of *Phaseolus* (fah-SEE-oh-luss) in Arizona. Photograph taken on Mogollon Rim near Woods Canyon Lake, August 9.

WRIGHT'S LIMABEAN 659
Phaseolus wrightii
Pea Family (Leguminosae)

Height:	Trailing vine.
Flowers:	Reddish pink and pea-shaped; to 3/8" wide; occurring singly or in small cluster; followed by limabeanlike, hairy pea pod.
Leaves:	Green, 3 leaflets with long, rounded lobes; reddish, hairy margins; to 2 1/4" wide.
Blooms:	Throughout the year.
Elevation:	1,000 to 4,000'.
Habitat:	Rocky slopes, canyons, and roadsides.
Comments:	Ten species of *Phaseolus* (fah-SEE-oh-luss) in Arizona. Photograph taken near Tortilla Flat, March 19.

WESTERN HONEY MESQUITE (mess-KEET)   87

Prosopis glandulosa

Pea Family (Leguminosae)

Height: To 20'.

Trunk: To 1' in diameter.

Bark: Brown and smooth, becoming rough with age.

Flowers: Creamy yellow and fragrant; to 1/4" long; in narrow cluster to 3" long; followed by spiraled or straight, beanlike pod to 8" long.

Leaves: Yellowish green, bipinnately compound; to 8" long; leaflets narrow, oblong, to 1 1/4" long, 1/8" wide.

Blooms: May.

Elevation: Below 4,500'.

Habitat: Plains, hillsides, and along washes.

Comments: A favorite of bees. Native Americans used pods for meal. A single or pair of white to yellowish spines, to 3 1/2" long, at large nodes on branches. Four species of *Prosopis* (pro-SOAP-iss) in Arizona. Photograph taken at Desert Botanical Garden, Phoenix, May 20. **HONEY MESQUITE** (*Prosopis glandulosa* var. *glandulosa*) has reddish spines and larger leaflets. Photograph (**PLATE 88**) taken in Tucson area, November 10.

SCREWBEAN MESQUITE (mess-KEET)   89

Fremont screwbean, tornillo, screwpod mesquite

Prosopis pubescens

Pea Family (Leguminosae)

Height: Shrub, or small tree to 20'.

Trunk: To 8" in diameter.

Bark: Light brown to reddish and smooth when young; when mature, separates into long, fibrous strips.

Flowers: Yellow and small; to 3/16" long; in dense, narrow, cylindrical cluster to 2" long; followed by a light greenish, tightly coiled, spiral pod to 2" long; on stalk in crowded cluster.

Leaves: Yellowish green, slightly hairy, bipinnately compound; to 3" long; 5 to 8 pairs of oblong leaflets, to 3/8" long, 1/8" wide.

Blooms: May–August.

Elevation: Below 4,000'.

Habitat: Flood plains and bottomlands along rivers.

Comments: Deciduous. Branches are twisted and spiny. Pods used by Native Americans for meal and also eaten by desert animals. Wood used for fence posts and fuel. Four species of *Prosopis* (pro-SOAP-iss) in Arizona, with several varieties. Photograph taken in vicinity of Scottsdale, August 25.

VELVET MESQUITE (mess-KEET)   90

Common mesquite, algaroba

Prosopis velutina

Pea Family (Leguminosae)

Height: A large shrub, or small tree to 30' or more.

Trunk: To 2' in diameter.

Bark: Dark brown, rough, separating into long, narrow strips.

Flowers: Greenish yellow, small and fragrant, in slender, cylindrical spikes to 4" long;

followed by narrow seed pods (brownish when mature) to 8" long.

Leaves: Yellow-green, bipinnately compound; leaflet to 1/2" long, leaf to 6" long.
Blooms: April; often again in August.
Elevation: Below 5,000'.
Habitat: Desert washes, alongside streams, and in areas where water table is reasonably high.
Comments: Deciduous shrub or tree, with straight 2" spines on branches. A legume that restores nitrogen to the soil. Roots penetrate ground to 60' in search of water. Often grows in dense thickets.

    A favorite of bees and other insects; its flowers are an excellent honey source. Ripened seed pods are eaten by livestock and wild animals; 80 percent of a coyote's diet in late summer and fall is mesquite beans. Native Americans ground a meal called *pinole* from seed pods, and used bark for basketry, fabrics, and medicine. Next to ironwood, mesquite is the best fuelwood in the desert; it burns slowly and is nearly smokeless. Used for cabinet-making; it also makes an aromatic charcoal for barbecuing.

    Along some desert rivers, such as the Verde, mesquite *bosques* (Spanish for "small forests") are still found; they provide excellent nesting sites for desert birds and habitat for mammals. Four species of *Prosopis* (pro-SOAP-iss) in Arizona. Photograph taken at Organ Pipe Cactus National Monument, April 9.

LEMON WEED   305
Lemon scurfpea
Psoralea lanceolata
Pea Family (Leguminosae)

Height: To 16".
Flowers: White with dark purple on lower lip; pealike; to 1/8" wide, 1/8" long; in dense, spikelike, terminal cluster, followed by a roundish, warty pod.
Leaves: Dark green, compound, with 3 linear segments; dotted with prominent glands; to 2" long.
Blooms: May–September.
Elevation: 5,500 to 7,500'.
Habitat: Sandy soil, clearings in pine forests, and mesas.
Comments: Perennial herb. Six species of *Psoralea* (soh-RAY-li-ah) in Arizona. Photograph taken north of St. Johns, June 28.

ROSARY BEAN   510
Rhynchosia texana (*Rhynchosia senna*)
Pea Family (Leguminosae)

Height: To 8", but mostly trailing.
Flowers: Yellow, pealike flower with sickle-shaped keel; to 1/8" wide, 1/4" long; occurring singly or in small cluster in leaf axils; followed by green, flat pea pod to 3/4" long.
Leaves: Dark green, pinnately divided into 3 elliptical segments; leaflet to 1 1/4" long, leaf to 2 1/4" long.
Blooms: May–September.
Elevation: 3,500 to 5,500'.
Habitat: Dry plains, mesas, and slopes.
Comments: Perennial herb. Ground cover, often controlling erosion. Two species of *Rhynchosia* (rin-KOH-zi-ah) in Arizona. Photograph taken at Lynx Lake, September 11.

NEW MEXICO LOCUST 97
Thorny locust, southwestern locust, rose locust, New Mexican locust
Robinia neomexicana
Pea Family (Leguminosae)

Height:	Large, spiny-branched shrub, or small tree to 25'.
Trunk:	To 8" in diameter.
Bark:	Grayish brown, smooth; becomes furrowed and scaly with age.
Flowers:	Purplish pink, pealike, fragrant; to 3/4" long; in dense, drooping clusters; followed by reddish brown, bristly haired, flat seed pod to 4 1/2" long.
Leaves:	Bluish green, pinnately compound, finely haired; to 12' long; 15 to 21 rounded leaflets, each to 1 1/2" long.
Blooms:	May–July.
Elevation:	4,000 to 8,500'.
Habitat:	Roadsides, canyons, and coniferous forests.
Comments:	At nodes, twigs have reddish brown, stout, curved, 1/2"-long, paired spines. Forms erosion-controlling thickets. Browsed by cattle and deer. Birds and small mammals eat seeds. Seeds, bark, and roots are poisonous to humans; New Mexican Indians ate flowers raw. Used medicinally by Hopi Indians. Fence posts are made from trunks. One species of *Robinia* (roh-BIH-nih-uh) in Arizona. Photograph taken at Lynx Lake, Prescott, May 27.

PINE THERMOPSIS 511
Golden pea
Thermopsis pinetorum
Pea Family (Leguminosae)

Height:	To 3'.
Flowers:	Bright yellow and pealike; to 1" long; in terminal, erect cluster; followed by long, slender pod, to 3" long.
Leaves:	Bright green, compound, with 3 broad, lance-shaped leaflets; to 4" long.
Blooms:	April–July.
Elevation:	6,000 to 9,500'.
Habitat:	Meadows and clearings in pine forests.
Comments:	Perennial herb; grows in clumps. One species of *Thermopsis* (ther-MOP-sis) in Arizona. Photograph taken near Hannagan Meadow, June 24.

TRIFOLIUM 547
Trifolium neurophyllum
Pea Family (Leguminosae)

Height:	To 2'.
Flowers:	Reddish purple and pealike; to 1/2" long; in large flowerhead to 1 3/4" long, 1 1/4" wide. Fading flowers turn downward on flowerhead.
Leaves:	Dark green above, lighter green and very hairy beneath; heavily veined; to 4 1/2" long; compound, with 3 narrowly elliptical, sharply pointed, finely toothed, stalkless leaflets to 2 1/4" long.
Blooms:	August.
Elevation:	8,000 to 8,500'.
Habitat:	Along mountain streams and in moist mountain meadows.
Comments:	More than a dozen species of *Trifolium* (trye-FOH-lih-uhm) in Arizona. Photograph taken at Luna Lake, August 5. Recognizable by large flowerheads and hairy stems.

COW CLOVER 548
Pine clover
Trifolium pinetorum
Pea Family (Leguminosae)

Height:	To 20".
Flowers:	Reddish lavender with whitish tips; pealike; to 1/8" wide, 1/2" long; flowerhead to 1 1/4" wide, has jagged-edged collar.
Leaves:	Dark green, toothed, narrowly elliptical; 2 1/2" long; compound, with leaflets usually in threes, to 1 1/4" long.
Blooms:	June–October.
Elevation:	6,500 to 9,000'.
Habitat:	Moist soil, streambanks, and wet meadows in coniferous forests.
Comments:	More than a dozen species of *Trifolium* (trye-FOH-lih-uhm) in Arizona. Photograph taken at Luna Lake, June 29.

RED CLOVER 748
Trifolium pratense
Pea Family (Leguminosae)

Height:	To 2'.
Flowers:	Deep pink to pink, pealike; 1/2" long; with 3 striped, bractlike stipules below each flowerhead; ball-shaped flowerhead, to 1 1/2" wide.
Leaves:	Dark green, hairy; to 4" wide; compound, with 3 oblong leaflets with lighter central chevron; leaflet to 2 1/2" long.
Blooms:	Summer.
Elevation:	Not available. Photograph taken at about 7,500'.
Habitat:	Roadsides, fields, and disturbed soil.
Comments:	Introduced from Europe, now naturalized in the U.S. Frequented by butterflies and bumblebees. More than a dozen species of *Trifolium* (trye-FOH-lih-uhm) in Arizona. Photograph taken at Forest Lakes, September 29.

WHITE CLOVER 306
White lawn clover
Trifolium repens
Pea Family (Leguminosae)

Height:	Creeper with flower stalks to 1' high.
Flowers:	White to pinkish, pealike; to 1/8" wide, 3/8" long; clustered in round flowerhead to 3/4" wide on leafless stem.
Leaves:	Dark green, finely toothed, to 1" wide; compound, with 3 oval, notched leaflets, each with a yellowish-green semicircle near the base.
Blooms:	April–October.
Elevation:	Throughout U.S.
Habitat:	Meadows, lawns, fields, and roadsides.
Comments:	Introduced from Europe. More than a dozen species of *Trifolium* (trye-FOH-lih-uhm) in Arizona. Photograph taken near Willow Springs Lake, September 14.

WHITETOP CLOVER 749
Trifolium variegatum
Pea Family (Leguminosae)

Height:	To 16".

Flowers:	Red-purple with white to pinkish tips; pealike; to 5/16" long; in roundish flowerhead of 2 to 10 or more flowers. Calyx lobes just below flowerhead are triangular; each has a sharp spine.
Leaves:	Dark green, with 3 narrow, oblong leaflets with saw-toothed margins; leaflets to 2" long.
Blooms:	April–July.
Elevation:	Not available. Photograph taken at 4,000'.
Habitat:	Areas with moist soil and wet canyons.
Comments:	More than a dozen species of *Trifolium* (trye-FOH-lih-uhm) in Arizona. Photograph taken north of Superior, April 20.

AMERICAN VETCH   660
Purple vetch
Vicia americana
Pea Family (Leguminosae)

Height:	A climber to 4'.
Flowers:	Pinkish to bluish purple; pealike; to 1 1/4" long, 4 to 9 in loose cluster on stalk in leaf axil; followed by pealike pod.
Leaves:	Green, pinnately compound, with 8 to 12 elliptical leaflets, each to 1 1/2" long. Leaf shape is variable.
Blooms:	May–September.
Elevation:	5,000 to 10,000'.
Habitat:	Clearings in ponderosa and mixed conifer forests.
Comments:	Perennial herb. Clings to other plants with its coiling tendrils. Six species of *Vicia* (VISS-i-ah) in Arizona. Photograph taken near Willow Springs Lake, June 11. A variety of **AMERICAN VETCH** (*Vicia americana* var. *linearis*) has very narrow leaflets to 1 1/4" long with the edges rolled under. Photograph (**PLATE 661**) taken at Luna Lake, August 5.

SWEET-CLOVER VETCH   307
Showy vetch
Vicia pulchella
Pea Family (Leguminosae)

Height:	Climbing or trailing to 3'.
Flowers:	White and pealike; to 1/4" long, 1/8" wide; in crowded, narrow raceme with flowers pointed downward, all facing in one direction. Raceme, to 5" long, bearing up to 20 flowers, followed by a flattened pod to 1 1/4" long.
Leaves:	Dark bluish green, pinnate; to 5" long; ending in a tendril; stipule at leaf base; up to 18 linear to oblong leaflets, each to 3/4" long.
Blooms:	July–September.
Elevation:	6,000 to 8,500'.
Habitat:	Ponderosa pine forests.
Comments:	Grooved, weak stems. Often a tangled mass. Six species of *Vicia* (VISS-i-ah) in Arizona. Photograph taken in vicinity of McNary, July 13.

RATANY FAMILY

Krameriaceae (kra-mee-ri-AY-see-ee)

Represented in Arizona by low shrubs.

Flowers: Irregular; 5 petals: upper 3 long-clawed; other 2 reduced and glandlike; 3 or 4 stamens; 1 pistil.

Fruit: Roundish, spiny.

Leaves: Alternate, simple.

WHITE RATANY   550A and B

Chacate

Krameria grayi

Ratany Family (Krameriaceae)

Height: Shrub to 2'.

Flowers: Reddish, very irregular, with 5 petals: 3 long, upper petals and 2 lower petals like lobes or oil glands; to 1/2" wide. Followed by small, round, burlike seed pod with 3 or 4 barbs at tip of each spine.

Leaves: Gray, finely haired, narrow; to 1/2" long.

Blooms: April–October.

Elevation: 500 to 4,000'.

Habitat: Dry desert foothills and mesas.

Comments: Partly parasitic on roots of such plants as creosote and bursage. More common than range ratany in the desert. Browsed by cattle and wildlife. Native Americans used powdered roots for treating sores. Three species of *Krameria* (kra-MEE-ri-ah) in Arizona. Photographs taken at Saguaro Lake, October 18. Unlike **RANGE RATANY** (*Krameria parvifolia*), its barbs occur only on the tips of spines of fruit.

CRAMERIA   549

Three fans, prostrate ratany, prairie-bur

Krameria lanceolata

Ratany Family (Krameriaceae)

Height: Trailing stems to 2' long.

Flowers: Dark, wine-colored red petals: 4 pointed upper petals, 1 larger, pointed lower petal curved forward. Three greenish, fan-shaped stigma lobes with reddish tips; flower to 3/4" long, 3/4" wide; followed by a round, spiny fruit to 5/16" in diameter.

Leaves: Grayish green, hairy, alternate; narrow and lance-shaped, elliptical or linear, to 1" long.

Blooms: May–August.

Elevation: 2,500 to 5,000'.

Habitat: Sandy slopes and dry, open plains.

Comments: Perennial herb. Spiny fruit can penetrate bare skin if stepped on. Three species of *Krameria* (kra-MEE-ri-ah) in Arizona. Photograph taken in vicinity of Fort Bowie, May 8.

RANGE RATANY   662

Chacate

Krameria parvifolia

Ratany Family (Krameriaceae)

Height: Shrub to 1 1/2'.

Flowers:	Pinkish, with 5 petals: 3 orangish, upper petals, 2 petals like lobes or oil glands; to 3/4" wide; followed by small, roundish, burlike seed pod with barbs along length of spines.
Leaves:	Small, grayish, alternate, and narrow; to 1/2" long.
Blooms:	April–October.
Elevation:	Below 5,000'.
Habitat:	Dry plains and mesas.
Comments:	Perennial; sprawling, many-branched, low shrub. Partly parasitic to other plants, absorbing water through their roots. Certain species of bees scrape oil glands for oil to bring to their eggs as food for the future offspring. Native Americans used twigs medicinally and made dyes from roots. Three species of *Krameria* (kra-MEE-ri-ah) in Arizona. Photograph taken at Coronado National Memorial, April 18. Distinguished from **WHITE RATANY** (*Krameria grayi*) by barbs along entire length of fruit spines.

GERANIUM FAMILY

Geraniaceae (ger-ray-nee-AY-see-ee)
Represented in Arizona by herbs.

Flowers:	Generally regular; usually with 5 separate petals; 5 sepals; 2 or 3 times as many stamens as petals; elongated style. Superior ovary, 3- to 5-celled.
Fruit:	Dry, 1-seeded pod.
Leaves:	Alternate, opposite, or basal; mostly simple, variously lobed.

FILAREE   593

Heron-bill, alfilaria, clocks, redstem stork's bill, pin-clover
Erodium cicutarium
Geranium Family (Geraniaceae)

Height:	To 15".
Flowers:	Pinkish violet, with 5 petals; to 1/4" wide; in loose cluster; followed by fruit with stiff, awl-shaped projection.
Leaves:	Dark green, mainly fernlike; forming basal rosette; to 4" long.
Blooms:	February–July.
Elevation:	Below 7,000'.
Habitat:	Desert flats, plains, mesas, and hillsides.
Comments:	Annual. Native to southern Europe, but introduced to this country by early Spanish settlers and now naturalized in the Southwest. Ripening seed pod (to 2" long) resembles a heron's beak, but when mature and dry it twists into a spiral. When moisture is available again, pod untwists, pushing point of seed pod into soil. Seeds are stored by harvester ants; foliage serves as forage for livestock. Three species of *Erodium* (eh-ROH-dee-uhm) in Arizona. Photograph taken in Superstition Mountains, February 4.

WILD GERANIUM   594

Cranesbill, purple geranium, James geranium, patita de leon
Geranium caespitosum
Geranium Family (Geraniaceae)

Height:	To 1 1/2'.
Flowers:	Deep reddish pink, with whitish streaks (occasionally all white); 5 petals flared

backward; partly hairy; to 1/2" wide.

Leaves:	Green, with 5 deeply cut lobes; both surfaces covered with soft hairs; to 1 1/2" wide.
Blooms:	May–September.
Elevation:	5,000 to 9,000'.
Habitat:	Rich soil in pine forests.
Comments:	Perennial herb. Seed pod looks like crane's bill; leaf looks like lion's paw (hence, *patita de leon*). Good forage for sheep. Eight species of *Geranium* (ger-RAY-ni-um) in Arizona. Photograph taken near Greer, July 20.

CAROLINA GERANIUM 595

Carolina cranesbill
Geranium carolinianum
Geranium Family (Geraniaceae)

Height:	To 16".
Flowers:	Pale pink, with 5 petals barely extending beyond the sepals; to 1/4" wide.
Leaves:	Grayish green, with 5 or 7 segments; divisions are cleft into narrowly oblong lobes; to 1 1/4" wide.
Blooms:	End of March–May.
Elevation:	2,000 to 5,500'.
Habitat:	Desert washes, slopes, and mesas.
Comments:	Pinkish stems. Eight species of *Geranium* (ger-RAY-ni-um) in Arizona. Photograph taken in Superstition Mountains, March 26.

RICHARDSON'S GERANIUM 193

Cranesbill, white geranium, white cranesbill
Geranium richardsonii
Geranium Family (Geraniaceae)

Height:	To 1 1/2'.
Flowers:	White to pale pink, with purplish veins; 5-petaled; to 1" wide.
Leaves:	Dark green, thin, palmately cleft into 5 to 7 main segments; on long stalks; to 4" wide.
Blooms:	April–October.
Elevation:	6,500 to 11,500'.
Habitat:	Moist soil of ponderosa pine and mixed conifer forests.
Comments:	Perennial herb. Often hybridizes with other species. "Cranesbill" refers to its long, beaklike seed capsule. Eight species of *Geranium* (ger-RAY-ni-um) in Arizona. Photograph taken in Greer area, June 20.

OXALIS FAMILY

Oxalidaceae (ox-al-i-DAY-see-ee)
Herbs.

Flowers:	Regular, 5 petals, 5 sepals, 10 stamens, 5 styles. Superior ovary, 5-celled.
Fruit:	Capsule seed pod.
Leaves:	Alternate, compound; often divided into 3 heart-shaped leaflets.

CREEPING WOOD SORREL   348
Little yellow sorrel, sour clover, wood shamrock, sheep sour
Oxalis corniculata
Oxalis Family (Oxalidaceae)
Height: Creeping stems to 8" long.
Flowers: Golden yellow, with 5 petals; to 1/2" wide; in cluster of 1 to 5 on slender stalk from
              leaf axil; followed by yellowish green, cylindrical, 5-angled, pointed, 1"-long seed
              pod.
Leaves: Dark green (sometimes tinged with purple); palmately compound with 3 notched
              leaflets; to 1" wide; folding together at night.
Blooms: February–November.
Elevation: 100 to 8,000'.
Habitat: Lawns, gardens, and fields.
Comments: Common garden weed; originated in Europe, now naturalized in the U.S. Roots at
              joints. Mature seed pods burst open, throwing seeds in all directions. Eight species
              of *Oxalis* (OX-ah-liss or ock-SAL-iss) in Arizona. Photograph taken at Chiricahua
              National Monument, April 24.

WOOD SORREL   596
Oxalis decaphylla (*Oxalis grayi*)
Oxalis Family (Oxalidaceae)
Height: To 5".
Flowers: Pink, with yellow throat, 5 petals; funnel-shaped; to 1/2" long, on leafless stem.
Leaves: Dark green, wedge-shaped, each is V-notched at tip; in umbrellalike arrangement; to
              1 3/4" wide.
Blooms: June–August.
Elevation: 5,000 to 9,500'.
Habitat: Clearings in pine and mixed coniferous forests.
Comments: Perennial herb. Eight species of *Oxalis* (OX-ah-lis or ock-SAL-iss) in Arizona.
              Photograph taken near Greer, June 22.

FLAX FAMILY
Linaceae (ly-NAY-see-ee)
Represented in Arizona by herbs.
Flowers: Regular, with 4 or 5 petals, 4 or 5 sepals; usually 4 or 5 stamens, 1 pistil, 2 to 5
              styles. Superior ovary, 2- to 5-celled.
Fruit: 4- to 10-valved capsule.
Leaves: Usually alternate, rarely opposite or whorled; simple.

WESTERN BLUE FLAX   687
Lewis flax, prairie flax
Linum lewisii
Flax Family (Linaceae)
Height: To 3'.
Flowers: Sky blue, often nearly white, with 5 petals; to 2" wide, in loose, terminal cluster.
Leaves: Grayish green, long, narrow, sharp-pointed; to 1" long; crowded along stem.
Blooms: April–September.
Elevation: 3,500 to 9,500'.

Habitat: Roadsides, clearings in ponderosa pine forests, and open mesas.
Comments: Perennial herb. Petals usually drop by noon. Fiber is used by Native Americans for
             cord, fishing nets, mats, and baskets. Cultivated flax is used to make linen; seeds are
             crushed to produce linseed oil. Six species of *Linum* (LY-num) in Arizona. Photo-
             graph taken on Mount Lemmon, April 30.

NEW MEXICAN YELLOW FLAX   353
Linum neomexicanum
Flax Family (Linaceae)
Height: To 2'.
Flowers: Yellow and starlike, with 5 petals; to 1/2" wide. Many grow on elongated flower
             stems to 1 1/2" long.
Leaves: Dark green, narrow; to 1/2" long; pointed upward, hugging stem; all along upward-
             pointing branches.
Blooms: June–September.
Elevation: 4,500 to 9,000'.
Habitat: Pine forests.
Comments: Six species of *Linum* (LY-num) in Arizona. Photograph taken in vicinity of Woods
             Canyon Lake, August 3.

PLAINS FLAX   532
Yellow flax
Linum puberulum
Flax Family (Linaceae)
Height: To 15".
Flowers: Orangish with reddish and white inner rings, 5 petals; to 2" wide.
Leaves: Grayish green, wiry, and very narrow; to 1" long; at intervals along the stem.
Blooms: April–October.
Elevation: 2,000 to 6,500'.
Habitat: Desert and mesas.
Comments: Six species of *Linum* (LY-num) in Arizona. Photograph taken at Tortilla Flat,
             April 1.

CALTROP FAMILY
Zygophyllaceae (zy-go-fill-LAY-see-ee)
Represented in Arizona by herbs and shrubs.
Flowers: Regular, usually 5 petals and 5 sepals; generaly 10 stamens, 1 pistil, simple style.
             Superior ovary, 2- to 12-celled.
Fruit: Usually a chambered capsule.
Leaves: Alternate or opposite; compound or pinnately dissected.

FAGONIA   597
Fagonia laevis (*Fagonia californica*)
Caltrop Family (Zygophyllaceae)
Height: To 18".
Flowers: Pinkish to lavender, 5 petals; to 1/2" wide; in leaf axils and branch ends.
Leaves: Dark green, narrow, each divided into 3 lance-shaped leaflets, each to 1/2" long.
Blooms: January–April.

Elevation:	Below 2,500'.
Habitat:	Dry, rocky slopes and mesas.
Comments:	Grows in low rounded mounds. Stems are angular and sticky. Flowers open early in day and close by early afternoon. Three species of *Fagonia* (fah-GO-ni-ah) in Arizona. Photograph taken at Cattail Cove State Park, February 24.

ARIZONA CALTROP   533

Arizona-poppy, orange caltrop, summer poppy
Kallstroemia grandiflora
Caltrop Family (Zygophyllaceae)

Height:	Sprawling to 3'.
Flowers:	Brilliant orange, crimson in center, with 5 broad, rounded petals forming bowl; deep orange stamens, hairy sepals; to 1" wide; facing upward on very hairy stems.
Leaves:	Grayish green, pinnately compound; opposite, to 2 1/2" long; oval leaflets, very hairy.
Blooms:	July–October.
Elevation:	Below 5,000'.
Habitat:	Roadsides, open plains, mesas, and desert slopes.
Comments:	Annual. Four species of *Kallstroemia* (kall-STROH-me-ah) in Arizona. Photograph taken in Phoenix area, August 16. This species distinguished from Mexican Gold Poppy (*Eschscholtzia mexicana*) mainly by 5 petals instead of 4, by its very hairy, compound leaves, and by its later blooming period.

CREOSOTE BUSH   354

Hediondilla, little stinker, gobernadora
Larrea tridentata (*Larrea divaricata*)
Caltrop Family (Zygophyllaceae)

Height:	Many-branched shrub to 10'.
Flowers:	Yellow, solitary, 5-petaled; to 1" in diameter; followed by a globe-shaped, fuzzy, white, dry capsule, to 1/4" in diameter.
Leaves:	Dark green to yellowish green, waxy, and strong-scented; resinous, 2 leaflets are joined at base; to 3/8" long.
Blooms:	Periodically; peaks March–April and November–December.
Elevation:	Below 4,500'.
Habitat:	Dry plains and mesas.
Comments:	Evergreen. Certain creosote plants are thought to be oldest living plants, at over 11,000 years old. Gives off musty odor after rain. When pollinated, petals twist 90 degrees. Varnishlike coating on leaves conserves water by slowing evaporation. During extreme drought plant grows tougher, smaller leaves. Resin from branches was used by Native Americans as a glue; other parts of plant were used medicinally. One species of *Larrea* (LAR-re-ah) in Arizona. Photograph taken at Cattail Cove State Park, February 24.

PUNCTURE VINE   355

Goat's head, puncture-weed, ground bur-nut, torrito, bull-head, tackweed
Tribulus terrestris
Caltrop Family (Zygophyllaceae)

Height:	Prostrate, to 2" high, 5' long.
Flowers:	Yellow, with 5 broad petals, to 1/2" wide; followed by hard, star-shaped fruit which

separates into 5 brownish gray nutlets, each bearing a pair of 1/4"-long spines.

Leaves: Dark green, opposite, pinnately compound; to 2" long; with leaflets to 1/2" long.
Blooms: March–October.
Elevation: Below 7,000'.
Habitat: Fields, wastelands, roadsides, and desert.
Comments: Annual weed. Two-spined segment of fruit resembles goat's head with horns. Native of Mediterranean region; now naturalized in Southwest. Spines injure livestock, puncture bicycle tires, are very painful to bare feet, and become embedded in fur and fabric. One species of *Tribulus* (TRIB-you-luss) in Arizona. Photograph taken at Saguaro Lake, October 18.

RUE FAMILY
Rutaceae (rew-TAY-see-ee)
Represented in Arizona by shrubs, small trees, and nearly herbaceous plants.

Flowers: Generally regular, with 4 or 5 petals, 4 or 5 sepals, 8 or 10 stamens (usually double the number of petals); 1 pistil. Superior ovary, 2- to 5-celled.
Fruit: Varying, depending on genus.
Leaves: Alternate or opposite, simple or compound.

NARROWLEAF HOPTREE   98
Common hoptree, three-leaved hoptree, western hoptree, shrubby trefoil, wafer-ash
Ptelea trifoliata (*Ptelea angustifolia*)
Rue Family (Rutaceae)

Height: Shrub, or small tree to 20'.
Trunk: To 8" in diameter.
Bark: Brownish gray, and smooth.
Flowers: White to yellowish green, fragrant, with 4 petals; to 1/2" wide, in cluster in leaf axils, followed by light brown, flat, roundish, winged, hoplike fruit, to 1/2" wide.
Leaves: Dark green, long-stalked; to 5 1/2" long; compound, with 3 ovate, slightly wavy-toothed leaflets, to 3" long.
Blooms: May–June.
Elevation: 3,500 to 8,500'.
Habitat: Canyons, pinyon-juniper woodlands, and ponderosa pine forests.
Comments: Deciduous. Plant parts have disagreeable odor. Fruit is used as hops substitute in brewing. One species of *Ptelea* (TEE-lee-uh) in Arizona, with many varieties. Photograph taken at Oak Creek Canyon north of Sedona, May 29.

TURPENTINE BROOM   684
Thamnosma montana
Rue Family (Rutaceae)

Height: To 4'.
Flowers: Deep blue-purple, cylinder-shaped, with 4 upright petals; to 1/2" long; followed by yellowish green, double, pea-sized, saclike fruit with gland-dotted skin.
Leaves: (When present) yellowish green, linear to spatula-shaped, sparse, short-lived.
Blooms: February–April.
Elevation: Below 4,500'.
Habitat: Desert slopes and mesas.
Comments: Yellowish green, shrubby plant, which conducts photosynthesis in its stems.

Aromatic glands on fruits yield an oily skin irritant. Crushed stems give off strong, citruslike odor. Native Americans used plant medicinally. Two species of *Thamnosma* (tham-NOS-mah) in Arizona. Photograph taken in Superstition Mountains, February 4.

SIMAROUBA FAMILY
Simaroubaceae (sy-mar-roo-BAY-see-ee)
Represented in Arizona by a tree and a shrub.

Flowers:	Generally small, with 3- to 8-lobed calyx; either 3 to 8 petals or petalless; 2 to 5 simple pistils.
Fruit:	Winged or drupelike.
Leaves:	Alternate, pinnately compound; or reduced to deciduous scales.

AILANTHUS   99
Tree of heaven, stinkweed, copal tree
Ailanthus altissima
Simarouba Family (Simaroubaceae)

Height:	To 80'.
Trunk:	To 2' in diameter.
Bark:	Dark gray, thin, rough.
Flowers:	Yellowish green; to 1/4" long; in large, dense, terminal cluster, to 10" long; followed by a reddish brown, twisted, winged fruit, to 1 1/2" long; in very large, dense cluster. Male and female flowers on separate trees.
Leaves:	Dark green, pinnately compound; to 2' long, with 6 to 12 pairs of broadly lance-shaped, pointed leaflets, to 5" long, 2" wide, toothed at base.
Blooms:	Spring.
Elevation:	Not available. Photograph taken at 3,300'.
Habitat:	Roadsides and wastelands.
Comments:	Deciduous; native of China. Escapes from cultivation in the Southwest. Spreads from seeds and root suckers. Clusters of seeds hang on tree most of winter. Flowers of male trees have objectionable odor. One species of *Ailanthus* (aye-LAN-thus) in Arizona. Photograph taken at Dead Horse Ranch State Park, September 9.

CRUCIFIXION THORN   834
Castela, corona-de-Cristo, rosario
Castela emoryi (*Holacantha emoryi*)
Simarouba Family (Simaroubaceae)

Height:	Small tree, or large shrub to 12'.
Flowers:	Yellowish green, hairy, with 4 to 8 petals; yellow stamens, pinkish buds; to 3/8" wide; occurring singly or in small cluster. Male and female flowers on separate plants; female flowers followed by a ring composed of 5 to 10 flattened, 1-seeded segments, to 1/4" long, persisting for years on plant.
Leaves:	Usually leafless; when present, very small or scalelike.
Blooms:	June–July.
Elevation:	500 to 2,000'.
Habitat:	Desert plains.
Comments:	Grayish green, smooth, rigid twigs, up to 8" long and about 1/4" in diameter, are

tipped with sharp spines. One species of *Castela* (KASS-tel-ah or kas-TELL-ah) in Arizona. Photograph in flower taken at Desert Botanical Garden, Phoenix, May 27. Plant native mostly to the southwestern part of Arizona and elsewhere in state.

TORCH WOOD FAMILY

Burseraceae (bur-ser-AY-see-ee)
Represented in Arizona by 2 species of shrubs or small trees.

Flowers:	Regular, tiny, with 3 to 5 petals, 3 to 5 calyx lobes, 6 to 10 stamens, 1 pistil. Ovary 3-celled.
Fruit:	Drupelike.
Leaves:	Alternate, pinnately compound.

ELEPHANT TREE   100

Torote, elephant bursera, copal, small-leaf elephant tree
Bursera microphylla
Torch Wood Family (Burseraceae)

Height:	To 20'.
Trunk:	To 1' in diameter.
Bark:	Whitish to gray, papery, peeling.
Flowers:	Whitish, less than 1/4" long; followed by red, 3-angled, 1/4"-long, very aromatic fruit.
Leaves:	Green, pinnately compound, aromatic; to 2" long; with 10 to 30 narrow leaflets each to 1/4" long.
Blooms:	July.
Elevation:	1,000 to 2,500'.
Habitat:	Rocky slopes of arid desert mountains.
Comments:	Very stout tree whose tapering branches resemble an elephant's trunk and legs. Branches are very sensitive to frost, but roots will produce new growth. Leaves produce *copal*, a resin once used as incense. Two species of *Bursera* (BUR-ser-ah) in Arizona. Photograph taken at Organ Pipe Cactus National Monument, October 23.

MALPIGHIA FAMILY

Malpighiaceae (mal-pig-i-AY-see-ee)
Represented in Arizona by woody vines.

Flowers:	Small, 5-petaled; with 5 sepals, 10 stamens, 3 styles. Superior ovary.
Fruit:	3 nutlike segments, sometimes winged.
Leaves:	Opposite, simple.

JANUSIA   356

Janusia gracilis
Malpighia Family (Malpighiaceae)

Height:	Twining, tangled vine climbing over cacti and trees up to 6', vine to 9' long horizontally.
Flowers:	Yellow, with 5 spoon-shaped petals; to 1/2" wide; occurring singly or in small cluster; followed by a 2- or 3-winged, reddish fruit similar to maple samara.
Leaves:	Grayish green, narrow, very hairy above and beneath; opposite, linear; to

1 1/4" long.

Blooms: April–October.
Elevation: 1,000 to 5,000'.
Habitat: Washes; dry, rocky slopes; and desert flats.
Comments: Very slender stems. One species of *Janusia* (jan-OO-see-ah) in Arizona. Photograph taken at Saguaro National Monument West, April 16.

MILKWORT FAMILY

Polygalaceae (pol-lig-a-LAY-see-ee)
Represented in Arizona by herbs and slightly shrubby plants.

Flowers: Irregular; 3 petals, often united at base; 5 sepals, sometimes united and colored; 6 to 8 stamens; 1 style with 1 to 4 stigmas. Superior ovary, mostly 1-celled.
Fruit: Mostly a flat, 1- or 2-celled capsule.
Leaves: Alternate, opposite, or whorled, simple.

WHITE MILKWORT   308

Polygala alba
Milkwort Family (Polygalaceae)

Height: To 14".
Flowers: White with greenish tinge at base; 3 petals; 5 sepals, 2 larger ones colored white like petals; to 1/8" long; in dense, narrow spike to 3" long; on top of slender stem.
Leaves: Dark green, linear, very narrow; in whorls at base, at intervals along upper stem; to 1 1/4" long.
Blooms: May–September.
Elevation: 5,000 to 7,500'.
Habitat: Roadsides and fields.
Comments: Does not produce a milky sap. It was once believed that if cattle ate the plant their milk production increased. Sixteen species of *Polygala* (pol-LIG-a-lah) in Arizona. Photograph taken at Heber, August 4.

SPURGE FAMILY

Euphorbiaceae (you-for-bi-AY-see-ee)
Represented in Arizona by herbs, shrubs, and trees.

Flowers: Usually small and inconspicuous, but bracts around and beneath them are often colorful. Flowers with or without petals or sepals; 1 stamen or many. Superior ovary, usually 3-celled.
Fruit: Mainly 3-lobed capsule.
Leaves: Alternate, opposite or whorled; simple or compound.

RATTLESNAKE WEED   283

White margin spurge
Euphorbia albomarginata
Spurge Family (Euphorbiaceae)

Height: Creeper, 1/2" high, with stems to 10" long.
Flowers: Tiny, white, flowerlike cups, to 1/8" wide; lacking sepals and petals; maroon pad at base of each cup, containing many simple flowers.
Leaves: Green, round or oblong; smooth, often edged with white; to 3/8" long.

Blooms:	February–October.
Elevation:	1,000 to 6,000'.
Habitat:	Open areas in grasslands, disturbed areas, roadsides, pinyon-juniper woodlands, and clearings in ponderosa forests.
Comments:	Perennial herb. New plants started when roots form at stem joints. Also reproduces by seed. Its milky sap may irritate skin on contact. At one time people believed plant to be an important snakebite remedy. More than 3 dozen species of *Euphorbia* (you-FOR-bi-ah) in Arizona. Photograph taken at Pine, September 2.

DESERT POINSETTIA   803
Threaded spurge
Euphorbia eriantha
Spurge Family (Euphorbiaceae)

Height:	To 15".
Flowers:	Greenish, tiny, clustered in center of floral leaves.
Leaves:	Bronze-green, slender; to 3" long; issue from stem. Threadlike floral leaves emerge from flower cluster.
Blooms:	February–October.
Elevation:	300 to 3,500'.
Habitat:	Dry desert areas in the shelter of small shrubs.
Comments:	Produces a milky sap. More than 3 dozen species of *Euphorbia* (you-FOR-bi-ah) in Arizona. Photograph taken at Usery Mountain Recreation Area, February 14.

EUPHORBIA   493
Euphorbia lurida
Spurge Family (Euphorbiaceae)

Height:	To 3'; usually shorter.
Flowers:	Yellowish bracts, petalless, male and female flowers occur together in a tiny cup formed by joined bracts; to 1/16" wide.
Leaves:	Light green, fleshy, numerous; wider than long, to 3/8" wide, 1/4" long.
Blooms:	April–August.
Elevation:	3,500 to 7,500'.
Habitat:	Roadsides, fields, and clearings.
Comments:	Stems have milky juice. More than 3 dozen species of *Euphorbia* (you-FOR-bi-ah) in Arizona. Photograph taken northeast of Superior, April 3.

LIMBER BUSH   835
Sangre-de-drago ("dragon's blood")
Jatropha cuneata
Spurge Family (Euphorbiaceae)

Height:	To 6'.
Flowers:	Pale yellowish; with deep yellow stamens; tubular, 5-lobed, narrow bell with rim curved backward; to 1/4" long, 1/8" wide; cluster at tips or on sides of branches.
Leaves:	Dark green, thick, fleshy, smooth; alternate, oval, with pointed base; creased down middle; to 3/4" long; in small clusters on branches. Usually leafless until after the summer rains.
Blooms:	July–August.
Elevation:	1,000 to 2,000'.
Habitat:	Dry mesas, plains, and slopes in southwestern Arizona.

Comments: Smooth, pliable branches give plant its common name. Fleshy stems and leaves store water for drought periods. Pinkish stems. Tannin in roots was once used for tanning hides. Reddish sap in roots was used to produce dye and medicine. Three percent rubber can be extracted from dry stems. Four species of *Jatropha* (JAT-row-fah) in Arizona. Photograph taken at Organ Pipe Cactus National Monument, August 25.

BOX FAMILY
Buxaceae (bucks-AY-see-ee)
Represented in Arizona by a shrub.

Flowers: Of 1 sex, petalless; with 4 to 6 sepals, 10 to 12 stamens, 3 styles. Superior ovary, 3-celled.
Fruit: Large, acorn-shaped capsule.
Leaves: Opposite, simple, thick, leathery.

JOJOBA (ho-HOH-ba)   836A and B
Coffee-bush, gray box bush, goatnut, deernut, wild-hazel, quinine-plant, coffeeberry
Simmondsia chinensis
Box Family (Buxaceae)

Height: Shrub to 7'.
Flowers: Greenish yellow, tiny; male and female flowers on separate plants; male (staminate) in dense cluster producing much pollen; female (pistillate) to 1/2" long; followed by a green, hard-shelled, acornlike capsule, to 1" long, turning tan at maturity.
Leaves: Grayish green, leathery, thick, and elliptical, to 1 1/2" long.
Blooms: December–July; extremely variable.
Elevation: 1,000 to 5,000'.
Habitat: Along washes, on alluvial fans, and dry, rocky slopes.
Comments: Evergreen. Browsed by deer and bighorn sheep; rodents eat seeds. Native Americans and pioneers used seeds as food and as substitute for coffee; their bitter taste improved with roasting. Waxy oil from seeds used commercially in medicines and cosmetics. One species of *Simmondsia* (sim-MOND-si-ah) in Arizona. Photographs taken in Mesa: of flowers, January 31; of plant with ripened fruit, September 10.

CASHEW-SUMAC (SOO-mack) FAMILY
Anacardiaceae (a-nuh-kar-dih-AY-see-ee)
Represented in Arizona by shrubs.

Flowers: Regular, small, with generally 5 petals, 5 sepals, 5 stamens, 1 pistil. Superior ovary, 1-celled.
Fruit: Small, 1-seeded drupe.
Leaves: Alternate; simple or compound.

MEARNS SUMAC   837
New Mexican evergreen sumac
Rhus choriophylla
Cashew or Sumac Family (Anacardiaceae)

Height: To 7'.
Flowers: White, oval; to 1/8" long, 1/16" wide; in cluster to 2" long, 2" wide; followed by

reddish to brown, hairy fruit, to 1/4" long.

Leaves: Dark green, shiny, evergreen, leathery; to 4" long; pinnately compound with 3 to 5 oval leaflets, reddish purple stems, leaflets to 2 1/2" long, 1 1/4" wide.

Blooms: July–September.

Elevation: 4,000 to 6,000' in southeastern Arizona.

Habitat: Rocky slopes and canyons.

Comments: Seven species of *Rhus* (RUSS) in Arizona. Photograph taken at Chiricahua National Monument, April 25.

SMOOTH SUMAC   101A and B

Common sumac, scarlet sumac
Rhus glabra
Cashew or Sumac Family (Anacardiaceae)

Height: To 20'.

Trunk: To 4" in diameter.

Bark: Brown; smooth or scaly.

Flowers: Whitish, 5 petals; to 1/8" wide; in dense, spikelike terminal cluster to 8" long; sexes usually on separate plants; followed by dark red, round fruit covered with short, sticky, red hairs; 1/8" in diameter; in upright, terminal cluster when mature.

Leaves: Shiny green above, creamy beneath; turning bright red in fall; pinnately compound; to 12" long; up to 31 lance-shaped, toothed leaflets, each to 4" long.

Blooms: June–August.

Elevation: 5,000 to 7,000'.

Habitat: Roadsides and rich soil in ponderosa pine forests.

Comments: Birds feed on fruits; fruits and twigs browsed by deer. If chewed, fruit quenches thirst; a lemonadelike drink is made from fruit. Seven species of *Rhus* (RUSS) in Arizona. Flower photograph taken in Oak Creek Canyon, June 18. Photograph in fruit taken in vicinity of Christopher Creek, August 11.

DESERT SUMAC   220A and B

Little leaf desert sumac
Rhus microphylla
Cashew or Sumac Family (Anacardiaceae)

Height: To 6'.

Flowers: Whitish, 5-petaled, with pinkish center; to 1/16" wide; in dense, roundish cluster to 1/4" wide; followed by egg-shaped, sticky, hairy, reddish fruit, to 1/4" long, in cluster.

Leaves: Green, pinnate, with 5 to 9 leaflets; hairy, winged leaflet stem; to 1 3/4" long (in shady locations) but closer to 3/4" in sunny locations, in clusters along stems.

Blooms: March–May.

Elevation: 3,500 to 6,000'.

Habitat: Dry slopes and mesas.

Comments: Sprawling, many-branched shrub with spine-tipped branches. Seven species of *Rhus* (RUSS) in Arizona. Photographs taken in Portal area: in flower, April 22; and in fruit, May 5.

SUGAR SUMAC   45

Chaparral sumac, sugarbush, mountain-laurel
Rhus ovata

Cashew or Sumac Family (Anacardiaceae)

Height:	Shrub, or small tree to 15'.
Trunk:	To 5" in diameter.
Bark:	Grayish brown, shaggy, rough, scaly.
Flowers:	Pinkish buds turning to cream color; 5 rounded petals; to 1/4" wide; in crowded, terminal cluster to 2" long, followed by reddish, hairy fruits to 1/8" in diameter.
Leaves:	Light green, shiny, thick, leatherlike; pinkish leaf stalk; oval, short-pointed at tip, rounded at base, curved upward at midvein; to 3 1/4" long.
Blooms:	February–March.
Elevation:	3,000 to 5,000'.
Habitat:	Mountain slopes in chaparral and in desert canyons.
Comments:	Broadleaf evergreen. Fruit used by Native Americans as a sweetener. Seven species of *Rhus* (RUSS) in Arizona. Photograph taken in Superstition Mountains, March 25.

POISON IVY   838

Poison oak, hiedra, mala
Rhus radicans var. *rydbergii*
Cashew or Sumac Family (Anacardiaceae)

Height:	An erect shrub to 2', or an ascending vine with aerial roots.
Flowers:	Greenish white; 1/4" wide; in loose clusters to 3" long at lower leaf axils; followed by cluster of yellowish white, 1/4" berrylike fruits.
Leaves:	Dark green, compound, divided into 3 leaflets; usually shiny; oblong to lance-shaped to oval; notched or toothed; to 4" long. Immature leaves have red tinge.
Blooms:	April–September.
Elevation:	3,000 to 8,000'.
Habitat:	Rich soils in canyons, ravines, and disturbed areas.
Comments:	Leaves turn reddish orange in fall. All parts of plant contain an oil that can cause skin eruptions. Remember: "Leaflets three, let it be." Seven species of *Rhus* (RUSS) in Arizona. Photograph taken at Oak Creek Canyon, June 9.

SKUNK BUSH   839

Squaw bush, lemonade sumac, limonita, lemonade berry, lemita, threeleaf sumac
Rhus trilobata
Cashew or Sumac Family (Anacardiaceae)

Height:	Shrub to 10'.
Flowers:	Yellow, appearing before leaves; to 3/4" wide; in dense cluster on spike; followed by cluster of sticky, bright, orange-red berries.
Leaves:	Dark green, shiny; compound with 3 oval, coarsely toothed, lobed leaflets; to 1 1/4" long.
Blooms:	March–June.
Elevation:	2,500 to 7,500'.
Habitat:	Pinyon-juniper areas, canyons, mesas, and slopes.
Comments:	Closely related to poison ivy. Leaves look like miniature poison ivy leaves and turn red in fall; emit strong odor when bruised. Berries not poisonous; small mammals and birds eat berries. Sheep, antelope, and deer browse on twigs and foliage. A lemonadelike drink is made from fruits. Native American women used stems in basket weaving. Seven species of *Rhus* (RUSS) in Arizona. Photograph taken near Nutrioso, August 3.

BITTERSWEET FAMILY

Celastraceae (see-lass-TRAY-see-ee)
Represented in Arizona by woody plants and shrubs.

Flowers:	Regular, small; 4 to 6 calyx lobes and 4 to 6 petals; as many or twice number of stamens as petals; 1 style. Superior or half inferior ovary, 2- to 5-celled.
Fruit:	Dry or fleshy, depending on genus.
Leaves:	Alternate or opposite; simple; often reduced to scales.

CANOTIA   46

Crucifixion-thorn
Canotia holacantha
Bittersweet Family (Celastraceae)

Height:	Spiny shrub, or small tree to 18'.
Trunk:	To 8" in diameter.
Bark:	Yellowish green; smooth when young, gray and rough with age.
Flowers:	Greenish white, 5 petals, 5 stamens; to 1/4" long; 3 to 5 in small cluster along branches; followed by reddish brown, egg-shaped, long-pointed, 5-valved capsule, to 1/2" long, later splitting along 10 lines.
Leaves:	Greenish, scalelike, short-lived, deciduous.
Blooms:	May–August.
Elevation:	2,000 to 4,500'.
Habitat:	Dry slopes and mesas in chaparral and desert.
Comments:	The most common of the crucifixion-thorns. Twigs are spine-tipped and form masses; very flexible when young, becoming rigid with age. Twigs and branches take the place of leaves in food manufacture. Fruit capsule persists until the following spring. One species of *Canotia* (can-OH-shah) in Arizona. Photograph taken at Sedona, June 18.

SANDPAPER BUSH   840

Mortonia scabrella
Bittersweet Family (Celastraceae)

Height:	To 4'.
Flowers:	White and small, with 5 petals; to 1/4" wide; in narrow cluster to 3" long.
Leaves:	Yellowish green, lighter green on margins; alternate; pointing upward on stems; elliptical, curved slightly inward; rough; to 3/8" wide, 1/2" long; crowded along stems in spiral arrangement, progressively smaller toward tips of branches.
Blooms:	March–September.
Elevation:	3,000 to 5,500'.
Habitat:	Mesas and dry plains.
Comments:	Many stiff, erect stems. One species of *Mortonia* (more-TOHN-i-ah) in Arizona. Photograph taken in vicinity of Tucson, November 12.

MOUNTAIN LOVER   819

Myrtle box-leaf, Oregon boxwood, mountain hedge, myrtle pachystima, mountain myrtle
Pachystima myrsinites
Bittersweet Family (Celastraceae)

Height:	Spreading shrub to 2', usually shorter.

Flowers:	Reddish brown, with 4 petals, 4 pointed sepals; to 1/8" wide; on 1/4"-long stem; 2 or 3 in cluster in leaf axils; followed by green, oval fruit to 1/8" long.
Leaves:	Dark green, shiny, thick; oval to elliptical, toothed; to 1" long.
Blooms:	May–July.
Elevation:	6,000 to 10,000'.
Habitat:	Coniferous forests in moist, shady locations.
Comments:	Prostrate evergreen ground cover. Woody at base, with brownish stems. Browsed by deer. Genus name sometimes referred to as *Paxistima*. One species of *Pachystima* (puh-KISS-tih-muh) in Arizona. Photograph taken south of Alpine, June 30.

MAPLE FAMILY

Aceraceae (ay-suh-RAY-see-ee)
Trees or large shrubs.

Flowers:	Small, either 4 or 5 petals or petalless; 4 or 5 sepals, 4 to 12 stamens, 1 pistil, 1 style with 2 stigmas. Superior ovary, 2-celled.
Fruit:	2-winged key ("samara," or seed case) united at base.
Leaves:	Opposite, single, palmately or pinnately compound.

ROCKY MOUNTAIN MAPLE   81

Dwarf maple, mountain maple, Douglas maple
Acer glabrum
Maple Family (Aceraceae)

Height:	Shrub, or small tree to 25'.
Trunk:	To 1' in diameter.
Bark:	Light brown to gray; smooth, thin.
Flowers:	Greenish yellow, small, in cluster; followed by paired, winged seed cases or "keys" to 1" long, set in narrow V. Male and female flowers usually on different trees.
Leaves:	Shiny, dark green above, lighter beneath; 3- to 5-lobed, toothed margins, red leaf stems; to 5" wide.
Blooms:	May–June.
Elevation:	5,000 to 9,000'.
Habitat:	Moist, rich soil along streams in ponderosa pine and spruce-fir forests.
Comments:	Foliage turns yellow and red in fall. Seeds eaten by rodents and foliage browsed by deer, elk, and cattle. Three species of *Acer* (AY-sur) in Arizona. Photograph taken at Woods Canyon Lake, August 3. Pointed teeth on leaf margins identify this maple.

BIGTOOTH MAPLE   82

Scrub maple, western sugar maple, canyon maple, dwarf maple
Acer grandidentatum
Maple Family (Aceraceae)

Height:	To 40'.
Trunk:	To 8" in diameter.
Bark:	Light brown to gray; smooth or scaly.
Flowers:	Yellow, 3/16" long; in drooping cluster, followed by greenish, U-shaped, paired, winged seeds or "keys" to 1 1/4" long. Male and female flowers on same tree.
Leaves:	Shiny, dark green above, lighter beneath; turning red and yellow in fall; red stems, 3 to 5 lobes, not toothed; often appearing on short stems along length of trunk; to 4" wide.

Blooms:	April.
Elevation:	4,700 to 7,000'.
Habitat:	Moist canyons, alongside streams, and in ponderosa pine forests.
Comments:	Has spreading, rounded crown. Browsed by livestock and deer. Used for fuel, and can be tapped for syrup in late winter. Three species of *Acer* (AY-sur) in Arizona. Photograph taken at Cave Creek, Portal, April 23. Toothless leaf margins identify this maple.

BOXELDER 102

Ash-leaved maple, inland boxelder, Rocky Mountain boxelder, Manitoba maple
Acer negundo
Maple Family (Aceraceae)

Height:	To 50'.
Trunk:	To 2 1/2' in diameter.
Bark:	Gray to brown, becoming deeply furrowed with age.
Flowers:	Yellowish green, 3/16" long, female flowers in hanging, terminal cluster; male flowers in flat-topped cluster; on separate trees; each followed by paired, clustered, long, V-shaped, winged seed cases ("keys") to 1 1/2" long.
Leaves:	Bright green above, lighter green and hairy beneath; thick, pinnately compound; to 6" long; 3 to 7 toothed leaflets to 4" long.
Blooms:	April–May.
Elevation:	3,500 to 8,000'.
Habitat:	Along streams, ponds, and lakes in oak woodlands and ponderosa pine forests.
Comments:	A rapid grower, but short-lived. Three species of *Acer* (AY-sur) in Arizona. Photograph taken at Oak Creek Canyon, September 9.

SOAPBERRY FAMILY

Sapindaceae (sa-pin-DAY-see-ee)
Represented in Arizona by a vine, shrub, and small tree.

Flowers:	Regular or nearly regular; 4 to 5 petals or petalless; 5 to 10 stamens; 1 style. Superior ovary, 2- to 4-celled.
Fruit:	Berrylike or dry, winged capsule.
Leaves:	Alternate, simple, or pinnately compound.

HOPBUSH 841

Switch-sorrel, akeake
Dodonaea viscosa
Soapberry Family (Sapindaceae)

Height:	Shrub to 12'.
Flowers:	Yellowish, small, without petals; in small, terminal raceme; followed by 2 to 4 creamy to pinkish, broad-winged fruits.
Leaves:	Green and oblong; to 4" long, 3/4" wide.
Blooms:	February–October.
Elevation:	2,000 to 5,000'.
Habitat:	Dry, rocky slopes and in canyons.
Comments:	Fruits used as substitute for hops. Contains saponin, a poisonous substance, used as laundry soap. One species of *Dodonaea* (do-do-NEE-ah) in Arizona. Photograph taken in Superstition Mountains, March 15.

WESTERN SOAPBERRY   103
Jaboncillo, cherioni, wild China-tree
Sapindus saponaria var. *drummondii*
Soapberry (Sapindaceae)

Height: To 50'; in Arizona, usually much shorter and often just a large-sized shrub.

Bark: Grayish brown and furrowed.

Flowers: White, with 5 round-tipped petals; to 1/4" wide; in large, branched, terminal cluster to 9" long; followed by a 1/2"-diameter, smooth fruit with a yellowish, translucent flesh.

Leaves: Light green splashed with yellow; smooth above, hairy beneath; alternate, deciduous, pinnate; 7 to 19 lance-shaped, unequal-sided leaflets; terminal leaflet smaller; toothless; leaflets to 4" long, leaf to 12" long.

Blooms: May–August.

Elevation: 2,400 to 6,000'.

Habitat: Canyon slopes, along streams, desert grasslands, and oak woodlands.

Comments: Slow grower, with hairy stems. Fruits contain saponin, a poisonous substance, and have been used as a soap for washing clothes. One species of *Sapindus* (sa-PIN-dus) in Arizona. Photograph taken in vicinity of Portal, May 5.

MELIA FAMILY
Meliaceae (mee-li-AY-see-ee)
Represented in Arizona by 1 tree species.

Flowers: Showy, with 4 to 5 united petals, 4 to 5 calyx lobes, 8 to 10 stamens, 1 pistil. Superior ovary, mostly 2- to 5-celled.

Fruit: Fleshy, single-seeded capsule.

Leaves: Alternate, compound.

CHINABERRY   104
Umbrella tree, China-tree, bead-tree, pride-of-India
Melia azedarach
Melia Family (Meliaceae)

Height: To 40'.

Trunk: To 30" in diameter, but usually less.

Bark: Dark brown to reddish brown, furrowed.

Flowers: Purplish, fragrant; to 3/4" wide; in loose cluster to 8" long; followed by round, yellowish, poisonous fruits to 1/2" in diameter, hanging on tree through winter.

Leaves: Bright green, bipinnately compound, to 2' long; with pointed, tooth-margined leaflets to 3" long.

Blooms: March–April.

Elevation: Not available. Photograph taken at 2,600'.

Habitat: Desert soils where a moderate amount of water is available.

Comments: Deciduous. Native of Southeast Asia. Escapee from home plantings. Rapid grower, but short-lived. Leaves turn golden in the fall. One species of *Melia* (MEE-li-ah) in Arizona. Photograph taken at Catalina State Park, April 15.

BUCKTHORN FAMILY

Rhamnaceae (ram-NAY-see-ee)

Represented in Arizona by shrubs and small trees.

Flowers: Regular, small, with 4 or 5 petals or petalless; 4 or 5 stamens; 4- or 5-lobed calyx. Superior or partly inferior ovary, 2- to 4-celled.

Fruit: A drupe or capsule.

Leaves: Alternate or opposite, simple.

FENDLER CEANOTHUS   221

Buckbrush, deer brier, Fendler buckbrush, deerbrush

Ceanothus fendleri

Buckthorn Family (Rhamnaceae)

Height: Spiny shrub to 6', but usually 3'.

Flowers: White to pinkish, with 5 petals, 5 stamens; to 3/16" wide, in terminal, pyramid-shaped cluster to 1 1/2" long; followed by reddish brown, dry, 3-lobed fruit, to 3/16" in diameter.

Leaves: Grayish green, somewhat thick; velvety surface, hairy beneath, prominent veins, elliptical, alternate; to 1" long.

Blooms: April–October.

Elevation: 5,000 to 10,000'.

Habitat: Pinyon-juniper woodlands and pine forests.

Comments: Forms thickets. Has gray, felty stems and straight, slender spines up to 1" long. Mature twigs are reddish brown. Browsed by deer and livestock. Foliage and stems are eaten by porcupines and rabbits. Native Americans used leaves for tea and fruits for food and medicines. Four species of *Ceanothus* (see-uh-NOH-thuss) in Arizona. Photograph taken in vicinity of Portal, April 22. This is the only species of *Ceanothus* with spines.

GREGG CEANOTHUS   222A and B

Desert ceanothus, buckbrush, mountain balm, wild lilac

Ceanothus greggii

Buckthorn Family (Rhamnaceae)

Height: To 8', but usually less.

Flowers: Whitish to pinkish, with 5 spoon-shaped, hooded petals; to 3/8" wide; in crowded cluster on branches; followed by cluster of fruit; each capsule to 3/16" in diameter.

Leaves: Shiny green above, grayish and felty beneath with a visible network; opposite, thick, leathery; to 1" long near base of shrub, in clusters along upper branches.

Blooms: March–May.

Elevation: 3,000 to 7,000'.

Habitat: Oak woodlands.

Comments: Light gray, felt-covered bark on old branches. Young wood is pinkish and felt-covered. Browsed by deer; seeds eaten by birds and small mammals. Four species of *Ceanothus* (see-uh-NOH-thuss) in Arizona. Photographs taken northeast of Superior: in flower, April 3; in fruit, April 20. Branches of this species are not spine-tipped.

DEERBRUSH 223
White lilac, California lilac, soapbush, mountain birch, white tea-tree,
Mogollon ceanothus
Ceanothus integerrimus
Buckthorn Family (Rhamnaceae)

Height: Shrub to 8'.
Flowers: White, occasionally pink or bluish, fragrant, 5-petaled; to 1/16" wide; in a spikelike flower cluster to 6" long; followed by cluster of dry, crested capsules.
Leaves: Dark green, elliptical, with 3 prominent main veins; to 1 1/2" long.
Blooms: May–October.
Elevation: 3,500 to 7,000'.
Habitat: Open woodland and chaparral.
Comments: Browsed by deer; wildlife feed on bark and seeds. Native Americans made a soapy mixture from the bark; root bark was used medicinally. Blooms are a source of honey. Four species of *Ceanothus* (see-uh-NOH-thuss) in Arizona. Photograph taken in a canyon north of Superior, April 20.

CALIFORNIA SNAKE BUSH 842
Snakewood
Colubrina californica
Buckthorn Family (Rhamnaceae)

Height: To 10'.
Flowers: Greenish or yellowish, inconspicuous; to 1/8" wide; solitary or in small cluster; followed by round, light brown, woody, 3-celled, drupelike seed capsule to 1/4" in diameter.
Leaves: Light green; finely haired, especially on margins; prominent sunken veins on upper surface; untoothed; oval, elliptical to oblong; to 1/2" long, 3/8" wide.
Blooms: June–August.
Elevation: 2,000 to 3,000'.
Habitat: Along desert washes and on dry, rocky slopes.
Comments: Young twigs are pinkish, with short hairs; older branches are light gray. Has spines at tips of branches. One species of *Colubrina* (kol-you-BRY-nah) in Arizona. Photograph taken in Kofa Mountains, March 6.

BITTER CONDALIA 47
Condalia globosa var. *pubescens*
Buckthorn Family (Rhamnaceae)

Height: Shrub, or small tree to 20'.
Trunk: To 1' in diameter.
Bark: Brownish gray, thin, fissured, shreddy.
Flowers: 5 yellowish green, pointed sepals; cup-shaped, petalless, fragrant; less than 1/8" wide; in leaf axils, followed by dark blue to blackish, juicy, bitter, berrylike fruit to 1/4" in diameter in spring, when maturing.
Leaves: Yellowish green, usually finely haired, toothless; spoon-shaped; to 1/2" long, 1/4" wide; occurring singly or in small clusters on branches.
Blooms: March or in the fall.
Elevation: 1,000 to 2,500'.
Habitat: Dry, sandy plains, along desert washes, and on rocky slopes.

Comments: Spine-tipped, many spreading branches. Four species of *Condalia* (kohn-DALE-ee-ah) in Arizona. Photograph taken at Desert Botanical Garden, Phoenix, March 23. Native to southwestern Arizona.

WARNOCK CONDALIA 843
Condalia warnockii var. kearneyana
Buckthorn Family (Rhamnaceae)

Height: To 5'.
Flowers: Tiny and petalless; solitary or in cluster; 5 stamens; followed by roundish, dark red fruit, to 1/4" in diameter.
Leaves: Dark green, alternate, spatula-shaped or elliptical; to 3/16" long, 1/16" wide; crowded together on branches.
Blooms: Spring.
Elevation: 2,500 to 4,500'.
Habitat: Sandy or gravelly slopes and mesas.
Comments: Has thorn-tipped branches. Four species of *Condalia* (kohn-DALE-ee-ah) in Arizona. Photograph taken at Catalina State Park, April 2.

BIRCHLEAF BUCKTHORN 844
Coffeeberry, ramno
Rhamnus betulaefolia
Buckthorn Family (Rhamnaceae)

Height: To 8'.
Trunk: Shrub to 4" in diameter.
Bark: Smooth, gray.
Flowers: Greenish, with 5 joined, pointed lobes; slightly hairy; to 1/8" wide; in clusters in leaf axils; followed by shiny, blackish purple fruits (in the fall); to 3/8" in diameter.
Leaves: Deciduous; bright green and shiny above, lighter green and very finely haired beneath; broadly oblong to egg-shaped; prominent veins beneath are reddish pink; blunt or short-pointed at tip; very finely toothed or not toothed; thin, edges not rolled under; to 4" long.
Blooms: May–June.
Elevation: 3,500 to 7,500'.
Habitat: Canyons, along streams in oak woodlands, and ponderosa pine forests.
Comments: Non-thorny, with reddish brown stems. (Older stems are dark red.) Leaves resemble birch leaves. Native Americans chewed inner bark as a medicine and ate the fruits. Fruits eaten by wildlife; foliage and twigs browsed by deer and other wildlife. Four species of *Rhamnus* (RAM-nuss) in Arizona. Photograph taken at Oak Creek Canyon, May 29. A similar species, **CALIFORNIA BUCKTHORN** (*Rhamnus californica*), has thicker, narrower, evergreen leaves, which are slightly rolled under on margins.

CALIFORNIA BUCKTHORN 845
Pigeonberry, coffeeberry
Rhamnus californica
Buckthorn Family (Rhamnaceae)

Height: To 20', but commonly to 10'.
Trunk: To 6" in diameter, generally less.
Bark: Pinkish when young, gray and smooth with age.

Flowers:	Greenish, with 5 joined, pointed lobes; slightly hairy; to 1/8" wide; in clusters in leaf axils; followed by shiny, juicy berries to 3/8" in diameter; in small cluster; changing from green to red to black in fall.
Leaves:	Dull green above, paler green and hairy beneath; elliptical to oval, short-pointed at tips; evergreen, very finely toothed; thick and leathery; prominent veins beneath; edges slightly rolled under; to 3" long; on pinkish stem.
Blooms:	May–June.
Elevation:	3,500 to 6,500'.
Habitat:	Canyons, ponderosa pine forests, and mountainsides.
Comments:	Birds, bears, and deer feed on fruits. Four species of *Rhamnus* (RAM-nuss) in Arizona. Photograph taken near Christopher Creek, September 27. A similar species, **BIRCHLEAF BUCKTHORN** (*Rhamnus betulaefolia*), has thinner, wider, deciduous leaves, which are not rolled under on margins.

HOLLYLEAF BUCKTHORN   846A and B
Hollyleaf redberry buckthorn
Rhamnus crocea
Buckthorn Family (Rhamnaceae)

Height:	Shrub, or small tree to 15'.
Bark:	Dark gray, rough, fissured.
Flowers:	Yellowish green, with 5 joined, pointed lobes; to 1/8" wide; in clusters in leaf axils, followed by bright red, 1/4" diameter, juicy fruits in fall. Male and female on different plants.
Leaves:	Shiny, yellow-green above, paler beneath; hollylike, oval to nearly round; spiny-toothed, leathery; to 1 1/2" long.
Blooms:	March–May.
Elevation:	3,000 to 7,000'.
Habitat:	Chaparral and lower elevation ponderosa pine forests.
Comments:	Evergreen. A slow grower. Browsed by bighorn sheep and deer. Native Americans consumed fruits. Four species of *Rhamnus* (RAM-nuss) in Arizona. Flower photograph taken in Superstition Mountains, April 6. Berry photograph taken in Oak Creek Canyon, September 9.

SAGERETIA   847
Sageretia wrightii
Buckthorn Family (Rhamnaceae)

Height:	Straggling shrub to 8'.
Flowers:	Cream-colored, starlike, with 5 petals; to 1/8" wide; followed by a small, fleshy drupe.
Leaves:	Dark green, shiny, oval, pointed at tip; to 1 1/4" long.
Blooms:	March–September.
Elevation:	1,500 to 5,000'.
Habitat:	Along washes and in canyons among rocks.
Comments:	Grayish, woolly stems. Somewhat spiny; spines to 1/4" long. One species of *Sageretia* (sa-ger-EE-ti-ah) in Arizona. Photograph taken in vicinity of Saguaro Lake, August 26.

GRAY THORN   848
Southwestern condalia
Ziziphus obtusifolia (*Condalia lycioides*)
Buckthorn Family (Rhamnaceae)

Height: Shrub to 10'.
Flowers: Whitish green, tiny, less than 1/8" long, in a stalked cluster, followed by round to elliptical fruits, to 1/4" long, maturing to blue-black.
Leaves: Dark green, oblong, finely haired; to 3/4" long, 3/8" wide.
Blooms: May–September.
Elevation: 1,000 to 5,000'.
Habitat: Desert, grassland, and mesas.
Comments: Spiny-branched with gray bark. Fruits eaten by birds, especially white-winged doves and Gambel's quail. Native Americans use parts of plant for medicinal purposes. Solution made from roots used as soap substitute. Some authorities place the one species of *Ziziphus* (ZIZ-i-fuss) under the genus *Condalia*. Photograph taken at Tortilla Flat, May 7.

GRAPE FAMILY
Vitaceae (vy-TAY-see-ee)
Represented in Arizona by woody vines.

Flowers: Regular, very small, with 4 or 5 petals, 4 or 5 calyx lobes, 4 or 5 stamens; 1 pistil, 1 style or none. Superior ovary, 2-celled.
Fruit: Berrylike.
Leaves: Alternate, simple or compound.

VIRGINIA CREEPER   849
Woodbine, American ivy, thicket creeper
Parthenocissus inserta
Grape Family (Vitaceae)

Height: A woody vine climbing tree trunks and over walls.
Flowers: Greenish, inconspicuous, in clusters opposite the leaves; followed by bunches of bluish black berries to 1/4" wide.
Leaves: Dark green, shiny; to 4" long; palmately compound, with 5 to 7 leaflets.
Blooms: May–September.
Elevation: 3,000 to 7,000'.
Habitat: Moist canyons and roadsides.
Comments: Deciduous; leaves turn red in fall. No aerial roots. Fruits eaten by birds and small mammals. One species of *Parthenocissus* (par-thenn-o-SIS-sus) in Arizona. Photograph taken at Walnut Canyon National Monument, September 7.

CANYON GRAPE   850
Arizona grape, vid, parra cimarrona
Vitis arizonica
Grape Family (Vitaceae)

Height: A sprawling, scrambling, woody vine, with tendrils, often covering entire trees.
Flowers: Greenish white, small; followed by juicy, purple-black clusters of grapes. Male and female flowers on separate plants.
Leaves: Dark green, broadly heart-shaped, coarsely toothed; to 6" long, 4 3/4" wide.

Blooms:	April–July.
Elevation:	2,000 to 7,500'.
Habitat:	Along streams and in canyons.
Comments:	Grapes used for making jelly, wine, and juice. Attractive to birds. One species of *Vitis* (VY-tis) in Arizona. Photograph taken at Lynx Lake area, September 11.

MALLOW FAMILY
Malvaceae (mal-VAY-see-ee)
Represented in Arizona by herbs and shrubs.

Flowers:	Regular, usually 5 broad petals and 5 sepals; numerous stamens united to form center column which surrounds style. Petals of buds twist. Superior ovary, 2- to many-celled.
Fruit:	Dry capsule splitting into several parts.
Leaves:	Alternate, simple; usually deeply lobed, cut, or dissected.

INDIAN MALLOW   534
Pelotazo
Abutilon incanum
Mallow Family (Malvaceae)

Height:	To 6'.
Flowers:	Orangish yellow, with 5 broad petals; to 1 1/2" wide; followed by roundish, segmented fruit with very short point.
Leaves:	Grayish green above, paler beneath; very finely haired, somewhat oval, with tapered point; scalloped or toothed; to 3" long.
Blooms:	March–October.
Elevation:	1,000 to 4,000'.
Habitat:	Dry slopes.
Comments:	Ten species of *Abutilon* (ah-BEW-ti-lon) in Arizona. Photograph taken below Horse Mesa Dam, Apache Lake, March 23.

PALMER'S ABUTILON   535
Indian mallow
Abutilon palmeri
Mallow Family (Malvaceae)

Height:	Bush to 8'.
Flowers:	Orange-yellow, with 5 petals, reddish brown center, bright yellow stamens; to 3/8" wide; followed by a short-pointed, hairy, round fruit with up to 7 segments.
Leaves:	Grayish green, woolly, velvetlike, heart-shaped, toothed; to 3" long.
Blooms:	March–May.
Elevation:	1,000 to 3,000'.
Habitat:	Dry, rocky slopes and deserts.
Comments:	Ten species of *Abutilon* (ah-BEW-ti-lon) in Arizona. Photograph taken in Superstition Mountains, March 26.

DESERT FIVE SPOT   626A and B
Lantern flower, Chinese lantern
Eremalche rotundifolium (*Malvastrum rotundifolium*)
Mallow Family (Malvaceae)

Height:	To 2'.
Flowers:	Pink to lilac globes, with 5 petals; opening at top to reveal cream-colored center with 5 carmine spots; to 1 1/4" wide.
Leaves:	Dark green to reddish, round to heart-shaped, with scalloped margins; to 2" wide.
Blooms:	March–May.
Elevation:	100 to 1,500'.
Habitat:	Dry, open desert and washes in sandy soil.
Comments:	Annual herb. When light passes through globe of petals flower resembles a lighted lantern. Two species of *Eremalche* (er-e-MAL-see) in Arizona. Photographs taken north of Yuma, March 29.

DESERT COTTON   194

Wild cotton, algodoncillo ("little cotton"), thurberia
Gossypium thurberi
Mallow Family (Malvaceae)

Height:	To 7'.
Flowers:	White to very pale pink, with 5 rounded, crinkly petals, each with a lavender spot near base; cup-shaped, with large filament tube in center; to 1" long, 1 1/2" wide; followed by dark brown capsule, to 1/2" in diameter.
Leaves:	Dark green above, paler green beneath; palmate, 3- to 5-lobed; to 7" wide, 7" long.
Blooms:	August–October.
Elevation:	2,500 to 5,000'.
Habitat:	Rocky slopes, washes, and canyons.
Comments:	Shrubby. An alternate host for the boll weevil. Bees and wasps are attracted to flower nectar; other insects feed on nectar produced by leaves and flower stalk. One species of *Gossypium* (gos-SIP-i-uhm) in Arizona. Photograph taken north of Superior, September 2.

HERISSANTIA   357

Herissantia crispa (*Bogenhardia crispa*) (*Gayoides crispum*)
Mallow Family (Malvaceae)

Height:	Straggly and weak-stemmed, to 2' long.
Flowers:	5 very pale yellow petals, orangish center, to 3/4" wide; followed by an angular, hairy, inflated, balloon-shaped fruit, to 1/2" wide, 3/8" high.
Leaves:	Grayish green, heart-shaped, toothed, hairy above and beneath; to 2" long.
Blooms:	Almost year-round.
Elevation:	Below 3,500'.
Habitat:	Dry slopes.
Comments:	Often vinelike. One species of *Herissantia* (her-is-SAN-ti-ah) in Arizona. Photograph taken at Saguaro National Monument West, March 31.

DESERT ROSE MALLOW   358

Coulter's hibiscus, pelotazo
Hibiscus coulteri
Mallow Family (Malvaceae)

Height:	To 4', but usually less.
Flowers:	Cream-colored or whitish with red basal spot, 5 rounded petals; cup-shaped; stamens joined at bases form tube surrounding style; to 2" wide.
Leaves:	Dark green and reddish-margined; toothed, hairy, glandular; 3-lobed upper leaves to

1" long, undivided lower leaves to 1 1/2" long.

Blooms:	Periodically throughout the year.
Elevation:	1,500 to 4,000'.
Habitat:	Canyons and rocky slopes.
Comments:	Straggling shrub with gray, woody stems. Frequented by bees. Three species of *Hibiscus* (hy-BISS-kuss) in Arizona. Photograph taken at Saguaro National Monument West, April 17.

ROCK HIBISCUS   598

Pale face, naked hibiscus
Hibiscus denudatus
Mallow Family (Malvaceae)

Height:	Straggly plant to 3' long.
Flowers:	Pale pink to lavender or white; deeper pink toward center; 5 broad, rounded petals; in center, dark pink, stamen column with pollen heads emerging from sides; to 1 1/2" wide; in upper leaf axils and tips of branches; followed by a 5-chambered capsule.
Leaves:	Yellowish green, densely woolly haired, somewhat oval to elliptical, with toothed margins; to 1 1/4" long.
Blooms:	January–October.
Elevation:	Below 2,000'.
Habitat:	Rocky slopes, flats, and washes in desert.
Comments:	Perennial herb with hairy stems; many-branched. Three species of *Hibiscus* (hy-BISS-kuss) in Arizona. Photograph taken at Saguaro Lake, February 6.

COMMON MALLOW   599

Roundleaf mallow, cheeses
Malva neglecta
Mallow Family (Malvaceae)

Height:	Spreading flat on ground, to 16" long.
Flowers:	Light pink striped with darker pink; 5 notched petals; cup-shaped; numerous stamens united into tube around style; to 3/4" wide; occurring singly or in clusters in leaf axils; followed by flat, disk-shaped fruit with up to 15 segments.
Leaves:	Dark green, hairy, roundish, crinkly; alternate, shallowly lobed, with scalloped margins; to 2" wide, 3" long including stem.
Blooms:	July–September.
Elevation:	3,500 to 7,500'.
Habitat:	Roadsides and wastelands.
Comments:	Introduced from Europe, now naturalized. Three species of *Malva* (MAL-vah) in Arizona. Photograph taken at Rainbow Lake, Lakeside, July 6.

CHEESEWEED   600

Little mallow
Malva parviflora
Mallow Family (Malvaceae)

Height:	To 4'.
Flowers:	Pinkish, 5 petals; to 1/4" wide; in small clusters at base of leaf stalks; followed by rounded, disklike seed pods, to 1/2" wide, containing 11 to 12 sections resembling cheese wedges.

Leaves:	Dark green, soft, almost circular, with 5 to 7 toothed lobes; to 5" wide, on stalks to 10" long.
Blooms:	March–September.
Elevation:	100 to 8,500'.
Habitat:	Fields, lots, and roadsides.
Comments:	Annual or biennial. Introduced from Europe. A common weed of fields and open lots. Boiled and eaten by Native Americans. Three species of *Malva* (MAL-vah) in Arizona. Photograph taken near Granite Reef Dam, March 1.

SIDA   359

Sida filicaulis (*Sida procumbens*)
Mallow Family (Malvaceae)

Height:	Sprawling vine.
Flowers:	Yellowish to yellowish orange or white, with bright yellow center; 5 flattened petals slightly indented at tips; to 7/8" wide; borne singly from leaf axil.
Leaves:	Dark green, hairy, elliptical, with scalloped margins; folded slightly upward; to 1" long.
Blooms:	April–October.
Elevation:	2,500 to 6,000'.
Habitat:	Plains and mesas in dry, sandy soil.
Comments:	Stems are pinkish and hairy. Seven species of *Sida* (sye-DAH) in Arizona. Photograph taken at Portal, April 23.

NEW MEXICAN CHECKERMALLOW   627

Prairie mallow, false mallow, alkali pink
Sidalcea neomexicana
Mallow Family (Malvaceae)

Height:	To 3'.
Flowers:	Deep pink to purple, with 5 petals; to 1 1/2" wide.
Leaves:	Yellowish green, lower leaves nearly round; rounded teeth; to 4" wide; upper leaves are smaller, palmately divided.
Blooms:	June–September.
Elevation:	5,000 to 9,500'.
Habitat:	Along streams and in wet meadows.
Comments:	Perennial. One species of *Sidalcea* (sye-DALL-see-ah) in Arizona. Photograph taken near Greer, July 20.

DESERT GLOBEMALLOW   536 and 601

Sore-eye poppy, globemallow, desert mallow, desert hollyhock, mal de ojo, apricot mallow, plantas muy malas ("very bad plants")
Sphaeralcea ambigua
Mallow Family (Malvaceae)

Height:	To 40".
Flowers:	Bright orange (variants occur in white, pink, purplish, or reddish hues), with 5 petals; to 1 1/2" wide; in clusters along upper stems.
Leaves:	Grayish, maplelike, 3-lobed; with scalloped edges; covered with starlike hairs; to 2 1/2" long; equally wide.
Blooms:	Year-round. (Each plant establishes its own time.)
Elevation:	Below 3,500'.

Habitat:	Roadsides, banks of sandy washes, and flats.
Comments:	Perennial herb that grows in large clumps. The most drought-tolerant of the globemallows. Browsed by bighorn sheep, domesticated sheep, and goats; attracts bees. Leaf hairs are an eye irritant to some people. Sixteen species of *Sphaeralcea* (sfee-RAL-see-ah) in Arizona. Photograph of orange flower taken at Apache Junction, March 22; pink flower photographed at Usery Mountain Recreation Area, March 10.

LITTLELEAF GLOBEMALLOW 537
Small leaf mallow
Sphaeralcea parvifolia
Mallow Family (Malvaceae)

Height:	To 3'.
Flowers:	Orange-red, with 5 petals; to 1" wide.
Leaves:	Green, broad, 3-lobed or none; whitish hairs, to 1 1/2" long.
Blooms:	May–September.
Elevation:	4,000 to 7,000'.
Habitat:	Roadsides and dry slopes.
Comments:	Perennial herb. Whitish hairs on stems. Sixteen species of *Sphaeralcea* (sfee-RAL-see-ah) in Arizona. Photograph taken at Wupatki National Monument, September 8.

ST. JOHN'S WORT FAMILY
Guttiferae (gut-TIFF-er-ree) (Hypericacae)
Represented in Arizona by 2 perennial herbs.

Flowers:	Regular, with 4 or 5 petals, 4 or 5 sepals, numerous stamens arranged in 3 or 5 distinct clusters, 2 to 5 styles. Superior ovary, 3-celled.
Fruit:	A capsule.
Leaves:	Opposite, simple, glandular-dotted.

TINKER'S PENNY 360
Hypericum anagalloides
St. John's Wort Family (Guttiferae) (Hypericacae)

Height:	Prostrate, to 8" long, 2" high.
Flowers:	Yellow to orangish yellow, with 5 petals, 5 sepals, many stamens; to 1/4" wide at branch tips.
Leaves:	Light green, opposite; round, slightly oval to elliptical; to 5/8" long; all along stems.
Blooms:	June–August.
Elevation:	7,500 to 8,000'.
Habitat:	Lakeshores and other wet areas.
Comments:	Perennial herb. Forms leafy mats. Prostrate stems root along their length. Two species of *Hypericum* (hy-PER-i-kum) in Arizona. Photograph taken at Woods Canyon Lake, July 7.

SOUTHWESTERN ST. JOHN'S WORT 361
Scouler's St. John's wort
Hypericum formosum
St. John's Wort Family (Guttiferae) (Hypericaceae)

Height:	To 28".

Flowers:	5 bright yellow petals above, reddish orange markings beneath; tiny, black dots on petal edges; numerous yellow stamens; to 1" wide.
Leaves:	Dull green, often tinged with pink; oblong to oval; paired around stem; black-dotted on margins (translucent dots all over leaf are oil and pigment glands); to 1" long.
Blooms:	July–September.
Elevation:	5,000 to 9,500'.
Habitat:	Along mountain streams and moist meadows in coniferous forests.
Comments:	Perennial herb. Reddish green erect stem, often with branches. Plant is named for St. John the Baptist. It was once believed if plants were hung in a home, inhabitants were protected from witches and thunder. Two species of *Hypericum* (hy-PER-i-kum) in Arizona. Photograph taken at Greer, July 5.

TAMARIX FAMILY

Tamaricaceae (tam-ah-ri-KAY-see-ee)
Large shrub or small tree.

Flowers:	Regular, very small, with 4 or 5 petals, 4 or 5 sepals, 4 or more stamens, 3 to 5 styles. Superior ovary, 1-celled.
Fruit:	3- to 5-valved capsule.
Leaves:	Alternate, small, scalelike.

SALT CEDAR   35

Tamarix, pino salado, tamarisco, tamarisk, five-stamen tamarisk
Tamarix pentandra
Tamarix Family (Tamaricaceae)

Height:	Shrub, or small tree to 15'.
Flowers:	Deep pink to nearly white; 1/16" long; crowded in narrow, 1- to 2"-long racemes grouped together in drooping, terminal clusters.
Leaves:	Bluish green, scalelike; narrow, pointed, and wiry; to 1/16" long.
Blooms:	March–August.
Elevation:	Below 5,000'.
Habitat:	Along streams, irrigation ditches, and other moist areas.
Comments:	Deciduous. Forms extensive thickets along rivers and lakes. Introduced from Eurasia; now naturalized in U.S. Robs native plants of water. Foliage salty to taste. Visited by bees. Two species of *Tamarix* (TAM-a-ricks) in Arizona. Photograph taken at Roper Lake State Park, April 20.

VIOLET FAMILY

Violaceae (vy-oh-LAY-see-ee)
Represented in Arizona by herbs.

Flowers:	Irregular; 5 petals, 4 arranged in pairs, lower petal larger and spurred; 5 sepals, 5 stamens. Superior ovary, 3-celled.
Fruit:	3-celled, many-seeded capsule.
Leaves:	Alternate or basal; simple or occasionally lobed.

WESTERN DOG VIOLET   751A and B

Blue violet, hook violet
Viola adunca

Violet Family (Violaceae)
Height: Flower stem to 4".
Flowers: Bluish violet, with 5 petals; 2 pointed upper petals; 2 side petals cupped forward with bases bearing tufts of hairs; lower petal whitish with purple, vertical veins at base; prominent backward spur extending beyond upper petals. Flower to 1" long, 1/2" wide.
Leaves: Dark green, spreading outward from stems, thick, round to oval; finely scalloped on margins; saw-toothed margins on lance-shaped stipules at bases of leaf stalks; to 1" wide, 1" long; leaf with stem to 2 1/2" long.
Blooms: June–July.
Elevation: 7,000 to 9,800'.
Habitat: Moist spruce-fir forests and borders of mountain meadows in shaded areas.
Comments: A variable species. Has hairy stem. Ten species of *Viola* (vy-OH-lah) in Arizona. Photograph A taken in mountains above Greer, July 11. Note small size, presence of main stem with side stems, and long spur. Photograph B, is a variation of this species, with crossed upper petals; found in large numbers in one area in the mountains above Greer, photographed July 3.

CANADA VIOLET   309

Viola canadensis
Violet Family (Violaceae)
Height: To 1', occasionally taller.
Flowers: White, growing from axils of upper leaves; bases of petals are yellow with purplish veins; fading to pinkish; broadly triangular lip petal; petals tinged with purple on back; flower to 3/4" wide.
Leaves: Dark green, broadly heart-shaped, with toothed margins; to 3" long.
Blooms: April–September.
Elevation: 6,000 to 11,500'.
Habitat: Rich, moist soil in coniferous forests.
Comments: Perennial. Nine species of *Viola* (vy-OH-lah) in Arizona. Photograph taken at Greer, June 18.

MEADOW VIOLET   752

Wanderer violet, northern bog violet, kidney-leaf violet
Viola nephrophylla
Violet Family (Violaceae)
Height: To 6".
Flowers: Deep bluish violet, with 5 petals, 3 lower petals with darker purple veins on white areas in throat and bearing tufts of hair at base; short-spurred flower to 3/4" long, 3/4" wide.
Leaves: Dark green, kidney-shaped to heart-shaped; broad, with rounded teeth; to 3 1/2" long (including stem), 3" wide.
Blooms: April–July.
Elevation: 5,000 to 9,500'.
Habitat: Moist meadows and moist mountain slopes in coniferous forests.
Comments: Nine species of *Viola* (vy-OH-lah) in Arizona. Photograph taken in mountains above Greer, July 8. Recognizable by absence of main stem; all leaves arise from base of plant.

STICK LEAF FAMILY

Loasaceae (low-a-SAY-see-ee)

Herbs or slightly woody plants.

Flowers: Regular, with 5 petals, 5 sepals and numerous stamens (outer stamens are often petallike). Inferior ovary, 1-celled.

Fruit: Dry pod (capsule).

Leaves: Alternate or pinnately cleft, simple, often with barbed hairs.

WHITE-BRACTED STICK LEAF   195

Sand blazing star

Mentzelia involucrata

Stick Leaf Family (Loasaceae)

Height: To 1'.

Flowers: White to pale cream, streaked inside with faint orange lines; translucent, erect, with 5 petals; to 1 1/2" wide, 1 1/4" long.

Leaves: Grayish green, lance-shaped, with irregular teeth on margins; very rough due to stiff hairs; to 4 1/2" long.

Blooms: February–May.

Elevation: Below 3,000'.

Habitat: Desert washes, slopes, and flat areas in dry, sandy soil.

Comments: Annual. Very rough, sandpapery leaves stick to fabric, making them difficult to remove. Eleven species of *Mentzelia* (ment-ZEE-lih-uh) in Arizona. Photograph taken north of Yuma, March 29.

VENUS BLAZING STAR   362

Stick leaf

Mentzelia nitens

Stick Leaf Family (Loasaceae)

Height: To 2', often prostrate.

Flowers: Bright yellow, 5 rounded petals, to 1/4" wide; in small, hairy clusters at tip of branches.

Leaves: Grayish green, rough, hairy; pinnately and deeply cleft into very narrow lobes; lower leaves to 6" long.

Blooms: February–May.

Elevation: Below 3,000'.

Habitat: Sandy deserts, often along rivers.

Comments: Several varieties of this species. Eleven species of *Mentzelia* (ment-ZEE-li-uh) in Arizona. Photograph taken along Bill Williams River below Alamo Lake Dam, February 26.

DESERT BLAZING STAR   363

Blazing star, bullet stick leaf, yellow mentzelia, evening star, moonflower

Mentzelia pumila

Stick Leaf Family (Loasaceae)

Height: To 3'.

Flowers: Bright yellow, star-shaped; outer stamens have broad, flattened filaments and resemble additional petals; to 2" wide; occurring at ends of branches; followed by bullet-shaped seed capsule.

Leaves:	Grayish green, sandpapery, long, narrow, many-lobed; to 4" long.
Blooms:	February–October.
Elevation:	100 to 8,000'.
Habitat:	Roadsides, dry stream beds, pinyon-juniper woods, and ponderosa forest clearings.
Comments:	Plant has whitish stems. Flowers open in late afternoon. This species has a bullet-shaped ovary below flowerhead. Leaves and stems cling to fabric like Velcro, due to hooked hairs. Native Americans ground seeds for meal. Eleven species of *Mentzelia* (ment-ZEE-li-uh) in Arizona. Photograph taken at Painted Rocks Dam, March 31.

CACTUS FAMILY
Cactaceae (kak-TAY-see-ee)
Represented in Arizona by mostly succulent, spiny, leafless plants with special organs (areoles) from which spines, stems, or flowers occur.

Flowers:	Mostly regular, with numerous petals and sepals forming funnel-shaped receptacle; many stamens; 1 style with several stigma lobes. Inferior ovary, 1-celled.
Fruit:	Large or small, fleshy or dry berry.
Leaves:	Leafless. Plants have varying numbers of stems and joints and various shapes.

SAGUARO (sah-WAR-oh)   109A, B, and C
Sahuaro, giant cactus
Cereus giganteus (*Carnegiea gigantea*)
Cactus Family (Cactaceae)

Height:	To 50', usually to 30' high; 2 1/2' in diameter; and weighing 9 tons.
Flowers:	Waxy-white, funnel-shaped, to 3" wide; in crownlike, terminal clusters on arms or main trunk; opening at night and remaining open part of the following day; egg-shaped, fleshy, green fruit (tinged with red), to 3" long, to 1 3/4" in diameter.
Stems:	Green, columnar, treelike trunk, 12 to 30 prominent ribs, branching well up on main trunk when older, branches to 20" in diameter.
Spines:	White-gray, sometimes tinged with pink; 15 to 30 per areole; to 3" long, the longest pointed downward.
Blooms:	May–June.
Elevation:	600 to 3,600'.
Habitat:	Rocky slopes and well-drained flats in the Sonoran Desert.
Comments:	The largest cactus in the U.S., the characteristic plant of the Sonoran Desert, and the state flower of Arizona. Three national monuments ensure the protection of these giant cacti: Saguaro National Monument East, Saguaro National Monument West, and Organ Pipe Cactus National Monument.

Saguaros grow very slowly, but live for 150 to 200 years. In their first year, they grow only about 1/2". They reach about 1' in 15 years; 10' in 40 to 50 years; and 12 to 20' in 75 to 100 years, when arm buds usually appear.

Young saguaros cannot survive either the heat of the desert sun or trampling; they usually grow under a "nurse" plant, such as a creosote bush or a paloverde tree. Spines on the stems of older plants provide shade to the trunk.

After a rain, the accordionlike pleats of a saguaro expand as it draws up water with its shallow roots, which often sprawl over a 50' radius. A mature plant may soak up to 200 gallons of water during a rainstorm. During droughts the saguaro becomes slim again.

On rare occasions a saguaro will experience abnormal growth. For some unknown reason the tissue growth becomes disorganized, causing the cactus to enlarge and flatten, producing a crest that looks like a giant, open fan of up to 6' across and 3' high. Such specimens are called "cristate" or "fasciated."

Once saguaros reach a height of about 8', the first flower buds appear. Flowers smell like ripe melon, and attract bees and other insects during the daytime, and bats and moths at night. Full-grown saguaros produce at least 100 fruits in a season. In July, when mature, the fruits split open, revealing their scarlet linings, deep red pulp, and up to 2,000 tiny, jet-black seeds.

Pulp and seeds provide food for birds, small rodents, harvester ants, and other insects. Fruits and seeds are used by Native Americans for food. The wooden ribs of dead plants are used for shelters, knick-knacks, hiking sticks, and corrals. Woodpeckers drill holes in saguaros for nest sites, where in summer the inside temperature is 30 degrees lower than the outside air. The injured saguaro lines the woodpecker hole with scar tissue, producing a boot-shaped structure. These "boots" are used by nesting elf owls and other birds.

Five species of *Cereus* (SEE-ree-us or SEER-ee-us) in Arizona. Full saguaro photograph taken at Usery Mountain Recreation Area, April 6. Cristate (or fasciated) saguaro taken at Organ Pipe Cactus National Monument, February 28. Saguaro flowers photographed at Saguaro National Monument, May 2.

SENITA CACTUS   110
Whisker cactus, old man
Cereus schottii (*Lophocereus schottii*)
Cactus Family (Cactaceae)

Height:	To 21'.
Flowers:	Pale pink, nocturnal; to 1 1/2" wide; often 2 or more at an areole, within hairlike area; followed by red, egg-shaped fruit to 1 1/4" long.
Stems:	Green to gray-green, to 5" in diameter; with clumps to 15' in diameter; 5 to 9 ribs.
Spines:	Upper branches: gray, bristlelike, to 50 per areole, to 3" long. Lower branches: gray, 8 to 10 per areole, to 3/8" long.
Blooms:	April–August.
Elevation:	1,000 to 2,000'.
Habitat:	Sandy soils of desert.
Comments:	Concentration of these at Senita Basin at Organ Pipe Cactus National Monument in southwestern Arizona. *Senita* means "old one" in Spanish. When stems age, upper spines become gray and hairlike. Five species of *Cereus* (SEE-ree-us or SEER-ee-us) in Arizona. Photograph taken at Organ Pipe Cactus National Monument, October 23.

ORGAN PIPE CACTUS   111A and B
Pitahaya dulce ("sweet cactus fruit")
Cereus thurberi (*Lemaireocereus thurberi*)
Cactus Family (Cactaceae)

Height:	To 20'.
Flowers:	Pale lavender, nocturnal, funnel-shaped; to 3" wide; on sides or tips of stems; followed (in July) by a red, edible, nearly round, 3"-diameter spiny fruit.
Stems:	Columnar cactus, free-branching, with stems arising from ground level; 12 to 20 ribs on stem; stems to 8" in diameter.

Spines:	Brown to black, 11 to 19 per brown-felted areole; straight, to 1/2" long; spreading in all directions.
Blooms:	May–June.
Elevation:	1,000 to 3,500'.
Habitat:	Stony desert and rocky hillsides of Organ Pipe Cactus National Monument.
Comments:	Resembles pipes of an organ. Organ Pipe Cactus National Monument in southwestern Arizona was established to preserve this species. Tohono O'Odham Indians harvest fruits for syrup, using pulp and seeds for winter food. Sanborn's long-nosed bats are the plant's most important pollinators. Five species of *Cereus* (SEE-ree-us or SEER-ee-us) in Arizona. Photograph taken at Organ Pipe Cactus National Monument, March 30. Cristate photograph taken at the Monument, May 5.

BEEHIVE CACTUS   119

Beehive nipple cactus, cushion cactus
Coryphantha vivipara var. *arizonica*
Cactus Family (Cactaceae)

Height:	To 8".
Flowers:	Pink, 2 1/2" wide, day-blooming; followed by green, oval fruit to 1" long, 5/8" in diameter.
Stems:	Green and globular, to 3" in diameter; forming dense clumps.
Spines:	Central spines: reddish to brown at tips, white at base, to 3/4" long. Radial spines: white, to 5/8" long.
Blooms:	May–July.
Elevation:	4,700 to 7,200'.
Habitat:	Rocky, sandy ground in juniper woodlands and ponderosa pine forests.
Comments:	Five species of *Coryphantha* (kor-ri-FAN-thah) in Arizona. Photograph taken in vicinity of Kohls Ranch, May 23.

TURK'S HEAD   120

Blue barrel, eagle's claw
Echinocactus horizonthalonius
Cactus Family (Cactaceae)

Height:	To 12"; usually closer to 8".
Flowers:	Pink, funnel-shaped, opening fully to 2 3/4" wide; followed by dry fruit, to 1" long, 1/2" in diameter, covered with woolly hairs.
Stems:	Bluish green, with flattened globe to short columnar shape; to 8" in diameter.
Spines:	Gray; central spine curving downward, to 1 1/4" long; radial spines, to 1" long, spreading in all directions.
Blooms:	May–June.
Elevation:	3,000 to 3,500'.
Habitat:	Desert.
Comments:	Eight-ribbed. This species may have been brought to Arizona by early miners. Two species of *Echinocactus* (ee-KY-no-kak-tus) in Arizona. Photograph taken at Tohono Chul Park, Tucson, April 15. Found in southwestern Pinal and north-central Pima counties.

ECHINOCACTUS   121

Echinocactus polycephalus var. *polycephalus*
Cactus Family (Cactaceae)

Height:	To 2'.
Flowers:	Yellow tinged with pink; to 2" wide; followed by a fruit densely covered with white, woolly hairs to 3/4" long; fruit to 1" long, 1/2" in diameter.
Stems:	Roundish to cylindrical, hidden by spines; to 2' long, 10" wide, with 13 to 21 ribs; numerous, in dense clumps of up to 30 branches, to 4' in diameter.
Spines:	Central spines: reddish to pink with gray, felty, deciduous hair covering; rather flat; 4 per areole (3 near-straight, the fourth, lower spine curving downward); to 3" long. Radial spines: 6 to 8 per areole; to 1 3/4" long.
Blooms:	February–March.
Elevation:	100 to 2,500'.
Habitat:	Rocky or gravelly slopes.
Comments:	A barrel cactus. Two species of *Echinocactus* (ee-KY-no-kak-tus) in Arizona. Photograph taken in Kofa Mountains, February 21.

STRAWBERRY HEDGEHOG   122

Strawberry cactus, hedgehog cactus, Engelmann's cactus, torch cactus, Engelmann hedgehog, strawberry echinocereus
Echinocereus engelmannii
Cactus Family (Cactaceae)

Height:	To 20".
Flowers:	Varying shades of magenta, with green stigma in center, cup-shaped; to 3" wide; bloom for several days, followed by green, spiny fruit (red when ripe), to 1 1/4" long, 1" in diameter.
Stems:	Green and cylindrical, to 3" in diameter, with 10 to 13 ribs; forming loose or dense cluster to 3' wide.
Spines:	Color varies from whitish to golden yellow to pinkish to black; straight, central spines to 2" long; radial spines to 1" long.
Blooms:	March–April.
Elevation:	To 5,000'.
Habitat:	Sandy and rocky flats and hillsides.
Comments:	Fruits are edible; they produce a sugary juice and may be eaten like strawberries. Six species of *Echinocereus* (ee-ky-no-SEER-ee-us) in Arizona. Photograph taken south of Phoenix, March 31.

RAINBOW CACTUS   123

Rainbow hedgehog, rainbow echinocereus, Arizona rainbow hedgehog
Echinocereus pectinatus
Cactus Family (Cactaceae)

Height:	To 1'.
Flowers:	Magenta to lavender, funnel-shaped, to 5" wide; 1 to 4 flowers, followed by green to greenish purple, oval fruit to 2 1/2" long.
Stems:	Usually single, erect, and columnar, with some red to white spines forming alternating horizontal bands on stem; 15 to 22 ribs; to 4" in diameter.
Spines:	Pink to gray to light brown; very dense, flat, comb-shaped, covering the entire stem.
Blooms:	June–August.
Elevation:	4,000 to 6,000'.
Habitat:	Grasslands, mountains, and limestone hills of southern Arizona.
Comments:	Six species of *Echinocereus* (ee-ky-no-SEER-ee-us) in Arizona. Photograph taken at Madera Canyon, June 10.

CLARET CUP CACTUS   124

Claret cup hedgehog, mound cactus, king's cup cactus, crimson hedgehog,
heart twister, strawberry cactus, spinemound
Echinocereus triglochidiatus var. *melanacanthus.*
Cactus Family (Cactaceae)

Height: To 6".
Flowers: Scarlet, to scarlet-orange, with bright green stigma in center; to 1 1/2" wide, 2 1/4" long; occurring at top of stem, followed by a 1"-long fruit with deciduous spines.
Stems: Green to bluish green, to 2 1/2" in diameter; with 9 to 10 ribs forming a crowded clump.
Spines: Grayish, tan, or white; central spine to 2 1/2" long.
Blooms: May–July.
Elevation: 4,000 to 9,000'.
Habitat: Open, rocky hillsides and ledges.
Comments: Numerous varieties of this cactus. Flowers remain open for several days. Six species of *Echinocereus* (ee-ky-no-SEER-ee-us) in Arizona. Photograph taken near Greer, June 15.

BARREL CACTUS   125

Arizona barrel cactus, candy barrel cactus, fishhook barrel, visnaga, compass barrel,
Wislizenus's barrel, biznaga, bisnagre
Ferocactus wislizenii
Cactus Family (Cactaceae)

Height: To 11' (usually much less), to 2' in diameter.
Flowers: Shades of orange to yellow to reddish; cup-shaped; day-blooming; to 2 1/2" wide; in crown at top of stem; followed by yellow, barrel-shaped, scaly fruit to 1 3/4" long, 1 3/8" in diameter.
Stems: Single, massive and cylindrical, with 20 to 28 ribs.
Spines: Grayish to reddish, in dense clusters along ribs; large, sharply hooked, flattened, central spine to 2" long, surrounded by slender, hairlike spines.
Blooms: July–September.
Elevation: 1,000 to 4,500'.
Habitat: Sandy desert and gravelly slopes in desert or grasslands.
Comments: Drawn toward direct sunlight; faster growth on the cactus' shady side causes barrels to lean in a southerly direction, hence the name "compass cactus." Instead of water, cactus is filled with a slimy alkaline juice. Yellow fruits persist all year, and are eaten by deer and rodents. Flowers attract bees. Pulp used as a basis for cactus candy. Native Americans used hooked spines as fishhooks. Three species of *Ferocactus* (FER-o-kak-tus) in Arizona. Photograph taken in vicinity of Mesa, July 13. The central spine on the similar **COVILLE'S BARREL** (*Ferocactus covillei*) is normally not hooked, and is surrounded by stout, stiff spines.

PINCUSHION CACTUS   126

Fishhook cactus, corkseed cactus, fishhook mammillaria, nipple cactus,
cabeza del viejo
Mammillaria microcarpa
Cactus Family (Cactaceae)

Height: To 6".
Flowers: Pink to lavender; to 1" wide; forming crown at top of stem; lasting several days;

followed by red, smooth, club-shaped fruit to 1" long.

Stems:	Cylindrical, with close-set "nipples" obscured by spines; solitary at first, then branching; to 2" in diameter.
Spines:	Grayish, dense, in clusters; central spine is dark reddish brown and hooked like an unbarbed fishhook.
Blooms:	April–August.
Elevation:	To 4,500'.
Habitat:	Dry, gravelly areas in deserts; usually under bushes.
Comments:	"Mammillaria" refers to nipplelike projections on stems. Pollinated by bees. Ten species of *Mammillaria* (mam-mill-AYE-ri-ah) in Arizona. Photograph taken in Mesa area, July 21.

BUCKHORN CHOLLA (CHOY-uh)   113

Yellow flowered cane cactus, deer-horn cactus
Opuntia acanthocarpa
Cactus Family (Cactaceae)

Height:	Shrubby to treelike, to 6'.
Flowers:	Variable, from yellow to orange to red; to 2 1/4" wide, followed by oval, dry fruit with long spines; to 1 1/2" long. When seeds mature, fruit falls from plant before winter.
Joints:	Green, cylindrical, to 20" long, 1 1/4" in diameter, with elongated tubercles or knoblike projections.
Spines:	Straw-colored, stout, 12 or more in a cluster; to 1 1/2" long.
Blooms:	Mid-April–late May.
Elevation:	500 to 3,500'.
Habitat:	Sandy soils of slopes and washes.
Comments:	Native Americans eat flower buds after steaming them. Twenty-eight species of *Opuntia* (oh-PUN-shuh or oh-PUN-tih-uh) in Arizona. Photograph taken at Usery Mountain Recreation Area, April 6.

PENCIL CHOLLA (CHOY-uh)   114

Opuntia arbuscula
Cactus Family (Cactaceae)

Height:	Shrubby to treelike, to 9', but usually much less.
Flowers:	Yellow, greenish or brownish red; to 1" long, 5/8" wide; followed by green fruit tinged with purple or red; smooth, spineless and elongated, to 1 1/2" long, 7/8" in diameter, lasting through winter.
Joints:	Green, nearly smooth; to 6" long, 1/2" in diameter.
Spines:	Reddish or tan, straight, up to 4 per cluster; largest spine facing downward; to 1 1/2" long.
Blooms:	May–June.
Elevation:	1,000 to 3,000'.
Habitat:	Gravelly and sandy plains, valleys, and washes.
Comments:	Twenty-eight species of *Opuntia* (oh-PUN-shuh or oh-PUN-tih-uh) in Arizona. Photograph taken at Saguaro National Monument West, March 31.

BEAVERTAIL CACTUS   132

Beavertail prickly pear
Opuntia basilaris

	Cactus Family (Cactaceae)
Height:	Grows in clumps 2' high and up to 6' in diameter.
Flowers:	Pink to magenta; to 3" wide; at upper end of pad; followed by grayish, oval fruit to 1" long, sparsely covered with glochids.
Stems:	Grayish green, with flat joint-pads; oval to spoon-shaped; spineless but with glochids; to 1' long, 6" wide, 1/2" thick.
Spines:	None; has clusters of very fine, brown to reddish brown glochids, to 1/8" long.
Blooms:	March–May.
Elevation:	200 to 4,000'.
Habitat:	Sandy or gravelly soils of canyons; washes or flats in desert.
Comments:	Glochids detach easily upon contact and are difficult to remove. Joint or pad resembles a beaver's tail. Pads root very easily. Native Americans use both fruits and pads for food. Pack rats feed on seeds. Twenty-eight species of *Opuntia* (oh-PUN-shuh or oh-PUN-tih-uh) in Arizona. Photograph taken at Cattail Cove State Park, March 18.

TEDDY BEAR CHOLLA (CHOY-uh)   115A and B

Silver cholla, teddybear cactus, jumping cholla
Opuntia bigelovii
Cactus Family (Cactaceae)

Height:	Shrubby to treelike, to 5'; rarely to 9'.
Flowers:	Greenish or yellowish streaked with lavender, to 1 1/2" wide; near end of joint; followed by yellowish, egg-shaped, knobby fruit to 3/4" long, 3/8" wide.
Joints:	Light green to bluish green, cylindrical; to 10" long, 2 1/2" in diameter; form arms at top of main stem.
Spines:	Silvery to golden when young, black when old; dense, backward-facing barbs; to 1" long.
Blooms:	February–May.
Elevation:	100 to 3,000'.
Habitat:	Desert to rocky hillsides.
Comments:	Joints detach very easily when brushed against, causing people to believe joints "jump off" plant. Detached joints root quickly in desert soil, creating dense thickets. Pack rats carry spiny joints to nest sites, often creating a huge pile to ward off enemies. Despite spines, cactus wrens favor this species and chain fruit cholla as nest sites. Twenty-eight species of *Opuntia* (oh-PUH-shuh or oh-PUN-tih-uh) in Arizona. Photographs taken at Usery Mountain Recreation Area, April 22.

SILVER CHOLLA (CHOY-uh)   128

Golden cholla
Opuntia echinocarpa
Cactus Family (Cactaceae)

Height:	To 4'.
Flowers:	Greenish yellow, outer parts streaked with red; to 2 1/2" wide; followed by green, egg-shaped fruit with spines on upper half; to 1 1/4" long, 3/4" wide; turning light tan at maturity.
Joints:	Green, cylindrical, with conspicuous tubercles to 3/8" long; joints generally to 6" long, 1 1/2" wide.
Spines:	Silvery or golden, very dense, 3 to 12 per areole; straight, pointing in all directions, narrow; tapering from base; to 1 1/2" long.

Blooms:	April.
Elevation:	1,000 to 4,000'.
Habitat:	Flats, slopes, and washes.
Comments:	Many-branched. Twenty-eight species of *Opuntia* (oh-PUN-shuh or oh-PUN-tih-uh) in Arizona. Photograph taken in Alamo Lake area, February 26.

MOHAVE PRICKLY PEAR 133
Porcupine prickly pear
Opuntia erinacea var. *erinacea*
Cactus Family (Cactaceae)

Height:	To 1'.
Flowers:	Reddish to pink to yellow; to 3" wide, followed by brownish, elliptical fruit, to 1 1/4" long, 1/2" wide.
Stems:	Bluish green, purplish on tips, elliptical to oblong; to 5" long, 2" wide.
Spines:	White, straight, long; longest at tip, reduced in size down joint; to 3 1/2" long.
Blooms:	May–June.
Elevation:	3,000 to 7,000'.
Habitat:	Sandy or gravelly soils in desert and woodlands.
Comments:	In sprawling clumps. Twenty-eight species of *Opuntia* (oh-PUN-shuh or oh-PUN-tih-uh) in Arizona. Photograph taken near Sunset Crater National Monument, May 31.

GRIZZLY BEAR CACTUS 134
Grizzly bear prickly pear
Opuntia erinacea var. *ursina*
Cactus Family (Cactaceae)

Height:	To 1'.
Flowers:	Rose to deep pink; to 3 5/8" wide; followed by brownish, spiny fruit to 1 1/4" long, 3/4" in diameter.
Stems:	Bluish green, elliptical to oblong; to 6" long, 3 1/2" wide, less than 1/2" thick; covered with long, curving, tangled, hairlike spines.
Spines:	White to pale gray, turned downward; to 4" long.
Blooms:	May–June.
Elevation:	4,000 to 5,500'.
Habitat:	Rocky, desert hillsides.
Comments:	Grows in clumps to 3' in diameter. Twenty-eight species of *Opuntia* (oh-PUN-shuh or oh-PUN-tih-uh) in Arizona. Photograph taken at the Arizona-Sonora Desert Museum at Tucson, November 12. Native chiefly to Mohave County.

CHAIN FRUIT CHOLLA (CHOY-uh) 116A and B
Chain cholla, choya, jumping cholla
Opuntia fulgida
Cactus Family (Cactaceae)

Height:	Shrubby to treelike, to 15', usually less.
Flowers:	Deep pink to lavender; to 3/4" wide; forming on previous year's pendent fruit, thus length of fruit chain increases each year. Fruit is green, oval, to 1 1/2" long, 1" in diameter.
Joints:	Light green, cylindrical; to 6" long; detach easily.
Spines:	Grayish to yellowish, barbed, 2 to 12 per areole; to 1 1/4" long.

Blooms:	May–August.
Elevation:	1,000 to 3,000'.
Habitat:	Deserts and hillsides.
Comments:	Joints seem to "jump" from plant when only slightly touched. Seeds are rarely fertile. Plant reproduces when fruit or segment falls to ground and forms roots, starting new plant. Fruits eaten by cattle; plant is pollinated by bees. Cactus wrens and curve-billed thrashers nest in this cactus. Twenty-eight species of *Opuntia* (oh-PUN-shuh or oh-PUN-tih-uh) in Arizona. Both photographs taken at Usery Mountain Recreation Area: January 24 (not in flower); and in bloom May 20.

DESERT CHRISTMAS CACTUS   129

Tesajo, Christmas cholla, pencil-joint cholla, holycross cholla, diamond cactus, darning needle cactus
Opuntia leptocaulis
Cactus Family (Cactaceae)

Height:	To 3' when growing in the open; taller and more vinelike when growing among desert trees.
Flowers:	Greenish yellow; to 1" wide; followed by bright red fruit, fleshy at maturity; to 1/2" long, 7/16" in diameter.
Joints:	Dark green, cylindrical, branched; to 16" long, 1/2" in diameter.
Spines:	Grayish, straight, to 2" long.
Blooms:	May–June.
Elevation:	1,000 to 4,000'.
Habitat:	Washes, slopes, and flat areas.
Comments:	Red fruits remain on stems much of winter. Twenty-eight species of *Opuntia* (oh-PUN-shuh or oh-PUN-tih-uh) in Arizona. Photograph taken at Tortilla Flat, November 1.

ENGELMANN'S PRICKLY PEAR   135A and B

Engelmann pricklypear, tuna, nopal, purple fruit prickly pear
Opuntia phaeacantha var. *discata* (*Opuntia engelmannii*)
Cactus Family (Cactaceae)

Height:	To 5'.
Flowers:	Yellow, orange, or reddish; to 3 1/4" wide; on edge of flat pad; followed by smooth, red to purplish, narrow-based, cylindrical fruit, to 3" long, 1 1/2" in diameter.
Stems:	Green to bluish green, with circular or oblong pad; to 16" long, to 9" wide; in upright or sprawling chains.
Spines:	Ash-gray to white, to 3" long, either flattened, curved, or straight. Areoles have brown or yellowish glochids.
Blooms:	April–June.
Elevation:	1,500 to 7,500'.
Habitat:	Sandy soils of flats, hills, and valleys in desert and grasslands.
Comments:	Most common prickly pear in Arizona. A wide, spreading cactus to 15' in diameter. Pollinated by bees. Fruits, called *tunas*, eaten by birds and rodents; also used for jelly and for making red dye. Javelinas eat pads. Stem pulp used to make face cream and water purifier. Glochids difficult to remove from skin. "Itching powder" was made from glochids. Twenty-eight species of *Opuntia* (oh-PUN-shuh or oh-PUN-tih-uh) in Arizona. Photograph of flowers taken at Usery Mountain Recreation Area, April 22; and of the fruit, August 21.

DIAMOND CHOLLA (CHOY-uh)   130

Opuntia ramosissima
Cactus Family (Cactaceae)

Height:	To 5', but usually less.
Flowers:	Apricot to brown with some lavender or red; to 1/2" wide; followed by brownish, spiny, elliptical fruit to 3/4" long, 1/2" in diameter.
Stems:	Grayish green, slender, flattened, and platelike; diamond-shaped, grooved or notched tubercles (projections on joints); to 4" long.
Spines:	Yellowish to tan part-way, grayish toward stem; barbed, thin, straight, set in a groove; to 2 1/4" long.
Blooms:	May–September.
Elevation:	100 to 2,000'; at times to 3,000'.
Habitat:	Washes and desert flats in sandy soil.
Comments:	Bushy, matted, many-branched. Twenty-eight species of *Opuntia* (oh-PUN-shuh or oh-PUN-tih-uh) in Arizona. Photograph taken in Kofa Mountains, February 22. Diamond-shaped, notched, or grooved tubercles are unique to this cholla.

CANE CHOLLA (CHOY-uh)   117

Cholla cane cactus, walkingstick cholla, handlegrip cholla, cardenche
Opuntia spinosior
Cactus Family (Cactaceae)

Height:	Shrubby to treelike, to 8'.
Flowers:	Variable in color, white or yellowish or red or purple; to 3" wide, followed by yellow, egg-shaped fruit to 1 3/4" long, to 1" in diameter; fruits persist through winter.
Joints:	Light green, to 12" long, 1" in diameter; with numerous, elongated tubercles or projections.
Spines:	Gray to pinkish, up to 20 per areole, straight, widely radiating, barbed, to 3/8" long.
Blooms:	May–June.
Elevation:	1,000 to 5,000'.
Habitat:	Desert grasslands and desert mountainsides.
Comments:	Fruits eaten by cattle; Native Americans ate fruits raw or cooked. Cactus wrens nest in branches. Twenty-eight species of *Opuntia* (oh-PUN-shuh or oh-PUN-tih-uh) in Arizona. Photograph taken at Roper Lake, May 2.

DEVIL CHOLLA (CHOY-uh)   127

Opuntia stanlyi
Cactus Family (Cactaceae)

Height:	To 6"; rarely to 1'.
Flowers:	Yellowish to greenish yellow; to 2" wide; followed by yellow, spiny fruit to 3" long, 3/4" in diameter.
Joints:	Cylindrical; to 6" long, 1 1/2" in diameter.
Spines:	Straw-colored to brownish, straight, 18 to 21 per areole; to 2" long.
Blooms:	May–June.
Elevation:	2,500 to 4,000'.
Habitat:	Plains and mesas in sandy soil.
Comments:	Belongs to the club/mat-forming cholla group. Plants form mats several yards in

diameter. There are several varieties of this species; the variety *kunzei* covers very large areas in the Kofa Mountain–Yuma area. Twenty-eight species of Op*untia* (oh-PUN-shuh or oh-PUN-tih-uh) in Arizona. Photograph taken at Roper Lake, May 2.

STAGHORN CHOLLA (CHOY-uh)   118
Tree cholla, deerhorn cholla
Opuntia versicolor
Cactus Family (Cactaceae)

Height:	Shrubby to treelike, to 15', usually less.
Flowers:	Orange, brown, yellow or red (very variable); to 2 1/4" wide; followed by green (tinged with purple to red), pear-shaped, fleshy, spineless fruit to 1 3/4" long, which remain attached during winter.
Joints:	Green, elongated, to 14" long, 1" in diameter, with long, knoblike projections.
Spines:	Gray or purplish, 7 to 10 in a cluster; to 5/8" long; spread at all angles.
Blooms:	May.
Elevation:	1,000 to 4,000'.
Habitat:	Sandy washes, plains, and canyons.
Comments:	Has forked branches resembling deer antlers. New fruits often develop on last year's fruits, occasionally a chain of 2 or 3 is seen. Twenty-eight species of *Opuntia* (oh-PUN-shuh or oh-PUN-tih-uh) in Arizona. Photograph taken in Tucson area, May 12.

PURPLE PRICKLY PEAR   136
Blue-blade, dollar cactus
Opuntia violacea var. *santa-rita*
Cactus Family (Cactaceae)

Height:	To 5'.
Flowers:	Pale yellow; to 3 1/2" wide; followed by red to purplish, smooth, slender fruit, to 1 1/2" long, 3/4" in diameter.
Stems:	Greenish blue to pink to pale violet-purple; thin, flat, almost round; to 8" wide.
Spines:	Few, if any. Reddish brown, to 3" long when present. Areoles, about 1" apart, have reddish brown glochids.
Blooms:	Spring.
Elevation:	Below 4,000'.
Habitat:	Sandy or gravelly soils.
Comments:	Color of pads varies with drought conditions or lower temperatures. Pads are eaten by rodents and cattle. This cactus is especially vulnerable to attack by tiny, cochineal scale insects, who reproduce and live under patches of sticky, white cottony fuzz, where they suck the juices from cactus pads. If fuzz is crushed a bright carmine red dye is produced. Twenty-eight species of *Opuntia* (oh-PUN-shuh or oh-PUN-tih-uh) in Arizona. Photograph taken at Patagonia Lake State Park, May 10.

WHIPPLE CHOLLA (CHOY-uh)   131
Opuntia whipplei
Cactus Family (Cactaceae)

Height:	To 2 1/2' when shrubby.
Flowers:	Pale yellow to lemon yellow; to 1 1/4" wide; followed by a yellow, spineless, nearly round to egg-shaped fruit; with shallow cavity at top; to 1 1/4" long, 3/4" wide; remaining through winter.
Joints:	Green, cylindrical, tubercles to 3/8" long; joint to 6" long, 3/4" wide.

Spines:	White to pinkish tan, needlelike; 7 to 14 per areole; 1 long spine in cluster to 2" long.
Blooms:	June–July.
Elevation:	4,500 to 7,000'.
Habitat:	Plains and grasslands.
Comments:	Plants often form mats or grow as low bushes. Twenty-eight species of *Opuntia* (oh-PUN-shuh or oh-PUN-tih-uh) in Arizona. Photograph taken at Wupatki National Monument, June 5.

DESERT NIGHT-BLOOMING CEREUS   112A and B

Arizona queen-of-the-night, reina-de-la-noche, deer-horn cactus
Peniocereus greggii (*Cereus greggii*)
Cactus Family (Cactaceae)

Height:	Erect or sprawling to 8', but usually less.
Flowers:	Waxy white, pointed, perianth segments; numerous white to yellow-tipped stamens; nocturnal, lasting only 1 night; very fragrant; to 4 1/2" wide, 8 1/2" long; followed by an orangish red, elliptical fruit with short spines, dulling with age, to 3" long, 1 1/2" in diameter.
Stems:	Lead-colored and slender, usually 4- to 5-ribbed; to 1/2" in diameter; unbranched or with up to 12 branches.
Spines:	Dark-colored, about 11 to 13 per areole; upper spines to 1/32" long, lower ones to 1/8" long; with some whitish color.
Blooms:	June–July.
Elevation:	1,000 to 3,500'.
Habitat:	Desert flats and washes under trees or shrubs.
Comments:	The inconspicuous, apparently dead stems are usually supported by branches of desert shrubs or trees. After dusk the flowers open in spasms, their aroma carrying as far as 100' and attracting moths and other night-feeding insects. The blossoms wilt shortly after sunrise the following morning. The tuberous root is turniplike; 27 roots weighed at the University of Arizona ranged from 1 1/2 to 43 pounds, but roots usually weigh 5 to 15 pounds. Tubers were once used as food by Native Americans and Mexicans. The seeds are eaten by birds. One species of *Peniocereus* (pen-i-oh-SEER-ee-us) in Arizona. Photographs taken at Desert Botanical Garden, Phoenix, June 25.

ELAEAGNUS or OLEASTER FAMILY

Elaeagnaceae (eh-lee-ag-NAY-see-ee)
Represented in Arizona by shrubs and small trees.

Flowers:	Regular, small, 4-toothed perianth, 4 to 8 stamens, long style. Superior ovary, 1-celled.
Fruit:	Dry nut or achene.
Leaves:	Alternate or opposite, simple, covered with minute, silvery or light brownish scales.

RUSSIAN OLIVE   48

Olive willow, oleaster
Elaeagnus angustifolia
Elaeagnus or Oleaster Family (Elaeagnaceae)

Height:	To 25'.
Trunk:	To 4".

Bark:	Grayish brown, fissured, shredding in long strips.
Flowers:	Pale yellow inside, silver on outer surface; petalless, bell-shaped, very fragrant; to 3/8" long; growing from leaf bases; followed by yellowish brown, silver-scaled, elliptical, 1/2"-long, berrylike fruit.
Leaves:	Grayish green above, gray beneath; velvety, toothless, lance-shaped or oblong; to 3 1/2" long.
Blooms:	Early summer.
Elevation:	3,000 to 7,000'.
Habitat:	Moist soils along streams and ponds.
Comments:	Deciduous, with reddish brown spines on branches and twigs to 2" long. Native of Europe and western Asia; now naturalized in areas of Arizona, crowding out native species. Fruits eaten by birds; occasionally used for making jelly. One species of *Elaeagnus* (eh-lee-AG-nuss) in Arizona. Photograph taken at Lyman Lake, August 4.

RUSSET BUFFALO BERRY   851
Shepherdia canadensis
Elaeagnus or Oleaster Family (Elaeagnaceae)

Height:	To 8'.
Flowers:	Yellowish, inconspicuous, petalless; to 1/16" wide; followed by reddish orange, fleshy, juicy, pockmarked, oval, berrylike fruit to 1/4" long.
Leaves:	Dull green and dusty-scaled above; silvery with rusty patches beneath; elliptical to oval; to 3" long.
Blooms:	April–June.
Elevation:	7,000 to 9,000'.
Habitat:	Moist coniferous forests.
Comments:	Thornless, sprawling shrub with grayish brown bark. Fruit tastes bitter; eaten by birds. Male and female flowers on separate plants. Three species of *Shepherdia* (sheh-PURD-ih-uh) in Arizona. Photograph taken at Greer, July 5.

ROUNDLEAF BUFFALO BERRY   852
Lead bush
Shepherdia rotundifolia
Elaeagnus or Oleaster Family (Elaeagnaceae)

Height:	To 5'.
Flowers:	Grayish green, petalless, tiny, inconspicuous; coated with grayish green scales; in leaf axils; followed by silvery, scaly, soft, juicy, egg-shaped berry to 3/8" long. Male and female flowers on separate plants.
Leaves:	Silvery gray and covered with silvery scales above, white or yellow-woolly and scaly beneath; curved under; thick, oval to roundish; to 1 1/4" long.
Blooms:	May–June.
Elevation:	5,000 to 8,000'.
Habitat:	Steep slopes in northern Arizona.
Comments:	Evergreen shrub. Ripened fruit contains sweet, watery, yellowish juice. Berries eaten by birds, bears, and small mammals; also used for making jelly. Salve made from plant to treat sheep eye irritation. Three species of *Shepherdia* (sheh-PURD-ih-uh) in Arizona. Photograph taken at North Rim of Grand Canyon National Park, June 25.

EVENING PRIMROSE FAMILY
Onagraceae (oh-nah-GRAY-see-ee)
Represented in Arizona by herbs and small shrubs.

Flowers:	Parts are usually regular and in fours: 4 petals, 4 sepals, 4 or 8 stamens, 4-lobed stigma, single style. Inferior ovary, 2- to 4-celled.
Fruit:	Usually a dry, 4-celled capsule.
Leaves:	Alternate, opposite, whorled or basal, simple.

HARTWEG EVENING PRIMROSE   333
Calylophus hartwegii (Oenothera greggii)
Evening Primrose Family (Onagraceae)

Height:	To 1'.
Flowers:	Bright yellow, with 4 very crinkly petals; to 2 1/2" wide; large buds are reddish with green stripes.
Leaves:	Gray-green, hairy, narrow, with wavy margins; to 2" long.
Blooms:	April–June.
Elevation:	3,000 to 7,000'.
Habitat:	Roadsides, hillsides, and plains.
Comments:	Perennial herb. Four species of *Calylophus* (kal-ee-LOH-fuss) in Arizona. Photograph taken in vicinity of Safford, April 20.

WOODY BOTTLE-WASHER   165
Camissonia boothii (Oenothera decorticans var. *condensata)*
Evening Primrose Family (Onagraceae)

Height:	To 20".
Flowers:	White, fading to pink, with 4 petals; long stamens curved inward toward center; to 1/2" wide on numerous long stems in center of plant; followed by splitting capsules on a woody core when mature and dry.
Leaves:	Dark green, with reddish purple blotches and spots; mainly basal; lance-shaped to elliptical; to 4" long.
Blooms:	February–May.
Elevation:	Below 2,500'.
Habitat:	Open desert.
Comments:	Annual. Fifteen species of *Camissonia* (ka-mis-SOHN-i-ah) in Arizona. Photograph taken at Golden Shores, February 25.

YELLOW CUPS   334
Sundrop, desert primrose, hierba del golpe
Camissonia brevipes (Oenothera brevipes)
Evening Primrose Family (Onagraceae)

Height:	To 22".
Flowers:	Bright yellow, with 4 petals; cup-shaped; to 1 1/2" wide; in broad raceme; followed by slender pod, to 3" long.
Leaves:	Green with reddish tinge, mostly in basal rosette; coarse, oval or pinnately lobed; to 5" long.
Blooms:	February–May.
Elevation:	Below 4,500'.
Habitat:	Desert slopes and washes.

Comments: Annual. Blooms at sunrise instead of sunset, like most evening primroses. Fifteen species of *Camissonia* (ka-mis-SOHN-i-ah) in Arizona. Photograph taken at Alamo Lake, February 13.

MUSTARD EVENING PRIMROSE   335
Camissonia californica
Evening Primrose Family (Onagraceae)

Height: To 3'.
Flowers: Yellow, 4-petaled; often with pinkish spots at bases of petals; to 3/4" wide; followed by a long, very narrow, mustardlike seed pod to 2 1/2" long.
Leaves: Dark green, narrow; linear on stems; lance-shaped with irregular margins toward base of plant; to 4" long.
Blooms: February–June.
Elevation: Below 4,500'.
Habitat: Washes, dry slopes, and plains.
Comments: Many-branched. Resembles members of the mustard family. Fifteen species of *Camissonia* (ka-mis-SOHN-i-ah) in Arizona. Photograph taken in Superstition Mountains, March 22.

CAMISSONIA   336
Camissonia micrantha (*Oenothera micrantha*)
Evening Primrose (Onagraceae)

Height: To 2'.
Flowers: Bright yellow, with orangish buds, 4 petals; to 1/2" wide.
Leaves: Gray-green, leathery with hairs; arrow-shaped; base clasps stem; to 2" long at base, smaller up along stem.
Blooms: March–May.
Elevation: Below 4,500'.
Habitat: Washes and desert flats.
Comments: Fifteen species of *Camissonia* (ka-mis-SOHN-i-ah) in Arizona. Photograph taken in vicinity of Saguaro Lake, May 20.

FIREWEED   579
Blooming Sally, giant willow-herb, French willow, brickweed
Epilobium angustifolium
Evening Primrose Family (Onagraceae)

Height: To 6'.
Flowers: Deep rose-purple, with 4 widely spreading petals; to 3/4" long, 1" wide; in long, terminal raceme; followed by slender pod to 3" long; each seed bearing a tuft of hairs.
Leaves: Green, lance-shaped, narrow; veins curved into scallops along margins; to 6" long.
Blooms: July–September.
Elevation: 7,000 to 11,500'.
Habitat: Roadsides, burned areas, and logged areas.
Comments: Perennial herb. Young shoots are potherbs. So named because it grows after forest fires. Ten species of *Epilobium* (ep-i-LOW-bi-uhm) in Arizona. Photograph taken at Greer, July 21.

EPILOBIUM   580

Epilobium halleanum
Evening Primrose Family (Onagraceae)

Height:	To 12".
Flowers:	Pink, striped with darker pink; with 4 deeply notched petals; to 1/8" wide; in cluster at upper leaf axil; followed by elongated, narrow, hairy, upright seed capsule to 1 3/4" long.
Leaves:	Dark green, clasping stem, pointing upward close to stem; lance-shaped, toothed, opposite; to 1 1/2" long.
Blooms:	July–August.
Elevation:	8,000 to 10,000'.
Habitat:	Wet mountain meadows and lakesides.
Comments:	Has reddish, hairy stems. Ten species of *Epilobium* (ep-i-LOW-bi-um) in Arizona. Photograph taken at Carnero Lake near Greer, July 11.

PARCHED FIREWEED   685

Epilobium paniculatum forma *adenocladon*
Evening Primrose Family (Onagraceae)

Height:	To 4'.
Flowers:	Rose to purplish, with 4 deeply cleft petals; to 1/2" wide, 1/4" long; in widely branching cluster on flower stalk to 1/2" long; followed by 4-sided seed pod to 1" long.
Leaves:	Dark green, linear, narrow, alternate; to 2" long. Clusters of shorter leaves in axils.
Blooms:	August–October.
Elevation:	5,000 to 8,500'.
Habitat:	Roadsides and dry, open, disturbed areas.
Comments:	Ten species of *Epilobium* (ep-i-LOW-bi-uhm) in Arizona. Photograph taken at McNary, August 10.

SCARLET GAURA   581

Scarlet beeblossom, plains gaura, butterflyweed
Gaura coccinea
Evening Primrose Family (Onagraceae)

Height:	To 20".
Flowers:	Reddish pink to white (lighter-colored in evening, becoming darker by mid-morning); irregular, shapeless; to 1/2" wide; on nodding spike blooming upward from base; followed by club-shaped, grooved seed capsule to 1/2".
Leaves:	Light green, narrowly lanceolate; to 2 1/2" long.
Blooms:	April–September.
Elevation:	2,000 to 8,000'.
Habitat:	Roadsides, fields, plains, and pine and juniper woodlands.
Comments:	Perennial herb. Light-colored, newly opened flowers attract pollinating moths at night. By morning, flowers are pink, deepening to reddish as day progresses. Three species of *Gaura* (GAU-rah) in Arizona. Photograph taken in Nutrioso area, July 23.

LIZARD-TAIL   582

Tall gaura, velvet leaved gaura, smallflower gaura
Gaura parviflora
Evening Primrose Family (Onagraceae)

Height:	To 6'.
Flowers:	Pink, tiny, 4-petaled; to 3/8" long, 3/16" wide; in dense, nodding, hairy, terminal spike to 18" long.
Leaves:	Dark green, lance-shaped, slightly toothed; to 8" long in basal rosette. Leaves on stem are lance-shaped, velvety-haired, alternate; to 4" long.
Blooms:	April–October.
Elevation:	100 to 6,800'.
Habitat:	Roadsides, fields, disturbed ground, and desert washes.
Comments:	Has hairy stems; 1 main stem with several smaller side branches. Three species of *Gaura* (GAU-rah) in Arizona. Photograph taken at Saguaro National Monument West, April 17.

PRAIRIE EVENING PRIMROSE   166
Oenothera albicaulis
Evening Primrose Family (Onagraceae)

Height:	To 16".
Flowers:	White (pink when aged), with 4 petals; to 1 1/2" wide.
Leaves:	Grayish green, to 2" long. Basal leaves are spoon-shaped; stem leaves are cleft into narrow lobes.
Blooms:	March–August.
Elevation:	2,500 to 7,500'.
Habitat:	Roadsides and dry, grassy, or sandy disturbed areas.
Comments:	Twenty-one species of *Oenothera* (ee-no-THEE-rah or ee-NOTH-er-rah) in Arizona. Photograph taken near Nutrioso, August 3.

STEMLESS PRIMROSE   167
Tufted evening primrose, sandlily, rockrose, white stemless evening primrose
Oenothera caespitosa
Evening Primrose Family (Onagraceae)

Height:	To 4".
Flowers:	White, turning to pink with age; 4 heart-shaped petals; long, yellow stamens and stigma; slightly fragrant; to 4" wide; opening in late afternoon, fading the following morning. Flower held above ground by long, thin calyx tube.
Leaves:	Grayish green, (some are tinged reddish), finely haired, narrow, with toothed margins; to 7" long, 1" wide; in basal rosette.
Blooms:	April–September.
Elevation:	3,000 to 7,500'.
Habitat:	Roadsides, ponderosa forest clearings, and dry, rocky slopes.
Comments:	Twenty-one species of *Oenothera* (ee-no-THEE-rah or ee-NOTH-er-ah) in Arizona. Photograph taken northeast of Superior, April 20.

WHITE PRIMROSE   168
Oenothera coronopifolia
Evening Primrose Family (Onagraceae)

Height:	To 18".
Flowers:	White, with 4 petals; to 1" wide.
Leaves:	Grayish green, linear and linear-lobed, toothed; to 3/4" long.
Blooms:	June–August.
Elevation:	3,000 to 8,000'.

Habitat:	Dry plains and sandy soil.
Comments:	Perennial herb. Twenty-one species of *Oenothera* (ee-no-THEE-rah or ee-NOTH-er-rah) in Arizona. Photograph taken at Lee's Ferry, June 23.

DUNE PRIMROSE   169
Oenothera deltoides
Evening Primrose Family (Onagraceae)

Height:	To 1 1/2'.
Flowers:	White, turning pink; yellow toward center; 4 petals; saucerlike; to 3 1/2" wide.
Leaves:	Pale green, hairy, sometimes grooved or cleft; to 4 1/2" long.
Blooms:	February–May, depending on variety.
Elevation:	Generally below 2,500', depending on variety.
Habitat:	Sandy deserts and other open areas.
Comments:	Sweet-scented and bushlike. There are numerous varieties of this species. The outer stems on some varieties curl upward and inward when they die, forming a cagelike structure. Twenty-one species of *Oenothera* (ee-no-THEE-rah or ee-NOTH-er-rah) in Arizona. Photograph taken near Tacna, March 29.

HOOKER'S EVENING PRIMROSE   337
Yellow flowered evening primrose
Oenothera hookeri
Evening Primrose Family (Onagraceae)

Height:	To 4'.
Flowers:	Yellow, becoming pink to orange the following day; 4 broad petals; to 3" wide; in a simple or branching raceme; followed by a slender pod to 2" long.
Leaves:	Green, long, lance-shaped or elliptical; to 9" long, graduating to smaller from base to top of stem.
Blooms:	July–October.
Elevation:	3,500 to 9,500'.
Habitat:	Roadsides, pinyon-juniper woodlands, and ponderosa pine clearings.
Comments:	Biennial herb. Seeds eaten by Native Americans. Flowers open in late afternoon and close by noon the following day. Twenty-one species of *Oenothera* (ee-no-THEE-rah or ee-NOTH-er-rah) in Arizona. Photograph taken near Willow Springs Lake, September 13.

BOTTLE EVENING PRIMROSE   338
Sundrop
Oenothera primiveris
Evening Primrose Family (Onagraceae)

Height:	Prostrate, to 4".
Flowers:	Yellow, 4 petals, notched; to 2" wide, opening in the evening, closing following morning.
Leaves:	Greenish gray, pinnate, broad, rounded lobes, basal; to 4" long.
Blooms:	Mid-February–May.
Elevation:	Below 4,500'.
Habitat:	Dry and open deserts.
Comments:	Twenty-one species of *Oenothera* (ee-no-THEE-rah or ee-NOTH-er-rah) in Arizona. Photograph taken at Organ Pipe Cactus National Monument, February 28.

YELLOW PRIMROSE 339
Oenothera taraxacoides
Evening Primrose (Onagraceae)

Height:	To 6".
Flowers:	Bright yellow (pink when faded), with 4 quilted petals, yellow stamens, long, yellowish green stigma with 4 threadlike branches; to 3 1/2" wide.
Leaves:	Dark green, very finely haired, deeply lobed; to 6" long.
Blooms:	May–August.
Elevation:	5,000 to 9,500'.
Habitat:	Sandy or moist soil along roadsides and in pine forests.
Comments:	Twenty-one species of *Oenothera* (ee-no-THEE-rah or ee-NOTH-er-rah) in Arizona. Photograph taken at Crescent Lake, July 2.

HUMMINGBIRD TRUMPET 551
Arizona trumpet, California fuchsia
Zauschneria californica ssp. *latifolia* (*Zauschneria latifolia*)
Evening Primrose Family (Onagraceae)

Height:	To 2'.
Flowers:	Reddish orange, tubular, crinkly, with 4 lobes notched in center; long stamens; to 1 1/2" long, hanging in clusters.
Leaves:	Dark green, hairy, narrowly elliptical, toothed; to 1" long, growing all along stems.
Blooms:	June–December.
Elevation:	2,500 to 7,000'.
Habitat:	Canyons, along washes, and in other damp areas.
Comments:	Perennial herb; shredding bark. Two species of *Zauschneria* (zaush-NEAR-i-ah) in Arizona. Photograph taken near Christopher Creek, September 27.

PARSLEY or CARROT FAMILY
Umbelliferae (um-bell-LIF-fer-ee)
Represented in Arizona by herbs.

Flowers:	Regular, with 5 petals, 5 sepals, 5 stamens, 2 styles. Usually small and in umbrella-shaped clusters. Inferior ovary, 2-celled.
Fruit:	2-ribbed or winged, 1-seeded pods with aromatic oil ducts.
Leaves:	Alternate or basal, pinnately compound; usually finely cut; strong-smelling.

WATER PARSNIP 270
Berula erecta
Parsley or Carrot Family (Umbelliferae)

Height:	To 3'.
Flowers:	White, tiny, with 5 rounded, twisted, notched petals; 5 long pink-tipped stamens; in compound umbel to 1 3/4" wide with bracts around umbel and flower clusters; followed by nearly round fruit, to 1/16" long, in umbel.
Leaves:	Light green, divided pinnately into segments; toothed or lobed, to 18" long; leaflets opposite, to 1 1/2" long.
Blooms:	June–August.
Elevation:	4,000 to 7,000'.

Habitat:	Streamsides, in streams, and in other wet places.
Comments:	Perennial. One species of *Berula* (BER-eu-lah) in Arizona. Photograph taken in vicinity of Lakeside, August 9.

WATER HEMLOCK   271

Douglas's water hemlock, western water hemlock, cowbane
Cicuta douglasii
Parsley or Carrot Family (Umbelliferae)

Height:	To 7'.
Flowers:	White, minute, in loose, flat-topped, terminal cluster to 5" wide.
Leaves:	Dark green, twice to three times pinnate, to 14" long; lance-shaped, sharply toothed leaflets to 4" long.
Blooms:	July–September.
Elevation:	6,000 to 9,000'.
Habitat:	Marshes, edges of streams, and low, wet areas.
Comments:	Perennial herb. Roots and young growth are very poisonous to warm-blooded animals if ingested. One species of *Cicuta* (sy-KEW-tah) in Arizona. Photograph taken at Nelson Reservoir, August 3.

HEMLOCK-PARSLEY   272

Conioselinum scopulorum
Parsley or Carrot Family (Umbelliferae)

Height:	To 4'.
Flowers:	Greenish white, with 5 wavy petals, green pistil; to 1/8" wide; in flat cluster or umbel to 4" wide; followed by flattened fruits with winged ribs, to 1/4" long.
Leaves:	Dark green, large, triangular-shaped; pinnately divided and cleft, clasping stem at base; to 9" long.
Blooms:	August–September.
Elevation:	6,000 to 9,500'.
Habitat:	Moist spruce-fir forests.
Comments:	Perennial herb. Attractive to flies. Two species of *Conioselinum* (koni-oh-sel-LIE-num) in Arizona. Photograph taken in vicinity of Hannagan Meadow, August 6.

POISON HEMLOCK   273

Winter fern
Conium maculatum
Parsley or Carrot Family (Umbelliferae)

Height:	To 10', but usually less.
Flowers:	White, 5-petaled; to 1/8" wide; in small cluster or umbel to 1/2" wide, grouped in compound umbel to 4" wide.
Leaves:	Dark green, fernlike, very finely divided; triangular-shaped, to 2' long, 2' wide at widest part.
Blooms:	May–August.
Elevation:	4,000 to 7,500'.
Habitat:	Moist ground near streams, waste areas, and roadsides.
Comments:	Biennial herb; many-branched. A native of Eurasia; now naturalized in U.S. Grayish green stems are hollow, grooved, and spotted or blotched with purple. All parts of plant contain very poisonous juices; an extract of this plant is what killed Socrates.

Some children have used this plant's hollow stems as whistles. Mouthing these "instruments" can be fatal. One species of *Conium* (ko-NYE-uhm or KOH-ni-uhm) in Arizona. Photograph taken in vicinity of Patagonia, May 10.

AMERICAN CARROT   274
Rattlesnake-weed
Daucus pusillus
Parsley or Carrot Family (Umbelliferae)

Height:	To 28".
Flowers:	Whitish, tiny, long, with lacy bracts below flower cluster; cluster to 2" wide.
Leaves:	Dark green, fernlike, lacy-lobed; to 3" long.
Blooms:	March–May.
Elevation:	Below 4,000'.
Habitat:	Disturbed soil and roadsides.
Comments:	Annual. A relative of the cultivated carrot; Native Americans ate roots raw and cooked. Two species of *Daucus* (DAH-kuss) in Arizona. Photograph taken at Patagonia Lake State Park, April 26.

OSHA   275
Chuchupate, Porter's lovage
Ligusticum porteri
Parsley or Carrot Family (Umbelliferae)

Height:	To 4'.
Flowers:	White or pinkish, with 5 notched petals; to 1/8" wide; bractless; in wide, flat umbel to 3" wide; secondary umbels or umbellets to 3/4" wide; followed by oblong fruit with narrow wings on ribs.
Leaves:	Dark green, triangular, alternate, and fernlike; pinnate, much-divided, toothed; with base of stalk sheathing stem; to 12" long.
Blooms:	June–August.
Elevation:	6,500 to 11,500'.
Habitat:	Moist areas in mountains and in coniferous forests.
Comments:	Perennial; hollow-stemmed. A forage plant. Roots used medicinally to treat numerous ailments. One species of *Ligusticum* (li-GUS-ti-cum) in Arizona. Photograph taken in mountains above Greer, July 8.

LOMATIUM   494
Biscuit-root, Indian-root
Lomatium foeniculaceum (*Lomatium macdougali*)
Parsley or Carrot Family (Umbelliferae)

Height:	To 1'.
Flowers:	Yellowish or purplish tinged, tiny, in umbel; followed by flat, oval fruit to 1/4" long, 3/16" wide on 3/8"-long stem; in cluster on long stem above leaves.
Leaves:	Grayish green, fernlike, much-dissected, hairy on both surfaces; very aromatic, triangular, basal; to 3" long.
Blooms:	March–June.
Elevation:	4,500 to 8,000'.
Habitat:	Oak-juniper woodlands and clearings in ponderosa forests.
Comments:	Perennial. Has hairy stems. Five species of *Lomatium* (lom-AISH-uhm) in Arizona. Photograph taken in vicinity of Ashurst Lake, June 2.

SWEET CICELY   804
Sweet root
Osmorhiza depauperata
Parsley or Carrot Family (Umbelliferae)

Height: To 30".

Flowers: Tiny, greenish white, with 5 petals; to 1/16" wide, 3/16" long; in clusters at ends of 2 to 5 long-spreading stalks; followed by narrow, hairy, cylindrical fruit with club-shaped tip, to 3/8" long, on slender stem to 3/8" long.

Leaves: Dark green, hairy, several times thrice-divided; toothed, lobed; to 4" long, 6" wide.

Blooms: May–October.

Elevation: 7,000 to 10,000'.

Habitat: Moist, shady coniferous forests.

Comments: Perennial. Roots have aniselike flavor. Three species of *Osmorhiza* (oz-moh-RISE-ah) in Arizona. Photograph taken in vicinity of Mormon Lake, June 1.

HOG FENNEL   276
Fendler cowbane
Oxypolis fendleri
Parsley or Carrot Family (Umbelliferae)

Height: To 2'.

Flowers: White, 5-petaled; to 1/16" wide; in loose, flat-topped umbel to 2" wide; followed by oblong to oval fruit with broad, thin, lateral wings, to 1/4" long.

Leaves: Dark green, smooth, alternate, once-pinnate; to 5" long; bases of leaf stalks are expanded and sheath stem; up to 9 coarsely toothed, elliptical leaflets, each to 1 1/2" long.

Blooms: July.

Elevation: 9,500 to 10,000'.

Habitat: Streambanks in partial shade.

Comments: Perennial herb. Unbranched, smooth stems. One species of *Oxypolis* (oks-IP-oh-liss) in Arizona. Photograph taken in Mount Baldy Wilderness, July 8.

PARISH'S YAMPAH   277
Perideridia parishii
Parsley or Carrot Family (Umbelliferae)

Height: To 3'.

Flowers: White and lacy, with 5 tiny petals; to 1/8" wide; in small cluster to 1/2" wide; entire cluster or umbel to 2" wide.

Leaves: Dark green, only 1 or 2 per stem, to 3 1/2" long; 1 to 3 leaflets with margins curved upward.

Blooms: July–September.

Elevation: 6,500 to 8,000'.

Habitat: Mountain meadows and moist pine forests.

Comments: Perennial. Its fleshy roots are edible, and were an important food source for Native Americans and pioneers. Raw roots have carrotlike flavor and can be ground into flour. One species of *Perideridia* (per-i-der-RID-i-ah) in Arizona. Photograph taken in vicinity of Woods Canyon Lake, August 2.

MOUNTAIN PARSLEY   473 and 552
Pseudocymopterus
Pseudocymopterus montanus
Parsley or Carrot Family (Umbelliferae)

Height: To 2', but highly variable.
Flowers: Minute; color varies greatly from yellow to reddish purple; in flat-topped, terminal cluster of variable size.
Leaves: Dark green, pinnately compound, varies substantially in shape and size.
Blooms: May–October.
Elevation: 5,500 to 12,000'.
Habitat: Ponderosa pine forests, mixed conifer forests, and grasslands.
Comments: Perennial herb. One species of *Pseudocymopterus* (soo-doh-sye-MOP-ter-us) in Arizona. Yellow flower in Willow Springs Lake area, August 19; red flower photographed at Lynx Lake, September 11.

DOGWOOD FAMILY
Cornaceae (kor-NAY-see-ee)
Represented in Arizona by 1 shrub.

Flowers: Regular, small, with 4 petals, 4 stamens, 1 pistil, 1 style. Inferior ovary, 1- or 2-celled.
Fruit: A drupe.
Leaves: Opposite, simple.

RED-OSIER DOGWOOD   170
Red-osier, red dogwood, kinnikinnick
Cornus stolonifera
Dogwood Family (Cornaceae)

Height: Normally a shrub to 8'; in rare instances, tree-sized.
Bark: Gray to brown, smooth or furrowed.
Trunk: To 3" in diameter.
Flowers: Creamy white, with 4 petals; less than 1/4" wide; in flat-topped cluster at tip of branch to 2 1/2" wide; followed by bluish white, 1/4" berrylike fruits.
Leaves: Dark green tinged with pink above; pale green or whitish beneath; oval to elliptical; to 5" long.
Blooms: May–July.
Elevation: 5,000 to 9,000'.
Habitat: Moist locations, along streams and in canyons, in ponderosa pine and Douglas fir forests.
Comments: Has reddish twigs and branches. Spreads by underground, prostrate stems, often forming very large clumps. Controls erosion on banks of streams. Stems are flexible and used for making baskets. One species of *Cornus* (KOR-nus) in Arizona. Photograph taken in vicinity of Mormon Lake, June 2.

SILK TASSEL FAMILY

Garryaceae (gair-ree-AY-see-ee)

Represented in Arizona by a small tree and a shrub.

Flowers: Regular, small, in dense, catkinlike spikes. Inferior ovary.
Fruit: Berrylike.
Leaves: Opposite, simple, thick, evergreen.

QUININE BUSH   49

Silk tassel bush, yellowleaf silk tassel
Garrya flavescens
Silk Tassel Family (Garryaceae)

Height: To 6'.
Flowers: Small, petalless, abundant; in a dense, drooping, grayish green tassel of bell-like, hairy bracts; tassel to 4" long; followed by a grapelike cluster of berrylike fruits. Each fruit is round to oval, downy-covered, pointed at tip; to 1/2" long, 5/16" wide; cluster is up to 3" long. Male and female flowers are on separate plants.
Leaves: Dull grayish green; leathery, thick; woolly hair is silky to the touch; untoothed, opposite, oval to elliptical; evergreen; to 4" long, to 2" wide.
Blooms: January–April.
Elevation: 2,500 to 7,000'.
Habitat: Dry mountain slopes and canyons in woodlands and chaparral.
Comments: Garryin, an alkaloid derived from several *Garrya* species, has medicinal uses. The leaves on *G. flavescens* are larger, covered with silky hairs, and appear much grayer than those of **WRIGHT SILK TASSEL** (*Garrya wrightii*). Two species of *Garrya* (GAIR-ree-uh) in Arizona. Photograph taken at Oak Creek Canyon, Sedona, June 8.

WRIGHT SILK TASSEL   50

Grayleaf dogwood, feverbush, coffeeberry-bush
Garrya wrightii
Silk Tassel Family (Garryaceae)

Height: To 15'.
Flowers: Small, petalless, few in number, in a loose, hanging, grayish green tassel; followed by roundish fruit to 1/3" in diameter, dark bluish purple when mature.
Leaves: Light greenish gray, elliptical, rough, evergreen; untoothed, leathery, opposite and alternate; to 2" long.
Blooms: March–August.
Elevation: 3,000 to 8,000'.
Habitat: Dry slopes.
Comments: A small amount of rubber can be extracted from this plant. Browsed by deer. Two species of *Garrya* (GAIR-ree-uh) in Arizona. Photograph taken on Mount Graham, May 3.

HEATHER FAMILY

Ericaceae (eh-rih-KAY-see-ee)

Herbs, shrubs, and small trees.

Flowers: Regular or nearly regular, bell-shaped, urn-shaped, or tubular, 4 to 5 lobes or petals, 4- to 5-lobed calyx, 8 to 12 stamens, 1 pistil, 1 style, 1 stigma.

	Superior or inferior ovary, 4- to 10-celled.
Fruit:	Dry or juicy.
Leaves:	Mostly alternate or basal; simple or scalelike.

ARIZONA MADRONE   51

Arizona madrono
Arbutus arizonica
Heather Family (Ericaceae)

Height:	To 40'.
Trunk:	To 1 1/2' in diameter.
Bark:	Light gray, in squarish plates.
Flowers:	White to pinkish, urn-shaped; to 1/4" long; in loose, terminal cluster to 2 1/2" long; followed by a cluster of orange-red, warty, berrylike fruit, 3/8" in diameter.
Leaves:	Shiny, light green above, paler beneath; lance-shaped, leathery, with reddish leaf stems; to 3" long, 1" wide.
Blooms:	April–September (usually June).
Elevation:	4,000 to 8,000'.
Habitat:	Oak woodlands in mountains of southeastern Arizona.
Comments:	Evergreen tree with compact, rounded crown. Related to manzanita, except reddish bark occurs only on smaller branches. One species of *Arbutus* (ar-BEW-tuss) in Arizona. Photograph taken at Cave Creek, Portal, April 22.

POINTLEAF MANZANITA   629A and B

Bearberry, pinguica, manzanilla, Mexican manzanita
Arctostaphylos pungens
Heather Family (Ericaceae)

Height:	To 6'.
Flowers:	White to pink, nodding, and bell-shaped; to 1/4" long, in clusters at tips of branches; followed by reddish brown, berrylike fruit, to 1/4" in diameter (resembling a miniature apple).
Leaves:	Green to bluish green, thick, leathery, elliptical; pointed at tip and base; to 1 1/2" long.
Blooms:	March–May.
Elevation:	4,000 to 8,000'.
Habitat:	Chaparral and dry hillsides and in ponderosa pine belt.
Comments:	Evergreen, with smooth, red bark and crooked branches. Often grows in dense thickets, preventing erosion. Rapidly reseeds or grows from root sprouts in burned areas. Leaves twist on stalks to a vertical position to prevent excess evaporation during drought periods. Infrequently browsed, though berries are eaten by rodents, bears, and birds. Flowers attract hummingbirds. Native Americans use berries for food and for making a beverage. Jelly is made from unripened fruits. *Manzanita* is Spanish for "little apple." Four species of *Arctostaphylos* (ark-toh-STAFF-ih-los) in Arizona. Photograph in flower taken north of Superior, April 20; in fruit, September 2. **PRINGLEI MANZANITA** (*Arctostaphylos pringlei*) is a tall shrub with rounded leaves, and is frequently found in chaparral with pointleaf manzanita. It blooms from April to June. Photograph **(PLATE 628)** taken near Christopher Creek, June 3. The **GREENLEAF MANZANITA** (*Arctostaphylos patula*), found at the North Rim of the Grand Canyon, is a low shrub to 3' tall, with bright green, nearly oval leaves.

WOODLAND PINEDROPS   820

Albany beechdrops, giant bird's nest
Pterospora andromedea
Heather Family (Ericaceae)

Height: To 40".
Flowers: Yellowish brown, urn-shaped, nodding; to 1/4" long; loosely scattered along erect hairy, sticky, reddish brown, leafless stem.
Leaves: Brown and scalelike.
Blooms: June–September.
Elevation: 6,000 to 9,500'.
Habitat: Rich soil in coniferous forests.
Comments: Lacks chlorophyll. A saprophytic herb feeding on decaying plant matter in soil. Roots are like matted hair. Plant feels sticky when touched. One species of *Pterospora* (ter-ROS-por-ah) in Arizona. Photograph taken at Greer, September 11.

ROCKY MOUNTAIN BLUEBERRY   738

Huckleberry, whortleberry
Vaccinium oreophilum
Heather Family (Ericaceae)

Height: To 1'.
Flowers: Pink and white, urn-shaped and waxy; to 1/8" long; followed by roundish, juicy berry with flattened base, reddish, ripening to bluish black, to 3/8" in diameter, hanging beneath leaves.
Leaves: Dark green, finely toothed, elliptical, thin; to 1 1/2" long.
Blooms: June–July.
Elevation: 8,000 to 11,000'.
Habitat: Coniferous forests and mountain slopes, often in very mossy forest areas.
Comments: A sprawling shrub, woody at base. Berries used in making jelly, pies, and other recipes. One species of *Vaccinium* (vak-SIHN-ih-uhm) in Arizona. Photograph taken in coniferous forest above Greer, August 12.

PYROLA FAMILY

Pyrolaceae (pir-oh-LAY-see-ee)
Herbs and saprophytes.

Flowers: Regular, with 4 or 5 petals, a calyx of 4 or 5 sepals, 8 to 12 stamens, 1 style. Superior or inferior ovary, 4- to 10-celled.
Fruit: Capsule.
Leaves: Alternate, basal, simple.

COMMON PIPSISSEWA   630

Prince's pine, western prince's pine, wintergreen
Chimaphila umbellata
Pyrola Family (Pyrolaceae)

Height: Flower stem to 8".
Flowers: Pinkish to white, waxy, with 5 widely spreading petals, 10 prominent stamens; bell-shaped, nodding; to 5/8" wide; in loose cluster at top of flower stalk.
Leaves: Dark green, shiny, thick, leathery; evergreen, lance-shaped, with toothed margins from tip to midleaf; to 3" long; whorled around stem.

Blooms:	July–August.
Elevation:	Above 6,500'.
Habitat:	Coniferous forests.
Comments:	Perennial herb. An ingredient in root beer. Two species of *Chimaphila* (ky-MAF-fill-ah) in Arizona. Photograph taken in Greer area, July 5.

WOOD NYMPH   196
One-flowered wintergreen, waxflower, single delight
Moneses uniflora
Pyrola Family (Pyrolaceae)

Height:	Flower stalk to 5".
Flowers:	White or very pale pink, waxy; 5 rounded, spreading petals with crinkly margins; 10 golden stamens with swollen bases; thick, green stigma with 5 pointed lobes; flower to 3/4" wide, solitary and downward-facing on curve tip of stem.
Leaves:	Dark green, roundish, finely toothed, thick; in basal cluster; to 3/4" long, 5/8" wide.
Blooms:	July–August.
Elevation:	9,500 to 11,500'.
Habitat:	Moist, cool spruce-fir forests.
Comments:	Perennial herb. Evergreen. One species of *Moneses* (moh-NEE-seez) in Arizona. Photograph taken in mountains above Greer, July 8.

WHITEVEIN WINTERGREEN   788A and B
Pyrola picta
Pyrola Family (Pyrolaceae)

Height:	Flower stalk to 8".
Flowers:	Greenish white or cream-colored, globe-shaped, waxy, nodding, 5-petaled; style turned to one side, flower to 1/4" long, to 1/2" wide, hanging in terminal raceme on pinkish stem.
Leaves:	Dark green with white or pinkish white veins above and pinkish below; shiny, oval to elliptical, with reddish stems; to 3" long, 1 1/2" wide; in basal rosette.
Blooms:	July–August.
Elevation:	8,000 to 9,500'.
Habitat:	Coniferous forests.
Comments:	Perennial herb. Four species of *Pyrola* (PIR-oh-lah) in Arizona. Photographs taken in mountains above Greer, August 9.

SIDE-BELLS PYROLA   789
One-sided pyrola, one-sided wintergreen, shinleaf
Pyrola secunda (Ramischia secunda)
Pyrola Family (Pyrolaceae)

Height:	Flower stalk to 6".
Flowers:	White to greenish white, bell-shaped; to 1/4" long, arranged on only one side of flower stem.
Leaves:	Dark green, shiny, basal; oval to elliptical; finely toothed; to 2 1/2" long.
Blooms:	July–August.
Elevation:	7,000 to 9,500'.
Habitat:	Moist coniferous forests.
Comments:	Herbaceous perennial; an evergreen. Four species of *Pyrola* (PIR-oh-lah) in Arizona. Photograph taken near Mexican Hay Lake, July 2.

GREEN PYROLA   790

Shortleaf wintergreen, shinleaf
Pyrola virens (Pyrola chlorantha)
Pyrola Family (Pyrolaceae)

Height: Flower stalk to 12" long.
Flowers: White to greenish white, bell-shaped, drooping; 5-petaled, with large style extending below petals; to 1/2" wide; occurring along leafless flower stalk.
Leaves: Dark green, roundish, basal; leaf blade to 1 1/2" wide, 1 1/2" long; to 3" long, including stem.
Blooms: July–August.
Elevation: 6,500 to 10,000'.
Habitat: Rich soil of coniferous forests.
Comments: Perennial herb; evergreen. Native Americans use plant medicinally and to make paint for ceremonials. Four species of *Pyrola* (PIR-oh-lah) in Arizona. Photograph taken near Willow Springs Lake, July 6.

PRIMROSE FAMILY

Primulaceae (prim-you-LAY-see-ee)
Herbs.

Flowers: Regular; mostly funnel-shaped or tubular and 4- or 5-lobed; with 5 sepals, generally 5 stamens (if corolla is 5-lobed), 1 pistil with single style and stigma. Superior ovary, 1-celled.
Fruit: Dry pod (capsule).
Leaves: Alternate, opposite, whorled, or in basal rosette; simple.

ROCK JASMINE   197

Umbrella rock jasmine, northern fairy candelabra
Androsace septentrionalis
Primrose Family (Primulaceae)

Height: To 10".
Flowers: White, funnel-shaped, starlike, with 5 roundish lobes; to 1/8" wide; on leafless, erect stems.
Leaves: Dark green to reddish green, lance-shaped, irregularly toothed; in basal rosette; to 1 1/4" long.
Blooms: April–September.
Elevation: 7,000 to 12,000'.
Habitat: Meadows and clearings in coniferous forests.
Comments: Many-stemmed. Two species of *Androsace* (an-DROS-ah-see) in Arizona. Photograph taken in Greer area, July 4.

WESTERN SHOOTING STAR   688

Few-flowered shooting star
Dodecatheon pulchellum
Primrose Family (Primulaceae)

Height: To 2'.
Flowers: Purplish pink with yellow at base; 4- or 5-lobed, with lobes sharply swept back; dark stamens forming cone-shaped tip, resembling a miniature rocket; nodding; to 3/4" long; in terminal cluster on leafless stem.

Leaves:	Dull green, broadly lance-shaped, but variable in shape; to 10" long.
Blooms:	June–August.
Elevation:	6,500 to 9,500'.
Habitat:	Moist meadows.
Comments:	Perennial herb. Three species of *Dodecatheon* (doh-de-KATH-ee-ahn) in Arizona. Photograph taken near Greer, June 17.

FRINGED LOOSESTRIFE   376
Lysimachia ciliata var. *validula*
Primrose Family (Primulaceae)

Height:	To 3'.
Flowers:	Shiny yellow, flattened; with 5 rounded, crinkly edged, toothed petals pinkish toward base; 5 green sepals showing between petals; 5 stamens; to 3/4" wide, on stalks in leaf axils.
Leaves:	Light green with pinkish margins; opposite, folded upward, lance-shaped to elliptical; to 2 3/4" long.
Blooms:	July–September.
Elevation:	6,000 to 7,500'.
Habitat:	Moist soil of meadows, pondsides, and streambanks.
Comments:	Perennial herb. Many-branched, with squarish stems. One species of *Lysimachia* (ly-si-MACK-i-ah) in Arizona. Photograph taken in vicinity of McNary, July 7.

PARRY'S PRIMROSE   631
Brook primrose, alpine primrose
Primula parryi
Primrose Family (Primulaceae)

Height:	Flower stalk to 18".
Flowers:	Magenta-pink, with 5 spreading lobes joined at base into narrow tube; yellow markings at throat of tube; to 3/4" wide; in loose, rounded umbel or cluster at top of dark stalk.
Leaves:	Dark green, oblong, basal; fleshy, usually erect; to 12" long.
Blooms:	June–August.
Elevation:	10,000 to 12,000'.
Habitat:	Moist rock crevices, wet meadows, and along mountain streams.
Comments:	Flowers smell like carrion. Four species of *Primula* (PRIM-you-lah) in Arizona. Photograph taken in Mount Baldy Wilderness, August 14.

OCOTILLO FAMILY
Fouquieriaceae (fo-ki-eer-ee-AY-see-ee)
Represented in Arizona by a thorny shrub.

Flowers:	Regular; 5 united petals forming 5-lobed tubular corolla; 5 sepals, 10 to 17 protruding stamens. Superior ovary.
Fruit:	3-celled capsule.
Leaves:	Alternate, simple, in clusters in axils of spines.

OCOTILLO (oh-ko-TEE-oh)   553A and B
Candlewood, slimwood, coachwhip, Jacob's staff, vine cactus, flamingsword
Fouquieria splendens
Ocotillo Family (Fouquieriaceae)

Height:	To 20' tall.
Flowers:	Red, tubular, about 1" long; in clusters to 10" long, at tips of canes.
Leaves:	Green, oval, to 2" long.
Blooms:	March–June.
Elevation:	Below 5,000'.
Habitat:	Desert, especially on rocky, well-drained slopes.
Comments:	Named for Pierre Fouquier, a French professor of medicine. Relative of the boojum tree of Baja. Despite spines on its stems, the ocotillo is not a cactus. Most of the year its canes are leafless, but after a heavy rain bright green leaves appear on the long stems. When arid conditions return, the leaves change to brown and fall. This drought-responsive process may be repeated several times during the warmer months. Sections of ocotillo planted in rows soon become living fences. Mature plants have up to 75 slender branches. One species of *Fouquieria* (fo-ki-EE-ri-ah) in Arizona. Flower closeup taken at Usery Mountain Recreation Area, March 18. Photograph of entire plant taken at Paradise Valley, April 25.

SAPOTE or SAPODILLA FAMILY
Sapotaceae (sa-poh-TAY-see-ee)
Represented in Arizona by a large shrub.

Flowers:	Regular and small, with 5 petals, 5 sepals, 10 stamens. Superior ovary.
Fruit:	1-seeded drupe.
Leaves:	Alternate, simple, leathery, and thick.

GUM BUMELIA   52
Chittamwood, gum elastic, false buckthorn
Bumelia lanuginosa var. *rigida*
Sapote or Sapodilla Family (Sapotaceae)

Height:	Shrub to 15' in Arizona.
Trunk:	To 8" in diameter.
Bark:	Gray, rough.
Flowers:	White, 5-petaled, bell-shaped; 5-lobed, fragrant; to 1/8" wide; clustered at leaf axils; followed by juicy, blackish, egg-shaped fruits to 3/8" long.
Leaves:	Shiny, dark green above, dense gray, matted hairs beneath; alternate or in small clusters; leathery; elliptical or lance-shaped; rounded at tip and narrowing to base; tiny, pinkish stems; to 2" long, to 1/2" wide.
Blooms:	June–July.
Elevation:	3,000 to 5,000'.
Habitat:	Along washes and streams.
Comments:	Forms dense thickets in some areas. Twigs are often tipped with straight spines. Gray spines at leaf clusters grow to 5/8" long. Gum from stem used as a chewing gum. Wood used for making tool handles and cabinets. One species of *Bumelia* (bew-MEE-lee-ah) in Arizona. Photograph taken at Catalina State Park, November 10.

OLIVE FAMILY

Oleaceae (oh-lee-AY-see-ee)

Herbs, shrubs, and trees.

Flowers: Regular; with tubular corolla, with 4 to 6 lobes, or 4 separate petals, or petalless; 2 to 4 stamens, 1 style. Superior ovary, 2-celled.

Fruit: Varying; drupe, winged samara, or capsule.

Leaves: Alternate or opposite; simple or pinnate.

NEW MEXICAN FORESTIERA 77

Wild privet, palo blanco, New Mexican olive, mountain privet, wild olive

Forestiera neomexicana

Olive Family (Oleaceae)

Height: Sprawling shrub to 6', or small tree to 10'.

Bark: Gray to light tan blotched with gray; reddish brown twigs.

Flowers: Tiny and petalless; followed by dark bluish green, oval fruits, to 1/4" long, 3/16" wide, in clusters on branches. Male and female on separate plants.

Leaves: Green to grayish green, opposite, alternate and in clusters; oval to elliptical but highly variable; minutely toothed or untoothed; to 1 1/2" long.

Blooms: March–May.

Elevation: 2,000 to 7,000'.

Habitat: Hillsides, mesas, and lakeshores.

Comments: Very hard wood. Navajo Indians use wood for prayersticks; the Hopi use wood as digging sticks. Two species of *Forestiera* (faw-ress-tih-EH-ruh) in Arizona. Photograph taken at Wupatki National Monument, June 5.

DESERT OLIVE 53

Wild olive, desert olive forestiera, tanglebush, tanglebrush

Forestiera shrevei (*Forestiera phillyreoides*)

Olive Family (Oleaceae)

Height: Shrub to 12'.

Bark: Gray or blackish, smooth.

Flowers: Greenish, dark purple anthers; to 1/4" long; in small clusters; followed by brownish, egg-shaped, 1-seeded, fleshy fruit, to 3/8" long. Male and female on separate plants.

Leaves: Green, finely haired on both surfaces, untoothed; opposite, margins rolled under, oblong or lance-shaped or reverse lance-shaped; to 1" long, 1/4" wide.

Blooms: December–March.

Elevation: 2,500 to 4,500'.

Habitat: Dry, rocky slopes and desert canyons.

Comments: Evergreen or nearly so. Often forms dense thickets. Named for Charles Le Forestier, a French naturalist and physician. Two species of *Forestiera* (faw-ress-tih-EH-ruh) in Arizona. Photograph taken in Kofa Mountains, February 22.

LOWELL ASH 105

Fraxinus lowellii

Olive Family (Oleaceae)

Height: Shrub, or small tree to 25'.

Trunk: To 6" in diameter.

Bark:	Grayish brown, deeply furrowed.
Flowers:	Greenish, 1/8" long, in clusters to 1 1/2" long; followed by light brown, long-winged, flattened "keys" (dry, 1-seeded, winged fruit); in clusters to 1 1/2" long. Male and female on separate trees.
Leaves:	Dark green, paired, pinnately compound; to 7" long; 3, 5, or 7 leaflets; oval but variable, with saw-toothed margins; slightly leathery; leaflets to 3" long.
Blooms:	March–May.
Elevation:	3,200 to 6,500'.
Habitat:	Along streams and in moist canyon soils in oak woodlands and upper desert areas in central Arizona.
Comments:	Named for Percival Lowell, the famous astronomer, who first found this ash in Oak Creek Canyon. Seven species of *Fraxinus* (FRAX-i-nuss) in Arizona. Photograph taken at Lowell Observatory in Flagstaff, June 22.

VELVET ASH   106
Desert ash, smooth ash, Arizona ash, Toumey ash, fresno
Fraxinus pennsylvanica ssp. *velutina* (*Fraxinus velutina*)
Olive Family (Oleaceae)

Height:	To 30'.
Trunk:	To 1' in diameter.
Bark:	Gray, and deeply furrowed into broad ridges.
Flowers:	Small; male and female on different trees. Male flower is yellow; female is greenish, in clusters, followed by elliptical, long-winged "keys" or samaras to 1" long.
Leaves:	Green, pinnately compound; with 5 to 9 elliptical to lance-shaped leaflets, each to 1 1/2" long; margins with or without teeth; leaf to 6" long. Leaves vary greatly in all characteristics. Young leaves feel velvety, but velvet soon disappears.
Blooms:	March–April.
Elevation:	2,000 to 7,000'.
Habitat:	Along streams, in moist canyons, and along moist washes.
Comments:	Deciduous; the most common ash of the Southwest; spreading branches and rounded crown. Flowers appear in spring before leaves. Birds and other animals eat seeds. Seven species of *Fraxinus* (FRAX-i-nuss) in Arizona. Photograph taken at Oak Creek Canyon, September 9.

YELLOW MENODORA   364
Rough menodora
Menodora scabra
Olive Family (Oleaceae)

Height:	To 1 1/2'.
Flowers:	Bright yellow and tubular, with 5 or 6 spreading lobes; to 3/4" wide; in loose clusters at branch tips; reddish buds, followed by 2 translucent, round fruits side by side, each to 1/4" in diameter.
Leaves:	Grayish green, thick, rough, and lance-shaped; to 1 1/2" long; occurring along the length of entire stem.
Blooms:	April–September.
Elevation:	1,500 to 7,500'.
Habitat:	Dry mesas and rocky slopes.

Comments: Perennial herb. Many-branched; browsed by wildlife. Three species of *Menodora* (meh-noh-DOH-ruh) in Arizona. Photograph taken at Dead Horse Ranch State Park, May 30.

GENTIAN FAMILY
Gentianaceae (jen-she-ah-NAY-see-ee)
Herbs.

Flowers: Regular, tubular or bell-shaped; corolla is usually 5-lobed, sometimes 4-lobed (rarely 12-lobed); 4 to 12 stamens alternating with corolla lobes and of same number; same number of sepals as petals; 1 style, 2-lobed stigma. Superior ovary, 1-celled.
Fruit: Many-seeded capsule.
Leaves: Generally opposite, simple.

BUCKLEY'S CENTAURY 602
Canchalagua, centaury, Rosita
Centaurium calycosum
Gentian Family (Gentianaceae)
Height: To 2'.
Flowers: Pink, with 5 pointed lobes, bright yellow anthers; to 1" wide; terminal and in forks of branches.
Leaves: Light green, opposite, lance-shaped, and succulent; clasping the stem; to 2 1/2" long.
Blooms: April–June. Year-round at lower elevations in protected areas.
Elevation: 150 to 6,000'.
Habitat: Moist meadows and along streams.
Comments: Two species of *Centaurium* (sen-TOR-ee-um) in Arizona. Photograph taken at Saguaro National Monument West, April 17.

CATCHFLY GENTIAN 706
Alkali chalice
Eustoma exaltatum
Gentian Family (Gentianaceae)
Height: To 2'
Flowers: Deep bluish purple, darker toward center; 5-petaled; to 1 1/4" wide, 1 1/4" long.
Leaves: Grayish green, leathery, smooth; oblong, stalkless, paired with bases surrounding stem; to 4" long.
Blooms: June–September.
Elevation: 500 to 2,500'.
Habitat: Along rivers, streams, and ditches.
Comments: Rare in Arizona. One species of *Eustoma* (you-STOH-mah) in Arizona. Photograph taken along Salt River north of Granite Reef Dam, August 20.

PLEATED GENTIAN 707
Marsh gentian
Gentiana affinis
Gentian Family (Gentianaceae)
Height: To 16".

Flowers:	Violet to bluish purple, 5-lobed, erect; in leaflike floral bracts; flower to 1" long, in elongated, terminal cluster along upper 1/3 of stem.
Leaves:	Dark green, opposite, narrowly lance-shaped; to 2" long, occurring all along stem.
Blooms:	August–October.
Elevation:	7,000 to 9,500'.
Habitat:	Mountain meadows.
Comments:	Perennial herb. Stems are reddish brown and clustered. Five species of *Gentiana* (jen-shi-AY-nah) in Arizona. Photograph taken in mountain meadow above Greer, September 12.

PARRY GENTIAN   689
Closed gentian
Gentiana parryi
Gentian Family (Gentianaceae)

Height:	To 16".
Flowers:	Deep blue, whitish within and streaked with green, 5-lobed corolla with fringed appendages between lobes. Flower to 2" long, 7/8" wide, in terminal cluster of 1 to 5 flowers.
Leaves:	Dark green, smooth, thick; leathery, opposite, to 1 1/2" long.
Blooms:	August–September.
Elevation:	8,500 to 11,500'.
Habitat:	Alpine and subalpine meadows.
Comments:	Has erect, pinkish stem. Five species of *Gentiana* (jen-shi-AY-nah) in Arizona. Photograph taken in mountain meadow above Greer, August 12.

NORTHERN GENTIAN   603
Gentianella amarella ssp. *acuta* (*Gentiana strictiflora*)
Gentian Family (Gentianaceae)

Height:	To 20".
Flowers:	Pink to lavender, tubular, with 5 spreading lobes; fringe of whitish hairs around center opening; to 1/2" long, 3/8" wide, numerous; in leaf axils along main stem.
Leaves:	Dark green, opposite, stalkless; lance-shaped and reddish tipped; at right angles to main stem; to 1 3/4" long.
Blooms:	June–September.
Elevation:	7,000 to 11,000'.
Habitat:	Moist coniferous forests.
Comments:	Main stem is reddish. Six species of *Gentianella* (jen-she-AH-nel-lah) in Arizona. Photograph taken in vicinity of Woods Canyon Lake, August 3.

GENTIANELLA   708
Gentianella amarella ssp. *heterosepala* (*Gentiana heterosepala*)
Gentian Family (Gentianaceae)

Height:	To 16".
Flowers:	Deep purple, tubular, with 5 spreading lobes; fringe of whitish hairs around center opening; to 1/4" wide, numerous; in leaf axils along main stem.
Leaves:	Light green, opposite, stalkless; elliptical, curled upright along main stem; to 1 1/2" long.
Blooms:	August–September.
Elevation:	7,000 to 11,500'.

Habitat: Moist mountain meadows.
Comments: Six species of *Gentianella* (jen-she-AH-nel-lah) in Arizona. Photograph taken in mountains above Greer, August 10.

SPUR GENTIAN   340
Spurred gentian
Halenia recurva
Gentian Family (Gentianaceae)
Height: To 20".
Flowers: Yellowish and pointed, with cylindrical corolla, 4 erect lobes, 4 short spurs at base; to 1/2" long, 1/2" wide; at leaf intervals along stem.
Leaves: Yellowish green, linear, in opposite pairs at intervals on erect stem; to 1 1/2" long.
Blooms: August–September.
Elevation: 7,500 to 10,000'.
Habitat: Mountain meadows and moist coniferous forests.
Comments: Annual herb. One species of *Halenia* (hah-LEEN-i-ah) in Arizona. Photograph taken near Willow Springs Lake, September 13.

FELWORT   709
Star swertia
Swertia perennis
Gentian Family (Gentianaceae)
Height: To 2'.
Flowers: Deep purple and starlike, with 5 or 6 pointed, petallike lobes; 2 fringed, hairy glands at base of each lobe; to 1" wide; on erect stems in leaf axils on main stem.
Leaves: Light green, sunken veins, elliptical base leaves on long slender stalk; to 8" long, 2 1/4" wide. Leaves on upper stem are opposite, smaller, and clasp stem.
Blooms: July–September.
Elevation: 9,000 to 10,000'.
Habitat: Mountain meadows and along shallow mountain streams in spruce-fir forests.
Comments: Perennial. Four species of *Swertia* (SWER-ti-ah) in Arizona. Photograph taken in mountains above Greer, August 12.

DEERS EARS   791
Swertia, green gentian, elkweed, monument plant
Swertia radiata
Gentian Family (Gentianaceae)
Height: To 6'.
Flowers: Greenish white dotted with purple; star-shaped; 4-lobed with 2 fringed glands on each lobe; in leaf axils on stem; to 1 1/2" wide, in elongated cluster.
Leaves: Light green, in whorls of 4 to 6; linear to lance-shaped; to 12" at base, diminishing in size upward on stem.
Blooms: May–August.
Elevation: 5,000 to 10,000'.
Habitat: Rich soil in open pine forests and mixed aspen-conifer forests.
Comments: Perennial herb. Four species of *Swertia* (SWER-ti-ah) in Arizona. Photograph taken near Payson, June 10.

UTAH SWERTIA   792
Swertia utahensis
Gentian Family (Gentianaceae)

Height: To 3'.
Flowers: Yellowish green with purple streaks and dots; greenish at tip of lobes; 4 lobes, each
               with an elongated, basal gland lined with yellowish hairs; to 1" wide; in loose,
               terminal raceme.
Leaves: Dark green with white margins; narrow-leaved, basal, wavy margined; to 3" long.
Blooms: June–September.
Elevation: 4,000 to 7,500'.
Habitat: Sandy washes and dunes.
Comments: Perennial herb. Has erect stem. Four species of *Swertia* (SWER-ti-ah) in Arizona.
               Photograph taken at Dead Horse Ranch State Park, May 28.

DOGBANE FAMILY
Apocynaceae (a-poss-i-NAY-see-ee)
Represented in Arizona by herbs and slightly woody plants.

Flowers: Regular, usually bell-shaped or funnel-shaped; generally 5 sepals, 5-lobed joined
               petals; occasionally a 4-lobed corolla; 5 stamens, 2 pistils; twisted in bud. Superior
               ovary, 2 with single style.
Fruit: Usually paired, dry pods.
Leaves: Alternate, opposite, or whorled; simple.

AMSONIA   199
Amsonia hirtella var. *pogonosepala*
Dogbane Family (Apocynaceae)

Height: To 2'.
Flowers: White to pale bluish gray, tubular, and starlike; 5 slightly twisted lobes; to 1/2"
               wide, 1/2" long; in terminal, branched cluster; followed by long, slender, cylindrical
               seed pod to 4" long; splitting into 2 sections when mature.
Leaves: Dark green, smooth, lance-shaped, with prominent midvein; to 3" long.
Blooms: March–April.
Elevation: 1,500 to 5,000'.
Habitat: Canyons and along streams.
Comments: Perennial herb. Stems contain a milky juice. Nine species of *Amsonia* (am-SOWN-i-
               ah) in Arizona. Photograph taken in Superstition Mountains, March 15. **AMSONIA
               HIRTELLA** is very similar but grows to a height of 3', is bushier, and has very
               hairy leaves and stems. Photograph (**PLATE 198**) taken east of Portal, May 5.

SPREADING DOGBANE   632
Honey bloom, wild ipecac, wandering milkweed
Apocynum androsaemifolium
Dogbane Family (Apocynaceae)

Height: To 20".
Flowers: Pale pink with deeper pink stripes within; bell-shaped; 5 flared lobes on rim, often
               curved backward; to 3/8" long, 5/16" wide; in loose, terminal cluster or in leaf axil;
               followed by slender pod to 7" long.
Leaves: Dark green above, paler or whitish beneath; oval, in drooping pairs; to 3 1/2" long.

Blooms:	June–August.
Elevation:	7,000 to 9,500'.
Habitat:	Clearings in ponderosa and mixed conifer forests.
Comments:	Perennial herb. Many-branched, with milky sap. Poisonous to livestock; once believed this plant was poisonous to dogs, hence its common name. Native Americans used stem fiber for making cloth, cordage, and fishing nets. Six species of *Apocynum* (a-POSS-i-num) in Arizona. Photograph taken at Greer, July 21.

INDIAN HEMP 633
Dogbane
Apocynum cannabinum
Dogbane Family (Apocynaceae)

Height:	To 5'.
Flowers:	White to very pale pink, with 5 pointed lobes; 3/16" long, 3/16" wide, in open, terminal, upright cluster; followed by a slender, cylindrical pod to 6" long.
Leaves:	Light green above, paler beneath; lance-shaped, opposite; on short leaf stalk; with whitish midvein; to 4" long.
Blooms:	June–September.
Elevation:	To 7,500'.
Habitat:	Clearings and borders of woodlands.
Comments:	Perennial herb. Reddish stems. A very variable species, as it interbreeds with other species of *Apocynum*. A low-grade heart stimulant was produced from the root. Six species of *Apocynum* (a-POSS-i-num) in Arizona. Photograph taken at Oak Creek Canyon, Sedona, June 9.

MYRTLE 690
Band-plant, cut-finger, vinca
Vinca major
Dogbane Family (Apocynaceae)

Height:	Trailing evergreen, often rooting at tips.
Flowers:	Bluish lavender, tubular, with 5 flat lobes twisted to left; solitary, stalked; to 2" wide, in axils of leaves.
Leaves:	Dark green, shiny, evergreen; oval, heart-shaped at base; to 3" long.
Blooms:	March–July.
Elevation:	Not available. Photograph taken at approximately 5,000'.
Habitat:	Light shade under trees.
Comments:	Perennial herb. Native of Europe. An escapee from cultivation in certain areas of Arizona. Becomes a weedy pest. Shoots used as styptic to stop bleeding. Photograph of *Vinca* (VIN-kah) taken in Oak Creek Canyon, June 18.

MILKWEED FAMILY
Asclepiadaceae (as-kleh-pih-a-DAY-see-ee)
Represented in Arizona by herbs and slightly woody plants.

| *Flowers:* | Regular, hourglass-shaped; 5 separate sepals; 5 joined petals, generally swept backward; with central column, 5 stamens. In roundish clusters or umbels. Two superior ovaries, each 1-celled. |

Fruit: Dry pod with seeds attached to tufts of hairs.
Leaves: Mostly opposite, occasionally whorled or alternate; simple. Normally produce a milky sap.

ANTELOPE HORNS   793
Spider antelope horns
Asclepias asperula (Asclepias capricornu)
Milkweed Family (Asclepiadaceae)
Height: To 1'.
Flowers: Greenish yellow with maroon tinges; fragrant; to 1/2" wide, in cluster to 3" wide; followed by stout, 6"-long, green pod with olive-green and pink streaks.
Leaves: Dark green and narrow, with grayish stripe down midvein; to 6" long.
Blooms: April–August.
Elevation: 3,000 to 9,000'.
Habitat: Dry plains, slopes, and clearings in oak woodlands and pine forests.
Comments: Perennial herb; used medicinally. Twenty-seven species of *Asclepias* (as-KLEH-pih-as) in Arizona. Photograph taken at Chiricahua National Monument, April 24.

CORN-KERNEL MILKWEED   377
Broadleaf milkweed
Asclepias latifolia
Milkweed Family (Asclepiadaceae)
Height: To 3'.
Flowers: Pale yellow and white, with 5 upward-pointing hoods above a pedestal; 5 downward-pointing petals below pedestal; very corn kernellike in appearance; to 3/8" wide, 1/2" long, followed by a broad, tapered pod to 5" long.
Leaves: Green to bluish green, roundish, smooth, and leathery; succulentlike; with reddish midvein, whitish side veins; to 6" long, 6" wide.
Blooms: June–August.
Elevation: 3,000 to 7,000'.
Habitat: Roadsides, plains, and mesas.
Comments: Perennial herb. Produces a milky sap. Twenty-seven species of *Asclepias* (as-KLEH-pih-as) in Arizona. Photograph taken north of Springerville, August 5.

PINE-NEEDLE MILKWEED   224
Asclepias linaria
Milkweed Family (Asclepiadaceae)
Height: To 5'.
Flowers: Whitish, with pinkish buds; 5 united petals; to 1/4" wide; with short-horned hoods; flowers in terminal cluster, to 1" wide; followed by smooth, shiny pod to 2" long.
Leaves: Light green, linear, alternate, and soft; to 1 1/2" long; crowded all along stems.
Blooms: March–November.
Elevation: 1,500 to 6,000'.
Habitat: Mesas and dry, rocky slopes.
Comments: Twenty-seven species of *Asclepias* (as-KLEH-pih-as) in Arizona. Photograph taken in vicinity of Tucson, November 10.

SHOWY MILKWEED   634A and B
Asclepias speciosa
Milkweed Family (Asclepiadaceae)

Height: To 4'.
Flowers: Dull pink, hairy, and starlike, with 5 darker pink sepals; 5 pink petals bent backward; 5 pink, pointed, wide-spreading hoods with incurved horns; flower to 1" wide; in clusters to 3" wide on stems in upper leaf axils and terminal; followed by white-woolly pod, to 4" long, with soft spines.
Leaves: Light green, short-stalked, thick, and leathery; shiny above, hairy beneath; prominent, whitish midvein; opposite; oblong to lance-shaped; to 8" long.
Blooms: June–August.
Elevation: 6,000 to 9,000'.
Habitat: Clearings in coniferous forests and roadsides.
Comments: Perennial herb. Produces milky sap. Has unbranched, woolly stems. Twenty-seven species of *Asclepias* (as-KLEH-pih-as) in Arizona. Photograph in flower taken in vicinity of McNary, July 7. Photograph in fruit taken in same locality, August 10.

LEAFLESS MILKWEED   378
Rush milkweed, bedstraw milkweed, desert milkweed
Asclepias subulata
Milkweed Family (Asclepiadaceae)

Height: To 4'.
Flowers: Yellowish; to 1/2" wide, in cluster to 2" wide; followed by a smooth, tapered seed pod to 4" long.
Leaves: Mostly leafless on mature plants. New growth has 2"-long leaves, which soon drop.
Blooms: April–October.
Elevation: Below 3,000'.
Habitat: Dry mesas, slopes, flats, and sandy washes.
Comments: Perennial herb. Has numerous, erect, gray-green stems that produce a milky sap. Each seed has a tuft of silky hairs. Twenty-seven species of *Asclepias* (as-KLEH-pih-as) in Arizona. Photograph taken at Usery Mountain Recreation Area, May 17.

POISON MILKWEED   225
Horsetail milkweed, whorled milkweed
Asclepias subverticillata
Milkweed Family (Asclepiadaceae)

Height: To 4'.
Flowers: White to cream-colored; to 1/2" wide; in round cluster to 1 1/4" wide; followed by a smooth, tapering seed pod to 4" long.
Leaves: Green, linear, to 5" long; in whorls at stem joints; tiny leaves in axils.
Blooms: May–September.
Elevation: 2,500 to 8,000'.
Habitat: Roadsides, sandy or rocky flats, and slopes.
Comments: Perennial herb. Each seed has a tuft of silky hairs. Stems have milky juice. Very poisonous to livestock. Queen and monarch butterfly caterpillars feed on the foliage of many milkweed species; ingested poisons are active in both caterpillars and adult butterflies, causing natural predators to avoid them. The foliage is fatal to other insects if eaten in large doses. Twenty-seven species of *Asclepias* (as-KLEH-pih-as) in Arizona. Photograph taken near Show Low, July 22.

BUTTERFLY WEED   379 and 538
Chiggerflower, orange milkweed, pleurisy-root
Asclepias tuberosa
Milkweed Family (Asclepiadaceae)

Height: To 3'.

Flowers: Brilliant orange to yellow; to 1/2" wide, 1/2" long; 5 small sepals, 5 petals (bent back) and 5 hoods, in flat-topped, erect, terminal cluster to 3" wide; followed by a narrow, tapered pod to 5" long.

Leaves: Light green, narrowly arrow-shaped; to 4 1/2" long.

Blooms: May–September.

Elevation: 4,000 to 8,000'.

Habitat: Dry, open grasslands and open areas in pine forests.

Comments: Perennial, bushy herb with stems hairy. Seeds have white, silky hairs. Unlike most milkweeds, sap of this species is not milky. Twenty-seven species of *Asclepias* (as-KLEH-pih-as) in Arizona. Photographs taken at Oak Creek Canyon, June 18.

CLIMBING MILKWEED   226
Sarcostemma cynanchoides (Funastrum cynanchoides)
Milkweed Family (Asclepiadaceae)

Height: Vine with stems to 10' long.

Flowers: White and starlike, with 5 petals, 5 sepals; to 1/2" wide, in cluster to 4" wide; followed by smooth, plump, brownish pod to 5/8" wide, 4" long; containing seeds with silky hairs attached.

Leaves: Dark green, arrow-shaped, to 2 1/2" long.

Blooms: May–September.

Elevation: 1,500 to 4,500'.

Habitat: Along streams, in washes, and on dry plains.

Comments: Perennial. Climbs on trees and shrubs. Has milky juice. Three species of *Sarcostemma* (sar-ko-STEM-mah) in Arizona. Photograph taken at Dead Horse Ranch State Park, September 9.

RAMBLING MILKWEED   635
Sarcostemma hirtellum (Funastrum hirtellum)
Milkweed Family (Asclepiadaceae)

Height: Climbs over shrubs and up into trees.

Flowers: Pale pink to purplish, creamy-colored in center; hairy, starlike, fragrant; 5 petals, 5 sepals; to 1/2" wide; in cluster, followed by velvety, long-tapering, plump seed pod to 3 1/2" long.

Leaves: Green, very narrow, linear to lance-shaped; to 2" long.

Blooms: March–October.

Elevation: Below 5,500'.

Habitat: Along desert washes.

Comments: Perennial. Seed pods smell like onion. Produces a milky juice. Its numerous stems often twist into a bluish green, living rope. Tohono O'Odham Indians consumed fruits. Three species of *Sarcostemma* (sar-ko-STEM-mah) in Arizona. Photograph taken at Usery Mountain Recreation Area, April 6.

MORNING GLORY FAMILY

Convolvulaceae (kon-voll-view-LAY-see-ee)
Represented in Arizona by herbs and slightly woody plants.

Flowers: Regular, with 4 or 5 united petals forming funnel-shaped or long, tubular corolla; 5 sepals, 5 stamens; 1 or 2 styles, 1 or 2 stigmas, usually twisted buds. Superior ovary, mostly 2-celled.

Fruit: Generally a capsule.

Leaves: Alternate, simple. Reduced to scales in species of dodder.

FIELD BINDWEED   200

Wild morning glory, possession vine, creeping Jenny
Convolvulus arvensis
Morning Glory Family (Convolvulaceae)

Height: Trailing vine to 4'.

Flowers: White or pinkish, funnel-shaped; to 1" wide; growing on one side of stalk; single; in leaf axil.

Leaves: Dark green, variable, arrow-shaped to triangular; growing on one side of stalk; to 2" long.

Blooms: May–September.

Elevation: Throughout Arizona.

Habitat: Roadsides, fields, and lots.

Comments: Perennial herb, from Europe; now naturalized. A troublesome, deep-rooted weed. Source of a blood-clotting material. Three species of *Convolvulus* (kon-VOLL-view-lus) in Arizona. Photograph taken at Nelson Reservoir, August 3.

HOARY BINDWEED   604

Convolvulus equitans (Convolvulus incanus)
Morning Glory Family (Convolvulaceae)

Height: Trailing to 3' long.

Flowers: Pale pink, funnel-shaped, 5 veins from center to lobes on edge; to 3/4" wide, 1" long.

Leaves: Grayish green, finely haired, narrow, with lobes at base; to 2" long.

Blooms: April–October.

Elevation: 3,000 to 6,000'.

Habitat: Roadsides, dry slopes, and mesas.

Comments: Three species of *Convolvulus* (kon-VOLL-view-lus) in Arizona. Photograph taken near Sierra Vista, April 26.

PRETTY DODDER   495

Cuscuta indecora
Morning Glory Family (Convolvulaceae)

Height: Twining, matted mass of yellowish stems ranging from several inches to several feet wide.

Flowers: Cream-colored, tiny, fleshy, and tubular; to 1/4" long; in small clusters.

Leaves: None.

Blooms: July–August.

Elevation: Not available. Photograph taken at 3,000'.

Habitat: Roadsides, canyons, and slopes.

Comments: Annual. A matted mass of yellowish stems. Parasitic; rootless. Seeds germinate in soil. Seedlings break contact with ground and twine about host plant, using suckers to absorb water and nutrients. Often spreads viral plant diseases. This species found on wide variety of shrubs and trees. Sixteen species of *Cuscuta* (kus-KYOO-tah) in Arizona. Photograph taken on Apache Trail, March 23.

ARIZONA BLUE EYES   691
Wild morning glory, evolvulus
Evolvulus arizonicus
Morning Glory Family (Convolvulaceae)

Height: To 1'.
Flowers: Sky blue, like those of a flattened morning glory; to 3/4" wide; on slender stalk; in upper leaf axil.
Leaves: Grayish green, lance-shaped, to 1" long.
Blooms: April–October.
Elevation: 3,500 to 5,000'.
Habitat: Deserts, grasslands, and pinyon-juniper woodlands.
Comments: Perennial herb. Four species of *Evolvulus* (eh-VOL-vu-lus) in Arizona. Photograph taken at Catalina State Park, April 15.

SILVER MORNING GLORY   201
Evolvulus sericeus
Morning Glory Family (Convolvulaceae)

Height: Prostrate, spreading; stems to 6" long.
Flowers: White or bluish (depending on variety); with funnel spreading into flattened disk; to 1/2" wide.
Leaves: Dark green, edged in silver above, gray beneath; tightly folded together; narrowly linear, pointed at both ends; to 1/2" long.
Blooms: May–September.
Elevation: 3,500 to 5,500'.
Habitat: Dry mesas and plains.
Comments: Sun-loving. Four species of *Evolvulus* (eh-VOL-vu-lus) in Arizona. Photograph taken at Lynx Creek Ruins, Prescott, May 27.

SCARLET CREEPER   554
Star glory, scarlet morning glory
Ipomoea coccinea (*Quamoclit coccinea*)
Morning Glory Family (Convolvulaceae)

Height: Long, twining vine.
Flowers: Bright reddish orange, tubular, and narrow; with white-tipped stamens; to 1" long, 1/2" wide.
Leaves: Dark green, heart-shaped or 3- to 5-lobed; to 2 1/4" wide, 2 1/2" long, not including stem.
Blooms: May–October.
Elevation: 2,500 to 6,000'.
Habitat: Canyons, woodlands, hillsides, and along streams.
Comments: Frequented by hummingbirds. Seventeen species of *Ipomoea* (ip-po-MEE-ah) in Arizona. Photograph taken at Clear Creek near Camp Verde, September 30.

WOOLLY MORNING GLORY   692
Ipomoea hirsutula (*Ipomoea desertorum*)
Morning Glory Family (Convolvulaceae)
Height: Twining vine.
Flowers: Purplish, tubular, with 5 pointed, hairy sepals; to 1 1/4" long, 1" wide.
Leaves: Dark green, hairy above and beneath; lacking lobes or with 3 pointed lobes; to 3" wide, to 3" long; on stems up to 5" long.
Blooms: July–November.
Elevation: 1,000 to 5,500'.
Habitat: Roadsides and fields.
Comments: Often becoming a weed. Has hairy stems. Seventeen species of *Ipomoea* (ip-po-MEE-ah) in Arizona. Photograph taken at Clear Creek near Camp Verde, September 30.

BIRD'S FOOT MORNING GLORY   605
Ipomoea leptotoma
Morning Glory Family (Convolvulaceae)
Height: Twining or spreading vine.
Flowers: Pink, bluish, or purple (rarely white) trumpet-shaped; to 1 1/2" long.
Leaves: Dark green, palmately cleft into 3 or 5 very narrow lobes; to 3" long.
Blooms: June–November.
Elevation: 2,500 to 4,500'.
Habitat: Washes; dry, grassy plains; and mesas.
Comments: Can be hairy stemmed. Seventeen species of *Ipomoea* (ip-po-MEE-ah) in Arizona. Photograph taken at Catalina State Park, November 10.

PHLOX FAMILY
Polemoniaceae (poh-lee-moh-ni-AY-see-ee)
Represented in Arizona by herbs and slightly woody plants.
Flowers: Mostly regular, tubular or funnel-shaped; with 5 corolla lobes or teeth, 5 sepals and 5 stamens alternating with corolla lobes; 1 style usually 3-lobed. Superior ovary, mostly 3-celled.
Fruit: Usually 3-celled capsule.
Leaves: Alternate or opposite; simple or compound.

MINIATURE WOOL STAR   693
Starflower
Eriastrum diffusum
Phlox Family (Polemoniaceae)
Height: To 4 1/2".
Flowers: Pale blue to whitish, tubular (long tube for tiny flower); to 1/2" long; in terminal clusters on bristle-tipped, woolly heads.
Leaves: Grayish green, very narrow, threadlike; to 3/4" long.
Blooms: March–June.
Elevation: 1,000 to 5,500'.
Habitat: Sandy areas, deserts, and mesas.
Comments: Annual. Stems are reddish brown. Two species of *Eriastrum* (air-ee-AH-strum) in Arizona. Photograph taken in Superstition Mountains, March 26.

BROAD-LEAVED GILIA   606
Starflower
Gilia latifolia
Phlox Family (Polemoniaceae)

Height:	To 20".
Flowers:	Pink, tubular, with 5 spreading lobes at right angles to narrow, funnel-shaped tube; to 1/2" long; terminal on stems.
Leaves:	Green, mostly basal, oblong, many-lobed, to 8" long.
Blooms:	February–April.
Elevation:	Below 2,000'.
Habitat:	Desert washes and slopes.
Comments:	Annual. Attractive to butterflies and hummingbirds. Eighteen species of *Gilia* (JILLY-ah; some prefer the Spanish pronunciation, HEEL-ee-uh) in Arizona. Photograph taken at Usery Mountain Recreation Area, February 18.

SKYROCKET   555
Scarlet gilia, skunk flower, polecat plant, hummingbird flower, desert trumpets, pink gilia, trumpet phlox, foxfire
Ipomopsis aggregata (*Gilia aggregata*)
Phlox Family (Polemoniaceae)

Height:	Flowering stem to 3'.
Flowers:	Bright red to deep pink, mottled with cream color; funnel-shaped; 5 flaring, pointed lobes; to 1 1/2" long; in leaf axils at tops of nearly leafless stems.
Leaves:	Dark green; pinnately divided into very narrow segments; mostly basal; to 2" long.
Blooms:	May–September.
Elevation:	5,000 to 9,000'.
Habitat:	Roadsides and openings in coniferous forests.
Comments:	Biennial; first year, produces rosette of leaves; in the second year, blooms. Has sticky stems; bruised leaves smell skunky. Attracts hummingbirds. Browsed by deer, pronghorn, and livestock. Native Americans used plant medicinally and for ceremonies. Nine species of *Ipomopsis* (eye-poh-MOP-sis) in Arizona. Photograph taken south of Alpine, July 23. **ARIZONA GILIA,** *Ipomopsis aggregata* var. *arizonica*, grows to 16" high, has red stems, trumpetlike flowers to 1" wide, 3/4" long, and hairy, basal, pinnately divided leaves to 1" long. It often grows on volcanic soil. Photograph **(PLATE 556)** taken at Sunset Crater National Monument, May 31.

BLUE GILIA   694
White-flowered gilia, blue starflower
Ipomopsis longiflora (*Gilia longiflora*)
Phlox Family (Polemoniaceae)

Height:	To 2'.
Flowers:	Pale blue to nearly white, with 5 spreading lobes at right angles to long, narrow tube; to 2" long; solitary or in pairs; on leafy cluster.
Leaves:	Green, threadlike, to 1" long; lower leaves with narrow segments; to 2" long.
Blooms:	May–November.
Elevation:	1,000 to 8,000'.

Habitat:	Dry mesas, plains, and roadsides.
Comments:	Often grows on limestone soil. Many-branched herb. Nine species of *Ipomopsis* (eye-poh-MOP-sis) in Arizona. Photograph taken in Tucson area, November 10.

MANY-FLOWERED GILIA   710
Ipomopsis multiflora (*Gilia multiflora*)
Phlox Family (Polemoniaceae)

Height:	Sprawling to 2'.
Flowers:	Violet-blue, tubular, with 5 flaring lobes, and 5 long stamens tipped with bright blue; to 1/2" wide, 1/2" long; in small, loose clusters along upper stems.
Leaves:	Dark green, downy, alternate; threadlike; pinnately divided into 3 to 5 lobes, or undivided; to 1 1/2" long, occurring along stems.
Blooms:	July–October.
Elevation:	4,000 to 9,000'.
Habitat:	Roadsides and dry slopes.
Comments:	Many-stemmed; attractive to bees. Native Americans used plant medicinally. Nine species of *Ipomopsis* (eye-poh-MOP-sis) in Arizona. Photograph taken near Heber, August 4.

YELLOW LINANTHUS   365
Desert gold
Linanthus aureus
Phlox Family (Polemoniaceae)

Height:	To 4".
Flowers:	Golden yellow, with bright orange center; 5-lobed, funnel-shaped, upright; to 1/2" wide.
Leaves:	Green, divided into 3 to 7 linear lobes; to 1/4" long; in rings at well-spaced intervals on stem.
Blooms:	March–June.
Elevation:	2,000 to 6,000'.
Habitat:	Dry plains, mesas, and oak woodlands.
Comments:	Annual. Threadlike, with reddish stalks. Six species of *Linanthus* (ly-NAN-thus) in Arizona. Photograph taken on Mount Graham, April 21.

LINANTHUS   202
Linanthus demissus
Phlox Family (Polemoniaceae)

Height:	To 4".
Flowers:	White, bell-shaped, with 5 flaring lobes, each with 2 reddish brown to purplish lines at base; to 1/2" wide, 1/4" long; in few-flowered clusters on branches.
Leaves:	Green, wiry, hairlike; to 3/8" long; surrounding bases of flowers.
Blooms:	March–May.
Elevation:	Below 2,000'.
Habitat:	Desert sands.
Comments:	Annual. Many-branched. Six species of *Linanthus* (ly-NAN-thus) in Arizona. Photograph taken in Kofa Mountains, March 29.

NUTTALL'S LINANTHUS 203

Linanthus nuttallii (*Linanthastrum nuttallii*)
Phlox Family (Polemoniaceae)

Height:	To 1'.
Flowers:	White, yellow in center; with 5 broad, flared lobes on narrow tube; to 1/2" wide; in terminal clusters on leafy stems.
Leaves:	Green, rigid, narrowly linear; leaves appear whorled on stems; to 1/2" long.
Blooms:	July–November.
Elevation:	5,500 to 8,000'.
Habitat:	Open ponderosa forests.
Comments:	Perennial herb. Six species of *Linanthus* (ly-NAN-thus) in Arizona. Photograph taken near Willow Springs Lake, August 19.

SLENDER PHLOX 607

Pink annual phlox
Microsteris gracilis
Phlox Family (Polemoniaceae)

Height:	To 8".
Flowers:	Rose to lavender, tubular, with 5 lobes, each notched in center; yellowish tube with long, slender, bright yellow-tipped stamens; flower to 1/8" wide, 1/2" long, in terminal cluster.
Leaves:	Dark green above, lighter green beneath; very hairy, lance-shaped, opposite; clasping stem; to 3/4" long.
Blooms:	February–May.
Elevation:	3,000 to 7,000'.
Habitat:	Moist areas.
Comments:	Annual. Pinkish and sticky, with hairy stems. One species of *Microsteris* (my-kro-STEE-riss) in Arizona. Photograph taken northeast of Superior, April 3.

SPREADING PHLOX 608

Phlox diffusa
Phlox Family (Polemoniaceae)

Height:	To 4".
Flowers:	Pure white to various shades of pink; upright trumpet with 5 broad, rounded lobes; to 5/8" wide; in large, colorful mats.
Leaves:	Greenish, sharp, needlelike, and stiff, to 5/8" long; occurring all along stem; hairy clusters at leaf bases.
Blooms:	May–August.
Elevation:	6,000 to 9,000'.
Habitat:	Plateaus and canyon rims.
Comments:	Woody, perennial herb. Eleven species of *Phlox* (FLOKS) in Arizona. Photograph taken at North Rim of Grand Canyon National Park, June 25. This low-growing species is distinguished by its broad, rounded petals and hairy clusters at leaf bases.

DESERT PHLOX 204

Vine phlox
Phlox tenuifolia
Phlox Family (Polemoniaceae)

Height:	To 3'.

Flowers:	White, funnel-shaped, with yellow inner tube; to 1" wide.
Leaves:	Dark green, linear, to 2" long.
Blooms:	February–May, rare instances in the fall after summer rains.
Elevation:	1,500 to 5,000'.
Habitat:	Along washes and on rocky slopes.
Comments:	Perennial. In partial shade, stems are vinelike and supported by neighboring shrubs. In the open, plants form tufts. Eleven species of *Phlox* (FLOKS) in Arizona. Photograph taken in Superstition Mountains, February 4.

WOODHOUSE'S PHLOX   609
Phlox woodhousei
Phlox Family (Polemoniaceae)

Height:	To 6".
Flowers:	Pink petal lobes (occasionally all white) above; white beneath; white center or "eye"; deeply notched; wedge-shaped petals; tubular with 5 or 6 petal lobes at right angles; to 3/4" wide.
Leaves:	Dark green, shiny, stiff, and thick; oblong, opposite, rough; to 2" long. Downy upper foliage.
Blooms:	Spring and autumn.
Elevation:	3,500 to 8,000'.
Habitat:	Open woods and pine forests.
Comments:	Has woody base. Eleven species of *Phlox* (FLOKS) in Arizona. Photograph taken at Upper Lake Mary, June 1. Notched petal lobes and white "eye" differentiate this species.

TOWERING POLEMONIUM   695
Jacob's ladder, leafy polemonium
Polemonium foliosissimum
Phlox Family (Polemoniaceae)

Height:	To 3'.
Flowers:	White, blue, or purple, with yellow center; shaped like a shallow bowl; to 1" wide; in terminal cluster.
Leaves:	Dark green, pinnate, with up to 25 elliptical to lance-shaped leaflets to 2 1/2" long.
Blooms:	July–August.
Elevation:	8,000 to 9,000'.
Habitat:	Moist soil along streams in mountains.
Comments:	Perennial herb with hairy stem. Five species of *Polemonium* (poh-lee-MOH-ni-uhm) in Arizona. Photograph taken south of Alpine, August 2.

WATERLEAF FAMILY
Hydrophyllaceae (hy-droh-fill-LAY-see-ee)
Represented in Arizona by herbs or shrubs.

Flowers:	Regular, often bell or funnel-shaped; in coils; 5 united petals forming 5 lobes; 5 united sepals, 5 stamens; 1 or 2 styles, 2 stigmas. Superior ovary, mostly 1-celled.
Fruit:	Many-seeded capsule.
Leaves:	Mostly alternate, often in basal rosettes, simple or pinnately compound.

WHISPERING BELLS   366
Yellow bells, golden bells
Emmenanthe penduliflora
Waterleaf Family (Hydrophyllaceae)

Height: To 20".
Flowers: Pale yellow, bell-shaped, and nodding; with 5 united petals; to 1/2" long; in loosely
                    branched cluster.
Leaves: Grayish green, long, narrow; pinnately lobed; to 4" long.
Blooms: March–June.
Elevation: Below 4,000'.
Habitat: Desert washes, slopes, and along streams.
Comments: Annual herb. Stems are covered with sticky hairs. So-named because when it is dry,
                    paper-thin flowers make rustling sounds in the wind. One species of *Emmenanthe*
                    (em-mee-NAN-thee) in Arizona. Photograph taken in the Superstition Mountains,
                    March 15.

YERBA SANTA   227
Mountain balm
Eriodictyon angustifolium
Waterleaf Family (Hydrophyllaceae)

Height: To 6 1/2'.
Flowers: White to pale lavender, funnel-shaped, 5-lobed, with dark-tipped stamens; to 3/8"
                    wide; in loose, terminal clusters on upper branches.
Leaves: Sticky, leathery, aromatic, evergreen; dull, dark green above (shiny when imma-
                    ture); lighter green and white-woolly beneath, with a prominent midvein and
                    network of veins; linear, often slightly toothed; margins rolled under; to 4" long.
Blooms: April–August.
Elevation: 2,000 to 7,000'.
Habitat: Dry hillsides, roadsides, and washes.
Comments: Woody at base. Browsed by mule deer. Infusion made from leaves is used medici-
                    nally to treat respiratory problems. One species of *Eriodictyon* (er-io-DICK-ti-on) in
                    Arizona. Photograph taken northeast of Superior, May 2.

SMALL-FLOWERED EUCRYPTA   696
Eucrypta micrantha
Waterleaf Family (Hydrophyllaceae)

Height: To 10".
Flowers: Bluish purple or white, bell-like, with 5 united petals; to 1/2" wide; in loose cluster
                    on slender, prickly stem.
Leaves: Dark green, prickly, pinnately lobed; clasping stem; to 2" long.
Blooms: February–May.
Elevation: Below 4,000'.
Habitat: Shade of shrubs and other sheltered areas.
Comments: Annual. Has very weak, prickly stems. Two species of *Eucrypta* (you-KRIP-tah) in
                    Arizona. Photograph taken at Alamo Lake State Park, February 26.

PURPLE MAT   610
Purple roll-leaf, nama
Nama demissum

Waterleaf Family (Hydrophyllaceae)
Height: To 3", with 8" stems in favorable years.
Flowers: Reddish pink, tubular, trumpetlike, with 5 rounded lobes; to 3/8" wide.
Leaves: Green, sticky, and narrow; hairy, spatula-shaped; to 1 1/2" long.
Blooms: February–May.
Elevation: Below 3,500'.
Habitat: Desert flats and washes.
Comments: Annual. In years of little rainfall, plant produces only a few flowers on very short stems. With plentiful rains, masses of these plants carpet broad areas of desert. Seven species of *Nama* (NAY-mah) in Arizona. Photograph taken at Organ Pipe Cactus National Monument, February 26.

DESERT BELL   697
Desert bluebell
Phacelia campanularia
Waterleaf Family (Hydrophyllaceae)
Height: To 2'.
Flowers: Dark blue to purplish blue, bell-shaped, tubular; 5 rounded lobes, each with white marking; purple filaments tipped with yellow-white anthers; hairy sepals; to 1" wide, 1 1/2" long; in loose flower cluster.
Leaves: Dark green above, edged in deep red; lighter green beneath; scalloped, ruffled, velvety-haired on both surfaces, oval to heart-shaped; to 3 1/2" long (including stem), 1 1/2" wide.
Blooms: February–April.
Elevation: Not available. Photograph taken at 2,700'.
Habitat: Washes and sandy areas.
Comments: Annual. Hairy, glandular plant with reddish stems. Branches freely. Thirty-eight species of *Phacelia* (fa-SEE-li-ah) in Arizona. Although this species is not listed in *A Catalogue of the Flora of Arizona*, it is apparently naturalized in the state. Photograph taken in a remote wash of the Santa Catalina Mountains, April 14. We have also seen the plant growing in the Santa Rita Mountains, May 11.

SCORPIONWEED   712
Common phacelia, caterpillar weed, scalloped phacelia
Phacelia crenulata
Waterleaf Family (Hydrophyllaceae)
Height: To 18".
Flowers: Violet-purple, bell-shaped, with 5 rounded, united petals; to 1/4" wide; in finely haired, terminal coils.
Leaves: Dark green, hairy, much-divided, variable; to 5" long.
Blooms: February–May.
Elevation: Below 4,000'.
Habitat: Roadsides, sandy washes, and desert flats.
Comments: Annual, with sticky, bristly stems. Emits onionlike odor when foliage is crushed. The name "scorpionweed" refers to curling flowerhead that resembles a scorpion's erect tail. Thirty-eight species of *Phacelia* (fa-SEE-li-ah) in Arizona. Photograph taken at Golden Shores, February 25. Another species, **PHACELIA CORRUGATA,** is found at 5,000 to 7,000'. Photograph (**PLATE 711**) taken at Nelson Reservoir, July 23.

WILD HELIOTROPE   713
Scorpionweed, blue phacelia
Phacelia distans
Waterleaf Family (Hydrophyllaceae)

Height: To 30".
Flowers: Pale blue and bell-shaped, with 5 rounded, united petals; to 1/4" wide; in finely haired, terminal coils.
Leaves: Green, finely haired, once or twice pinnately divided; highly variable; to 3" long.
Blooms: February–May.
Elevation: 1,000 to 4,000'.
Habitat: Along washes and slopes.
Comments: Annual, with reddish, hairy, branching stems. Straggly, often growing in tangles among shrubs. Thirty-eight species of *Phacelia* (fa-SEE-li-ah) in Arizona. Photograph taken at Saguaro National Monument, March 31.

VARILEAF PHACELIA   228
Phacelia magellanica (Phacelia heterophylla)
Waterleaf Family (Hydrophyllaceae)

Height: To 4'.
Flowers: White to greenish yellow, with long stamens; 5-lobed; to 1/2" wide; in coiled, terminal cluster.
Leaves: Grayish green, very hairy, oval on upper stem; pinnately divided into 3 to 5 sharp-pointed leaflets; to 4" long on lower stem.
Blooms: May–October.
Elevation: 4,000 to 9,500'.
Habitat: Moist coniferous forests.
Comments: Pinkish purple, prickly, hairy stems. Thirty-eight species of *Phacelia* (fa-SEE-li-ah) in Arizona. Photograph taken in Oak Creek Canyon, May 29.

BRITTLE PHACELIA   205
Phacelia neglecta
Waterleaf Family (Hydrophyllaceae)

Height: To 4".
Flowers: White, bowl-shaped, with 5 united petals; to 1/4" wide.
Leaves: Dark green, broadly oval, slightly scalloped; hairy, thick, succulent, brittle; to 1 1/4" long.
Blooms: March–April.
Elevation: Below 1,500'.
Habitat: Stony desert soils frequently of volcanic origin.
Comments: Thirty-eight species of *Phacelia* (fa-SEE-li-ah) in Arizona. Photograph taken north of Yuma, March 29.

FORGET-ME-NOT or BORAGE FAMILY
Boraginaceae (bore-aj-i-NAY-see-ee)
Represented in Arizona by herbs and slightly shrubby plants.

Flowers: Regular; 5 petals united into trumpetlike tube flared at top, with 5 lobes, 5 sepals, 5 calyx lobes, 5 stamens. Mostly small, on 1-sided, rolled up, coiled spike that gradually unfolds. Superior ovary.

Fruit: Divides into 4, 1-seeded nutlets.
Leaves: Mostly alternate, simple.

FIDDLENECK   380
Tarweed, saccato gordo, coast fiddleneck
Amsinckia intermedia
Forget-me-not or Borage Family (Boraginaceae)
Height: To 20".
Flowers: Yellow-orange, funnel-shaped; to 1/8" wide; in coiled spike.
Leaves: Green, narrow, with bristly hairs; 6" at base, graduating upward to 3/4" at tips
              of stem.
Blooms: March–May.
Elevation: Below 4,000'.
Habitat: Fields, roadsides, and dry, open areas.
Comments: Annual. At start of blooming, flowerhead is coiled in a manner resembling the neck
              of a violin; as individual flowers open, the coil uncurls. Two species of *Amsinckia*
              (am-SIN-ki-ah) in Arizona. Photograph taken at Usery Mountain Recreation Area,
              March 7.

NARROW-LEAVED POPCORN FLOWER   229
Narrow-leaved cryptantha
Cryptantha angustifolia
Forget-me-not or Borage Family (Boraginaceae)
Height: To 10".
Flowers: White, with 5 united petals; to 1/8" wide; in coiled cluster.
Leaves: Grayish, hairy, narrow; to 1 1/2" long.
Blooms: February–June.
Elevation: Below 4,000'.
Habitat: Creosote bush desert in dry, sandy, or gravelly soil in western and southern Arizona.
Comments: A bristly plant. Thirty-five species of *Cryptantha* (krip-TAN-thah) in Arizona.
              Photograph taken north of Yuma, March 29.

BRISTLY HIDDENFLOWER   230
Cryptantha setosissima
Forget-me-not or Borage Family (Boraginaceae)
Height: To 3'.
Flowers: White, with 5 united petals, light yellow center; to 1/4" wide; in bristly haired,
              coiled flower cluster.
Leaves: Grayish green, bristly haired, lance-shaped to linear-lobed; to 5" long.
Blooms: May–September.
Elevation: 6,000 to 8,500'.
Habitat: Pine belt.
Comments: Perennial, with bristly haired stems. Thirty-five species of *Cryptantha* (krip-TAN-
              thah) in Arizona. Photograph taken at North Rim of Grand Canyon National Park,
              June 25.

MANY-FLOWERED STICKSEED   714
Bare-stickseed, wild forget-me-not
Hackelia floribunda

Forget-me-not or Borage Family (Boraginaceae)

Height: To 3'.

Flowers: Pale blue, tubular; yellow center of tiny teeth surrounding tube opening; 5-lobed; to 1/4" wide; in cluster on curving flower stalk and on stems at leaf axils; followed by nutlet with barbed prickles on margins.

Leaves: Grayish green, velvet-haired, with sunken midvein; alternate, narrowly lance-shaped, gradually becoming smaller up the stem; to 5" long.

Blooms: July–August.

Elevation: Above 7,000'.

Habitat: Moist meadows, streambanks, and clearings in coniferous forests.

Comments: Biennial, with hairy stem. Hooks on nutlets adhere to fabric and fur. Three species of *Hackelia* (hack-ELL-i-ah) in Arizona. Photograph taken near Green's Peak, Greer area, August 9. Barbed prickles on margins of nutlets help identify this species. **PINE STICKSEED** (*Hackelia pinetorum*) has wider leaves and prickles all over nutlets.

SWEET-SCENTED HELIOTROPE   206

Phlox heliotrope, false morning glory
Heliotropium convolvulaceum
Forget-me-not or Borage Family (Boraginaceae)

Height: To 1'.

Flowers: White, fragrant, broadly funnel-shaped, with yellow "eye" in center; 5 lines of hairs beneath flower; to 3/4" wide; in terminal clusters, or singly in leaf axils, or on stem between two leaves.

Leaves: Green, very hairy; short-stalked, oval (broadest below middle); to 1 1/2" long.

Blooms: March–October.

Elevation: 4,500 to 6,000'.

Habitat: Roadsides and other dry, sandy areas.

Comments: Low, spreading herb with rigid hairs lying flat on stems and leaves. Three species of *Heliotropium* (hee-li-oh-TRO-pi-uhm) in Arizona. Photograph taken near St. Johns, August 4.

SALT HELIOTROPE   231

Quail plant, cola de mico, Chinese-pusley, monkey-tail
Heliotropium curassavicum
Forget-me-not or Borage Family (Boraginaceae)

Height: To 16".

Flowers: White to pinkish white, with yellowish center; funnel-shaped; 5 rounded lobes; to 3/16" wide; in paired, coiled flower cluster.

Leaves: Bluish green, thick, wavy, and fleshy; smooth, spatula-shaped, covered with bluish wax; to 1 1/2" long.

Blooms: Most of the year.

Elevation: Below 6,000'.

Habitat: Moist, saline soil and dried ponds.

Comments: Pima Indians used powdered root to treat wounds. Quail feed on fruits. Three species of *Heliotropium* (hee-li-oh-TRO-pi-uhm) in Arizona. Photograph taken at Lyman Lake, June 28.

MOUNTAIN GROMWELL   381

Puccoon

Lithospermum cobrense

Forget-me-not or Borage Family (Boraginaceae)

Height:	To 1'.
Flowers:	Pale yellow, funnel-shaped, 5-lobed; to 3/4" wide; clustered together on erect coil.
Leaves:	Gray, lancelike, covered with short hairs; to 2" long.
Blooms:	July–August.
Elevation:	5,000 to 9,000'.
Habitat:	Ponderosa pine forests.
Comments:	Biennial or short-lived perennial. Five species of *Lithospermum* (lihth-oh-SPUR-muhm) in Arizona. Photograph taken at Vernon, June 13.

FRINGED GROMWELL   382

Puccoon, narrowleaf gromwell

Lithospermum incisum

Forget-me-not or Borage Family (Boraginaceae)

Height:	To 16".
Flowers:	Yellow, fringed, and trumpet-shaped; 5 united petals; to 1 1/4" long, 3/4" wide.
Leaves:	Grayish green, narrowly lanceolate, to 2 1/2" long.
Blooms:	March–May.
Elevation:	4,000 to 7,500'.
Habitat:	Foothills, open plains, and slopes.
Comments:	Used by the Hopi Indians to produce medicine. Five species of *Lithospermum* (lihth-oh-SPUR-muhm) in Arizona. Photograph taken at Chiricahua National Monument, April 24.

MANYFLOWER PUCCOON   383

Manyflower gromwell, purple gromwell

Lithospermum multiflorum

Forget-me-not or Borage Family (Boraginaceae)

Height:	To 2'.
Flowers:	Yellow to yellowish orange, funnellike, with 5 short, rounded petal lobes; to 1/2" wide; in nodding, coiled, terminal clusters.
Leaves:	Grayish green, sandpapery, and covered with stiff hairs; linear to slightly lance-shaped; to 2" long.
Blooms:	June–September.
Elevation:	6,000 to 9,500'.
Habitat:	Slopes, flats, and clearings in pinyon-juniper woodlands and ponderosa pine forests.
Comments:	Perennial, with hairy stems. Native Americans obtained purple dye from roots. Five species of *Lithospermum* (lihth-oh-SPUR-muhm) in Arizona. Photograph taken at Mormon Lake, June 2.

GREEN-FLOWERED MACROMERIA   384

Macromeria viridiflora

Forget-me-not or Borage Family (Boraginaceae)

Height:	To 3'.
Flowers:	Yellowish to greenish white, narrow, 5-lobed; very hairy, trumpet-shaped, and drooping; to 2 1/2" long, in clusters at ends of branches.

Leaves:	Grayish green, prominently veined, very hairy, lance-shaped; to 7" long.
Blooms:	July–September.
Elevation:	6,000 to 9,000'.
Habitat:	Roadsides, rocky slopes, and valleys in coniferous forests.
Comments:	Dried flowers and leaves mixed with wild tobacco are used by Hopi Indians during rainmaking ceremonies. One species of *Macromeria* (mak-roh-MEER-i-ah) in Arizona. Photograph taken south of Alpine, June 30.

FRANCISCAN BLUEBELLS   715
Lungwort
Mertensia franciscana
Forget-me-not or Borage Family (Boraginaceae)

Height:	To 3'.
Flowers:	Dark to pale blue (can be pinkish or white); tubular, with hairy sepal margins; pendent, in loose clusters; to 5/8" long.
Leaves:	Dark green, lance-shaped, narrowing to a point; with short, flattened hairs on upper surface; to 5" long.
Blooms:	June–September.
Elevation:	Above 7,000'.
Habitat:	Moist, shaded areas in ponderosa and spruce-fir forests.
Comments:	Two species of *Mertensia* (mer-TEN-si-ah) in Arizona. Photograph taken south of Alpine, August 2. The very similar species, **MACDOUGALL'S BLUEBELLS** (*Mertensia macdougalii*), has hairless sepal margins and hairless leaves.

SHRUBBY COLDENIA   611
Oreja de perro
Tiquilia canescens (*Coldenia canescens*)
Forget-me-not or Borage Family (Boraginaceae)

Height:	To 8".
Flowers:	Pinkish to white, single, tubular, and 5-lobed; to 3/8" long, 1/4" wide.
Leaves:	Grayish green, woolly, oval, and numerous; to 3/8" long.
Blooms:	February–May.
Elevation:	Below 3,500'.
Habitat:	Dry, sunny mesas and slopes.
Comments:	Woody shrub often forming mats or mounds. Five species of *Tiquilia* (te-KILL-i-ah) in Arizona. Photograph taken in Kofa Mountains, February 21.

CRINKLE MATS   698
Plicate coldenia
Tiquilia plicata (*Coldenia plicata*)
Forget-me-not or Borage Family (Boraginaceae)

Height:	To 10".
Flowers:	Pale lavender to blue, funnellike, 5-lobed; to 1/4" wide, 1/4" long.
Leaves:	Dark green, oval, and crinkly, with deep ridges lined with grayish, feltlike hairs; to 1/4" long.
Blooms:	March–October.
Elevation:	Below 2,000'.
Habitat:	Sandy flats, rocky ridges, and dry river bottoms.
Comments:	Perennial. Forms rounded mounds to 2' wide. Five species of *Tiquilia* (te-KILL-i-ah) in Arizona. Photograph taken near Yuma, March 29.

VERBENA or VERVAIN FAMILY

Verbenaceae (ver-bee-NAY-see-ee)
Represented in Arizona by herbs or shrubs.

Flowers: Usually irregular, tubular or funnel-shaped; with 4 to 5 lobes or 2-lipped; generally 4 stamens (2 shorter), 5 sepals, 1 style, 1 to 2 stigmas. Superior ovary, 2-, 4-, or 5-celled.
Fruit: A drupe or a fruit with 2 to 4 nutlets.
Leaves: Opposite or whorled; simple or compound.

GOODDING'S VERBENA   636

Southwestern vervain, verbena, desert verbena
Glandularia gooddingii (*Verbena gooddingii*)
Verbena or Vervain Family (Verbenaceae)

Height: To 12".
Flowers: Pink to lavender, 5-notched, with joined petals; to 1/2" wide, in headlike cluster to 1 1/4" wide.
Leaves: Dark green, very hairy above and beneath; to 1 1/2" long; cleft into 3 main lobes, which are many times toothed or cleft.
Blooms: February–October.
Elevation: Below 5,000'.
Habitat: Dry slopes, mesas, and roadsides.
Comments: Perennial. Square stems. A favorite of butterflies and moths. *Glandularia* (glan-dew-LAY-ri-ah) species are very difficult to identify; 3 species in Arizona. Photograph taken at Desert Botanical Garden, Phoenix, March 22.

TEXAS FROG FRUIT   310

Lippia, fog fruit
Phyla incisa (*Lippia incisa*)
Verbena or Vervain Family (Verbenaceae)

Height: Creeping stems to 2' or more.
Flowers: White, 4-lobed; to 1/6" wide; arranged in circle, alternating from white with 1 yellowish orange lobe to white with 1 lavender lobe; compact flowerhead to 1/2" wide, on long stem in leaf axil.
Leaves: Dark green, hairy, rough, and granular; prominent midvein; 2-toothed on each margin near pointed tip; oblong to wedge-shaped; to 1" long.
Blooms: April–November.
Elevation: 400 to 7,000'.
Habitat: Open ground along lakesides, riverbanks, and in damp woodlands.
Comments: Plant roots at nodes; has hairy stems. Four species of *Phyla* (FYE-lah) in Arizona. Photograph taken at Lyman Lake State Park, June 28.

DAKOTA VERBENA   638

Vervain, small-flowered verbena
Verbena bipinnatifida
Verbena or Vervain Family (Verbenaceae)

Height: To 18".
Flowers: Pink, fragrant, and tubular, with 5 abruptly flaring lobes; each with a notch; to 1/2" wide; in somewhat flat, terminal cluster.

Leaves:	Dark green, long-haired, with edges curled under; sunken veins; much-divided or pinnately cleft into linear lobes; to 1 1/2" long.
Blooms:	May–September.
Elevation:	5,000 to 10,000'.
Habitat:	Roadsides and clearings in coniferous forests.
Comments:	Forms a mounded bush. Stems are very hairy. Frequented by bees and butterflies. Nineteen species of *Verbena* (ver-BEE-nah) in Arizona. Photograph taken north of Springerville, August 5.

PROSTRATE VERVAIN 716
Verbena bracteata
Verbena or Vervain Family (Verbenaceae)

Height:	To 5", stems spread out on ground.
Flowers:	Lavender to purple, small; to 1/8" wide, on a broad spike.
Leaves:	Dark green, hairy, 3-lobed, jagged-toothed; to 3" long.
Blooms:	May–September.
Elevation:	1,000 to 7,500'.
Habitat:	Roadsides, disturbed ground, and dry river bottoms.
Comments:	Plant is quite hairy. Nineteen species of *Verbena* (ver-BEE-nah) in Arizona. Photograph taken near Woods Canyon Lake, August 5.

MEXICAN VERVAIN 637
Sweet William, vervain
Verbena ciliata
Verbena or Vervain Family (Verbenaceae)

Height:	To 1 1/2', with sprawling stems.
Flowers:	Pink to purple, with 5 unequal-sized lobes; to 1/2" wide; in terminal cluster.
Leaves:	Dark green, once or twice pinnately cut into toothed lobes; to 3" long.
Blooms:	April–July.
Elevation:	2,000 to 7,000'.
Habitat:	Mesas, plains, and clearings in ponderosa pine forests.
Comments:	Hairy stems. Nineteen species of *Verbena* (ver-BEE-nah) in Arizona; many hybridize, making identification difficult. Photograph taken at Pine, April 29.

NEW MEXICAN VERVAIN 769
Spike verbena, tall verbena
Verbena macdougalii
Verbena or Vervain Family (Verbenaceae)

Height:	To 3'.
Flowers:	Lavender to purple; 5-lobed, with 3 lobes bent downward, 2 bent upward; to 1/4" wide; on long, erect spike. Flowers open first at bottom of stalk and progress upward.
Leaves:	Dark green, lance-shaped, prominently veined, irregularly toothed; to 4" long.
Blooms:	June–September.
Elevation:	6,000 to 7,500'.
Habitat:	Open flats, valleys, and roadsides.
Comments:	Square-stemmed like a mint. Native Americans used plant for medicinal and ceremonial purposes. Nineteen species of *Verbena* (ver-BEE-nah) in Arizona. Photograph taken near Nutrioso, July 23.

HILLSIDE VERVAIN 770
Verbena neomexicana
Verbena or Vervain Family (Verbenaceae)

Height: To 30".
Flowers: Lavender, 2-lipped, 5-lobed; to 1/2" long, 3/8" wide; in long, slender, interrupted spike with flowers opening from base upward.
Leaves: Grayish green, hairy, opposite; pinnately lobed to sharply toothed; to 3 1/2" long.
Blooms: March–October.
Elevation: 2,000 to 6,000'.
Habitat: Canyons and foothills.
Comments: Natural hybrids are common in this genus. Nineteen species of *Verbena* (ver-BEE-nah) in Arizona. Photograph taken at Saguaro National Monument West, April 17.

LILAC CHASTE-TREE 717
Indian spice, monk's pepper tree, hemp tree
Vitex agnus-castus
Verbena or Vervain Family (Verbenaceae)

Height: To 20'.
Flowers: Lavender to lavender-blue, tubular, 5-lobed (lower lobe largest); 4 long stamens; to 3/8" wide, 5/16" long; in dense, terminal spike to 7" long, 1 1/4" wide; followed by brownish, round fruit to 3/16" in diameter.
Leaves: Dark green above, grayish beneath; long-stalked, opposite, palmately compound; to 5" long; 5 to 7 lance-shaped leaflets, center leaflet longest.
Blooms: May–October.
Elevation: Not available. Photograph taken at 1,300'.
Habitat: Undocumented in Arizona; this specimen and others were found growing in moist soil of a cove at north end of Saguaro Lake.
Comments: Deciduous; has reddish brown stems. Native of China and India. This species not previously recorded for Arizona; escapees from cultivation. Photograph of *Vitex* (VY-tex) taken at Saguaro Lake, October 18.

MINT FAMILY
Labiatae (lay-bee-AY-tee)
Represented in Arizona by herbs and shrubs.

Flowers: Irregular, with 5-lobed corolla, usually 2-lipped: upper lip 2-lobed, lower lip 3-lobed. Four stamens, 2 longer than others. Superior ovary, 2-celled, 4-lobed.
Fruit: Four 1-seeded nutlets.
Leaves: Opposite, rarely whorled, with fragrant oil glands; simple; 4-angled or square stems.

HORSE-MINT 311
Yellow mint
Agastache pallidiflora
Mint Family (Labiatae)

Height: To 3'.
Flowers: White to pale yellowish green to pinkish, depending on subspecies; tubular, 2-lipped, yellowish green bracts; to 1/2" long; in thick, terminal cluster.
Leaves: Yellowish green above, paler green beneath; opposite, with round-toothed margins; triangular, deeply veined; to 1 1/2" long.

Blooms:	July–October.
Elevation:	7,000 to 10,000'.
Habitat:	Moist soil in coniferous forests and along mountain streams.
Comments:	Perennial herb. Has square stems. Six species of *Agastache* (ah-GAH-sta-kee) in Arizona. Photograph taken at Luna Lake, August 5.

SWEET SCENT   771
Hedeoma hyssopifolium
Mint (Labiatae)

Height:	To 20".
Flowers:	Lavender; gaping throat whitish with purplish blotches inside; upper lip projecting; to 1/2" long; in pairs along stem.
Leaves:	Green, narrow, numerous, opposite; to 3/4" long; occurring at intervals along stem.
Blooms:	May–October.
Elevation:	5,000 to 9,500'.
Habitat:	Ponderosa pine forests, hillsides, and canyons.
Comments:	Seven species of *Hedeoma* (hee-dee-OH-mah) in Arizona. Photograph taken near Willow Springs Lake, July 6.

MOCK-PENNYROYAL   772
Hedeoma oblongifolium
Mint Family (Labiatae)

Height:	To 20".
Flowers:	Purple to rose-purple, white throat with purple stripes; tubular; to 1/8" wide, 1/2" long; clustered in leaf axils.
Leaves:	Bright green, oval, hairy, untoothed; to 1/2" long.
Blooms:	March–September.
Elevation:	1,800 to 8,000'.
Habitat:	Desert washes, along streams, and in woodlands.
Comments:	Perennial herb, with stiff and square stem. Seven species of *Hedeoma* (hee-dee-OH-mah) in Arizona. Photograph taken at Tortilla Flat, March 19.

DESERT LAVENDER   773
Lavender
Hyptis emoryi
Mint Family (Labiatae)

Height:	Shrub to 15'.
Flowers:	Violet-blue, to 1"; in clusters in leaf axils.
Leaves:	Gray-green and oval, with irregularly serrated margins; covered with woolly hairs; to 2 1/2" long.
Blooms:	Any time of year.
Elevation:	Below 5,000'.
Habitat:	Desert washes and dry, rocky slopes.
Comments:	Deciduous to semi-deciduous, with ash gray bark and lavender-scented foliage. Frost-sensitive. Browsed by livestock; a valuable bee plant. Seeds used as food by wildlife. Minty leaves used to flavor tea. One species of *Hyptis* (HIP-tiss) in Arizona. Photograph taken at Usery Mountain Recreation Area, February 14.

HOREHOUND 312
Marrubio
Marrubium vulgare
Mint Family (Labiatae)

Height: To 3'.
Flowers: White, tiny; to 1/4" long; in whorls in leaf axils.
Leaves: Grayish green, oval, veiny, crinkly surfaced above, white-woolly beneath; in pairs; to 1 1/2" long; on stem below each flower whorl.
Blooms: April–September.
Elevation: Throughout the state.
Habitat: Disturbed places, roadsides, fields, and pastures.
Comments: Perennial herb, and a weed. Stems are white, woolly, and 4-angled. Horehound used as flavoring in candy. Introduced from Europe, now naturalized in U.S. One species of *Marrubium* (mar-REW-bi-um) in Arizona. Photograph taken at Harshaw, April 27.

FIELD MINT 774
Wild mint, corn mint, wild pennyroyal
Mentha arvensis
Mint Family (Labiatae)

Height: To 2'.
Flowers: Pale pink to lavender, bell-shaped; to 1/4" long, 1/8" wide; clustered in axils of foliage leaves at intervals along stem.
Leaves: Dark green, aromatic, slightly downy; ovate to lanceolate, tapering on both ends; to 3" long.
Blooms: July–October.
Elevation: 5,000 to 9,500'.
Habitat: Moist woods and streambanks.
Comments: Strong-scented perennial. Produces runners to 2' long. Native Americans used leaves for flavoring. Mints recognizable by opposite leaves, square stems, and irregular flowers. Three species of *Mentha* (MEN-thah) in Arizona. Photograph taken at Nelson Reservoir, August 3.

BERGAMOT 663
Horsemint, mintleaf beebalm
Monarda menthaefolia
Mint Family (Labiatae)

Height: To 3'.
Flowers: Pinkish, tubular, 2-lipped; 1" long; in single, dense, globular, terminal cluster above whorl of purplish green leaves.
Leaves: Yellowish green with purplish tinge in places; lance-shaped, opposite, toothed; to 2 1/2" long.
Blooms: July–August.
Elevation: 5,000 to 9,000'.
Habitat: Roadsides and moist pine and spruce-fir forests.
Comments: Perennial. Square stem tinged with purple. Leaves have strong, mint odor when crushed. Three species of *Monarda* (mo-NAR-dah) recorded for Arizona. Photograph taken south of Alpine, July 23.

PLAINS BEEBALM   664
White horsemint, pagoda plant, wild bergamot, pony mint
Monarda pectinata
Mint Family (Labiatae)

Height:	To 1'.
Flowers:	Light rose to white; to 1/2"; in clusters at intervals on a spike; each separated by a spinelike bract and a whorl of leaves.
Leaves:	Dark green, oblong to lance-shaped, finely toothed; to 1 1/2" long.
Blooms:	August–September.
Elevation:	5,000 to 7,000'.
Habitat:	Dry soil of plains and pastures.
Comments:	Square stem. Three species of *Monarda* (mo-NAR-dah) recorded for Arizona. Photograph taken south of Alpine, July 23.

SPOTTED HORSEMINT   313
Monarda
Monarda punctata
Mint (Labiatae)

Height:	To 16".
Flowers:	White, long, narrow, hairy; 2-lipped, with upper lip arched upward, lower lip curved downward and speckled with lavender; to 1" long; in circular clusters around stem; surrounded by 8 broad, purplish bracts covered with a white down.
Leaves:	Grayish green, opposite, lance-shaped; folded upward from center vein; tinged with lavender at base; slightly toothed, curved downward from stem; to 2" long; in clusters surrounding stem.
Blooms:	End of June–August.
Elevation:	5,000 to 7,000'.
Habitat:	Dry, sandy soil.
Comments:	Square stem. Three species of *Monarda* (mo-NAR-dah) recorded for Arizona. This species not previously recorded for Arizona. Photograph taken 28 miles north of St. Johns, June 28.

HEAL ALL   753
Self heal
Prunella vulgaris
Mint Family (Labiatae)

Height:	To 12", sometimes prostrate.
Flowers:	Lavender to purple; 2-lipped, with upper lip forming a hood, lower lip drooping; green bracts between flowers; to 1/2" long; in terminal spike.
Leaves:	Dark green, oval to lance-shaped, toothed; to 4" long.
Blooms:	June–September.
Elevation:	5,000 to 9,000'.
Habitat:	Moist meadows along streams, lake shores, and roadsides.
Comments:	Perennial herb. Introduced from Europe; now naturalized. Square-stemmed. Flower spikes elongate after blooming. One species of *Prunella* (pru-NELL-ah) in Arizona. Photograph taken south of Alpine, July 10.

CHIA   775
California chia, desert sage, desert chia
Salvia columbariae
Mint Family (Labiatae)

Height: To 20".
Flowers: Deep blue, prominent upper and lower lips; to 1/2" long; in dense, rounded clusters on terminal spike.
Leaves: Green, mostly basal, oblong, much-divided; to 4" long.
Blooms: March–May.
Elevation: Below 3,500'.
Habitat: Sandy washes and desert slopes.
Comments: Annual; smells skunky. Like most members of the mint family, chia has square stems. When placed in water, seeds form sticky, mucilaginous mass, believed to aid in germination. Native Americans used seeds for food and to make mucilaginous poultices and certain beverages. Fifteen species of *Salvia* (SAL-vi-ah) in Arizona. Photograph taken in Superstition Mountains, March 26.

MARSH SKULLCAP   776
Scutellaria galericulata
Mint Family (Labiatae)

Height: To 2'.
Flowers: Lavender, slipper-shaped, 2-lipped, tubular; lower lobe facing downward; to 3/4" long; 1 flower in each upper leaf axil.
Leaves: Light green, opposite, slightly scalloped on margins; lance-shaped, pinkish, with sunken veins; granular-feeling; clasping stem; to 1 1/2" long, 1/2" wide.
Blooms: June–August.
Elevation: 6,000 to 9,500'.
Habitat: Moist ground of wet meadows and swampy areas.
Comments: Perennial herb. Square stems. Four species of *Scutellaria* (skew-te-LAIR-i-ah) in Arizona. Photograph taken in vicinity of McNary, July 7.

TEXAS BETONY   557A and B
Scarlet sage, scarlet hedge nettle
Stachys coccinea
Mint Family (Labiatae)

Height: To 3'.
Flowers: Scarlet, tubular; 2-lipped, with upper lip erect, lower lip 3-lobed and spreading; to 1 1/4" long; in whorls around stem.
Leaves: Grayish green, oval to triangular, toothed; hairy, with netlike surface; opposite; to 3" long.
Blooms: March–October.
Elevation: 1,500 to 8,000'.
Habitat: Slopes and canyons in rich soil.
Comments: Perennial herb. Square stems. Four species of *Stachys* (STACK-iss) in Arizona. Photograph A taken below Kitt Peak, April 18. A number of plants with pink flowers were found growing below Horse Mesa Dam, shown in photograph B, taken March 23.

HEDGE NETTLE   777
Stachys palustris
Mint Family (Labiatae)

Height: To 2'.

Flowers: Pale lavender with darker lavender markings; short upper lip projecting like a hood, 3-lobed lower lip long and bent downward; to 1" long, 1/4" wide; in whorls of 6 at intervals on terminal spike to 10" tall.

Leaves: Pale green, opposite, thin, spreading hairs, clasping stem, deeply veined, broadly lance-shaped, toothed margins, to 3" long.

Blooms: July–August.

Elevation: 7,000 to 9,000'.

Habitat: Moist, shady areas.

Comments: Perennial herb. Four-sided, hairy stem. Tubers can be eaten. Four species of *Stachys* (STACK-iss) in Arizona. Photograph taken near Greer, August 15.

NIGHTSHADE or POTATO FAMILY
Solanaceae (so-lah-NAY-see-ee)
Represented in Arizona by herbs and shrubs.

Flowers: Regular, bell or funnel-shaped; 5 united lobes folded lengthwise in bud; 5 stamens, 1 style, 1- or 2-lobed stigma. Superior ovary, 2-celled.

Fruit: Dry capsule or berry, often very poisonous.

Leaves: Alternate, simple or pinnately compound; lobed or dissected.

SMALL GROUNDCHERRY   207
Chamaesaracha coronopus
Nightshade or Potato Family (Solanaceae)

Height: To 10" tall, spreading on ground to 1 1/2'.

Flowers: Whitish to yellowish green, flat, wheel-shaped with 5 spreading lobes; to 3/4" wide; on stems in leaf axils; followed by yellow, berrylike seed pod, to 1/4" in diameter.

Leaves: Dark green, rough, thick, alternate; covered with scaly down; narrowly oblong, occasionally shallowly lobed; to 4" long.

Blooms: April–September.

Elevation: 2,500 to 7,500'.

Habitat: Dry plains, mesas, roadsides, and disturbed ground.

Comments: Perennial herb; many-branched. Native Americans eat seed pods. Two species of *Chamaesaracha* (kah-mee-sah-RACK-ah) in Arizona. Photograph taken at Dead Horse Ranch State Park, May 28.

DINGY CHAMAESARACHA   367
Velvet five-eyes
Chamaesaracha sordida
Nightshade or Potato Family (Solanaceae)

Height: To 1'; usually much less because plant hugs the ground.

Flowers: Pale yellowish or whitish above, purplish streaks beneath; flat, with 5 spreading lobes; 5 greenish bands radiating outward from center; eyelike markings at base of each lobe; to 1/2" wide, in upper leaf axils.

Leaves: Dull green, glandular, very sticky, and hairy; lance-shaped to oblong, often pinnately cleft or toothed, with wavy margins; to 1 1/2" long.

Blooms: March–October.
Elevation: 3,500 to 5,500'.
Habitat: Dry mesas and plains.
Comments: Because of stickiness, foliage is often covered with pollen dust or soil particles. Two species of *Chamaesaracha* (kah-mee-sah-RACK-ah) in Arizona. Photograph taken in vicinity of Fort Bowie, May 8.

SACRED DATURA 208
Thornapple, western jimson, giant jimson, moon lily, jimsonweed, tolguacha
Datura meteloides
Nightshade or Potato Family (Solanaceae)

Height: To 4'.
Flowers: White tinged with lavender; trumpet-shaped, united petals; to 6" long; followed by prickly seed capsule to 2" in diameter.
Leaves: Grayish green, oval to heart-shaped, to 6" long.
Blooms: April–November.
Elevation: 1,000 to 6,000'.
Habitat: Washes and roadsides from deserts to mesas.
Comments: Perennial herb. Flowers open in early evening and close following day when struck by the sun's rays. All parts of plant extremely poisonous if ingested. *Datura* (dah-TOOR-rah) was one of most important medicinal plants to early Native Americans. Four species of *Datura* in Arizona. Photograph taken north of Payson, September 2.

ANDERSON THORNBUSH 699A and B
Anderson wolfberry, Anderson lycium, tomatillo
Lycium andersonii
Nightshade or Potato Family (Solanaceae)

Height: To 9', but usually less.
Flowers: Pale lavender or whitish, narrow, and tubular; usually 5-lobed (sometimes 4), with hairy calyx, stigma doesn't protrude beyond lobes; stamens level with or protruding beyond lobes; flower to 1/2" long; followed by reddish orange, fleshy, juicy, egg-shaped, many-seeded fruit to 3/8" long.
Leaves: Dark green, very finely haired, succulent, and leathery; rather thick, spatula-shaped; to 1 3/4" long.
Blooms: February–March.
Elevation: Below 5,500'.
Habitat: Flats and along desert washes.
Comments: Has spine-tipped branches. Older branches are grayish; newer growth is brownish. Birds and small mammals feed on fruit. Flowers attract bees and other insects. Ten species of *Lycium* (LISS-i-uhm) in Arizona. There are several varieties of this species, differing in flower length and in leaf thickness and size. Photograph in flower taken in Superstition Mountains, February 4. Photograph in fruit taken near Granite Reef Dam, March 28.

BERLANDIER WOLFBERRY 700
Lycium berlandieri
Nightshade or Potato Family (Solanaceae)
Height: To 7'.

Flowers:	Bluish to lavender, funnel-shaped (flaring at top); 4- or 5-lobed, with protruding stamens; flower to 3/8" long; solitary or in clusters; followed by roundish berry, to 5/16" in diameter, red at maturity.
Leaves:	Green, minutely hairy, linear to spatula-shaped; to 1 1/4" long.
Blooms:	March–November.
Elevation:	Below 3,000'.
Habitat:	Plains and rocky hillsides.
Comments:	Shrub with spines on branches and branch tips. Favorite of butterflies and bees. Ten species of *Lycium* (LISS-i-uhm) in Arizona. Photograph taken in Tucson area, November 12.

FREMONT THORNBUSH 701A and B
Lycium fremontii
Nightshade or Potato Family (Solanaceae)

Height:	To 9'.
Flowers:	Purplish to lavender, tubular, erect, 5-lobed; to 3/8" long; followed by orangish red, fleshy, juicy fruit to 3/8" long.
Leaves:	Light green, spatula-shaped, succulent, glandular-hairy; to 1" long, 1/4" wide; occurring all along branches.
Blooms:	Throughout year, but primarily January–March.
Elevation:	Below 2,500'.
Habitat:	Desert.
Comments:	Has sharp-pointed branches. Fruits are eaten by desert Native Americans. Ten species of *Lycium* (LISS-i-uhm) in Arizona. Photograph in flower and in fruit taken at Organ Pipe Cactus National Monument, March 7.

DESERT THORN 794
Wolfberry
Lycium macrodon
Nightshade or Potato Family (Solanaceae)

Height:	To 10'.
Flowers:	Greenish white, tubular, with 5 pointed lobes; to 1/2" long; followed by fruit constricted below middle; 2- to 4-seeded.
Leaves:	Dark green, linear to spatula-shaped, narrow; to 1 1/2" long, 1/4" wide.
Blooms:	February–May.
Elevation:	500 to 2,000'.
Habitat:	Desert and plains.
Comments:	Branches end in spines. Immature twigs are woolly. Ten species of *Lycium* (LISS-i-uhm) in Arizona. Photograph taken at Desert Botanical Garden, Phoenix, March 3. This species native to Pinal County and southern Arizona.

RABBIT THORN 795
Pale lycium
Lycium pallidum
Nightshade or Potato Family (Solanaceae)

Height:	To 6'.
Flowers:	Greenish yellow, funnel-shaped, and 5-lobed, with lobes flaring outward; 5 stamens extending beyond corolla tube; to 3/4" long, 5/8" wide; followed by round, orange to red, juicy fruit, to 1/4" in diameter.

Leaves:	Bluish white to bluish green, spatula-shaped to elliptical or oval; leathery, covered with bloom; to 3" long, 1/2" wide; in clusters on branches.
Blooms:	April–June.
Elevation:	3,500 to 7,000'.
Habitat:	Dry plains and slopes.
Comments:	Has spines along branches. Browsed by livestock. The bitter fruits are eaten by birds, small animals, and people. Ten species of *Lycium* (LISS-i-uhm) in Arizona. Photograph taken in vicinity of Fort Bowie, May 8.

TREE TOBACCO   385

Shrub tobacco
Nicotiana glauca
Nightshade or Potato Family (Solanaceae)

Height:	To 20'.
Flowers:	Pale yellow, tubular; to 2" long; in loose clusters at ends of branches.
Leaves:	Bluish green, long-stalked, oval, and smooth; to 7" long.
Blooms:	Throughout the year.
Elevation:	Below 3,000'.
Habitat:	Roadsides, washes, hillsides, and rocky canyons.
Comments:	Grows as an open shrub or small tree. Contains the poisonous alkaloid nicotine. Plant also contains anabasine, another potent poison. An insecticide for aphids is brewed by soaking plant parts in water, and then using solution on infected plant. Native to South America, now naturalized in Arizona. The name *Nicotiana* is in honor of Jean Nicot, who introduced tobacco plants to the French royalty. Four species of *Nicotiana* (ni-koh-shi-AY-nah) in Arizona. Photograph taken in vicinity of Crown King, May 4.

DESERT TOBACCO   209

Tabaquillo ("little tobacco"), punche
Nicotiana trigonophylla
Nightshade or Potato Family (Solanaceae)

Height:	To 3'.
Flowers:	White to greenish white, trumpet-shaped; to 3/4" long; in loosely branched clusters.
Leaves:	Dark green, sticky, oval to lance-shaped; to 6" long; upper leaves stalkless, with 2 lobes clasping sticky stem.
Blooms:	Throughout the year.
Elevation:	Below 6,000'.
Habitat:	Washes and other sandy areas.
Comments:	Perennial herb. Leaves contain nicotine. Four species of *Nicotiana* (ni-koh-shi-AY-nah) in Arizona. Photograph taken at Usery Mountain Recreation Area, March 18.

THICK-LEAVED GROUND CHERRY   368

Ground cherry
Physalis crassifolia
Nightshade or Potato Family (Solanaceae)

Height:	To 2'.
Flowers:	Tawny yellow, bell-shaped, with spreading lobes; petals joined; to 1/2" wide; followed by a silvery, inflated, 3/4"-long, lantern-shaped calyx containing the berry of seeds.

Leaves:	Dark green, triangular to heart-shaped; to 1" wide.
Blooms:	February–October.
Elevation:	Below 3,000'.
Habitat:	Dry, rocky slopes and washes.
Comments:	Perennial herb. Plant forms small bush. Ten species of *Physalis* (FISS-a-lis) in Arizona. Photograph taken at Cattail Cove State Park, March 8.

PURPLE GROUND CHERRY   702
Husk tomato
Physalis lobata
Nightshade or Potato Family (Solanaceae)

Height:	Usually prostrate, to 16" high.
Flowers:	Purple, saucer-shaped; to 1" wide; on slender flower stalks in leaf axils; bright yellow, knobby anthers; followed by 1/4" berry.
Leaves:	Dark green, lance-shaped, pinnately lobed; to 4" long.
Blooms:	March–September.
Elevation:	1,000 to 5,000'.
Habitat:	Desert roadsides, flats, and mesas.
Comments:	Ten species of *Physalis* (FISS-a-lis) in Arizona. Photograph taken near Pisinimo, March 30.

SILVERLEAF NIGHTSHADE   703
White horse nettle, silver horse nettle, bull nettle, desert nightshade, trompillo
Solanum elaeagnifolium
Nightshade or Potato Family (Solanaceae)

Height:	To 3'.
Flowers:	Violet to bluish violet; starlike with 5 points; bright yellow anthers in center; to 1 1/2" wide; followed by yellow, 1/2"-diameter berry.
Leaves:	Silvery, oblong to lance-shaped, wavy-margined, spines on underside; to 4" long.
Blooms:	May–October.
Elevation:	1,000 to 5,500'.
Habitat:	Roadsides and fields.
Comments:	Perennial herb, and a poisonous weed. Spines on stem. Plant produces a protein-digesting enzyme; in cheese-making, Native Americans added crushed berries to curdle milk. Fifteen species of *Solanum* (so-LAY-num) in Arizona. Photograph taken at Hassayampa River Preserve, Wickenburg, May 7.

WILD POTATO   210
Solanum jamesii
Nightshade or Potato Family (Solanaceae)

Height:	To 1'.
Flowers:	White, deeply 5-cleft, with 5 orange stamens; to 3/4" wide, in loose cluster.
Leaves:	Dark green, alternate, sparsely haired; to 4 3/4" long; pinnately compound; 5 to 9 leaflets.
Blooms:	July–September.
Elevation:	5,500 to 8,500'.
Habitat:	Coniferous forests, clearings, and wooded slopes.

Comments: Perennial herb. Has small tubers, and was once used as food by Native Americans. Fifteen species of *Solanum* (so-LAY-num) in Arizona. Photograph taken in vicinity of Nutrioso, August 3.

WHITE NIGHTSHADE   232
Solanum nodiflorum
Nightshade or Potato Family (Solanaceae)

Height: To 30".
Flowers: White, with 5 starlike, united petals with yellow beak of stamens; to 3/4" wide; followed by a shiny, black, pea-sized berry.
Leaves: Light green, triangular, lobed; to 3 1/2" long.
Blooms: March–December.
Elevation: Not available. Photograph taken at 2,000'.
Habitat: Wasteland and roadsides in Maricopa and Pinal counties and probably elsewhere.
Comments: Introduced from tropical America. Fifteen species of *Solanum* (so-LAY-num) in Arizona. Photograph taken in Superstition Mountains, March 26.

BUFFALO-BUR   369
Texas thistle, Colorado bur, Mexican thistle
Solanum rostratum
Nightshade or Potato Family (Solanaceae)

Height: To 2 1/2'.
Flowers: Bright yellow, starlike, with 5 crinkly lobes, 5 yellow anthers form cone in center; to 1" wide; followed by spiny bur to 1" wide.
Leaves: Dark green, deeply cut into 5 to 7 pinnate lobes; stalks and vein backs covered with spines; to 6" long.
Blooms: May–August.
Elevation: 1,000 to 7,000'.
Habitat: Roadsides, fields, and disturbed areas.
Comments: Annual herb. Probably the original host of the Colorado potato beetle. Entire plant is covered with straight, sharp, straw-colored spines, to 1/2" long, which cause pain if touched. Leaves and seed pods are poisonous. Fifteen species of *Solanum* (so-LAY-num) in Arizona. Photograph taken at Dead Horse Ranch State Park, May 29.

PURPLE NIGHTSHADE   704
Solanum xanti
Nightshade or Potato Family (Solanaceae)

Height: To 3'.
Flowers: Deep violet to dark lavender, starlike, 5 united petals, crinkled; to 1" wide; 5 bright yellow stamens attached in center; in small cluster, followed by round, green berry to 1/2" in diameter.
Leaves: Dark green, very hairy, alternate; oval to elliptical, occasionally lobed; to 3" long.
Blooms: April–November.
Elevation: 3,500 to 5,500'.
Habitat: Rocky slopes, mostly in chaparral.
Comments: Perennial herb. A bushy plant, woody at base. Fifteen species of *Solanum* (so-LAY-num) in Arizona. Photograph taken in vicinity of Sedona, June 9.

SNAPDRAGON or FIGWORT FAMILY

Scrophulariaceae (skroff-yew-lay-ri-AY-see-ee)
Represented in Arizona by herbs and shrubs.

Flowers: Generally irregular, with 5 united petals; tubular; usually 2-lipped, with upper lip 2-lobed (sometimes hooked) and lower lip 3-lobed; often with 3 sacs. Usually 4 stamens, 2 shorter than the others; forked or unforked style. Superior ovary, mostly 2-celled.
Fruit: Generally a 2-celled capsule.
Leaves: Alternate, opposite, or basal; simple or pinnate.

NUTTALL'S SNAPDRAGON   778

Antirrhinum nuttallianum
Snapdragon or Figwort Family (Scrophulariaceae)
Height: To 3'.
Flowers: Violet with a few cream-colored markings; snapdragonlike; 2 upper lobes (erect, sharply pointed, earlike, darker violet), 3 lower lobes (flaring outward, ruffled, lighter violet); flower stalks as long or longer than calyx; flower to 3/8" wide, 3/8" long; in long spike with side branches.
Leaves: Dark green, hairy, and sticky; lance-shaped, opposite and alternate; to 1" long.
Blooms: March–May.
Elevation: Below 4,000'.
Habitat: Canyons.
Comments: Very hairy, sticky plant. Four species of *Antirrhinum* (an-tir-RYE-num) in Arizona. Photograph taken at Saguaro National Monument West, April 17.

FOOTHILL KITTENTAILS   665

Besseya plantaginea
Snapdragon or Figwort Family (Scrophulariaceae)
Height: To 20".
Flowers: Pinkish, purplish, or white; 4-lobed (one forming upper lip and others, lower lip); conspicuous bracts; to 1/2" long; in dense, terminal spike to 16" long.
Leaves: Green, often with reddish veins and tints of red; mostly basal; finely haired, finely scalloped, and oblong, to 8" long.
Blooms: June–August.
Elevation: 7,000 to 9,500'.
Habitat: Moist meadows and mixed coniferous forests.
Comments: Perennial herb. Two species of *Besseya* (BESS-e-yah) in Arizona. Photograph taken south of Alpine, June 30. A similar species, **ARIZONA BESSEYA** (*Besseya arizonica*) has small, rounded leaves and a shorter flower stem.

DESERT PAINTBRUSH   558

Painted-cup
Castilleja chromosa
Snapdragon or Figwort Family (Scrophulariaceae)
Height: To 16".
Flowers: Reddish to orangish bracts, shorter and wider than leaves; hairy; in terminal cluster. Flowers are inconspicuous and generally hidden within bracts.
Leaves: Reddish green, grayish haired, linear to linear-lobed; to 2" long.

Blooms:	March–September.
Elevation:	2,000 to 8,000'.
Habitat:	Roadsides, chaparral, and clearings in ponderosa pine forests.
Comments:	Removes selenium from soil. Over a dozen species of *Castilleja* (cass-til-LAY-yah) in Arizona; the species of this genus are difficult to identify. Photograph taken at Mormon Lake, September 3.

WOOLLY PAINTBRUSH   559
Painted-cup
Castilleja lanata
Snapdragon or Figwort Family (Scrophulariaceae)

Height:	To 2'.
Flowers:	Red to reddish orange, with somewhat narrow bracts, some lobed, very hairy, in terminal cluster. Flowers inconspicuous and generally hidden within bracts.
Leaves:	Reddish green, hairy, margins curved upward; to 2" long; linear to linear-lobed; bunches of small leaves in leaf axils.
Blooms:	March–August.
Elevation:	2,500 to 7,000'.
Habitat:	Arid slopes and desert.
Comments:	Over a dozen species of *Castilleja* (cass-til-LAY-yah) in Arizona; the species of this genus are difficult to identify. Photograph taken in desert area below Superstition Mountains, March 15.

MOGOLLON INDIAN PAINTBRUSH   512
Painted-cup
Castilleja mogollonica
Snapdragon or Figwort Family (Scrophulariaceae)

Height:	To 14".
Flowers:	Pale yellow; 3-toothed bracts, each 1" long, with pinkish, pointed tips, center tooth wider than others; very hairy, clustered on 4"-long erect spike. Flowers inconspicuous and generally hidden within bracts.
Leaves:	Light green, finely haired, narrow; to 1 1/4" long.
Blooms:	July–August.
Elevation:	Around 9,500'.
Habitat:	Wet alpine meadows.
Comments:	Stem is very hairy. Over a dozen species of *Castilleja* (cass-til-LAY-yah) in Arizona. Photograph taken in mountain meadow above Greer, August 8.

MAIDEN BLUE-EYED MARY   314
Blue lips, blue eyes
Collinsia parviflora
Snapdragon or Figwort Family (Scrophulariaceae)

Height:	To 1', but usually less.
Flowers:	Two whitish, rounded, upper lobes flaring upward; 2 deep blue lower lobes; bent forward, with a folded, purplish lobe between them; tubular; to 1/8" wide, 3/8" long; in terminal, leafy cluster on stem.
Leaves:	Dark green above, bright maroon beneath; lance-shaped; in whorls at flower clusters, opposite on lower stem, to 1 1/2" long.
Blooms:	February–June.

Elevation:	4,000 to 8,000'.
Habitat:	Areas moist in the spring.
Comments:	Annual herb, with reddish stems. One species of *Collinsia* (kol-LIN-si-ah) in Arizona. Photograph taken northeast of Superior, April 3.

CLUB-FLOWER 666
Birdbeak
Cordylanthus parviflorus
Snapdragon or Figwort Family (Scrophulariaceae)

Height:	To 3', sprawling to 4' wide.
Flowers:	Pink with yellow at tip; tubular with white, tonguelike projection along upper surface at tip; hairy; to 3/4" long, 5/16" wide; terminal on branches. Flower is actually turned upside down with lower lip longer and uppermost.
Leaves:	Dark green, linear, alternate; hairy and sticky; to 5/8" long.
Blooms:	August–October.
Elevation:	2,500 to 7,000'.
Habitat:	Rocky slopes and mesas.
Comments:	Annual. Many-branched. Partially root-parasitic. All parts of plant are glandular and very sticky. Five species of *Cordylanthus* (kor-di-LAN-thus) in Arizona. Photograph taken at Oak Creek Canyon, October 1.

WRIGHT'S BIRDBEAK 513
Club-flower
Cordylanthus wrightii
Snapdragon or Figwort Family (Scrophulariaceae)

Height:	To 2'.
Flowers:	Yellowish green, beaklike, narrow; upper and lower lips nearly equal; surrounded by long bracts; to 1 1/4" long, in clusters at branch ends.
Leaves:	Light green, tinged with pink; hairlike, divided into very narrow, curly segments; to 2" long; occurring all along stems.
Blooms:	June–October.
Elevation:	5,000 to 7,500'.
Habitat:	Roadsides, sandy mesas, and flats, often growing among junipers.
Comments:	Annual. Partially root-parasitic. Many-branched, spindly, and bushlike. Five species of *Cordylanthus* (kor-di-LAN-thus) in Arizona. Photograph taken north of St. Johns, August 4.

BUSH PENSTEMON 514
Keckiella antirrhinoides ssp. *microphylla* (*Penstemon microphyllus*)
Snapdragon or Figwort Family (Scrophulariaceae)

Height:	Sprawling shrub to 8'.
Flowers:	Bright yellow, snapdragonlike, with 2 upper lobes, 3 lower lobes; 4 yellow stamens curved upward in throat, upper surface of fifth stamen (sterile, lacking anther) heavily bearded; flower to 1" long, 3/8" wide; all along stems and side branches.
Leaves:	Light green, hairy, elliptical to oblong; to 3/4" long; in small clusters along branches.
Blooms:	March–May.
Elevation:	1,500 to 5,000'.

Habitat:	Rocky slopes.
Comments:	Only occasionally browsed by livestock. One species of *Keckiella* (kec-ki-EL-ah) in Arizona. Photograph taken south of Superior, April 9.

BUTTER AND EGGS 515
Dalmatian toadflax
Linaria dalmatica
Snapdragon or Figwort Family (Scrophulariaceae)

Height:	To 4'.
Flowers:	Pale yellow, snapdragonlike; long, slender, basal spur; 2 lobes of upper lip pointing upward, 2 lobes of lower lip pointing downward; orange palate (in throat); to 2" long; in elongated cluster along stem.
Leaves:	Bluish green, broad, leathery; oval to lance-shaped; clasping stem at regular intervals; to 3" long.
Blooms:	May–September.
Elevation:	5,500 to 7,500'.
Habitat:	Roadsides, fields, and waste areas.
Comments:	Perennial herb. Orange palate serves as a honey guide for bees. Naturalized from Eurasia. Three species of *Linaria* (ly-NAY-ri-ah) in Arizona. Photograph taken in Lynx Lake area, May 26.

BLUE TOADFLAX 779
Old-field toadflax, Texas toadflax
Linaria texana
Snapdragon or Figwort Family (Scrophulariaceae)

Height:	To 32".
Flowers:	Blue-violet, with 2-lipped, long, slender spur projecting backward; to 3/8" long; loosely grouped on slender stems.
Leaves:	Dark green, shiny, linear; to 1 1/4" long.
Blooms:	February–May.
Elevation:	1,500 to 5,000'.
Habitat:	Roadsides, plains, and mesas.
Comments:	Annual. Three species of *Linaria* (ly-NAY-ri-ah) in Arizona. Photograph taken near Sells, March 30.

MABRYA 315
Mabrya acerifolia (*Maurandya acerifolia*)
Snapdragon or Figwort Family (Scrophulariaceae)

Height:	Prostrate, to 10" long.
Flowers:	White to greenish white, 5-lobed, tubular; to 1" long.
Leaves:	Dark green, downy, sticky; heart-shaped to kidney-shaped; coarsely toothed; to 1" wide, wider than long.
Blooms:	March–May.
Elevation:	About 2,000'.
Habitat:	Shaded cliffs and rock ledges.
Comments:	Mat-forming plant with brittle stems. Stems often hang down from moist, rock ledges. One species of *Mabrya* (mah-BRY-ah) in Arizona. Photograph taken in Superstition Mountains, April 6.

TWINING SNAPDRAGON   667

Snapdragon vine, little snapdragon vine, violet twining
Maurandya antirrhiniflora
Snapdragon or Figwort Family (Scrophulariaceae)

Height:	Vine; twining over bushes to 8'.
Flowers:	Reddish pink, snapdragonlike; white in throat with pinkish lines; side lobes flare outward, upper lobes paired and flare upward; to 1" long, 5/8" wide.
Leaves:	Dark green, arrow-shaped; leathery, strong network; rounded at tip on lower leaves, pointed at tip on younger leaves; to 1 1/4" wide, 2" long.
Blooms:	April–October.
Elevation:	1,500 to 6,000'.
Habitat:	Among shrubs in washes, on rocky slopes, and in pinyon-juniper woodlands.
Comments:	Perennial herb. Stems of flowers and leaves twist in all directions. Three species of *Maurandya* (mau-RAN-dee-ah) in Arizona. Photograph taken at Dead Horse Ranch State Park, May 30.

BIGELOW MIMULUS   668

Bigelow's monkey flower
Mimulus bigelovii
Snapdragon or Figwort Family (Scrophulariaceae)

Height:	To 10".
Flowers:	Pink with darker pink in center; tubular; 5 crinkled lobes with white hairs; bright yellow stamens fused to lower petal; lower petal projecting slightly forward; hairy calyx, flower to 1" long, 1" wide.
Leaves:	Dark green tinged with pink; hairy, broadly elliptical; to 2" long.
Blooms:	February–April.
Elevation:	500 to 2,500'.
Habitat:	Sandy desert washes and open, sandy plains.
Comments:	Hairy stems. Fourteen species of *Mimulus* (MIM-you-luss) in Arizona. Photograph taken at Cattail Cove State Park, March 8.

CRIMSON MONKEY FLOWER   560

Scarlet monkey flower
Mimulus cardinalis
Snapdragon or Figwort Family (Scrophulariaceae)

Height:	To 3'.
Flowers:	Crimson red to reddish orange, tubular; 2-lipped, with 3 lobes of lower lip notched, upper lip arched upward; yellow stamens, hairy sepals; to 2" long, 1" wide; terminal, on 2"-long stem.
Leaves:	Dark green, hairy, opposite; oblong to oval, coarsely toothed, sticky; clasping stem; to 4 1/4" long.
Blooms:	March–October.
Elevation:	1,800 to 8,000'.
Habitat:	Seeps, springs, along flowing streams, and in wet canyons.
Comments:	Stems hairy. Fourteen species of *Mimulus* (MIM-you-luss) in Arizona. Photograph taken along West Fork of Oak Creek Canyon, October 1.

COMMON MONKEY FLOWER   516

Seep-spring monkey flower, spotted monkey flower, yellow monkey flower
Mimulus guttatus
Snapdragon or Figwort Family (Scrophulariaceae)

Height:	To 3'.
Flowers:	Bright yellow, hairy throat spotted with reddish pink; 2 lobes of upper lip point upward, 3 lobes of lower lip point downward; to 1 1/2" long, 1 1/4" wide; in upper leaf axils.
Leaves:	Dark green, oval, opposite; margins toothed; to 4" long, upper leaves lack stalks.
Blooms:	March–September.
Elevation:	500 to 9,500'.
Habitat:	Along brooks, springs, and other wet places.
Comments:	Perennial herb with hollow stems. Variable in size from tall and spindly to large and bushy. Native Americans used leaves for salad greens. Fourteen species of *Mimulus* (MIM-you-luss) in Arizona. Photograph taken at Organ Pipe Cactus National Monument, April 1.

GHOST FLOWER   517

Mohavea confertifolia
Snapdragon or Figwort Family (Scrophulariaceae)

Height:	To 16".
Flowers:	Pale cream-colored to yellowish, with pinkish purple dots on inside surface of roughly fringed lobes; cuplike; lower petal has reddish purple spot with 2 bright yellow stamens curving upward over spot; lower lip deeply indented on underside by hairy calyx; flower to 1 1/2" long; in clusters among leaves.
Leaves:	Light green, succulent, hairy on upper surface; elliptical to lance-shaped; to 4" long.
Blooms:	February–April.
Elevation:	Below 2,500'.
Habitat:	Sandy desert washes and rocky talus slopes.
Comments:	Annual. One main stem with many side stems. Translucent appearance of flower gives it its common name. Two species of *Mohavea* (mo-HAV-ee-ah) in Arizona. Photograph taken at Cattail Cove State Park, March 8.

YELLOW OWL'S CLOVER   518

Buttered owl's clover
Orthocarpus luteus
Snapdragon or Figwort Family (Scrophulariaceae)

Height:	To 16".
Flowers:	Golden yellow; 2-lipped, with upper lip forming short beak, saclike lower lip; to 1/2" long; in axils of hairy, 3-lobed bracts on single spike; flowering section of spike to 3" long.
Leaves:	Dark green to reddish green, alternate, spiraling up stem; linear or at times narrowly 3-lobed; to 1" long.
Blooms:	July–September.
Elevation:	7,000 to 9,500'.
Habitat:	Coniferous forests and moist meadows and hillsides.
Comments:	Annual. Erect stem. Three species of *Orthocarpus* (or-thoh-KAHR-puhs) in Arizona. Photograph taken in vicinity of Greer, August 8.

OWL CLOVER   669A and B
Escobita, common owl's clover, Mohave owl clover
Orthocarpus purpurascens
Snapdragon or Figwort Family (Scrophulariaceae)

Height: To 16".

Flowers: Rose-purple upper and lower lips, lower lip with white or yellow tip; surrounded by 5- to 7-lobed, rose-purple bracts, each to 1" long; flowers to 1 1/4" long; in dense, erect spike.

Leaves: Greenish to purplish and hairy; threadlike, with threadlike segments; to 2" long.

Blooms: March–May.

Elevation: 1,500 to 4,500'.

Habitat: Open mesas, slopes, and desert.

Comments: Annual. *Escobita* means "little broom" in Spanish. Can be partly parasitic on roots of other desert wildflowers. Three species of *Orthocarpus* (or-thoh-KAHR-puhs) in Arizona. Photographs taken in Superstition Mountains, March 19.

TWOTONE OWL'S CLOVER   316
Purple-white owl's clover
Orthocarpus purpureo-albus
Snapdragon or Figwort Family (Scrophulariaceae)

Height: To 12".

Flowers: White and pinkish purple, with lower lip greatly inflated; small, hooked beak above; to 3/4" long; spaced loosely along stem.

Leaves: Dark green, threadlike, 3-lobed; to 1 1/4" long, growing all along stem.

Blooms: July–September.

Elevation: 5,500 to 9,000'.

Habitat: Pinyon-juniper woodlands and ponderosa forests.

Comments: Annual. Three species of *Orthocarpus* (or-thoh-KAHR-puhs) in Arizona. Photograph taken near Ashurst Lake, September 5.

WOOD BETONY   754
Juniper lousewort
Pedicularis centranthera
Snapdragon or Figwort Family (Scrophulariaceae)

Height: To 4 1/2".

Flowers: White; 2-lipped with purplish tips on upper and lower lips; 4 stamens curled under upper lip, with tips of anthers projecting like tiny, upper teeth; flower to 1 3/4" long, 1/4" wide; in short, dense, terminal cluster of very hairy bracts.

Leaves: Grayish green with reddish midrib; pinnate, finely dissected into toothed lobes, fernlike; to 4" long; mainly in basal rosette.

Blooms: April–June.

Elevation: 5,000 to 8,000'.

Habitat: Ponderosa pine forests. .

Comments: Perennial herb. *Pediculus* means "louse" in Latin; in Roman times seeds were used to kill lice. Five species of *Pedicularis* (pe-dick-you-LAY-riss) in Arizona. Photograph taken in vicinity of Willow Springs Lake, April 22.

GRAY'S LOUSEWORT 519

Fern-leaf
Pedicularis grayi
Snapdragon or Figwort Family (Scrophulariaceae)

Height:	To 5'.
Flowers:	Yellowish with red-brown lines; 2-lipped, tubular, short-beaked; to 3/4" long, in a dense, bracted, terminal spike.
Leaves:	Dark green, fernlike, twice pinnate; to 1 1/2' long.
Blooms:	July–August.
Elevation:	8,000 to 10,000'.
Habitat:	Rich soil in coniferous forests.
Comments:	Five species of *Pedicularis* (pe-dick-you-LAY-riss) in Arizona. *Pediculus* means "louse" in Latin; in Roman times seeds were used to kill lice. Photograph taken in Greer area, July 21.

ELEPHANT HEAD

Elephanthead pedicularis, bull elephants head, little elephant, little red elephants
Pedicularis groenlandica
Snapdragon or Figwort Family (Scrophulariaceae)

Height:	To 3'.
Flowers:	Pink or reddish purple, shaped like a miniature elephant's head; to 1/2" long without "trunk"; twisted, long upper lip forms "trunk," shorter lower side lobes form "ears"; flowers arranged along upper half of erect stem.
Leaves:	Green, long, narrow, alternate; pinnately divided into sharply toothed segments; to 10" long.
Blooms:	August.
Elevation:	8,000 to 10,000'.
Habitat:	Wet meadows and cold streams.
Comments:	Perennial herb. *Pediculus* means "louse" in Latin; in Roman times seeds were used to kill lice. This species is included here without a photograph. After four years of searching for this plant in "sure-to-find" places (wet, mountain meadows), we never found it. We had better luck in Africa photographing the "real thing." Five species of *Pedicularis* (pe-dick-you-LAY-riss) in Arizona.

PARRY PEDICULARIS 317

Parry lousewort, fern leaf
Pedicularis parryi
Snapdragon or Figwort Family (Scrophulariaceae)

Height:	To 20".
Flowers:	White to yellowish white; narrow; upper lip compressed sideways and arched; lower lip 3-lobed and bent downward; to 1" long; on tall spike to 8" long.
Leaves:	Dark green with some red; fernlike and narrow; deeply lobed and toothed; to 5" long, 1/2" at widest; mainly basal.
Blooms:	June–September.
Elevation:	7,500 to 12,000'.
Habitat:	Moist mountain meadows and streambanks.
Comments:	Perennial herb; partially root-parasitic. *Pediculus* means "louse" in Latin; in Roman times seeds were used to kill lice. Five species of *Pedicularis* (pe-dick-you-LAY-riss) in Arizona. Photograph taken in Greer area, July 3.

BUSH PENSTEMON 670

Plains penstemon, moth penstemon, cow-tobacco
Penstemon ambiguus
Snapdragon or Figwort Family (Scrophulariaceae)

Height: To 3'.
Flowers: Pale pink, tubular, with 5 united petals; tube is curved with 2 large, upper petal lobes bent backward and 3 lower lobes projecting forward; to 3/4" wide, 1/2" long.
Leaves: Green, linear, grasslike, opposite; to 1" long; occurring up along stem.
Blooms: June–July.
Elevation: 4,500 to 6,500'.
Habitat: Sandy mesas and grasslands.
Comments: Branches freely forming a large, rounded, colorful bush when in bloom. More than 3 dozen species of *Penstemon* (pen-STEH-mohn or pen-STEE-mohn) in Arizona. Photograph taken near Page, June 26. Note the oblique angle of the lobes to the tubular section of the flower, thus distinguishing this species from all other penstemons.

GOLDEN-BEARD PENSTEMON 561

Southwestern penstemon, scarlet penstemon, beardlip penstemon, red penstemon, hummingbird flowers
Penstemon barbatus
Snapdragon or Figwort Family (Scrophulariaceae)

Height: To 4'.
Flowers: Scarlet red, narrow, and tubular; with upper lip projecting forward, lower lip bent downward with sides flared backward; to 1 1/2" long; in open, terminal raceme mostly on one side of stem.
Leaves: Gray-green, narrow, smooth; to 5" long.
Blooms: June–October.
Elevation: 4,000 to 10,000'.
Habitat: Roadsides, oak woods, and coniferous forests.
Comments: Native Americans use plant for medicinal and ceremonial purposes. Pollinated by hummingbirds. More than 3 dozen species of *Penstemon* (pen-STEH-mohn or pen-STEE-mohn) in Arizona. Photograph taken south of Alpine, August 2.

PINK PENSTEMON 671

Penstemon clutei
Snapdragon or Figwort Family (Scrophulariaceae)

Height: To 20".
Flowers: Deep pink to rose-purple, very hairy, tubular; tube widens gradually; 2 small, earlike upper lobes; 3 larger, rounded lower lobes; to 1" long, 3/4" wide; in elongated cluster.
Leaves: Grayish green, lance-shaped, opposite; crinkled margins, toothed; to 2" long; clasping stem.
Blooms: June–July.
Elevation: About 7,000'.
Habitat: Volcanic cinders.
Comments: In Arizona found only at Sunset Crater National Monument. More than 3 dozen species of *Penstemon* (pen-STEH-mohn or pen-STEE-mohn) in Arizona. Photograph taken at Sunset Crater National Monument, June 5.

EATONI PENSTEMON   562
Scarlet bugler (a name also given to another species)
Penstemon eatoni
Snapdragon or Figwort Family (Scrophulariaceae)
Height: Flower stalk to 2'.
Flowers: Bright scarlet red, tubular, with width of tube fixed; flaring lobes about equal;
               to 1" long; in elongated cluster.
Leaves: Dark green, leathery, mainly basal; to 2 1/2" long.
Blooms: February–June.
Elevation: 2,000 to 7,000'.
Habitat: Roadsides, desert slopes, and mesas.
Comments: Stems are purplish. Several subspecies. More than 3 dozen species of *Penstemon*
               (pen-STEH-mohn or pen-STEE-mohn) in Arizona. Photograph taken in Alamo Lake
               area, February 27. *P. eatoni* is similar to scarlet bugler, but its tubes are shorter.

NARROWLEAF PENSTEMON   780
Linarialeaf penstemon, toadflax penstemon, beardtongue
Penstemon linarioides
Snapdragon or Figwort Family (Scrophulariaceae)
Height: To 18".
Flowers: Lavender to bluish purple, tubular; 2 upper lobes flaring upward, 3 lower lobes
               flaring downward; whitish throat with yellow hairs; to 3/4" long, 1/2" wide; all
               facing in one direction on long, narrow flower stalk.
Leaves: Grayish green, linear, very narrow, pointing upward; to 3/4" long; occurring all
               along stem.
Blooms: June–August.
Elevation: 4,500 to 9,000'.
Habitat: Dry slopes and clearings in woodlands and pine forests.
Comments: Shrubby growth; has branching root system. More than 3 dozen species of
               Penstemon (pen-STEH-mohn or pen-STEE-mohn) in Arizona. Photograph taken at
               Oak Creek Canyon, June 18. The variety *viridis* forms a small mound to 6" tall, and
               is woody at base. Photograph (**PLATE 781**) taken along roadside at McNary,
               August 10.

PALMER'S PENSTEMON   672
Pink wild snapdragon, balloon flower, scented penstemon
Penstemon palmeri
Snapdragon or Figwort Family (Scrophulariaceae)
Height: Flower stem to 5'.
Flowers: Pale pink, fragrant, tubular; 2 upper lobes flared backward, 3 lower lobes flared
               downward; flower tube swollen; to 1 1/8" wide, 1 1/2" long; in long, narrow cluster
               often bending under the weight of buds and flowers.
Leaves: Grayish green, with waxy, blue coating; leathery, toothed, wavy; upper leaves paired
               together surrounding stem; to 5" long on each side, to 10" long for pair.
Blooms: March–September.
Elevation: 3,500 to 6,500'.
Habitat: Roadsides, washes, and mountain slopes.

Comments: A spectacular *Penstemon* (pen-STEH-mohn or pen-STEE-mohn). More than
3 dozen species of *Penstemon* in Arizona. Photograph taken on Mingus Mountain,
May 28.

PARRY'S PENSTEMON   673
Beardtongue, wind's flower
Penstemon parryi
Snapdragon or Figwort Family (Scrophulariaceae)

Height: To 4'.
Flowers: Pinkish to lavender, broadly funnel-shaped; petal lobes short and round, lower petal
lobes project forward; to 3/4" long; in long, open, terminal cluster.
Leaves: Bluish green, fleshy, without stalks; smooth, narrowly triangular; to 5" long.
Blooms: March.
Elevation: 1,500 to 5,000'.
Habitat: Well-drained slopes, mountain canyons, and roadsides.
Comments: Perennial herb. Well-scattered, does not grow in clumps. Flowers attract humming-
birds, bees, and other insects. More than 3 dozen species of *Penstemon*
(pen-STEH-mohn or pen-STEE-mohn) in Arizona. Photograph taken at Horseshoe
Lake Dam, March 21.

ARIZONA PENSTEMON   674
Nevada penstemon, Mohave beard tongue
Penstemon pseudospectabilis
Snapdragon or Figwort Family (Scrophulariaceae)

Height: To 4'.
Flowers: Bright lavender-red; wide throat with lower, one-sided bulge; to 3/4" long,
in clusters along stem.
Leaves: Gray, triangular, leathery, and toothed; bases joined together around stem;
to 3" long.
Blooms: February–May.
Elevation: 2,000 to 7,000'.
Habitat: Roadsides, hillsides, and canyons.
Comments: More than 3 dozen species of *Penstemon* (pen-STEH-mohn or pen-STEE-mohn)
in Arizona. Photograph taken in Superstition Mountains, March 15.

PORCH PENSTEMON   782
Penstemon strictus
Snapdragon or Figwort Family (Scrophulariaceae)

Height: To 32".
Flowers: Purple to violet-blue, tubular; 2 upper petals project forward like roof of a porch,
lower petals slope downward; stamen heads with white, twisted hairs; flower
to 1" long, spaced along stem in loose raceme.
Leaves: Dark green, narrow to lance-shaped, to 3" long.
Blooms: June–July.
Elevation: 7,000 to 8,000'.
Habitat: Roadsides and dry, gravelly slopes.
Comments: A variable species. More than 3 dozen species of *Penstemon* (pen-STEH-mohn
or pen-STEE-mohn) in Arizona. Photograph taken near Nutrioso, June 23.

SCARLET BUGLER 563
Penstemon subulatus
Snapdragon or Figwort Family (Scrophulariaceae)

Height: To 3'.

Flowers: Bright red, tubular, with 5 short lobes rounded at tips; to 1 1/4" long; on one side all along upper stems.

Leaves: Dark green, smooth, thick; lance-shaped to spatula-shaped, opposite; to 3" long.

Blooms: March–June.

Elevation: 600 to 4,500'.

Habitat: Dry hillsides and cliffs.

Comments: Stem is pinkish. More than 3 dozen species of *Penstemon* (pen-STEH-mohn or pen-STEE-mohn) in Arizona. Photograph taken near Apache Lake, March 29.

WANDBLOOM PENSTEMON 675
Penstemon virgatus
Snapdragon or Figwort Family (Scrophulariaceae)

Height: To 30".

Flowers: Pale pinkish violet, light purplish lines within; funnel-shaped, 2-lipped, 2 lobes above, 3 lobes below; to 3/4" wide, 1" long; along only 1 side of stem.

Leaves: Dark green, narrow, linear; to 4" long.

Blooms: June–September.

Elevation: 5,000 to 11,000'.

Habitat: Pine forests and mountain meadows.

Comments: Very variable species. More than 3 dozen species of *Penstemon* (pen-STEH-mohn or pen-STEE-mohn) in Arizona. Photograph taken near Willow Springs Lake, August 5.

WHIPPLE'S PENSTEMON 783
Whipple's beardtongue, dusky beardtongue
Penstemon whippleanus
Snapdragon or Figwort Family (Scrophulariaceae)

Height: To 2'.

Flowers: Whitish to lavender to deep purple; sticky-haired; yellow-orange in throat; strongly 2-lipped, with 2 lobes of upper lip flaring forward and upward, 3 lower lobes spread apart and projecting forward more than upper lobes; to 1" long; in several downward-facing clusters on stem.

Leaves: Dark green; basal leaves elliptical, to 4" long; stem leaves opposite and lance-shaped, to 1" long.

Blooms: July–August.

Elevation: 6,500 to 12,000'.

Habitat: Moist meadows and rocky slopes.

Comments: Plants in Arizona are in the purple color range. More than 3 dozen species of *Penstemon* (pen-STEH-mohn or pen-STEE-mohn) in Arizona. Photograph taken in mountains above Greer, July 3. This species of *Penstemon* identifiable by its longer lower lip and by downward-facing arrangement of flower clusters on stem.

YELLOW RATTLE   520
Rhinanthus rigidus
Snapdragon or Figwort Family (Scrophulariaceae)

Height:	To 8".
Flowers:	Yellow, with arched upper lip, 3-lobed lower lip; to 1/2" long; in dense, elongated cluster; followed by enlarged, bladderlike, oval calyx, to 3/8" thick, 5/8" long, 1/2" wide.
Leaves:	Light green streaked with reddish purple; opposite, lance-shaped, toothed; to 2" long.
Blooms:	August–September.
Elevation:	9,000 to 9,500'.
Habitat:	Streamsides and moist mountain meadows.
Comments:	Annual. Erect, 4-angled stems. Plant used as an insecticide. One species of *Rhinanthus* (rin-AN-thuss) in Arizona. Photograph taken in Mount Baldy Wilderness, August 13.

MOTH MULLEIN   522
Verbascum blattaria
Snapdragon or Figwort Family (Scrophulariaceae)

Height:	To 5'.
Flowers:	Yellow (sometimes white), with 5 rounded, slightly unequal lobes; flat; red-orange anthers with purplish hairs on stamen filaments; to 1 1/4" wide; clustered along slender, erect spike.
Leaves:	Dark green, straplike, lobed or toothed; to 5" long in basal rosette, decreasing in length toward flowers.
Blooms:	August–September.
Elevation:	6,000 to 7,000'.
Habitat:	Fields, roadsides, and wastelands.
Comments:	Biennial weed. Introduced from Europe; now naturalized in U.S. Hairy stamen filaments resemble a moth's antennae; the flattened flowers on the stem resemble resting moths; hence the name "moth mullein." Three species of *Verbascum* (ver-BAS-kum) in Arizona. Photograph taken near Prescott, September 11.

COMMON MULLEIN   521A and B
Flannel mullein, blanketweed, woolly mullein, velvet plant, flannel-leaf, candlewick
Verbascum thapsus
Snapdragon or Figwort Family (Scrophulariaceae)

Height:	To 6'.
Flowers:	Yellow, with 5 slightly unequal lobes, 5 orange-tipped stamens; to 1" wide; in tightly wedged, spikelike cluster; to 20" long.
Leaves:	Grayish green, oblong, feltlike, grayish-haired; basal leaves in rosette; to 16" long, shorter on stem.
Blooms:	June–September.
Elevation:	5,000 to 7,000'.
Habitat:	Roadsides, open areas, and disturbed places.
Comments:	Biennial; naturalized from Europe. Seeds eaten by birds. Leaves used as wicks. For warmth, colonists and Native Americans lined footwear with leaves. Various parts of plant used medicinally. Three species of *Verbascum* (ver-BAS-kum) in Arizona. Photographs taken in vicinity of Woods Canyon Lake, August 7.

AMERICAN BROOKLIME   784

American speedwell
Veronica americana
Snapdragon or Figwort Family (Scrophulariaceae)

Height: To 2'.
Flowers: Blue streaked with lavender; 4-lobed with lower lobe narrowest; to 1/2" wide; in loose clusters arising from leaf axils.
Leaves: Dark green, shiny, broadly lance-shaped to oval; toothed margins variable; short-stalked; to 3" long.
Blooms: May–August.
Elevation: 1,500 to 9,500'.
Habitat: In and around springs and along streamsides.
Comments: Semi-aquatic succulent with creeping, reddish stems. Spreads easily, forming dense areas. Named for Saint Veronica. Nine species of *Veronica* (ver-RON-i-kah) in Arizona. Photograph taken in Hannagan Meadow area, June 30.

THYME SPEEDWELL   785

Veronica serpyllifolia
Snapdragon or Figwort Family (Scrophulariaceae)

Height: To 6".
Flowers: Pale blue; 4-lobed with lower lobe narrowest; to 1/4" wide, arising from leaf axils.
Leaves: Dark green, oval to oblong, hairy, and toothed; to 1" long.
Blooms: June–August.
Elevation: 8,000 to 10,000'.
Habitat: Moist areas in coniferous forests.
Comments: Creeping, hairy stems. Introduced from Eurasia; now naturalized in U.S. Named for Saint Veronica. Nine species of *Veronica* (ver-RON-i-kah) in Arizona. Photograph taken at Lee Valley Reservoir area, June 30.

BIGNONIA FAMILY

Bignoniaceae (big-known-i-AY-see-ee)
Represented in Arizona by shrubs or small trees.

Flowers: Irregular, tubular or funnel-shaped; 2-lipped (2-lobed upper lip and 3-lobed lower lip); usually 4 stamens, in 2 sets; 5-lobed calyx; 1 style, usually 2-lobed stigma. Superior ovary, 2-celled.
Fruit: Dry, elongated, 2-valved capsule.
Leaves: Opposite, simple, or compound.

SOUTHERN CATALPA   54

Indian bean, common catalpa, catawba, bean-tree, cigar-tree
Catalpa bignonioides
Bignonia Family (Bignoniaceae)

Height: To 40'.
Trunk: To 2' in diameter.
Bark: Brownish gray, scaly.
Flowers: White outside; white inside with 2 yellow stripes and spots and stripes of purplish brown; bell-shaped; 5 rounded, fringed lobes; to 1 1/2" long, 1 1/2" wide; in

branched clusters to 9" long; followed by dark brown, very narrow, cylindrical seed capsule to 14" long.

Leaves: Dull green above, paler green and hairy beneath; heart-shaped, opposite, pointed at tip; to 10" long, 7" wide.

Blooms: June–July.

Elevation: Not available. Photograph taken at approximately 5,000'.

Habitat: Clearings and roadsides.

Comments: Fast-growing; has soft wood. Introduced to the state. One species of *Catalpa* (ka-TAL-pah) in Arizona. Photograph taken in Oak Creek Canyon, Sedona, June 8.

DESERT WILLOW 55

Mimbre, jano, desert catalpa, flowering willow
Chilopsis linearis
Bignonia Family (Bignoniaceae)

Height: Large shrub, or small tree to 25'.

Trunk: To 1' in diameter.

Bark: Dark brown, scaly, ridged.

Flowers: Whitish, tinged with lavender and yellow, tubular, orchidlike; to 1 1/2" long; fragrant, in 3- to 4-inch clusters; followed by very narrow, brown seed capsules, to 1/4" wide, 8" long.

Leaves: Light green, very narrow, untoothed; to 6" long, to 3/8" wide.

Blooms: April–August.

Elevation: 1,500 to 5,000'.

Habitat: Along washes and other waterways in desert, grasslands, foothills, and mesas.

Comments: Deciduous; has spreading crown. Desert willows help control erosion by forming dense thickets along washes. Not a true willow, but related to catalpa, which has very similar flowers and seed capsules (although catalpa leaves are very large and heart-shaped). Wood was used for bows by Native Americans. One species of *Chilopsis* (ky-LOP-sis) in Arizona. Photograph taken in vicinity of Scottsdale, May 7.

YELLOW TRUMPET BUSH 523

Yellow bells, yellow elder, trumpetflower, yellow trumpet, esperanza, palo del arco, minones, tronadora, minona
Tecoma stans (Stenolobium stans)
Bignonia Family (Bignoniaceae)

Height: Small shrub to 15'.

Flowers: Bright yellow, trumpet-shaped, with ruffled lobes; to 2" long; in clusters; followed by a narrow capsule to 8" long, 1/4" wide.

Leaves: Dark green, glossy, lance-shaped to oval; pointed at tips, toothed; to 6" long; pinnately compound, with 5 to 13 leaflets.

Blooms: May–October.

Elevation: 3,000 to 5,500'.

Habitat: Dry, gravelly hillsides in southeastern Arizona.

Comments: Evergreen in frost-free areas. Browsed by bighorn sheep. Cultivated as an ornamental. One species of *Tecoma* (te-KOH-mah) in Arizona. Photograph taken at Mesa, May 9.

UNICORN PLANT FAMILY

Martyniaceae (mar-tin-i-AY-see-ee)
Annual herbs.

Flowers: Irregular with 2 lips and lobes; large, funnel-shaped; 4 to 5 calyx lobes, 4 stamens. Superior ovary, 1-celled.

Fruit: Capsule with curved beak.

Leaves: Alternate or opposite, simple, sticky, hairy.

DEVIL'S CLAW   676A and B

Unicorn plant, una de gato, torito, guernito, elephant tusks, red devil's claw
Proboscidea parviflora
Unicorn Plant Family (Martyniaceae)

Height: Sprawling stems to 3' long.

Flowers: Reddish purple to pinkish with yellowish, striped throat; tubular, 5-lobed, hairy; to 1 1/2" long, 3/4" wide; followed by dark green, very sticky, hairy, fleshy fruit with curved tip; fruit to 12" along the curve. When mature, each fruit sheds its fleshy skin and splits open, revealing a black, woody shell ending in two curved prongs.

Leaves: Dark green, very hairy and sticky, triangular; to 7" long, 7" wide; on pinkish stem to 1' long.

Blooms: April–October.

Elevation: 1,000 to 5,000'.

Habitat: Roadsides, mesas, plains, and disturbed areas.

Comments: Annual herb. Entire plant is very sticky. Prongs on fruits hook on passing animals. Immature fruits are eaten as a vegetable. Black mature pods used by Native Americans in basketry. Three species of *Proboscidea* (pro-bos-SID-i-ah) in Arizona. Photographs taken at Dead Horse Ranch State Park, October 3.

BROOMRAPE FAMILY

Orobanchaceae (or-oh-ban-kee-AY-see-ee)
Represented in Arizona by root-parasitic herbs with fleshy stems and lacking chlorophyll.

Flowers: Irregular, tubular; 5 united petals forming 2-lobed upper lip and 3-lobed lower lip; 4 stamens in pairs, 2 to 5 sepals, 1 style. Superior ovary, 1-celled.

Fruit: Many-seeded, chambered capsule.

Leaves: Alternate, simple, scalelike.

SQUAWROOT   524

Mexican squawroot, cancer-root
Conopholis alpina var. *mexicana*
Broomrape Family (Orobanchaceae)

Height: To 12".

Flowers: Yellowish, curved with protruding stigmas; in several rows on elongated spike; to 1/2" long.

Leaves: Yellow (lack chlorophyll); scalelike.

Blooms: April–June.

Elevation: 5,000 to 6,000'.

Habitat: The humus in pine, oak, cypress, and madrone areas.

Comments: Plant resembles a large pine cone. A saprophyte on decaying vegetation. One species of *Conopholis* (ko-NO-foh-lis) in Arizona. Photograph taken in vicinity of Cave Creek, Portal, April 22.

BURRO WEED STRANGLER   786
Broomrape, Louisiana broomrape, cancer-root
Orobanche cooperi (*Orobanche ludoviciana*)
Broomrape Family (Orobanchaceae)

Height: To 15".
Flowers: Purplish, tubular, with 2-lobed upper lip and 3-lobed lower lip; to 1" long; many on erect, conelike spike.
Leaves: Purplish brown, scalelike bracts.
Blooms: February–September.
Elevation: 200 to 5,000'.
Habitat: Sandy deserts and washes.
Comments: Lacks chlorophyll. Parasitic herb usually on roots of bursage and other composites. Used by Native Americans for food and medicine. Four species of *Orobanche* (or-oh-BAN-kee) in Arizona. Photograph taken at Cattail Cove State Park, February 23.

CLUSTERED BROOMRAPE   525
Cancer-root
Orobanche fasciculata var. *lutea*
Broomrape Family (Orobanchaceae)

Height: To 4".
Flowers: Yellowish with slight pinkish color on lobes; tubular, 5-lobed; pointed, hairy calyx lobes; glandular hairs on flower and calyx; 2 pair of very hairy, yellow stamens; flower to 3/8" wide, 1" long.
Leaves: Cream-colored scales.
Blooms: May–August.
Elevation: 4,000 to 8,000'.
Habitat: Chaparral and coniferous forests, frequently in volcanic cinders.
Comments: Cream-colored, hairy, separate stems in cluster. A root parasite. Four species of *Orobanche* (or-oh-BAN-kee) in Arizona. Photograph taken at Sunset Crater National Monument, June 4.

BLADDERWORT FAMILY
Lentibulariaceae (len-tib-you-lair-i-AYE-see-ee)
Represented in Arizona by an aquatic herb.

Flowers: Irregular, prominently 2-lipped; 2 stamens, spurred. Superior ovary, 1-celled.
Fruit: 1-celled capsule.
Leaves: Have threadlike segments; submerged in water.

COMMON BLADDERWORT   526
Greater bladderwort
Utricularia vulgaris
Bladderwort Family (Lentibulariaceae)

Height: To 8" above surface of water.
Flowers: Yellow, 2-lipped, snapdragonlike; large palate faintly striped with red; spurred; to

	1/2" wide, 3/4" long; in a sparsely flowered, terminal cluster on a stout, leafless stem.
Leaves:	Dark green, finely dissected, hairlike; floating or submerged; provided with scattered, 1/8"-wide bladders; to 2" long.
Blooms:	July–August.
Elevation:	8,000 to 9,500'.
Habitat:	Mainly shallow water of ponds and lakes.
Comments:	Only insectivorous plant in Arizona. The bladders resemble minute bubbles. Each is equipped with a tiny door and a sensitive trigger, which when touched opens the door. The vacuum inside the bubble sucks an organism in, then digestive enzymes disintegrate the prey. Water fleas and mosquito larvae are common victims. One species of *Utricularia* (you-trik-you-LARE-ee-ah) in Arizona. Photograph taken at Carnero Lake near Greer, July 11.

ACANTHUS FAMILY

Acanthaceae (ah-kan-THAY-see-ee)
Represented in Arizona by herbs or shrubs.

Flowers:	Irregular, 4 to 5 united petals, often 2-lipped (2-lobed upper and 3-lobed lower); 5-part calyx, 2 to 4 stamens. Pistil with long style and usually 2 stigmas. Superior ovary, 2-celled.
Fruit:	2-celled capsule.
Leaves:	Opposite, simple, occasionally lobed.

DESERT HONEYSUCKLE   539

Chuparosa
Anisacanthus thurberi
Acanthus Family (Acanthaceae)

Height:	Shrub to 6'.
Flowers:	Vermilion or orange, with long slender tube; to 1 1/4" long.
Leaves:	Dark green, short-stemmed, elliptical; to 2 1/2" long, 3/4" wide.
Blooms:	Chiefly in spring, but also other times of year.
Elevation:	2,500 to 5,500'.
Habitat:	Along sandy washes and in canyons.
Comments:	Has woody stems and shreddy bark. Browsed by sheep and cattle; pollinated by hummingbirds. One species of *Anisacanthus* (ah-neese-uh-KAN-thus) in Arizona. Photograph taken at Patagonia, April 27.

CHUPAROSA   564

Hummingbird bush, honeysuckle
Beloperone californica (*Justicia californica*)
Acanthus Family (Acanthaceae)

Height:	To 6'.
Flowers:	Dull red, tubular; 2-lobed upper and 3-lobed lower lip; anther with large, white point at tip; to 2" long, in terminal clusters; followed by two-celled capsule.
Leaves:	(When present) grayish green, covered with soft hairs; oval to egg-shaped; to 1" long; falling during drought or cold.
Blooms:	On and off throughout year.
Elevation:	1,000 to 2,500'.

Habitat:	Rocky slopes and along washes.
Comments:	Stems are soft and hairy. A favorite with hummingbirds (*Chuparosa* is Spanish for "hummingbird"). One species of *Beloperone* (bel-o-per-OWN-ee) in Arizona. Photograph taken at Usery Mountain Recreation Area, March 7. Distinguished from *Jacobinia ovata* by terminal clusters of flowers, more narrow tube without prominent white throat markings, and by presence of white point at anther tip.

PURPLE SCALY STEM   755
Elytraria imbricata
Acanthus Family (Acanthaceae)

Height:	To 10".
Flowers:	Blue to lavender; 2 upright, earlike lobes; 2 cleft side lobes; 1 cleft lower lobe; to 5/16" long, 5/16" wide; on long narrow, scaly flower stem.
Leaves:	Dark green, scalelike.
Blooms:	April–September.
Elevation:	3,500 to 5,000'.
Habitat:	Among rocks on slopes or mesas.
Comments:	Numerous upright or spreading flower stems forming a clump. One species of *Elytraria* (el-i-TRAR-i-ah) in Arizona. Photograph taken at Patagonia Lake State Park, May 10.

JACOBINIA   565
Jacobinia ovata
Acanthus Family (Acanthaceae)

Height:	Sprawling shrub to 5'.
Flowers:	Deep red with white markings in throat; tubular, 2-lobed upper and 3-lobed lower tube; petals united for about two-thirds of tube; lower lobes wide, notched, and curving downward; anther lacks large white point at tip; flower to 1 1/2" long, in upper leaf axils; followed by 2-celled capsule.
Leaves:	Grayish green with deep purplish brown markings; covered with soft hairs; oval to sharply pointed; to 1 1/2" long, 3/4" wide.
Blooms:	On and off throughout year.
Elevation:	1,500 to 3,500'.
Habitat:	Rocky foothills, washes, and canyons.
Comments:	One species of *Jacobinia* (jack-oh-BIN-i-ah) in Arizona. Photograph taken below Horse Mesa Dam, Apache Lake, March 23.

SIPHONOGLOSSA   318
Siphonoglossa longiflora
Acanthus Family (Acanthaceae)

Height:	To 8".
Flowers:	White, tubular; with 1 notched, smaller upper lip; 3-lobed, larger lower lip; brown-tipped stamens; flower to 2" long, 1/2" wide; clustered in leaf axils.
Leaves:	Dark green, opposite, margins curled slightly upward; short-stalked, lance-shaped, to 2" long.
Blooms:	April–October.
Elevation:	3,000 to 4,000'.
Habitat:	Canyons and rocky slopes.

Comments: Flowers open in evening and close the following morning. Browsed by livestock and wild animals. One species of *Siphonoglossa* (sye-fon-oh-GLOS-sah) in Arizona. Photograph taken in Molino Canyon, Mount Lemmon, May 14.

PLANTAIN FAMILY
Plantaginaceae (plant-ah-gin-AY-see-ee)
Herbs.

Flowers: Regular, small; calyx and corolla are 4-divided or 4-lobed; 2 to 4 stamens. Superior ovary, 2- to 4-celled.
Fruit: A capsule.
Leaves: Basal.

BUCKHORN PLANTAIN   805
Ribwort, English plantain, narrow-leafed plantain
Plantago lanceolata
Plantain Family (Plantaginaceae)

Height: To 24".
Flowers: Greenish white, to 1/8" long; spirally arranged in a dense, terminal spike, to 1 1/2" long, on tall, leafless stalk; stamens projecting from hairlike stalks with cream-colored anthers at ends; followed by tiny, brown, 2-seeded capsule.
Leaves: Dark green; lancelike, in basal cluster; to 16" long.
Blooms: April–September.
Elevation: Widely distributed.
Habitat: Meadows, fields, and lawns.
Comments: Considered a weed. Native to Europe; now naturalized in U.S. Eleven species of *Plantago* (plan-TAY-goh) in Arizona. Photograph taken at Nelson Reservoir, August 3.

PURSH PLANTAIN   284
Indian wheat, woolly plantain
Plantago purshii
Plantain Family (Plantaginaceae)

Height: Flower stem to 8".
Flowers: Buff-colored with brownish tinge toward center; 4 narrow, pointed petals; to 1/8" wide; flowers spaced on woolly bracted spike to 1 1/4" long.
Leaves: Grayish green, very hairy, narrow, and basal; to 4" long.
Blooms: February–July.
Elevation: 1,000 to 7,000'.
Habitat: Dry slopes and mesas.
Comments: Very hairy plant. Browsed by livestock. Eleven species of *Plantago* (plan-TAY-goh) in Arizona. Photograph taken in Superstition Mountains, March 25.

MADDER FAMILY

Rubiaceae (rew-bih-AY-see-ee)

Represented in Arizona by herbs and shrubs.

Flowers: Regular or nearly regular, with 4- to 5-lobed united corolla, 4 to 5 sepals, 4 to 5 stamens, 1 style. Inferior ovary, mostly 2-celled.

Fruit: Capsule, berry, or drupe.

Leaves: Opposite or whorled, simple. Square stems.

SMOOTH BOUVARDIA 566

Bouvardia glaberrima

Madder Family (Rubiaceae)

Height: Small shrub to 3'.

Flowers: Bright reddish orange, narrow, tubular, flaring into 4 lobes; honeysucklelike; to 1 1/4" long, 5/16" wide; in clusters.

Leaves: Dark green, lance-shaped, hairy; generally in whorls of 3, to 3" long.

Blooms: May–October.

Elevation: 3,000 to 9,000'.

Habitat: Slopes and canyons.

Comments: Visited by hummingbirds. Used medicinally in Mexico. One species of *Bouvardia* (boo-VAR-di-ah) in Arizona. Photograph taken at Madera Canyon, May 11.

BUTTONBUSH 171

Globe-flower, honey-balls, button-willow, snowball

Cephalanthus occidentalis var. *californicus*

Madder Family (Rubiaceae)

Height: Shrub, or small tree to 10'.

Trunk: To 4" in diameter.

Bark: Brown or gray, ridged, scaly.

Flowers: White with very tiny, brownish dots; narrow, tubular, with very long stamens tipped with yellow; white buds with yellow tips; fragrant, 4-lobed; to 1/2" long, 1/8" wide; clustered in round ball, to 1 1/2" in diameter. Followed by a rough button of seeds, green turning to brown; to 3/4" in diameter.

Leaves: Shiny, dark green above, slightly paler beneath; finely toothed, with prominent midvein; broadly lance-shaped to elliptical; pointed; opposite or in whorls of 3; to 5" long, 2 1/2" wide.

Blooms: June–September.

Elevation: 1,000 to 5,000'.

Habitat: Wet ground bordering lakes and streams.

Comments: Deciduous. Has green stems with warts; poisonous foliage. Bark is used medicinally. Waterfowl feed on seeds. Plant is a source for honey. One species of *Cephalanthus* (seh-fuh-LAN-thuss) in Arizona. Photograph taken at Saguaro Lake, August 26.

COMMON BEDSTRAW 172

Goosegrass bedstraw, cleavers, reclining bedstraw

Galium aparine

Madder Family (Rubiaceae)

Height: Sprawling to 3'.

Flowers:	White to greenish, with 4 petals; to 1/8" wide; in small clusters on stems rising from the leaf axils.
Leaves:	Dark green, hairy, linear to lance-shaped; to 3" long; 6 to 8 in whorls around stem.
Blooms:	March–May.
Elevation:	2,000 to 8,000'.
Habitat:	Along streams, in canyons, and in woodlands.
Comments:	Weak-stemmed annual supported by other plants. Barbed stems cleave to fabric and fur. Early settlers used plants as mattress stuffing. Seeds used as a coffee substitute. More than a dozen species of *Galium* (GAY-li-um) in Arizona. Photograph taken in Superstition Mountains, March 26. This species has leaves in whorls of 6 to 8 and 4-angled, spiny stems.

NORTHERN BEDSTRAW   173
Northern snow bedstraw
Galium boreale
Madder Family (Rubiaceae)

Height:	To 2'.
Flowers:	White, with 4 petals; to 1/8" wide; in dense, round-topped clusters.
Leaves:	Dark green, narrow, nearly smooth; lance-shaped to linear, with 3 prominent veins; to 2" long; in whorls of 4 around stem, smaller side shoots arise from main stems.
Blooms:	July–September.
Elevation:	6,000 to 9,500'.
Habitat:	Rocky slopes and clearings in pine forests.
Comments:	More than a dozen species of *Galium* (GAY-li-um) in Arizona. Photograph taken in Greer area, July 4. This species has leaves in whorls of 4 and a nearly smooth stem and leaves.

DESERT BEDSTRAW   174
Galium stellatum
Madder Family (Rubiaceae)

Height:	To 2'.
Flowers:	Cream-colored, with dark yellow stamens; 4 petals joined at base; starlike; to 1/8" wide, in loose clusters.
Leaves:	Dark green, lance-shaped, sharp-pointed, and rough; in whorls of 4 or 5 on lower stems; to 1/4" long.
Blooms:	January–May.
Elevation:	Below 3,000'.
Habitat:	Dry, rocky slopes.
Comments:	Many-branched shrubby plant with reddish, square stems. More than a dozen species of *Galium* (GAY-li-um) in Arizona. Photograph taken in Superstition Mountains, March 26.

WRIGHT'S BLUETS   583
Hedyotis pygmaea (*Houstonia wrightii*)
Madder Family (Rubiaceae)

Height:	To 8".
Flowers:	Purplish, pinkish, or white; funnel-shaped; 4 flaring lobes; to 1/4" wide; closely clustered.
Leaves:	Dark green, thick, narrow, numerous; to 1/2" long.

Blooms:	May–September.
Elevation:	5,000 to 9,000'.
Habitat:	Slopes, dry mesas, and edges of coniferous forests.
Comments:	Four species of *Hedyotis* (hay-DEE-oh-tis) in Arizona. Photograph taken in Hannagan Meadow area, June 24.

HOUSTONIA   584
Hedyotis rubra (*Houstonia rubra*)
Madder Family (Rubiaceae)

Height:	To 3".
Flowers:	Bright pink, tubular, 4 lobes spreading at right angles; to 1/2" wide, 1" long.
Leaves:	Grayish green, linear, thick, and succulent; to 1" long.
Blooms:	April–August.
Elevation:	4,000 to 6,000'.
Habitat:	Washes, mesas, and rocky hillsides.
Comments:	Perennial. Dense, baseball-shaped mound of leaves and flowers. Four species of *Hedyotis* (hay-DEE-oh-tis) in Arizona. Photograph taken in wash at Dead Horse Ranch State Park, May 28.

HONEYSUCKLE FAMILY
Caprifoliaceae (kap-rih-foh-lih-AY-see-ee)
Herbs, vines, shrubs, and small trees.

Flowers:	Regular or irregular; bell, funnel or tube-shaped; 4- to 5-lobed corolla, 4- to 5-toothed or lobed calyx; 4 to 5 stamens, 1 style, 1 to 5 stigmas. Inferior ovary, 2- to 5-celled.
Fruit:	Berry, drupe, or capsule.
Leaves:	Opposite, simple, or compound.

TWINFLOWER   612
Northern twinflower
Linnaea borealis
Honeysuckle Family (Caprifoliaceae)

Height:	Trailing to 2', upright flower stem to 4".
Flowers:	Pink, bell-like, narrow; nodding, fragrant, tubular, 5-lobed; in twin pair on forked stalk; flower to 1/4" wide to 1/2" long.
Leaves:	Dark green to yellowish green, opposite, broadly elliptic; thick; 2 shallow teeth on each leaf margin toward tip; shiny, basal, to 3/4" long.
Blooms:	June–August.
Elevation:	In 9,000' range.
Habitat:	Moist spruce-fir forests.
Comments:	Evergreen. Eaten by deer and grouse. Genus is named for Carl Linnaeus, the famous botanist. One species of *Linnaea* (lin-NEE-ah) in Arizona. Photograph taken in mountains above Greer, July 8.

ARIZONA HONEYSUCKLE   567
Madreselva
Lonicera arizonica
Honeysuckle Family (Caprifoliaceae)

Height:	A stiff, trailing vine to 3' or more.
Flowers:	Red outside, with orange throat inside; trumpet-shaped; in small, terminal, whorled cluster arising from 2 joined leaves; followed by cluster of red berries.
Leaves:	Bluish green above, paler beneath; very finely haired; oval; joined together in pairs; to 2" wide, 2 3/4" long.
Blooms:	June–July.
Elevation:	6,000 to 9,000'.
Habitat:	Open coniferous forests.
Comments:	Has scaly, brown trunk. A favorite of hummingbirds. Berries eaten by birds and small mammals. Six species of *Lonicera* (lah-NIH-seh-ruh) in Arizona. Photograph taken near Willow Springs Lake, June 11.

CHAPARRAL HONEYSUCKLE 527
Lonicera interrupta
Honeysuckle Family (Caprifoliaceae)

Height:	Trailing.
Flowers:	Creamy white, tubular, with swollen throat; upper lobe rolled backward, lower lobe in watchspring-shaped curl; 4 very long stamens; to 3/4" long; in elongated, terminal cluster.
Leaves:	Dark green above, lighter green beneath; opposite, oval; to 1 3/4" long.
Blooms:	May–June.
Elevation:	4,000 to 6,000'.
Habitat:	Along streams in juniper-oak woodlands.
Comments:	Has reddish stems. Six species of *Lonicera* (lah-NIH-seh-ruh) in Arizona. Photograph taken north of Payson along East Verde River, June 3.

BEARBERRY HONEYSUCKLE 739
Black twinberry, ink-berry, pigeon-bush, twin-flower, skunkberry, madreselva
Lonicera involucrata
Honeysuckle Family (Caprifoliaceae)

Height:	To 7'.
Flowers:	Yellow tinged with red; tubular; to 1/2" long; in pairs, with 2 large bracts at base; followed by a pair of shiny, purplish black, pea-sized berries.
Leaves:	Dark green, glandular-dotted, oval, and hairy; to 5" long.
Blooms:	June–July.
Elevation:	7,500 to 10,500'.
Habitat:	Along streams and in moist coniferous forests.
Comments:	Often forms thickets. Frequented by hummingbirds. Birds and mammals eat its sour berries. Six species of *Lonicera* (lah-NIH-seh-ruh) in Arizona. Photograph taken in Greer, July 20.

UTAH HONEYSUCKLE 370A and B
Red twinberry, twinberry honeysuckle
Lonicera utahensis
Honeysuckle Family (Caprifoliaceae)

Height:	Shrub to 5'.
Flowers:	Creamy white, trumpet-shaped, long-stamened, 5-lobed; to 3/4" long; paired, on thin, 1/2"-long flower stem; followed by twin, orangish yellow to red, oval berries.

Leaves:	Pale green above, lighter green and powdery beneath; broadly elliptical; to 1 1/2" long.
Blooms:	June–July.
Elevation:	8,000 to 11,000'.
Habitat:	Openings in coniferous forests.
Comments:	Berries are poisonous to humans but eaten by birds and other wildlife. Six species of *Lonicera* (lah-NIH-seh-ruh) in Arizona. Photograph of flowers taken in Greer area, July 3. Photograph of plant in berry taken in same area, August 9.

BLUEBERRY ELDER   107
Elderberry, blue elderberry
Sambucus glauca (Sambucus coerulea)
Honeysuckle Family (Caprifoliaceae)

Height:	Shrub, or small tree to 20'.
Trunk:	To 1' in diameter.
Bark:	Brown or gray, furrowed.
Flowers:	Yellowish white; to 1/4" wide; in dense, flat-topped cluster to 8" wide; followed by loose cluster of dark blue, 1/4"-diameter berries covered with a powdery coating.
Leaves:	Dark green, pinnately compound, evenly toothed, to 8" long; with 5 to 9 lance-shaped leaflets, to 4" long.
Blooms:	July–August.
Elevation:	6,500 to 9,500'.
Habitat:	Openings in moist coniferous forests and meadows.
Comments:	Forms clumps. Foliage browsed by livestock and deer. Berries attractive to birds; edible and used for wine, jelly, and pies. Bark used for fever medication. Five species of *Sambucus* (sam-BEW-kuss) in Arizona. Photograph taken south of Alpine, July 23.

MEXICAN ELDER   108
Arizona elder, desert elderberry, sauco, tapiro, New Mexican blueberry elder
Sambucus mexicana
Honeysuckle Family (Caprifoliaceae)

Height:	To 30'.
Trunk:	To 18" in diameter.
Bark:	Light brown to gray with long, narrow, scaly ridges.
Flowers:	Yellowish white, fragrant; to 1/4" wide; in flat-topped cluster to 8" wide; followed by dark blue to blackish fruits (with a whitish powdery coating). Fruits are sweet, juicy, edible, 1/4" in diameter and grow in a cluster.
Leaves:	Green above, paler green beneath, pinnately compound, to 14" long; with 3 or 5 leaflets, elliptical or oval, finely saw-toothed, thick, leathery, to 3" long, 1 1/2" wide.
Blooms:	March–June.
Elevation:	1,000 to 4,000'.
Habitat:	Along streams and rivers in woodlands, deserts, and desert grasslands.
Comments:	Evergreen, but deciduous during long droughts. One of the largest of the native elders. Grows at lower elevations than any elder in Arizona. Fruits eaten by birds; used in pies and jellies; Native Americans dried fruits for future uses. Five species of *Sambucus* (sam-BEW-kuss) in Arizona. Photograph taken at Patagonia, April 27.

REDBERRIED ELDER   233A and B
Scarlet elderberry, red elderberry, bunchberry elder, European red elder
Sambucus microbotrys (*Sambucus racemosa*)
Honeysuckle Family (Caprifoliaceae)

Height: To 5'.
Flowers: White to cream-colored, fragrant, 5-petaled; to 1/2" wide; in pyramidal cluster; followed by cluster of shiny, bright red, roundish berries to 1/4" in diameter.
Leaves: Dark green, pinnate, to 10" long; 5 to 7 leaflets, each folded upward slightly lengthwise, toothed.
Blooms: June–July.
Elevation: 7,500 to 10,000'.
Habitat: Moist forests.
Comments: Berries eaten by birds. Foliage browsed by deer and livestock. Reportedly parts of this plant and its berries are poisonous if mouthed or eaten raw. Five species of *Sambucus* (sam-BEW-kuss) in Arizona. Photographs taken at Lee Valley Reservoir: July 2 (in flower) and August 7 (in berry).

LONG-FLOWERED SNOWBERRY   613
Longflower snowberry
Symphoricarpos longiflorus
Honeysuckle Family (Caprifoliaceae)

Height: To 40".
Flowers: Pink, trumpetlike, with 5 spreading lobes; to 1/2" long; followed by white, pea-sized berry.
Leaves: Pale green, with whitish bloom above, prominent veins on underside; opposite, lance-shaped to oval; to 1/2" long, 1/4" wide.
Blooms: April–August.
Elevation: 4,000 to 8,000'.
Habitat: Pine forests, canyons, and foothills.
Comments: Birds and small mammals feed on berries. Six species of *Symphoricarpos* (sim-foh-rih-KAR-pus) in Arizona. Photograph taken at North Rim of Grand Canyon National Park, June 25.

MOUNTAIN SNOWBERRY   614
Symphoricarpos oreophilus
Honeysuckle Family (Caprifoliaceae)

Height: To 4 1/2'.
Flowers: Pinkish, tubular, slender, with 5 spreading lobes; to 1/2" long; followed by white, egg-shaped fruit; to 3/8" long.
Leaves: Pale green, smooth above, pale green below with prominent veins; opposite, oval, thin; to 1" long.
Blooms: May–August.
Elevation: 5,500 to 9,000'.
Habitat: Pine forests.
Comments: Deciduous. Has grayish bark, smooth twigs. Browsed by deer and livestock. Fruits are eaten by small mammals and birds. Six species of *Symphoricarpos* (sim-foh-rih-KAR-pus) in Arizona. Photograph taken south of Alpine, June 30.

ROUNDLEAF SNOWBERRY   615
Symphoricarpos rotundifolius
Honeysuckle Family (Caprifoliaceae)

Height: To 3 1/2'.
Flowers: Pinkish, tubular, slender, lobed at tip; to 1/2" long; in clusters of up to 6 in leaf axils; followed by a round, white berry to 1/2" in diameter.
Leaves: Grayish green above, paler beneath; prominent network, thick, finely haired, oval, toothed or untoothed, to 1 1/2" long, 3/4" wide.
Blooms: May–June.
Elevation: 4,000 to 10,000'.
Habitat: Rocky slopes, and clearings in ponderosa pine forests.
Comments: Twigs are brown and finely haired. Stems pinkish on new growth. Berries remain for most of winter. Foliage browsed by livestock and deer. Six species of *Symphoricarpos* (sim-foh-rih-KAR-pus) in Arizona. Photograph taken on Mingus Mountain, Prescott, May 28.

VALERIAN FAMILY
Valerianaceae (va-leer-i-a-NAY-see-ee)
Herbs.

Flowers: Irregular and tubelike, with 4 to 5 lobes, generally 3 stamens, 1 style. Inferior ovary, 3-celled.
Fruit: Achenelike, 1-seeded.
Leaves: Opposite.

ARIZONA VALERIAN   639
Tobacco-root
Valeriana arizonica
Valerian Family (Valerianaceae)

Height: To 14".
Flowers: Pinkish white to lavender, tubular, 5-lobed; white stamens and anthers extend beyond lobes; to 1/4" wide, 1" long (including stamens); in rounded cluster to 2" wide.
Leaves: Dark green, thin, basal, broadly elliptical; to 2" long. Stem leaves are clasping, arrow-shaped, divided into a pair or pairs of narrow lobes, with end lobe largest and pointed. Leaf to 2 1/2" long; leaf and stalk to 6 1/2" long.
Blooms: April–July.
Elevation: 4,500 to 8,000'.
Habitat: Moist coniferous forests.
Comments: Perennial. Has smooth, hollow stem. When dried, plants give off unpleasant odor. Some species used as food by Native Americans. Five species of *Valeriana* (va-leer-i-AYE-nah) in Arizona. Photograph taken at Sharp Creek, northeast of Christopher Creek, April 22.

GOURD FAMILY
Cucurbitaceae (kew-kur-bi-TAY-see-ee)
Herbs.

Flowers: Regular, small and inconspicuous; or large and funnel-shaped; or of 5 separate petals; calyx joined to 5-lobed ovary; 3 or 5 stamens (2 pairs united), 1 style, usually 3 stigmas. Inferior ovary, 1- to 4-celled.

Fruit: Varying; generally berrylike or gourdlike.

Leaves: Alternate, simple or compound.

FINGER-LEAVED GOURD   371
Finger leaf gourd
Cucurbita digitata
Gourd Family (Cucurbitaceae)

Height: Trailing vine.

Flowers: Yellow, bell-shaped tube, to 1 1/2" long; followed by a dark green, roundish gourd, with vertical, whitish stripes and blotches; to 3 1/2" in diameter. Matures to pale yellow.

Leaves: Grayish green with central silvery white markings on 5 narrow, fingerlike segments; very hairy beneath; side lobes vary in shape and size; to 10" long including stem.

Blooms: June–October.

Elevation: Below 5,000'.

Habitat: Sandy washes, mesas, and dry plains.

Comments: Has very hairy stems. Four species of *Cucurbita* (kew-KUR-bi-tah) in Arizona. Photograph taken at Catalina State Park, November 9.

BUFFALO GOURD   372
Calabazilla, stinking gourd, fetid gourd, Missouri gourd, wild pumpkin, calabacilla loca
Cucurbita foetidissima
Gourd Family (Cucurbitaceae)

Length: Prostrate to 20' long.

Flowers: Yellow, funnel-shaped, to 4" long; followed by smooth, round, light and dark green striped 4" gourd that turns yellow when mature.

Leaves: Gray-green above, whitish beneath; triangular, finely toothed, long-stalked; to 1' long.

Blooms: May–August.

Elevation: 1,000 to 7,000'.

Habitat: Roadsides and dry or sandy areas.

Comments: Perennial, with huge taproots and foul-smelling leaves. Flowers open very early in day. Pollinated by bees. Gourds are edible before they dry. Native Americans used oil extracted from seeds for cooking, and dried gourds for ceremonial rattles. Four species of *Cucurbita* (kew-KUR-bi-tah) in Arizona. Photograph taken in vicinity of Vernon, August 4. The **COYOTE MELON** (*Cucurbita palmata*) has similar flowers and round gourds, but its leaves are fingerlike instead of triangular.

WILD CUCUMBER   211
Big-root, gila manroot
Marah gilensis
Gourd Family (Cucurbitaceae)

Height:	Long vine climbing over shrubs and small trees.
Flowers:	White to cream, star-shaped; to 3/8" wide; followed by round, green, fleshy fruit with stout, smooth spines, to 2" in diameter.
Leaves:	Dark green, pointy or rounded lobes, to 3" wide.
Blooms:	March–April.
Elevation:	Below 5,000'
Habitat:	Thickets along washes and streams.
Comments:	Perennial. Very large tuberlike root. One species of *Marah* (MAR-ah) in Arizona. Photograph taken at Bartlett Dam area, March 24.

BELLFLOWER or BLUEBELL FAMILY
Campanulaceae (kam-pan-yew-LAY-see-ee)
Represented in Arizona chiefly by herbs.

Flowers:	Regular or irregular, mostly bell-shaped with 5 flaring lobes and 5 stamens; or tubular and 2-lipped with stamens joined. One style with 2 to 5 stigmas; 5 sepals. Inferior ovary, 1- to 5-celled.
Fruit:	Dry pod (capsule).
Leaves:	Alternate or basal, simple.

HAREBELL   705A and B
Bluebell, bluebell of Scotland, witches' thimble
Campanula rotundifolia
Bellflower or Bluebell Family (Campanulaceae)

Height:	To 20".
Flowers:	Blue to violet, bell-shaped, 5-lobed; drooping on slender stem; to 1" long.
Leaves:	Green, roundish, basal; withering before flowers appear; to 3" long. Leaves along stem very narrow.
Blooms:	June–September.
Elevation:	8,000 to 12,000'.
Habitat:	Meadows and rocky slopes.
Comments:	Two species of *Campanula* (kam-PAN-yew-lah) in Arizona. Photograph A taken at Greer, July 20. Occasionally, harebell will have 8 lobes. Photograph B taken in Mount Baldy Wilderness, July 8. The flowers of a similar species, **PARRY BELLFLOWER** (*Campanula parryi*), are erect and basal leaves are lance-shaped, tapering at base.

MOUNTAIN LOBELIA   787
Southwestern blue lobelia
Lobelia anatina
Bellflower or Bluebell Family (Campanulaceae)

Height:	To 18".
Flowers:	Deep lavender, tubular; 2 smaller upper lobes, crossed, 3 larger flaring lower lobes; to 3/4" wide, 3/4" long; with about 8 flowers on slender, erect stem.
Leaves:	Dark green, lance-shaped to linear, toothed; to 3" long.

Blooms: July–October.
Elevation: 5,500 to 9,000'.
Habitat: Moist mountain meadows, marshy places, and along streams.
Comments: Perennial herb. Visited by bees and hummingbirds. Four species of *Lobelia* (lo-BEE-li-ah) in Arizona. Photograph taken at Luna Lake, August 5.

CARDINAL FLOWER 568
Scarlet lobelia
Lobelia cardinalis
Bellflower or Bluebell Family (Campanulaceae)

Height: To 5'.
Flowers: Bright red, tubular, with 2 small upper lobes, 3 larger lower lobes; stamens united in column; to 1 1/2" long; in elongated cluster on erect stalk.
Leaves: Dark green, oblong, toothed; to 5" long.
Blooms: June–October.
Elevation: 3,000 to 7,500'.
Habitat: Wet areas and along streams.
Comments: Perennial herb. Attracts hummingbirds. Four species of *Lobelia* (lo-BEE-li-ah) in Arizona. Photograph taken in Tucson area, August 23.

TEASEL FAMILY
Dipsacaceae (dip-sah-KAY-see-ee)
A weedy herb.

Flowers: Small, in bracted heads; tubular, 4- or 5-lobed; 5 sepals, 4 stamens, threadlike style. Inferior ovary, 1-celled.
Fruit: Dry achene.
Leaves: Opposite, simple.

TEASEL 750
Dipsacus sylvestris
Teasel Family (Dipsacaceae)

Height: To 6'.
Flowers: Lavender, tubular, 4-lobed; to 1/16" wide, 1/2" long; clustered on thistlelike cone, surrounded by short, spiny bracts and numerous very long, upward-pointing, spiny bracts with straight tips; cluster to 4" long, 2" wide.
Leaves: Light green above, with a row of spines on each side of white midvein; sharp spines beneath on midvein; spined margins; lance-shaped, opposite, basal leaves in rosette, to 14" long, 2 1/2" wide; smaller leaves up stem.
Blooms: July–October.
Elevation: Not available. Photograph taken at 5,800'.
Habitat: Roadsides and old fields.
Comments: Biennial. The first flowers start blooming in a belt around center. Succeeding blooms open daily above and below this band; soon 2 bands of flowers form. Outdoors, dried plants weather rain and snow. Introduced from Europe, plant was once cultivated for its dried, spiny heads which were used in teasing wool to raise nap. Dried stem with spiny flowerhead used for dried floral arrangements. In various areas escapees are found. Photograph taken along roadside near Christopher Creek, August 11. *Dipsacus* (DIP-sa-kus) not previously recorded for Arizona.

SUNFLOWER FAMILY
Compositae (kom-PAH-zih-tee)
Represented in Arizona by herbs or shrubs.

Flowers: Regular or irregular, in heads surrounded by bracts, scales, or bristles. Individual florets are tiny to small, composed of outer straplike, flat ray flowers (as in the petals of the daisy) and tiny to small, tubular disk flowers (as at the center of the daisy). Some are rayless, with 5 united petals forming tube. Usually 5-stamened. Inferior ovary, 1-seeded.

Fruit: An achene.

Leaves: Alternate or opposite, occasionally whorled; simple, lobed, or dissected.

WESTERN YARROW   245
Milfoil
Achillea millefolium var. *lanulosa* (*Achillea lanulosa*)
Sunflower Family (Compositae)

Height: To 40".

Flowers: White (sometimes pinkish), to 1/8" wide; in flat-topped cluster of ray and disk flowers.

Leaves: Light green, finely dissected, fernlike; to 8" long at base.

Blooms: June–September.

Elevation: 5,500 to 11,500'.

Habitat: Fields, roadsides, clearings in pine forests, and waste ground.

Comments: Perennial herb. Native Americans and Spaniards used plant medicinally. Zuni use plant before fire ceremonies. Named for Achilles, said to have discovered healing powers of yarrow. One species of *Achillea* (ak-ih-LEE-ah) in Arizona. Photograph taken near Willow Springs Lake, July 21.

DESERT HOLLY   285
Acourtia nana (*Perezia nana*)
Sunflower Family (Compositae)

Height: To 10", but usually 4 to 5".

Flowers: Whitish to pinkish, tiny, 15 to 24 per head; with purplish, diamond-shaped bracts; flowerhead to 1" long; borne singly.

Leaves: Grayish green, hollylike, stalkless, spiny-toothed; somewhat round, stiff, brittle, and alternate; to 2" long, 2" wide.

Blooms: March–June.

Elevation: Below 6,000'.

Habitat: Slopes and dry plains.

Comments: Perennial herb. Flowers smell like violets. Three species of *Acourtia* (ah-KOR-tee-uh) in Arizona. Photograph taken in vicinity of Portal, May 5.

PEREZIA   677
Acourtia wrightii (*Perezia wrightii*)
Sunflower Family (Compositae)

Height: To 3'.

Flowers: Pinkish lavender, to 3/4" wide, in loosely branched, terminal cluster; followed by numerous tawny bristles.

Leaves:	Dark green, leathery, oval or oblong; wrinkled; toothed with spiny teeth; base of leaf clasping stem; to 5" long.
Blooms:	January–June.
Elevation:	Below 6,000'.
Habitat:	Foothills and canyons.
Comments:	Perennial herb. Attracts butterflies and bees. Three species of *Acourtia* (ah-KOR-tee-uh) in Arizona. Photograph taken at Catalina State Park, April 30.

AGERATINA   262
Ageratina herbacea (*Eupatorium herbaceum*)
Sunflower Family (Compositae)

Height:	To 2'.
Flowers:	White, rayless, with 5 starlike, pointed lobes; long white stamens; flower to 1/16" wide, flowerhead to 3/8" wide; in terminal cluster.
Leaves:	Light green, heart-shaped, toothed, prominently veined; to 3" long (including stem), to 1 3/4" wide.
Blooms:	June–October.
Elevation:	5,000 to 9,000'.
Habitat:	Clearings in pine forests.
Comments:	One species of *Ageratina* (a-jer-ah-TI-nah) in Arizona. Photograph taken in vicinity of Woods Canyon Lake, September 14.

ORANGE AGOSERIS   540
Orange mountain-dandelion
Agoseris aurantiaca
Sunflower Family (Compositae)

Height:	To 2'.
Flowers:	Burnt orange, all rays, with shorter rays toward center; stamens stand upright; flowerhead to 1" wide; solitary on erect, leafless flower stem; followed by seeds topped with silvery bristles.
Leaves:	Grayish green, narrow, widest above middle; with or without teeth or lobes; to 10" long.
Blooms:	June–August.
Elevation:	5,000 to 9,500'.
Habitat:	Meadows and clearings in coniferous forests.
Comments:	Perennial herb; has pinkish stem. Produces milky sap. Four species of *Agoseris* (AH-goh-ser-is) in Arizona. Photograph taken in Greer area, August 8.

PALE AGOSERIS   446
Mountain dandelion, pale mountain dandelion, false dandelion
Agoseris glauca
Sunflower Family (Compositae)

Height:	Flowering stem to 18".
Flowers:	Yellow; all ray flowers, center ones shorter; to 1 1/2" wide; single; terminal on erect, leafless stem; followed by round seedheads with soft, white bristles attached.
Leaves:	Dark green, basal, producing milky sap when crushed; shape varies from narrow to broadly lance-shaped; toothed or not, or deeply pinnately divided; to 14" long.
Blooms:	May–October.
Elevation:	6,500 to 10,000'.

| Habitat: | Mountain meadows and coniferous forests. |
| Comments: | Perennial herb. Four species of *Agoseris* (AH-goh-ser-is) in Arizona. Photograph taken at Lake Mary, June 1. |

CANYON RAGWEED 806A and B
Ambrosia ambrosioides (*Franseria ambrosioides*)
Sunflower Family (Compositae)

Height:	To 40".
Flowers:	Yellowish green, to 3/8" wide, in terminal spike; followed by clusters of cocklebur-like fruit with slender spines; to 1" long.
Leaves:	Green above and below, hairy, elongated to lance-shaped, saw-toothed; to 5" long, 1" wide.
Blooms:	February–May.
Elevation:	Below 4,500'.
Habitat:	Sandy washes and canyons.
Comments:	Branches are reddish brown with long white hairs. Twelve species of *Ambrosia* (am-BROH-si-ah) in Arizona. Photograph taken at Usery Mountain Recreation Area, February 14. Close-up photograph taken in Superstition Mountains, March 26. A similar species, **GIANT RAGWEED** (*Ambrosia trifida*), is found in fields and along roadsides. Its abundant airborne pollen is dreaded by those who suffer with hay fever. Photograph (**PLATE 809**) taken in vicinity of McNary, August 10.

TRIANGLE BURSAGE 807
Rabbit bush, burrobush
Ambrosia deltoidea (*Franseria deltoidea*)
Sunflower Family (Compositae)

Height:	To 2'.
Flowers:	Greenish, petalless, to 1/4" wide; in terminal spike, followed by 1/4"-long, burlike fruits with hook-tipped spines.
Leaves:	Grayish green above, white and woolly beneath; triangular-shaped, finely toothed; to 1 1/4" long.
Blooms:	December–April.
Elevation:	1,000 to 3,000'.
Habitat:	Washes, gravelly slopes, and desert flats.
Comments:	Perennial shrub. Causes severe hay fever in spring. Stabilizes soil. A "nurse" shrub for young cacti growing in its shade. Twelve species of *Ambrosia* (am-BROH-si-ah) in Arizona. Photograph taken at Usery Mountain Recreation Area, February 14.

WHITE BURSAGE 808
Burrobush, burroweed
Ambrosia dumosa (*Franseria dumosa*)
Sunflower Family (Compositae)

Height:	To 2'.
Flowers:	Greenish, petalless, to 1/8" wide, in terminal spike; followed by 1/4"-long spiny fruits (not hooked).
Leaves:	Smoky-colored due to dense, short hairs; pinnately divided several times into small divisions; to 3/4" long.
Blooms:	Late March–November.
Elevation:	Below 3,000'.

Habitat: Dry plains and mesas.

Comments: Rounded, many-branched shrub with short, dense, white hairs on branches. Eaten by burros, horses, and sheep. Twelve species of *Ambrosia* (am-BROH-si-ah) in Arizona. Photograph taken at Salome, March 28.

PEARLY EVERLASTING 286
Everlasting
Anaphalis margaritacea
Sunflower Family (Compositae)

Height: To 3'.

Flowers: Minute, pearly white bracts surrounding yellowish center of disk flowers; flowerhead to 3/8" wide; in sprawling, terminal cluster.

Leaves: Shiny, dark green above, woolly white beneath; alternate, linear to linear-oblong, clasping stem, prominent midvein; to 5" long.

Blooms: July–October.

Elevation: 4,500 to 8,500'.

Habitat: Roadsides, open woodlands and forests, along streams, and in canyons.

Comments: Perennial herb; has woolly stems. Flowers last a long time, and dry well for floral arrangements. One species of *Anaphalis* (a-NAFF-a-liss) in Arizona. Photograph taken along West Fork of Oak Creek Canyon, October 1.

ROCKY MOUNTAIN PUSSYTOES 287
Cat's foot, mountain pussytoes
Antennaria parvifolia
Sunflower Family (Compositae)

Height: To 6".

Flowers: Dirty white, tubular, minute; small heads in loose cluster; cluster to 1" wide.

Leaves: Gray, woolly, in basal rosette; spatula-shaped; about 3/4" long, narrower on flower stalk.

Blooms: May–August.

Elevation: 5,000 to 12,000'.

Habitat: Open, sandy areas in coniferous forests.

Comments: Perennial herb. Native Americans use plant medicinally and for ceremonies. Five species of *Antennaria* (an-ten-AR-ee-ah) in Arizona. Photograph taken near Greer, June 20.

PUSSYTOES 288
Antennaria rosulata
Sunflower Family (Compositae)

Height: To 1".

Flowers: Grayish white with brown stamens; minute; in cluster to 1/4" wide. Flowerheads single or up to 3, surrounded by leaves.

Leaves: Gray, woolly, spoon-shaped; to 1/2" long, in basal rosette.

Blooms: May–July.

Elevation: 5,500 to 11,000'.

Habitat: Ponderosa pine clearings and meadows.

Comments: Perennial herb. Five species of *Antennaria* (an-ten-AR-ee-ah) in Arizona. Photograph taken near Ashurst Lake, June 1.

MEADOW ARNICA   394
Leafy arnica
Arnica chamissonis (*Arnica foliosa*)
Sunflower Family (Compositae)

Height: To 2 1/2'.
Flowers: Yellow rays notched at tips, with brownish yellow to orangish disks; to 1 1/2" wide; single or up to 3 terminal flowerheads. Bracts on flowerhead have tufts of white hairs inside tips.
Leaves: Grayish green, felty-haired, opposite; clasping stem; 5 to 12 pairs; toothed, oblong to lance-shaped; to 4 1/2" long.
Blooms: July–August.
Elevation: 8,000 to 9,500'.
Habitat: Moist mountain meadows and mountain lakesides.
Comments: Single-stemmed, sticky-haired plant. Two species of *Arnica* (AR-ni-kah) in Arizona. Photograph taken at Lee Valley Reservoir in mountains above Greer, August 7. A similar species, **HEARTLEAF ARNICA** (*Arnica cordifolia*), has pointed ray flowers, heart-shaped leaves, and solitary flowerheads.

SAND SAGEBRUSH   289
Artemisia filifolia
Sunflower Family (Compositae)

Height: To 5'.
Flowers: White to yellow, tiny, in terminal spikes to 8" long; followed by tiny seeds.
Leaves: Grayish green, threadlike, covered with silvery hairs; occurring all along stems.
Blooms: August–November.
Elevation: 4,000 to 6,500'.
Habitat: Loose, sandy soil.
Comments: Many-branched shrub. A valuable browse plant. Used medicinally by Native Americans and pioneers. Fourteen species of *Artemisia* (are-teh-MEE-sih-uh) in Arizona. Photograph taken at Wupatki National Monument, September 8.

RAGWEED SAGEBRUSH   290
Artemisia franserioides
Sunflower Family (Compositae)

Height: To 2' with flower stalk.
Flowers: Tiny, to 3/16" wide; in a long, slightly drooping, terminal cluster, to 6" long.
Leaves: Light green above, grayish beneath, with fine hairs; bipinnate, alternate, very fragrant when rubbed; to 6" long.
Blooms: August–September.
Elevation: 8,000 to 10,000'.
Habitat: Clearings in coniferous forests.
Comments: Leaves are very soft and velvety. Fourteen species of *Artemisia* (are-teh-MEE-sih-uh) in Arizona. Photograph taken at Lee Valley Reservoir in mountains above Greer, August 7.

WHITE ASTER   248
Aster commutatus
Sunflower Family (Compositae)

Height: To 2'.

Flowers:	White rays, yellow disks; to 1/2" wide; numerous flowerheads on branches.
Leaves:	Grayish green, hairy, alternate, narrow; to 1/4" long; growing all along stems.
Blooms:	August–October.
Elevation:	5,000 to 8,000'.
Habitat:	Roadsides and clearings in pine forests.
Comments:	Perennial herb, with hairy stems. This species absorbs selenium from soil and may be toxic to livestock. More than a dozen species of *Aster* (ASS-ter) in Arizona. Photograph taken at Upper Lake Mary, September 2.

LEAFYBRACT ASTER   718

Leafy aster, leafyhead aster
Aster foliaceus
Sunflower Family (Compositae)

Height:	To 18".
Flowers:	Narrow, with lavender to purple rays, yellow disks, and large, leafy bracts around flowerhead; flowerhead to 2" wide.
Leaves:	Dark green, with hairy margins; lance-shaped at base; to 6" long, 1/2" wide. Leaves clasping on upper stem, alternate, elongate, to 2" long.
Blooms:	August–September.
Elevation:	7,500 to 10,000'.
Habitat:	Mountain meadows and coniferous forests.
Comments:	Stems are reddish and hairy. More than a dozen species of *Aster* (ASS-ter) in Arizona. Photograph taken at Lee Valley Reservoir in mountains above Greer, August 14.

YERBA-DE-PASMO   263

Baccharis pteronioides
Sunflower Family (Compositae)

Height:	Shrub to 3' tall, 3' wide.
Flowers:	Cream-colored, rayless, flowerhead to 1/4" wide; 1/4" long; heads on short, leafy branches arranged like a raceme.
Leaves:	Dark green, sandpapery, sticky, lobed; to 5/8" long; clustered along many-branched stems.
Blooms:	April–September.
Elevation:	3,500 to 6,000'.
Habitat:	Slopes and plains.
Comments:	Spanish name, *yerba-de-pasmo*, means "chill weed." Infusions from leaves were supposedly used for chills. Browsed by livestock. Eleven species of *Baccharis* (BAK-a-ris) in Arizona. Photograph taken near Prescott, May 27.

SEEP WILLOW   264

Seepwillow baccharis, rosin brush, water-motie, broom baccharis, water-wally, water-willow, hierba del pasmo, batamote
Baccharis salicifolia (*Baccharis glutinosa*)
Sunflower Family (Compositae)

Height:	To 12'.
Flowers:	Creamy white, rayless, male and female flowers on separate plants; in clusters at ends of branches; followed (on female flowers) by seeds with silky tails.
Leaves:	Dark green, shiny, waxy, sticky; lance-shaped, toothed; to 6" long, 1/2" wide.

Blooms:	March–December.
Elevation:	2,000 to 5,500'.
Habitat:	Along washes, streams, and seepage channels.
Comments:	Not a true willow, but has willowlike growth. Leaves have a distinctive odor. Controls river and stream erosion by forming dense stands along watercourses. Acts as a "nurse" plant by protecting willow and cottonwood seedlings. Parts of plant used medicinally. Eleven species of *Baccharis* (BAK-a-ris) in Arizona. Photograph taken at Granite Reef Dam area, March 1.

DESERT BROOM   265

Broom baccharis, rosin brush, hierba del pasmo, Mexican broom
Baccharis sarothroides
Sunflower Family (Compositae)

Height:	Shrub to 10'.
Flowers:	Whitish, rayless, small; male and female on separate plants; to 3/8" long; in terminal clusters. Female plants develop white, silky, airborne seeds.
Leaves:	Bright green, smooth, sticky; to 1 1/2" long, 1/8" wide.
Blooms:	September–February.
Elevation:	1,000 to 5,500'.
Habitat:	Sandy washes, hillsides, along streams, and bottomlands.
Comments:	Shrub with fast-growing, stiff stems. Important in erosion control. Certain Native Americans chew stems to ease toothaches. Branches used as brooms by pioneers and Native Americans. Eleven species of *Baccharis* (BAK-a-ris) in Arizona. Photograph taken at Stewart Dam area, October 18.

BAHIA   395

Bahia absinthifolia
Sunflower Family (Compositae)

Height:	To 16".
Flowers:	Bright yellow rays, thick, orange disk flowers; to 2" wide.
Leaves:	Grayish, hairy, 3-lobed, to 2 1/2" long.
Blooms:	April–October.
Elevation:	2,500 to 5,500'.
Habitat:	Mesas, plains, and slopes.
Comments:	Five species of *Bahia* (baa-EE-ah) in Arizona. There are varieties and intermediates of this species which vary in leaf and flower characteristics. Photograph taken in Tucson area, April 18.

WILD CHRYSANTHEMUM   396

Ragleaf, ragleaf bahia, yellow ragweed
Bahia dissecta
Sunflower Family (Compositae)

Height:	To 3'.
Flowers:	Yellow rays, darker yellow disks; to 3/4" wide; numerous; in open, branched cluster.
Leaves:	Green, pinnate, divided 2 or 3 times; basal leaves deeply lobed, to 3 1/4" long.
Blooms:	August–October.
Elevation:	5,000 to 9,000'.

Habitat: Roadsides, pinyon-juniper woodlands, and clearings in ponderosa pine forests.
Comments: Biennial or short-lived perennial. Five species of *Bahia* (baa-EE-ah) in Arizona. Photograph taken in vicinity of Mormon Lake, September 3.

DESERT MARIGOLD   397

Wild marigold, paperdaisy, desert baileya, baileya del desierto, hierba amarilla.
Baileya multiradiata
Sunflower Family (Compositae)

Height: To 2'.
Flowers: Yellow, daisylike; to 2" wide; on long, nearly leafless stem.
Leaves: Grayish, woolly, well-divided, and lobed; to 3" long.
Blooms: March–October at various intervals; year-round under ideal conditions.
Elevation: To 5,000'.
Habitat: Roadsides, slopes, and sandy, gravelly areas.
Comments: Annual herb. On overgrazed land, sheep and goats are frequently poisoned by feeding on this marigold. With age, flower petals become bleached and tissue-paper-like. Three species of *Baileya* (BAY-lee-ah) in Arizona. Photograph taken at Usery Mountain Recreation Area, March 18.

CHUCKWALLA'S DELIGHT   457

Bebbia, sweet bush
Bebbia juncea
Sunflower Family (Compositae)

Height: To 4', usually straggly.
Flowers: Yellow, rayless, with hairy bracts; tubular, sweet-smelling; flowerhead to 1/2" wide, 5/8" long; solitary or several; terminal on many branches.
Leaves: (When present) dark green, sparse, alternate; linear to lance-shaped; lobed, rough, hairy; to 2" long.
Blooms: Much of the year.
Elevation: Below 4,000'.
Habitat: Canyons, rocky slopes, sandy washes, and roadsides.
Comments: Bushy, slender-branched plant with hairy stems. Attracts butterflies. One species of *Bebbia* (BEBB-i-ah) in Arizona. Photograph taken in vicinity of Granite Reef Dam, April 25.

GREENEYES   398

Chocolate flower
Berlandiera lyrata
Sunflower Family (Compositae)

Height: To 4'.
Flowers: Yellow rays (5 to 12) veined with reddish tint beneath; maroon disk; prominent, nearly flat, broad bracts; flowerhead to 1 1/2" wide.
Leaves: Grayish green, velvetlike; deeply lobed or pinnately divided into segments, with largest at end; to 5" long.
Blooms: April–October.
Elevation: 4,000 to 5,000'.
Habitat: Roadsides and fields of southeastern Arizona.
Comments: Perennial herb. Gives off a faint smell of chocolate when rays are pulled from

flowerhead. Native Americans used flowerheads as food seasoning. One species of *Berlandiera* (ber-lan-dee-AIR-ah) in Arizona. Photograph taken in vicinity of Sierra Vista, April 26.

COULTER'S BRICKELLIA 458
Brickellia coulteri
Sunflower Family (Compositae)

Height:	To 3'.
Flowers:	Yellowish green, rayless, with brownish to pinkish bracts; slender flowerhead to 5/8" long, 1/4" wide; approximately 15 flowers in loose, terminal cluster.
Leaves:	Light green, triangular-shaped, tapering to tip; toothed, opposite, to 1 1/2" long.
Blooms:	March–November.
Elevation:	2,000 to 4,000'.
Habitat:	Canyons and dry, rocky slopes.
Comments:	Forms a roundish shrub with brownish, hairy, brittle stems. Sticky plant. More than 2 dozen species of *Brickellia* (brik-KELL-lih-uh) in Arizona. Photograph taken at King Canyon, Tucson, April 17.

BRICKELLIA 267
Brickellia floribunda
Sunflower Family (Compositae)

Height:	To 4 1/2'.
Flowers:	White to cream-colored, petalless; flowerhead to 3/8" wide, 1/2" long.
Leaves:	Light green, heart-shaped; to 4" long (including stalk), 2" wide.
Blooms:	September–October.
Elevation:	3,000 to 5,500'.
Habitat:	Rich soil in canyons.
Comments:	Entire plant very glandular, sticky, and has odd odor. More than 2 dozen species of *Brickellia* (brik-KELL-lih-uh) in Arizona. Photograph taken in vicinity of Christopher Creek, September 14.

LARGE-FLOWERED BRICKELLBUSH 266
Brickellia, tassel-flower, sheath flower, large-flowered thoroughwort
Brickellia grandiflora
Sunflower Family (Compositae)

Height:	To 3'.
Flowers:	Whitish, upright to nodding, rayless; to 3/8" long; 20 to 40 flowers in a head, hanging at tips of stalks in various-sized clusters.
Leaves:	Dark green, triangular, with toothed, prominent veins; to 4" long, smaller on upper stem.
Blooms:	August–October.
Elevation:	5,000 to 9,000'.
Habitat:	Rocky slopes and coniferous forests.
Comments:	More than 2 dozen species of *Brickellia* (brik-KELL-lih-uh) in Arizona. Photograph taken at Sunset Crater National Monument, September 6.

WHITE TACKSTEM 260
White cupfruit
Calycoseris wrightii

Sunflower Family (Compositae)
Height: To 12".
Flowers: White, with pinkish streaks or dots on back of petals; to 1 1/2" wide.
Leaves: Grayish green, narrow; with narrow lobes near base of plant, sparser and smaller lobes toward ends of stems; to 3" long.
Blooms: March–May.
Elevation: 500 to 4,000'.
Habitat: Sandy soil of mesas, plains, and hillsides.
Comments: Annual. Named "tackstem" for its tack-shaped glands on stems. Two species of *Calycoseris* (kal-i-ko-SER-is) in Arizona. White flower photograph taken in Kofa Mountains, March 29. **YELLOW TACKSTEM** (*Calycoseris parryi*), a similar species, has yellow flowers. Photograph (**PLATE 447**) taken at Organ Pipe Cactus National Monument, March 30.

NODDING THISTLE 644
Bristle thistle, musk thistle
Carduus nutans
Sunflower Family (Compositae)
Height: To 3'.
Flowers: Pink to reddish lavender, rayless, and nodding; flowerhead surrounded by series of spiny-toothed bracts; to 2 1/2" wide; single; followed by seeds with long, white bristles at top.
Leaves: Green, deeply lobed, spiny, stalkless, to 8" long.
Blooms: June–October.
Elevation: 5,000 to 9,000'.
Habitat: Roadsides, fields, and rangeland.
Comments: Biennial. Native to Europe; now naturalized in certain areas of U.S. One species of *Carduus* (KARD-you-us) in Arizona. Photograph taken in vicinity of Mexican Hay Lake, July 21.

BRISTLEHEAD 640
Carphochaete bigelovii
Sunflower Family (Compositae)
Height: To 2'.
Flowers: Light pink to lavender, darker pink toward center; tubular, with 5 pointed lobes; to 1/2" wide; in terminal cluster to 1 1/4" wide.
Leaves: Grayish green, gland-dotted, hairy; opposite, linear to elliptical; clasping stem; to 3/4" long.
Blooms: March–July.
Elevation: 4,000 to 7,000'.
Habitat: Canyons and rocky slopes.
Comments: Woody at base with reddish brown stems. Browsed by deer and livestock. One species of *Carphochaete* (KAR-foh-kee-tee) in Arizona. Photograph taken northeast of Superior, April 3.

RUSSIAN KNAPWEED 728
Star-thistle
Centaurea repens
Sunflower Family (Compositae)

Height:	To 3'.
Flowers:	Lavender, tubular; in spineless, thistlelike flowerhead, to 3/4" wide, 1" long; surrounded by overlapping, silvery bracts; solitary at tips of leafy branches, followed by seeds with white bristles on top.
Leaves:	Grayish green, rough, thick, deeply lobed at base, to 4" long; narrowly oblong, sharp-pointed, toothed; to 2 1/2" long on stem.
Blooms:	May–October.
Elevation:	1,000 to 7,000'.
Habitat:	Roadsides, waste places, fields, lots, and farmland.
Comments:	Perennial weed. Introduced from Europe and Asia; now naturalized throughout West. Difficult to control due to horizontal roots that produce new plants. Nine species of *Centaurea* (sen-TOR-ree-ah) in Arizona. Photograph taken at Dead Horse Ranch State Park, May 28.

YELLOW STAR THISTLE   459
Barnaby thistle
Centaurea solstitialis
Sunflower Family (Compositae)

Height:	To 20".
Flowers:	Bright yellow disk flowers, erect; to 1/2" wide; yellowish spines to 3/4" long extending from green bracts surrounding flowerhead; followed by seeds attached to hairy fluff.
Leaves:	Grayish green, finely haired, spineless; wavy, divided at base; to 2" long; linear and decreasing in size along stem; grasping and extending like wings along entire stem.
Blooms:	May.
Elevation:	Below 4,000'.
Habitat:	Disturbed areas, roadsides, and fields.
Comments:	Annual weed. Well-branched. Native of Europe; now naturalized in parts of U.S. Nine species of *Centaurea* (sen-TOR-ree-ah) in Arizona. Photograph taken in vicinity of Granite Reef Dam, May 14.

FREMONT'S PINCUSHION   268
Morning bride
Chaenactis fremontii
Sunflower Family (Compositae)

Height:	To 16".
Flowers:	White or pinkish, rayless; disk flowers forming pincushionlike flowerhead; to 1" wide.
Leaves:	Green, divided into linear lobes; to 3" long.
Blooms:	March–June.
Elevation:	1,000 to 3,500'.
Habitat:	Plains and mesas.
Comments:	Six species of *Chaenactis* (kee-NAK-tis) in Arizona. Photograph taken near Salome, March 28.

ESTEVE'S PINCUSHION   269
False yarrow, broad-leaved chaenactis
Chaenactis stevioides
Sunflower Family (Compositae)

Height:	To 1'.
Flowers:	White and rayless; disk flowers form pincushion with raylike outer disks, flowerhead to 3/4" wide, 5/8" long.
Leaves:	Grayish green, woolly, divided twice into many short, thick, very narrow segments; to 2" long.
Blooms:	March–May.
Elevation:	1,000 to 6,500'.
Habitat:	Dry mesas and plains.
Comments:	Six species of *Chaenactis* (kee-NAK-tis) in Arizona. Photograph taken in vicinity of Kitt Peak, April 18.

OXEYE DAISY   249
Field daisy, common daisy, white daisy
Chrysanthemum leucanthemum
Sunflower Family (Compositae)

Height:	To 2'.
Flowers:	White rays, yellow disks; to 2" wide; growing singly, on long stem.
Leaves:	Dark green, coarsely toothed or pinnately lobed; basal, to 6" long; growing along stem to 3" long.
Blooms:	June–October.
Elevation:	Throughout Arizona.
Habitat:	Roadsides and fields.
Comments:	Introduced from Europe; now naturalized. Two species of *Chrysanthemum* (kris-SAN-thee-mum) in Arizona. Photograph taken at Hannagan Meadow area, June 30.

GOLDEN RABBIT BRUSH   460
Chamisa, rubber rabbit brush, chamiso blanco, false goldenrod, rabbitbush
Chrysothamnus nauseosus
Sunflower Family (Compositae)

Height:	To 5'.
Flowers:	Yellow, feathery, slender, and rayless; to 1/4" wide, 1/2" long; in terminal cluster; followed by seeds with white bristles attached.
Leaves:	Grayish green, linear, very narrow; to 2 1/2" long; at intervals along stem of soft, matted hairs.
Blooms:	July–October.
Elevation:	3,000 to 9,000'.
Habitat:	Dry plains, dry mountainsides, grassland, open woodlands, and roadsides.
Comments:	Perennial shrub, with slender, flexible branches. Twigs are covered with feltlike hairs. Eaten by rabbits and browsed by deer, elk, and pronghorn. Provides shelter for birds and small mammals. Flowers attract insects, and yield yellow dye used by Navajo Indians. Inner bark is a source of green dye. The Hopi use plant for kiva fuels and wind breaks, and in arrow and wicker work. Latex obtained from plant is of no commercial value. Nine species of *Chrysothamnus* (krih-soh-THAM-nuss) in Arizona; this species has many varieties. Photograph taken at Upper Lake Mary, September 2.

COMMON CHICORY   725
Succory, coffeeweed, blueweed, blue dandelion, blue sailors
Cichorium intybus

Sunflower Family (Compositae)

Height:	To 4'.
Flowers:	Light blue to bluish lavender, square-tipped ray flowers, each with 5 small teeth; prickly bracts; flowerheads to 2" wide; close, on well-branched stems.
Leaves:	Grayish green, wavy; clasping stem, nearly leafless above, lower leaves variable: lance-shaped, pinnately toothed, or lobed, with prickly margins; to 8" long.
Blooms:	June–October.
Elevation:	Below 7,000'.
Habitat:	Fields, roadsides, and waste areas.
Comments:	Perennial herb; produces milky sap. Each flower lasts only one day. Introduced from Europe; now naturalized. Immature leaves used as vegetable or for salad. Roots are ground and roasted as coffee additive or substitute. One species of *Cichorium* (sick-KOR-i-um) in Arizona. Photograph taken near Show Low, July 6.

ARIZONA THISTLE   569
Cirsium arizonicum
Sunflower Family (Compositae)

Height:	To 4'.
Flowers:	Bright red or carmine, with slender flowerheads; to 2" long.
Leaves:	Grayish green, very hairy, alternate; spiny-toothed and tipped; to 2" long.
Blooms:	May–October.
Elevation:	3,000 to 7,000'.
Habitat:	Roadsides, chaparral, and clearings in ponderosa pine forests.
Comments:	Native Americans use thistles medicinally. Seventeen species of *Cirsium* (SIR-si-uhm) in Arizona. This species hybridizes with *Cirsium nidulum,* producing intermediate specimens. Photograph taken at Lynx Lake, October 5.

NEW MEXICO THISTLE   645
Cirsium neomexicanum
Sunflower Family (Compositae)

Height:	To 6'.
Flowers:	Pink-purple flowerhead of tiny, tubular, disk flowers; to 2" wide; surrounded by long, spine-tipped bracts, with outer bracts pointing downward.
Leaves:	Dark green, shiny, straplike; spiny, coarsely pinnately lobed, to 7" long.
Blooms:	March–September.
Elevation:	1,000 to 6,500'.
Habitat:	Foothills, mesas, and plains.
Comments:	Has spiny stems. Native Americans use thistle plants medicinally. Seventeen species of *Cirsium* (SIR-si-uhm) in Arizona. Photograph taken in Superstition Mountains, April 6.

YELLOW SPINE THISTLE   730
Santa Fe thistle
Cirsium ochrocentrum
Sunflower Family (Compositae)

Height:	To 3'.
Flowers:	Purple to rose to cream-colored flowerhead of tiny, tubular, disk flowers; broad flowerhead to 3" wide, 2" tall; usually occurring singly at tips of branches.
Leaves:	Grayish green and very woolly above, white and very hairy beneath; thick, deeply

lobed, with yellowish spines on edges of leaves; to 7" long.

Blooms:	May–October.
Elevation:	4,500 to 8,000'.
Habitat:	Roadsides and clearings in pinyon-juniper woodlands.
Comments:	Has woolly haired stem. Seventeen species of *Cirsium* (SIR-si-uhm) in Arizona. Photograph taken in vicinity of Heber, August 4.

PARRY'S THISTLE   461
Cirsium parryi
Sunflower Family (Compositae)

Height:	To 40".
Flowers:	Yellowish green, very narrow, hairy; in flowerhead with outer bracts fringed with bristles and a spine; flowerhead to 1 1/4" wide; occurring singly or several in a cluster.
Leaves:	Dark green above, grayish green beneath, hairy, spiny-margined; to 10" long.
Blooms:	July–September.
Elevation:	7,500 to 9,500'.
Habitat:	Clearings in coniferous forests and mountain meadows.
Comments:	Has hairy stems. Seventeen species of *Cirsium* (SIR-si-uhm) in Arizona. Photograph taken in mountain clearing above Greer, August 8.

WAVYLEAF THISTLE   646
Cirsium undulatum
Sunflower Family (Compositae)

Height:	To 16".
Flowers:	Pink flowerhead of tiny, tubular, disk flowers; to 2" long, 2" wide; long, narrow bracts with yellow spines.
Leaves:	Grayish green, wavy, yellow-spined; gray-haired on both surfaces; to 8" long, becoming smaller on upper stems.
Blooms:	June–October.
Elevation:	7,000 to 9,500'.
Habitat:	Roadsides and fields.
Comments:	Seventeen species of *Cirsium* (SIR-si-uhm) in Arizona. Photograph taken in vicinity of Nutrioso, July 23.

BULL THISTLE   729
Cirsium vulgare
Sunflower Family (Compositae)

Height:	To 4'.
Flowers:	Rose-purple flowerhead of tiny, tubular, disk flowers; spiny, yellow-tipped bracts; flowerhead to 2" wide, 2" long.
Leaves:	Dark green above, white beneath; pinnately lobed, very spiny; clasping stem and extending onto stem, forming spiny wings; to 6" long.
Blooms:	June–September.
Elevation:	Not available. Photograph taken at 7,500'.
Habitat:	Roadsides, fields, and disturbed areas.
Comments:	Biennial. Seventeen species of *Cirsium* (SIR-si-uhm) in Arizona. Photograph taken in vicinity of Woods Canyon Lake, September 14.

WHEELER THISTLE   731
Cirsium wheeleri
Sunflower Family (Compositae)

Height:	To 4'.
Flowers:	Rose-purple or lavender flowerhead of tiny, tubular, disk flowers; bracts wide and oval-shaped; loose flowerhead to 1 1/2" wide, 2" long; occurring singly, at branch tips.
Leaves:	Dark green above, white-woolly beneath; alternate and narrow, with widely spaced, spiny lobes; to 6" long at base, smaller on upper stem.
Blooms:	June–October.
Elevation:	5,000 to 9,000'.
Habitat:	Clearings in pine forests.
Comments:	Native Americans use thistles medicinally. Seventeen species of *Cirsium* (SIR-si-uhm) in Arizona. Photograph taken in vicinity of Christopher Creek, September 27.

CALLIOPSIS   399
Goldenwaves, tickseed, garden coreopsis
Coreopsis tinctoria
Sunflower Family (Compositae)

Height:	To 3'.
Flowers:	Yellow with reddish brown at base; 5 to 7 rays; to 1 1/4" wide.
Leaves:	Dark green; pinnate, with 2 to 3 pairs of linear lobes; to 4" long.
Blooms:	June–September.
Elevation:	Not available. Photograph taken at 7,000'.
Habitat:	Moist fields, waste areas, and roadsides.
Comments:	Annual. An escapee from cultivation. Three species of *Coreopsis* (koh-ree-OP-sis) in Arizona. Photograph taken at Upper Lake Mary, September 2.

COSMOS   643
Cosmos parviflorus
Sunflower Family (Compositae)

Height:	To 2 1/2'.
Flowers:	Has 8 pale pink ray flowers, bright yellow disk flowers; 8 long, narrow sepals; flower to 1" wide, on long, leafless stem; followed by seeds with stiff bristles.
Leaves:	Dark green, linear, very finely divided; to 3" long.
Blooms:	July–October.
Elevation:	4,000 to 9,000'.
Habitat:	Clearings in ponderosa pine forests and hillsides.
Comments:	Annual, with reddish stem. One species of *Cosmos* (KOS-mus) in Arizona. Photograph taken at McNary, August 10.

WESTERN SNEEZEWEED   400A and B
Owl-claws, mountain helenium, orange sneezeweed, Hoopes sneezeweed, yellow weed
Dugaldia hoopesii (*Helenium hoopesii*)
Sunflower Family (Compositae)

Height:	To 3'.
Flowers:	Yellow to orange-yellow, narrow, straggly, droopy ray flowers, each tipped with 3 teeth; flat flowerhead to 3" wide.

Leaves:	Grayish green, long, narrow, and woolly; progressively smaller toward flowerhead; to 1' long.
Blooms:	June–September.
Elevation:	7,000 to 11,000'.
Height:	Mountain meadows and coniferous forests.
Comments:	Has woolly stems. Causes illness in sheep and is poisonous to cattle if eaten. Some people are allergic to pollen. Root is used medicinally. Yellow dye made from flowerheads. One species of *Dugaldia* (doo-GALL-di-ah) in Arizona. Closeup photograph taken at Lee Valley Reservoir, July 2. Photograph of entire plant taken south of Alpine, July 23.

NEEDLELEAF DOGWEED   401
Dyssodia acerosa
Sunflower Family (Compositae)

Height:	To 1'.
Flowers:	Yellow rays (usually 8), slightly darker yellow disks; flower bracts dotted with yellowish glands; to 3/4" wide, terminal on branches.
Leaves:	Dark green, narrowly linear, needlelike, opposite or alternate, dotted with yellowish glands; to 1/2" long, all along stems.
Blooms:	March–October.
Elevation:	3,500 to 6,000'.
Height:	Washes; dry, rocky slopes; and mesas.
Comments:	Perennial herb. Many-branched, rounded bush; woody at base. Has glands on pinkish brown stems. Seven species of *Dyssodia* (dye-SOH-dee-uh) in Arizona. Photograph taken at Dead Horse Ranch State Park, October 3.

FIVE-NEEDLE FETID MARIGOLD   402
Common dogweed
Dyssodia pentachaeta
Sunflower Family (Compositae)

Height:	To 8".
Flowers:	Bright yellow rays and disks; bracts dotted with orangish brown glands; to 1/2" wide; on leafless stalks above leaves.
Leaves:	Dark green, mostly opposite, stiff, pinnately cleft into very narrow lobes with spiny tips; to 1/2" long.
Blooms:	March–September.
Elevation:	2,500 to 4,500'.
Habitat:	Desert and dry slopes.
Comments:	Plant forms low mound. Foliage has disagreeable odor when handled. Seven species of *Dyssodia* (dye-SOH-dee-uh) in Arizona. Photograph taken at Catalina State Park, April 15.

SAN FELIPE DYSSODIA   480
Dyssodia porophylloides
Sunflower Family (Compositae)

Height:	To 2'.
Flowers:	Yellowish orange, to 3/16" long; bracts have dark glands; large flowerhead to 1/2" wide, 1" long.

Leaves:	Dark green, opposite and alternate; pinnately 3- or 5-parted into narrow lobes; to 1" long, 7/8" wide.
Blooms:	March–October.
Elevation:	500 to 3,000'.
Height:	Mesas, washes, and rocky slopes.
Comments:	A straggly bush. When crushed, plant gives off disagreeable odor. Seven species of *Dyssodia* (dye-SOH-dee-uh) in Arizona. Photograph taken at King Canyon, Tucson, April 17.

BRITTLEBUSH 403

Incienso, rama blanca, hierba del vaso, hierba del gusano, white brittlebush
Encelia farinosa
Sunflower Family (Compositae)

Height:	To 4'.
Flowers:	Bright yellow, daisylike rays and disks; to 2" wide, in branched clusters; on tall, brittle stems forming a yellow canopy above foliage.
Leaves:	Greenish gray to silvery gray and woolly; oval, oblong or triangular-shaped; to 4" long; leaves are smaller during dry conditions.
Blooms:	November–May (in frost-free areas).
Elevation:	Below 3,000'.
Habitat:	Slopes, washes, and flats.
Comments:	Shrubby perennial. A rounded bush. During drought, leaves turn brown and drop, and are replaced by tiny new leaves. Stems are easily broken; exude a resin or gum which was chewed by Native Americans and burned as incense (*incienso*) in early missions. Three species of *Encelia* (en-SEE-li-ah) in Arizona. In some areas of Arizona, a variety of this species has flowerheads with brownish centers or disk flowers. Photograph taken at Usery Mountain Recreation Area, March 7.

RAYLESS ENCELIA 462

Green brittle bush
Encelia frutescens
Sunflower Family (Compositae)

Height:	To 3'.
Flowers:	Yellowish orange, rayless, dome-shaped; flowerhead to 3/4" wide; solitary; on hairy stem.
Leaves:	Dark green, very shiny above, hairy on margins and beneath; wavy-margined, rough, oval to oblong; to 1/2" wide, 2" long.
Blooms:	January–September.
Elevation:	Below 4,000'.
Habitat:	Mesas and rocky slopes.
Comments:	Low, branching shrub often to 3' wide. Young stems are pinkish, older stems are whitish. Three species of *Encelia* (en-SEE-li-ah) in Arizona. Photograph taken near Salome, March 28.

ENGELMANN'S DAISY 404

Engelmann's sunflower
Engelmannia pinnatifida
Sunflower Family (Compositae)

| Height: | To 3'. |

Flowers:	Bright yellow, usually with 8 rays, slightly curled under at tips; yellow disks; to 1 1/4" wide; in loose, terminal cluster on upper stems.
Leaves:	Dark green above, lighter green beneath; alternate, very rough and hairy, deeply pinnately lobed; clasping stem; basal leaves to 8" long, becoming shorter on upper stems.
Blooms:	May–September.
Elevation:	4,000 to 6,500'.
Habitat:	Dry prairies and hills.
Comments:	Perennial herb. Hairy-stemmed. One species of *Engelmannia* (eng-guhl-MAHN-ee-ah) in Arizona. Photograph taken in vicinity of Portal, May 4.

TURPENTINE BRUSH   481

Turpentine bush, larch-leaf goldenweed
Ericameria laricifolia (*Aplopappus laricifolius*) or (*Haplopappus laricifolius*)
Sunflower Family (Compositae)

Height:	Bush to 40".
Flowers:	Golden yellow, with up to 11 ray flowers, up to 13 disk flowers; to 3/8" long, 3/8" wide; in dense cluster; terminal on leafy branches.
Leaves:	Light green to grayish green; linear, leathery, crowded, glandular-dotted; to 3/4" long, 1/16" wide.
Blooms:	August–December.
Elevation:	3,000 to 6,000'.
Habitat:	Canyons, rocky slopes, and mesas.
Comments:	Foliage smells like turpentine when crushed. Plant contains small amount of rubber. Attractive to bees and other insects. Two species of *Ericameria* (air-i-cuh-MER-ee-ah) in Arizona. Photograph taken east of Camp Verde, September 30.

PRINCELY DAISY   719

Erigeron formosissimus
Sunflower Family (Compositae)

Height:	To 16".
Flowers:	Lavender to blue, with very narrow rays, yellow disks; flowerhead to 1 1/2" wide.
Leaves:	Grayish green, hairy. Spatula-shaped, basal leaves to 3" long. Stem leaves shorter, alternate, lance-shaped, clasping stem, progressively smaller.
Blooms:	July–September.
Elevation:	5,500 to 10,500'.
Habitat:	Coniferous forests, meadows, and edges of aspen-spruce forests.
Comments:	Stems hairy. There are more than 2 dozen species of *Erigeron* (eh-RIJ-er-on) in Arizona. Photograph taken in mountains above Greer, August 13.

ASPEN FLEABANE   720

Wild-daisy, blue aspen daisy
Erigeron macranthus
Sunflower Family (Compositae)

Height:	To 3', but usually closer to 2'.
Flowers:	Pale bluish lavender rays, very long and narrow; orangish yellow disks (large for a fleabane); to 1 1/2" wide; numerous flowerheads.
Leaves:	Dark green, hairy, wavy; lance-shaped, alternate, to 6" long.
Blooms:	July–October.

Elevation: 6,000 to 9,500'.
Habitat: Oak thickets and pine forests.
Comments: Hairy stems. Fleabanes are usually difficult to identify; they come in all sizes and range in color from white to pink to bluish lavender. Some bloom in spring, others in summer and fall. In general, they are easily distinguished from asters by their numerous, very narrow ray flowers. There are more than 2 dozen species of *Erigeron* (eh-RIJ-er-on) in Arizona. Photograph taken in Greer area, July 5.

FLEABANE   250
Erigeron oreophilus
Sunflower Family (Compositae)
Height: To 16".
Flowers: White, very narrow rays, yellow disk flowers; flowerhead to 1" wide.
Leaves: Grayish green, very hairy on both surfaces; alternate, 5- to 7-lobed, to 1" long.
Blooms: May–October.
Elevation: 4,500 to 9,500'.
Habitat: Oak woodlands and clearings in ponderosa forests.
Comments: Herb, with very hairy stem. More than 2 dozen species of *Erigeron* (eh-RIJ-er-on) in Arizona. Photograph taken in vicinity of Willow Springs Lake, August 19.

WOOLLY DAISY   251
Woolly eriophyllum
Eriophyllum lanosum
Sunflower Family (Compositae)
Height: To 1 1/2".
Flowers: White, woolly, with yellow centers; to 1/4" wide; at ends of woolly stems.
Leaves: Grayish white, woolly, linear; to 1/4" long.
Blooms: February–May.
Elevation: 1,000 to 3,000'.
Habitat: Dry, gravelly slopes and mesas.
Comments: Annual. Five species of *Eriophyllum* (eh-ri-o-FILL-uhm) in Arizona. Photograph taken near Salome, March 28.

PRINGLE'S WOOLLYLEAF   496
Pringle eriophyllum
Eriophyllum pringlei
Sunflower Family (Compositae)
Height: To 2".
Flowers: Yellow, all disk flowers; to 1/16" wide, in 1/4"-wide clusters.
Leaves: Grayish green, woolly haired, linear, 3-lobed at tips; to 3/16" long; surrounding flower cluster.
Blooms: March–May.
Elevation: 1,500 to 3,000'.
Habitat: Sandy desert flats and slopes.
Comments: Grows in tufts. Five species of *Eriophyllum* (eh-ri-o-FILL-uhm) in Arizona. Photograph taken at Catalina State Park, April 2.

SLENDER GAILLARDIA   405
Reddome blanketflower, pinnate-leaved gaillardia
Gaillardia pinnatifida
Sunflower Family (Compositae)

Height: To 20".
Flowers: Yellow ray flowers; reddish to greenish disk flowers in rounded dome; to 1 3/4" wide.
Leaves: Green, pinnately lobed, to 3" long.
Blooms: May–October.
Elevation: 3,500 to 7,000'.
Habitat: Fields, plains, mesas, and clearings in ponderosa pine forests.
Comments: Perennial herb. Hopi Indians use this species as a diuretic. Five species of *Gaillardia* (gay-LAR-di-ah) in Arizona. Photograph taken at Portal, April 23.

BLANKETFLOWER   406
Firewheel, Indian blanket, gaillardia
Gaillardia pulchella
Sunflower Family (Compositae)

Height: To 2'.
Flowers: Reddish purple, wedge-shaped ray flowers tipped with bright yellow; broad ends of rays divided into 3 sharp lobes; reddish purple disk flowers in dome-shaped center; to 3" wide.
Leaves: Green; upper leaves oblong, lower ones lobed; to 3" long.
Blooms: April–September.
Elevation: 3,500 to 5,500'.
Habitat: Roadsides, fields, and clearings in pinyon-juniper woodlands and ponderosa forests.
Comments: Annual. Five species of *Gaillardia* (gay-LAR-di-ah) in Arizona. Photograph taken at Payson, September 12.

DESERT SUNFLOWER   407
Desert sunshine, desert gold, hairy-headed sunflower
Geraea canescens
Sunflower Family (Compositae)

Height: To 3'.
Flowers: Yellow rays, golden orange disks, to 2" wide; terminal on branches.
Leaves: Grayish green, very hairy, diamond-shaped, with toothed margins; to 3" long.
Blooms: January–June; abundant in April.
Elevation: Below 3,000'.
Habitat: Sandy desert roadsides and flats.
Comments: Annual. Fragrant; attractive to bees and hummingbird moths. Seeds are a food source for small rodents and birds. One species of *Geraea* (je-REE-ah or je-RAY-ah) in Arizona. Photograph taken north of Yuma, March 29.

ARIZONA CUDWEED   291
Gnaphalium arizonicum
Sunflower Family (Compositae)

Height: To 2'.
Flowers: Whitish gray, rayless, tipped with yellowish brown; in slender heads; to 1/4" long; to 47 per head, in cluster to 1/2" wide.

Leaves:	Grayish, woolly, margins curled under; linear, alternate, pointing upward on stem; to 1" long.
Blooms:	August–October.
Elevation:	5,000 to 7,500'.
Habitat:	Pine forests.
Comments:	Herb. Has woolly stems. Dried flower stalks last a long time. Ten species of *Gnaphalium* (na-FAY-li-uhm) in Arizona. Photograph taken in Woods Canyon Lake area, September 14.

RAYLESS GUMWEED   463
Mountain gumplant
Grindelia aphanactis
Sunflower Family (Compositae)

Height:	To 16".
Flowers:	Yellow, rayless, ball-shaped flowerhead of rounded, linear, semi-hooked, sticky bracts; to 1 1/4" wide.
Leaves:	Dark green, narrow, straplike, sticky, with toothed margins, to 2 3/8" long.
Blooms:	June–October.
Elevation:	5,000 to 7,000'.
Habitat:	Roadsides, fields, and clearings in ponderosa forests.
Comments:	Annual or biennial. Sticky-gummy plant. Five species of *Grindelia* (grin-DEE-lee-ah) in Arizona. Photograph taken at Nelson Reservoir, August 3. Recognizable by its absence of ray flowers.

CURLYCUP GUMWEED   408
Rosinweed, tarweed, sticky heads, broadleaf gumplant
Grindelia squarrosa
Sunflower Family (Compositae)

Height:	To 3'.
Flowers:	Yellow rays, darker yellow disk flowers; daisylike; tips of bracts surrounding flowerhead are rolled back and very sticky; to 1 1/2" wide.
Leaves:	Dark green, oblong, stemless, clasping stem at base, to 4" long.
Blooms:	July–September.
Elevation:	4,000 to 7,500'.
Habitat:	Dry, open fields, and waste places.
Comments:	Perennial herb; sticky-gummy plant. Plant used medicinally. Invades overgrazed ranchland. Five species of *Grindelia* (grin-DEE-lee-ah) in Arizona. Photograph taken near Show Low, August 5. Recognizable by presence of ray flowers.

GUARDIOLA   234
Guardiola platyphylla
Sunflower Family (Compositae)

Height:	To 4'.
Flowers:	White, with 1 to 5 rays, 3 to 8 white disk flowers; flower to 1/2" wide; in loose, terminal clusters.
Leaves:	Dark green, opposite, leathery; heart-shaped to oval; sharp-toothed, very short-stalked, prominent network; to 2" long.
Blooms:	February–September.
Elevation:	3,000 to 5,000'.

Habitat:	Rocky slopes and canyons.
Comments:	Branching perennial. Mature stems are gray; immature stems, reddish. One species of *Guardiola* (GARD-i-oh-lah) in Arizona. Photograph taken in vicinity of Kitt Peak, April 18.

BROOM SNAKEWEED 409

Turpentine weed, matchweed, matchbrush, resin-weed, broom-weed, yerba de San Nicolas, broombrush
Gutierrezia sarothrae
Sunflower Family (Compositae)

Height:	To 2'.
Flowers:	Yellow, tiny, 3 to 8 ray flowers to 1/8" long; 2 to 8 disk flowers; flowerheads to 1/4" long; in dense clusters at ends of branches.
Leaves:	Dark green, very narrow, to 1/8" wide, 2 1/2" long; at intervals along stem.
Blooms:	July–December.
Elevation:	3,000 to 8,000'.
Habitat:	Plains, pinyon-juniper woodlands, ponderosa forest clearings, and roadsides.
Comments:	Perennial herb. Plant forms mound. Where abundant, it indicates overgrazed land. Flowerheads resemble matchheads, hence the common name. Poisonous to livestock; causes abortion of fetuses. Seeds eaten by birds. Once used medicinally on sheep for snakebite. Dried stems made into primitive brooms. Chewed leaves were once placed on ant, bee, or wasp stings to reduce swelling. Five species of *Gutierrezia* (goo-tih-ehr-REE-zih-uh) in Arizona. Photograph taken at Canyon de Chelly National Monument, July 27. A similar species, *Gutierrezia microcephala*, has fewer and more slender flowerheads.

GYMNOSPERMA 497

Gymnosperma glutinosum (Selloa glutinosa)
Sunflower Family (Compositae)

Height:	To 4'.
Flowers:	Yellow, with inconspicuous rays; flower to 3/8" wide, 1/2" long; in clusters on stems off main stem; followed by minute pappus (hairs).
Leaves:	Dark green, alternate, linear; rough, curled a bit, to 2" long; occurring all up stem; smaller leaves in clusters at base of leaf stem.
Blooms:	March–December.
Elevation:	1,000 to 6,000'.
Habitat:	Rocky canyons and slopes.
Comments:	A slightly woody plant toward base; has light brown stem. Plant used medicinally in Mexico. One species of *Gymnosperma* (jim-noh-SPURM-ah) in Arizona. Photograph taken at Organ Pipe Cactus National Monument, November 14.

ARIZONA SNEEZEWEED 410

Helenium arizonicum
Sunflower Family (Compositae)

Height:	To 4'.
Flowers:	Yellow, 3-lobed ray flowers; purplish brown, globular disk flowers; to 2" wide; occurring singly at tips of stems.
Leaves:	Dark green, narrow, to 5" long; becoming smaller on upper stems.
Blooms:	July–September.

Elevation:	7,000 to 8,000'.
Habitat:	Roadsides and clearings in ponderosa forests.
Comments:	Three species of *Helenium* (hell-LEE-ni-um) in Arizona. Photograph taken at Willow Springs Lake area, July 21.

ASPEN SUNFLOWER   411
Five-nerve helianthella, five-veined sunflower
Helianthella quinquenervis
Sunflower Family (Compositae)

Height:	To 4'.
Flowers:	Pale yellow rays, with greenish yellow disks; sunflowerlike, hairy bracts; to 3" wide; solitary or in few-flowered cluster.
Leaves:	Grayish green, hairy, with 5 prominent veins; broadly lance-shaped; to 10" long; mostly basal.
Blooms:	July–October.
Elevation:	5,000 to 10,000'.
Habitat:	Mountain meadows, slopes, and coniferous clearings, often near aspen groves.
Comments:	Perennial herb. Wildlife graze on flowerheads. Three species of *Helianthella* (he-li-an-THELL-lah) in Arizona. Photograph taken in Greer area, July 5. A similar species, **PARRY HELIANTHELLA** (*Helianthella parryi*) has narrower leaves and smaller flowers.

COMMON SUNFLOWER   412
Kansas sunflower, mirasol, annual sunflower
Helianthus annuus
Sunflower Family (Compositae)

Height:	To 9'.
Flowers:	Bright yellow ray flowers, maroon disk flowers; to 5" wide.
Leaves:	Dull green, stiff hairs; lower leaves are broadly triangular to heart-shaped; irregularly toothed; to 12" long.
Blooms:	May–October.
Elevation:	100 to 7,000'.
Habitat:	Roadsides and fields.
Comments:	Annual; state flower of Kansas. Frost-sensitive. Flowers are heliotropic (face the sun as it moves across sky). Seeds eaten by birds, rodents, and humans. Native Americans use seeds to make purple and black dye; yellow dye is made from the flowers. Eight species of *Helianthus* (hee-li-AN-thus) in Arizona. Photograph taken near Mexican Hay Lake, July 21.

PRAIRIE SUNFLOWER   413
Narrowleaf sunflower, sand sunflower
Helianthus petiolaris
Sunflower Family (Compositae)

Height:	To 4'.
Flowers:	Yellow rays, reddish brown disk flowers; to 2" wide.
Leaves:	Green, oblong to lance-shaped, toothed; to 2" long.
Blooms:	April–October.
Elevation:	1,000 to 7,500'.
Habitat:	Roadsides, fields, and cultivated land.

Comments: Annual. Has hairy stems. Eight species of *Helianthus* (hee-li-AN-thus) in Arizona. Photograph taken at Sunset Crater National Monument, September 7. Shorter plant, with more compact flowerheads than common sunflower, *Helianthus annuus.*

CAMPHORWEED   414A and B
Telegraph plant
Heterotheca psammophila (*Heterotheca subaxillaris*)
Sunflower Family (Compositae)

Height: To 5'.
Flowers: Bright yellow rays, orange disk flowers, to 1" wide; in loose clusters on branches on a single, erect stem resembling a telegraph pole; followed by seedheads like tiny, mature dandelions.
Leaves: Light green, wavy, egg-shaped; thick, toothed, with clasping bases; to 3 1/2" long.
Blooms: March–November.
Elevation: 1,000 to 5,500'.
Habitat: Roadsides, pastures, vacant lots, and other disturbed places.
Comments: Crushed leaves smell like camphor. Six species of *Heterotheca* (het-ero-THEE-kah) in Arizona. Photographs taken at Oak Creek Canyon, September 9.

HAIRY GOLDEN ASTER   415
Rosinweed
Heterotheca villosa (*Chrysopsis villosa*)
Sunflower Family (Compositae)

Height: 30".
Flowers: Yellow rays varying in number, darker yellow disks; to 1" wide; terminal, in cluster.
Leaves: Gray to grayish green, woolly haired; alternate, oblong to spoon-shaped (widest toward tip); crinkled; to 1 1/4" long; occurring all along stems.
Blooms: May–October.
Elevation: 1,500 to 8,500'.
Habitat: Plains, mesas, and clearings in ponderosa pine forests.
Comments: Brownish, hairy stems. Six species of *Heterotheca* (het-ero-THEE-kah) in Arizona. There are numerous varieties of this species, differing in hairiness and other characteristics. Photograph taken at Black Canyon Lake, September 29.

FENDLER'S HAWKWEED   448
Hieracium fendleri
Sunflower Family (Compositae)

Height: To 20".
Flowers: Yellow, small, all rays; to 1/2" wide, 3/4" long.
Leaves: Green above, lighter green beneath; very hairy, in basal rosette; widest between middle and tip; to 5" long.
Blooms: May–August.
Elevation: 6,000 to 9,500'.
Habitat: Pine forests.
Comments: Perennial herb. Stem is very hairy, with 1/8"-long hairs. Five species of *Hieracium* (hy-er-RAY-see-um) in Arizona. Photograph taken in vicinity of Ashurst Lake, June 1.

BURRO BRUSH   853
Cheeseweed
Hymenoclea salsola
Sunflower Family (Compositae)

Height: To 4'.
Flowers: Silvery white, tufted, in leaf axils of upper leaves; also terminal; to 3/8" wide;
              followed by fruit with silvery white wings.
Leaves: Dark green, very slender; lower leaves have 3 or more threadlike divisions;
              to 3" long.
Blooms: March–April.
Elevation: Below 4,000'.
Habitat: Arroyos, sandy washes, and rocky slopes.
Comments: Feathery branches. Has cheesy odor when foliage is crushed. Pollen can cause hay
              fever. Two species of *Hymenoclea* (hy-meh-NOCK-li-ah) in Arizona. Photograph
              taken near Salome, March 28.

FINELEAF WOOLLYWHITE   464
Yellow cut-leaf
Hymenopappus filifolius
Sunflower Family (Compositae)

Height: To 30".
Flowers: Bright yellow, petalless; disk flowers enlarged with long stamens and style
              projecting upward and outward; flowerhead to 7/8" wide; number of
              flowerheads varies.
Leaves: Grayish green above, gray beneath; feltlike hairs; pinnately divided into threadlike
              segments; leaves 3" to 8" long, depending on variety; basal in some varieties; in
              others 1 to 7 leaves extend up stem.
Blooms: May–September.
Elevation: Varies depending on variety.
Habitat: Rocky slopes or sandy soil or clearings in ponderosa pine forests depending
              on variety.
Comments: Very variable species. Photograph taken in Ashurst Lake Area, September 5. Four
              species of *Hymenopappus* (hy-men-oh-PAP-pus) in Arizona. The flowers of
              MEXICAN WOOLLYWHITE (*Hymenopappus mexicanus*) are very similar, but
              the basal, woolly leaves are single, lance-shaped to partly lobed, and up to 6" long,
              1/2" wide. Plant is 3' tall with lower reddish stem. Photograph (**PLATE 465**) taken
              in mountain meadow above Greer, August 8.

WRIGHT BEEFLOWER   678
Hymenothrix wrightii
Sunflower Family (Compositae)

Height: To 3'.
Flowers: Pinkish, with two circles of flower bracts, outer ones narrow, short, and pointed;
              inner ones broad, long, and blunt; flower to 5/16" long; flowerhead to 1/2" wide;
              numerous on widely spread top stems.
Leaves: Dark green, hairy, divided into very narrow segments; to 1 1/2" long, graduating to
              smaller up stem.
Blooms: June–October.
Elevation: 4,000 to 8,000'.

Habitat:	Roadsides, dry slopes in scrub-oak and pine belts.
Comments:	Perennial herb. Has a hairy stem. Three species of *Hymenothrix* (hy-men-NOTH-rix) in Arizona. Photograph taken east of Camp Verde, September 30.

BITTERWEED   416
Hymenoxys bigelovii
Sunflower Family (Compositae)

Height:	To 16".
Flowers:	Yellow, notched rays; orange disks to 3/4" wide; flowerhead to 2" wide.
Leaves:	Dark green, very narrow; with whitish midvein in grooved, upper surface; hairy beneath, very hairy at base; clasping stem; mainly basal, to 7" long; with a few shorter, alternate leaves on upper stem.
Blooms:	April–July.
Elevation:	5,500 to 7,500'.
Habitat:	Pine forests.
Comments:	Flower resembles a tall, sparsely leaved gaillardia. Twelve species of *Hymenoxys* (hy-men-OX-siss) in Arizona. Photograph taken in vicinity of Upper Lake Mary, June 2.

COOPER'S GOLDFLOWER   417
Hymenoxys cooperi
Sunflower Family (Compositae)

Height:	To 3'.
Flowers:	Bright yellow, straggly rays, orangish disks; to 1" wide, on stalks up to 4" long; numerous stalks of flowers on plant.
Leaves:	Grayish green, woolly, pinnate, with linear lobes in some varieties, wider leaves in others; to 3" long.
Blooms:	May–September.
Elevation:	2,000 to 8,000'.
Habitat:	Dry, rocky areas.
Comments:	Many varieties of this species. Woolly stems. Twelve species of *Hymenoxys* (hy-men-OX-siss) in Arizona. Photograph taken at North Rim of Grand Canyon National Park, July 13.

JIMMYWEED   482
Rayless-goldenrod, goldenbush
Isocoma wrightii (Haplopappus heterophyllus)
Sunflower Family (Compositae)

Height:	To 3' high, 3' wide.
Flowers:	Yellow, to 1/2" wide, 1/2" long; flowerhead to 15 flowers, in terminal clusters on stems.
Leaves:	Grayish green, very rough, linear with shorter linear leaf cluster on stem at base; alternate; to 2 1/4" long, all along stem.
Blooms:	June–September.
Elevation:	Below 5,000'.
Habitat:	Roadsides, plains, and mesas.
Comments:	A weed. Often takes over on overgrazed land. If large amounts are eaten by cattle, it causes "milk-sickness" or "trembles," a disease transmitted through milk to humans. Four species of *Isocoma* (eye-soh-COH-mah) in Arizona. Photograph taken at Usery

Mountain Recreation Area, August 20. A similar species, **BURROWEED** (*Isocoma tenuisecta*) is common in the Tucson area. Its leaves are glandular and linear with prominent side lobes.

PRICKLY LETTUCE   449
Wild lettuce
Lactuca serriola
Sunflower Family (Compositae)

Height:	To 6'.
Flowers:	Yellow, composed solely of ray flowers; to 1/3" wide; on short stalks, on branched, upper flowering stems; followed by miniature, dandelionlike tufts.
Leaves:	Bluish green, clasping stem; with prominent white midvein smooth above, prickly veins beneath; prickly on margins, cut into deep, irregular lobes; to 10" long at base, graduating to smaller size on upper stems.
Blooms:	May–October.
Elevation:	1,000 to 8,000'.
Habitat:	Roadsides and disturbed soil.
Comments:	A weed. Stems filled with milky juice; main stem branches where flowering occurs. Introduced from Europe; now naturalized. Five species of *Lactuca* (lak-TOO-kah) in Arizona. Photograph taken at Ashurst Lake, September 4.

GOLDFIELDS   418
Desert goldfields, fly flower
Lasthenia chrysostoma (*Baeria chrysostoma*)
Sunflower Family (Compositae)

Height:	To 8".
Flowers:	Yellow ray flowers notched at tips; darker yellow disk flowers; to 1" wide; terminal on slender stems.
Leaves:	Light green, hairy on both surfaces; narrow, linear, opposite; to 1 1/2" long.
Blooms:	March–May.
Elevation:	1,500 to 4,500'.
Habitat:	Deserts, mesas, and plains.
Comments:	Annual herb. Often grows in dense patches, forming carpets of gold. Grazed by horses. Fragrant flowers attract a species of small fly. One species of *Lasthenia* (las-THEE-ni-ah) in Arizona. Photograph taken in Superstition Mountains, March 22.

TIDYTIPS   252
White layia, white tidytips
Layia glandulosa
Sunflower Family (Compositae)

Height:	To 18".
Flowers:	White ray flowers tipped with 3 equal teeth; yellow disk flowers; terminal; to 1 1/2" wide.
Leaves:	Green, narrow, with sticky hairs; basal leaves with 1 to 5 pairs of short lobes; to 3" long; stem leaves narrow and elliptical.
Blooms:	February–April.
Elevation:	Up to 5,000'.

| Habitat: | Desert washes, dry slopes, and mesas. |
| Comments: | Annual. One species of *Layia* (LAY-i-ah) in Arizona. Photograph taken at Usery Mountain Recreation Area, March 1. |

BABY ASTER 253
White aster
Leucelene ericoides (*Aster hirtifolius*)
Sunflower Family (Compositae)

Height:	To 6".
Flowers:	White rays, orange disks; to 5/8" wide; on tips of branches; fading to pale pink.
Leaves:	Grayish green, finely haired, linear; to 1/4" long, tightly adhering to the entire stem.
Blooms:	March–September.
Elevation:	3,500 to 7,000'.
Habitat:	Dry slopes and mesas.
Comments:	One species of *Leucelene* (lew-SELL-ee-nee) in Arizona. Photograph taken at Portal, April 23.

MACHAERANTHERA 721
Machaeranthera asteroides var. *asteroides*
Sunflower Family (Compositae)

Height:	To 4'.
Flowers:	Purple rays, orange disk flowers, to 1" wide.
Leaves:	Grayish green, linear, sandpapery, with spines on margins; to 3" long.
Blooms:	April–May.
Elevation:	1,500 to 2,500'.
Habitat:	Washes and desert flats.
Comments:	More than a dozen species of *Machaeranthera* (mack-uh-RAN-the-rah) in Arizona. Photograph taken in vicinity of Saguaro Lake, May 20. Another variety, *Machaeranthera asteroides* var. *glandulosa* reaches up to 3' tall, has large flowers to 1 1/4" wide, and toothed leaves to 5 1/2" long. Photograph (**PLATE 722**) taken in Superstition Mountains, April 6.

YELLOW SPINY DAISY 419
Goldenweed, yellow daisy
Machaeranthera gracilis (*Aplopappus* or *Haplopappus gracilis*)
Sunflower Family (Compositae)

Height:	To 1'.
Flowers:	Yellow rays and disks; to 1 1/4" wide; terminal on upper branches.
Leaves:	Grayish green, hairy, narrow; angled upward, toothed, with spiny bristle at tip of each tooth; lowest leaves have a few lobes; to 3/4" long.
Blooms:	February–December.
Elevation:	Below 7,000'.
Habitat:	Dry plains, mesas, and rocky slopes.
Comments:	Annual herb. More than a dozen species of *Machaeranthera* (mack-uh-RAN-the-rah) in Arizona. Photograph taken at Apache Lake, March 19. Recognizable by spiny bristle at tip of each leaf tooth.

TANSYLEAF SPINE ASTER 723
Tahoka daisy
Machaeranthera tanacetifolia (*Aster tanacetifolius*)
Sunflower Family (Compositae)

Height:	To 16".
Flowers:	Bluish purple rays, yellow disks; to 2" wide.
Leaves:	Grayish green, sticky-hairy, much-divided, fernlike, pinnate leaves tipped with tiny spines, leaf to 3" long.
Blooms:	June–October.
Elevation:	1,000 to 8,000'.
Habitat:	Roadsides, fields, and disturbed soil.
Comments:	Perennial herb. Hairy, pinkish stems. More than a dozen species of *Machaeranthera* (mack-uh-RAN-the-rah) in Arizona. Photograph taken near Nutrioso, August 7. Fernlike leaves with tiny spines at leaf tips help identify this species.

MOHAVE ASTER 724
Desert aster
Machaeranthera tortifolia (*Aster abatus*)
Sunflower Family (Compositae)

Height:	To 2 1/2'.
Flowers:	Pale lavender to almost white rays; yellow disk flowers; terminal, to 2 1/2" wide.
Leaves:	Grayish green, grayish-haired, narrowly lance-shaped; spiny teeth along margins, leaf tipped with a spine; to 3" long.
Blooms:	March–May.
Elevation:	2,000 to 3,500'.
Habitat:	Dry, rocky hills and slopes.
Comments:	Perennial herb. As many as 20 flowerheads on one plant. More than a dozen species of *Machaeranthera* (mack-uh-RAN-the-rah) in Arizona. Photograph taken at Alamo Lake, February 27.

DESERT DANDELION 450
Malacothrix californica var. *glabrata* (*Malacothrix glabrata*)
Sunflower Family (Compositae)

Height:	To 16".
Flowers:	Pale yellow rays, no disk flowers, centers are red until all petals expand; to 1 3/4" wide.
Leaves:	Green, linear, pinnately lobed, mostly basal; to 5" long.
Blooms:	March–June.
Elevation:	Below 7,000'.
Habitat:	Dry, sandy flats of low desert and mesas.
Comments:	Annual herb. Seven species of *Malacothrix* (MAL-ah-koh-thricks) in Arizona. Photograph taken near Golden Shores, March 9.

FENDLER'S DANDELION 451
Desert dandelion, cliff aster, yellow saucers
Malacothrix fendleri
Sunflower Family (Compositae)

Height:	To 6".
Flowers:	Yellow, notched petals, pink-striped on back; to 1" wide.

Leaves:	Grayish green, pinnate, triangularly lobed, to 2" long.
Blooms:	March–June.
Elevation:	2,000 to 5,000'.
Habitat:	Foothills, sandy plains, and mesas.
Comments:	Annual herb. Seven species of *Malacothrix* (MAL-ah-koh-thricks) in Arizona. Photograph taken at Portal, April 23.

BLACKFOOT DAISY   254
Desert daisy, plains blackfoot, ash-gray blackfoot
Melampodium leucanthum
Sunflower Family (Compositae)

Height:	To 20".
Flowers:	White ray flowers, 8 to 10, with purple veins; yellow disk flowers; to 1 1/2" wide; numerous flowerheads on rounded, shrublike plant.
Leaves:	Ash-gray, narrow, opposite; to 2" long.
Blooms:	March–December.
Elevation:	2,000 to 5,000'.
Habitat:	Dry, rocky slopes, desert grassland, and oak woodlands.
Comments:	Perennial herb. Three species of *Melampodium* (mel-am-POH-dee-um) in Arizona. Photograph taken in Superstition Mountains, March 15.

MICROSERIS   452
Microseris lindleyi
Sunflower Family (Compositae)

Height:	Flower stem to 1 1/2'.
Flowers:	Yellow, all rays, flowerhead to 5/8" wide; occurring singly on long, hollow, leafless stem; followed by large, round, silvery seedhead to 1 1/2" wide.
Leaves:	Dark green, onionlike, and basal; to 8" long.
Blooms:	Photograph taken in June.
Elevation:	Not available. Photograph taken at 5,500'.
Habitat:	Pine forests.
Comments:	Three species of *Microseris* (my-kroh-SER-is) in Arizona. Photograph taken in vicinity of Pine, June 3.

SILVER PUFFS   453
Starpoint
Microseris linearifolia
Sunflower Family (Compositae)

Height:	To 12".
Flowers:	Yellow rays, dandelionlike; flowerhead bracts extend beyond rays as sharp points; to 1" wide; followed by delicate, silvery, pufflike seedhead.
Leaves:	Grayish green; linear to partly linear, or pinnately lobed; to 5" long.
Blooms:	March–May.
Elevation:	Below 5,000'.
Habitat:	Foothills, plains, and mesas.
Comments:	Hollow stemmed. Three species of *Microseris* (my-kroh-SER-is) in Arizona. Photograph taken at Saguaro National Monument West, April 17.

MOHAVE DESERT STAR   255
Desert daisy, rock daisy
Monoptilon bellioides
Sunflower Family (Compositae)

Height:	To 2" high with tussocks to 10" wide.
Flowers:	White to pinkish rays; yellow disk; to 3/4" wide.
Leaves:	Grayish green, narrow, stiffly haired; to 1" long.
Blooms:	February–April.
Elevation:	200 to 3,500'.
Habitat:	Sandy or rocky slopes, mesas, and desert flats.
Comments:	Winter annual herb; in good years, often producing large patches of white on desert floor. Two species of *Monoptilon* (mon-OP-til-on) in Arizona. Photograph taken at Organ Pipe Cactus National Monument, March 30.

SPANISH NEEDLES   647
Palafoxia arida (Palafoxia linearis)
Sunflower Family (Compositae)

Height:	To 3'.
Flowers:	Pinkish, petalless, with 10 to 20 disk flowers in pincushionlike flowerhead; to 3/4" high, 1/2" wide; followed by seeds with needlelike bristles.
Leaves:	Grayish green, hairy, narrow, and linear; to 2 1/2" long.
Blooms:	February–November.
Elevation:	Below 2,000'.
Habitat:	Sandy washes, plains, mesas, and dunes.
Comments:	Annual herb. One species of *Palafoxia* (pal-ah-FOX-ee-ah) in Arizona. Photograph taken north of Yuma, March 29.

CROWDED RAYWEED   235
Mariola
Parthenium confertum
Sunflower Family (Compositae)

Height:	To 2'.
Flowers:	White and buttonlike, with 5 tiny, cuplike ray flowers around outer margin; to 1/4" wide; in clusters along upper stems.
Leaves:	Grayish green, hairy, alternate; pinnately cleft with blunt, rounded lobes; to 3" long at base, smaller up along stem.
Blooms:	April–October.
Elevation:	2,500 to 6,000'.
Habitat:	Dry plains and mesas.
Comments:	Has hairy stem. Sap contains rubber. This species common in southeastern Arizona. Two species of *Parthenium* (par-THEE-ni-uhm) in Arizona. Photograph taken near Portal, April 22.

FETID-MARIGOLD   420
Lemonweed, lemon-scented pectis
Pectis angustifolia
Sunflower Family (Compositae)

Height:	To 6".
Flowers:	Bright yellow, 8 to 10 rays; to 1/4" wide; clustered at end of branches.

Leaves:	Dark green, smooth, linear, with 3 to 5 pairs of linear lobes; to 1 1/2" long.
Blooms:	August–November.
Elevation:	700 to 7,000'.
Habitat:	Dry, sandy, or gravelly mesas.
Comments:	Hopi Indians extract a dye from plant, and also consume the plant raw or dried. Ten species of *Pectis* (PEK-tiss) in Arizona. Photograph taken at Painted Rocks State Park, November 12.

TAILLEAF PERICOME   466
Taperleaf, yerba de chivato
Pericome caudata
Sunflower Family (Compositae)

Height:	To 5'.
Flowers:	Yellow to orange-yellow, rayless, to 1/2" wide; in branched clusters to 2" wide.
Leaves:	Dark green, triangular, tip tapers to long slender tail; limp, drooping; to 5" long, 2 1/2" wide at widest part.
Blooms:	July–October.
Elevation:	6,000 to 9,000'.
Habitat:	Roadsides and slopes in pine forests.
Comments:	Perennial herb; named by Spaniards *yerba de chivato* ("herb of the he-goat") because of its goatlike smell. Plant used for treating ailments. Bushes often grow to 6' wide, forming mound of yellow flowers. One species of *Pericome* (per-ih-COMB-ee) in Arizona. Photograph taken at Mormon Lake, September 3.

EMORY'S ROCK DAISY   256
Emory rock daisy
Perityle emoryii
Sunflower Family (Compositae)

Height:	To 2'.
Flowers:	White rays, yellow disks, to 1/2" wide.
Leaves:	Dark green, finely haired, brittle, succulent; broadly triangular, with deeply toothed margins; to 1 1/2" wide.
Blooms:	February–May, and possibly to October.
Elevation:	To 3,000'.
Habitat:	Rocky desert slopes, cliffs, and washes.
Comments:	Twelve species of *Perityle* (per-ih-TYE-lee) in Arizona. Photograph taken at Cattail Cove State Park, February 25.

PERITYLE   467
Perityle lemmoni (*Laphamia dissecta*)
Sunflower Family (Compositae)

Height:	To 1', but generally prostrate.
Flowers:	Yellow, rayless; to 1/2" long, to 1/4" wide.
Leaves:	Dark green edged in brown; woolly haired, opposite, maplelike; cleft into narrow lobes; to 3/8" long, 1/4" wide.
Blooms:	May–October.
Elevation:	3,000 to 7,000'.

Habitat: Crevices of boulders and cliffs.
Comments: Brittle, hairy stems. Twelve species of *Perityle* (per-ih-TYE-lee) in Arizona. Photograph taken at Molino Canyon, Mount Lemmon, May 13.

DESERT FIR   468
Fir leaf, pigmy cedar
Peucephyllum schottii
Sunflower Family (Compositae)
Height: Shrub to 4 1/2'.
Flowers: Yellow, petalless, 1/2" wide; occurring at tips of branches.
Leaves: Green, hairlike, stiff, and dense; to 3/4" long.
Blooms: Mid-February–June.
Elevation: Below 5,000'.
Habitat: Dry, rocky slopes, and along washes.
Comments: Perennial; many-branched shrub. One species of *Peucephyllum* (pe-YOU-seff-i-lum or pe-you-SEFF-i-lum) in Arizona. Photograph taken at Cattail Cove State Park, February 23.

MARSH FLEABANE   732
Arrow weed, arrowweed pluchea
Pluchea purpurascens var. *purpurascens* (*Pluchea sericea*)
Sunflower Family (Compositae)
Height: To 10'.
Flowers: Reddish purple to lavender, petalless, to 1/4" wide; in clusters at branch ends; followed by whitish, tufted seedheads.
Leaves: Grayish, silvery-haired, linear to lance-shaped; to 1 1/4" long, 1/4" wide, occurring all along stem.
Blooms: May.
Elevation: Below 3,000'.
Habitat: Along rivers and streams.
Comments: Willowlike; forms dense thickets. Twigs covered with silvery, soft, flat hairs. Rank-smelling. Browsed by horses, cattle, and deer. Source of honey. Native Americans use stems for building huts and making baskets. One species of *Pluchea* (PLUE-keah) in Arizona. Photograph taken near Scottsdale, May 7.

ODORA   733
Poreleaf, hierba del venado ("herb of the deer")
Porophyllum gracile
Sunflower Family (Compositae)
Height: To 28".
Flowers: Purplish to purplish white, streaked with dark purple lines; petalless; flowerhead to 5/8" wide, 3/4" long, single at ends of branches; followed by numerous, gray bristles.
Leaves: Dark green, narrowly linear to threadlike, to 2" long.
Blooms: March–October.
Elevation: Below 4,000'.
Habitat: Dry, rocky slopes, mesas, and washes.
Comments: Perennial; many-branched; rank odor when crushed. Browsed by cattle and deer. Two species of *Porophyllum* (por-oh-FILL-uhm) in Arizona. Photograph taken at Saguaro National Monument East, April 15.

COOPER'S PAPERFLOWER 421
Paper daisy
Psilostrophe cooperi
Sunflower Family (Compositae)

Height: To 2'.
Flowers: Bright yellow, with varying number of broad rays, notched into 3 lobes; small disk flowers; to 1" wide; terminal on branches; turning papery with age; remaining on plant for weeks.
Leaves: Grayish green, woolly, linear; to 2 1/2" long.
Blooms: Most of the year.
Elevation: 2,000 to 5,000'.
Habitat: Plains, mesas, and along washes.
Comments: Forms a bushy mound with tangled branches. Three species of *Psilostrophe* (sye-loh-STROH-fee) in Arizona. Photograph taken in Superstition Mountains, March 26.

PAPERFLOWER 422
Paper daisy, woolly paperflower
Psilostrophe tagetina
Sunflower Family (Compositae)

Height: To 18".
Flowers: Bright yellow, with 3 to 5 petals; 3-lobed; to 3/4" wide, in clusters at ends of branches; becoming straw-colored and papery with age.
Leaves: Grayish green, very woolly, oblong to lance-shaped; twisted, growing along stems, to 2 1/2" long.
Blooms: May–October.
Elevation: 4,000 to 7,500'.
Habitat: Plains, mesas, and pine forest clearings.
Comments: A many-branched, aromatic, rounded plant. Poisonous to sheep. Three species of *Psilostrophe* (sye-loh-STROH-fee) in Arizona. Photograph taken near Nutrioso, August 18.

ORANGE SKYFLOWER 541
Pyrrocoma crocea (*Aplopappus croceus*) (*Haplopappus croceus*)
Sunflower Family (Compositae)

Height: To 16".
Flowers: Saffron-colored to dull orange rays, yellowish orange disks; to 2" wide; usually single, but occasionally up to 3 per stem.
Leaves: Dark green above, with prominent midvein beneath; alternate, clasping stem; basal; linear leaves to 6" long; smaller, arrow-shaped leaves on stem, to 1 1/2" long.
Blooms: July–October.
Elevation: 6,000 to 9,500'.
Habitat: Clearings in coniferous forests and mountain meadows.
Comments: Reddish, hairy stem. One species of *Pyrrocoma* (pye-roh-KOH-mah) in Arizona. Photograph of orange flower taken in vicinity of Greer, August 8. A yellow-rayed variety, *Pyrrocoma crocea* var. *genuflexa* (**PLATE 423**), photographed in vicinity of Willow Springs Lake, September 14.

DESERT-CHICORY   261
Desert-dandelion, goatsbeard, New Mexico plumeseed
Rafinesquia neomexicana
Sunflower Family (Compositae)

Height:	To 20".
Flowers:	White, ray flowers only; flowerheads to 1 1/2" wide.
Leaves:	Dark green, narrowly lobed, to 6" long at base, smaller on upper stem.
Blooms:	Mid-February–May.
Elevation:	200 to 3,000'.
Habitat:	From deserts to mesas.
Comments:	A weak-stemmed annual that usually grows among shrubs for support. Flower is similar to that of tackstem. Two species of *Rafinesquia* (raff-in-ESS-ki-ah) in Arizona. Photograph taken at Alamo Lake, February 26.

MEXICAN HAT   424
Upright prairie coneflower, yellow coneflower
Ratibida columnaris
Sunflower Family (Compositae)

Height:	To 3'.
Flowers:	Drooping rays, yellow with reddish brown or all reddish brown, to 1 1/2" long; disks are purplish brown and tubular, covering a cone-shaped column to 1 1/2" long; terminal flowerhead to 3" wide.
Leaves:	Green, narrow, pinnately cleft into 5, 7, or 9 narrow segments; to 6" long.
Blooms:	June–October.
Elevation:	5,000 to 8,500'.
Habitat:	Roadsides, fields, and open clearings in pine forests.
Comments:	Perennial herb. Two species of *Ratibida* (rat-i-BID-ah) in Arizona. Yellow flower photograph taken at Greer, July 21. Reddish flower, *Ratibida columnaris* var. *pulcherrima* (**PLATE 570**), photographed near Show Low, August 4.

CUTLEAF CONEFLOWER   425
Brown-eyed Susan
Rudbeckia laciniata
Sunflower Family (Compositae)

Height:	To 7'.
Flowers:	Yellow ray flowers arching downward to 2" long; tiny, greenish yellow disk flowers forming cone. Flowerhead to 5" wide.
Leaves:	Dark green, pinnate, leaves with 3 to 7 deeply toothed lobes; to 8" long.
Blooms:	July–September.
Elevation:	5,000 to 8,500'.
Habitat:	Rich soil in meadows, along mountain streams, and in moist canyons.
Comments:	Perennial herb. Poisonous to livestock. One species of *Rudbeckia* (rood-BECK-i-ah) in Arizona. Photograph taken south of Alpine, August 2.

NODDING GROUNDSEL   469
Bigelow groundsel
Senecio bigelovii
Sunflower Family (Compositae)

Height:	To 3'.
Flowers:	Yellow, all disk flowers; nodding flowerhead to 1/2" wide, 5/8" long, each on separate stalk; flowerheads on elongated cluster; followed by seedlike fruits with fine, white hairs attached.
Leaves:	Dark green, leathery, lance-shaped, toothed; clasping stem, alternate; to 7" long at base, progressively shorter toward flowerheads.
Blooms:	July–September.
Elevation:	7,000 to 11,000'.
Habitat:	Moist soil of roadsides, mountain meadows, and clearings in coniferous forests.
Comments:	Twenty-four species of *Senecio* (seh-NEE-sih-oh) in Arizona. Photograph taken in mountain meadow above Greer, August 10.

SAND WASH GROUNDSEL 426
Groundsel, comb butterweed
Senecio douglasii var. *douglasii* (*Senecio monoensis*)
Sunflower Family (Compositae)

Height:	To 5'.
Flowers:	Yellow rays, orange disks, to 1 1/2" wide.
Leaves:	Yellowish green, pinnate with linear lobes curling upward; comblike; to 2 1/2" long.
Blooms:	Most of the year.
Elevation:	2,500 to 7,500'.
Habitat:	Washes, dry slopes, mesas, and plains.
Comments:	Twenty-four species of *Senecio* (seh-NEE-sih-oh) in Arizona. Photograph taken in Tucson area, March 3. The comblike leaves help to identify this species.

THREADLEAF GROUNDSEL 427
Felty groundsel, old man, Douglas ragwort, creek senecio, squaw-weed
Senecio douglasii var. *longilobus* (*Senecio longilobus*)
Sunflower Family (Compositae)

Height:	To 4'.
Flowers:	8 to 13 yellow rays, yellowish orange disks; woolly bracts side by side; floppy petals; to 1 1/8" wide; in clusters.
Leaves:	Grayish green, very woolly, linear; divided into very narrow lobes; to 4" long.
Blooms:	Throughout most of year at lower elevations; May–November elsewhere.
Elevation:	2,500 to 7,500'.
Habitat:	Sandy washes, plains, and mesas.
Comments:	Many-branched, woolly stemmed shrub. Once used medicinally by Native Americans. Very poisonous if eaten by cattle or horses. Twenty-four species of *Senecio* (seh-NEE-sih-oh) in Arizona. Photograph taken near Portal, May 5. Unlike **BROOM GROUNDSEL** (*Senecio spartioides*), this species has woolly bracts and stems and divided, woolly leaves.

GROUNDSEL 428
Senecio eremophilus var. *macdougalii* (*Senecio macdougalii*)
(*Senecio ambrosioides*)
Sunflower Family (Compositae)

Height:	To 3'.
Flowers:	5 to 8 yellow rays, darker yellow disks; stamens curling upward; long, slender bracts tipped with black; flowerhead to 5/8" wide, 3/8" long.

Leaves:	Dark green, lance-shaped, slightly hairy; lobes deeply cleft almost to midvein; leaf to 5" long toward base; alternate and graduating in size upward on stem.
Blooms:	July–October.
Elevation:	6,500 to 10,500'.
Habitat:	Coniferous forests and clearings in aspen groves.
Comments:	Recognizable as a *Senecio* by its few ray flowers and as this particular species by its black-tipped bracts and its leaf shape. Twenty-four species of *Senecio* (seh-NEE-sih-oh) in Arizona. Photograph taken in mountains above Greer, August 13.

SENECIO   429
Senecio franciscanus
Sunflower Family (Compositae)

Height:	To 4", in tufts to 3" wide.
Flowers:	Yellow rays, orange disks; flowerhead to 1/2" wide, single or a few at tips of stems.
Leaves:	Grayish green, edged in reddish purple; oval to roundish, downy, crinkly, toothed; to 2" long.
Blooms:	July–August on San Francisco Peaks.
Elevation:	On San Francisco Peaks up to 12,000'.
Habitat:	Tundra on San Francisco Peaks.
Comments:	Stems are reddish. Found only in Arizona, this species is federally protected. Twenty-four species of *Senecio* (seh-NEE-sih-oh) in Arizona. Photograph taken at The Arboretum at Flagstaff, June 3.

LEMMON'S BUTTERWEED   430
Senecio lemmoni
Sunflower Family (Compositae)

Height:	To 3'.
Flowers:	Yellow rays, orange disks, to 1 1/8" wide.
Leaves:	Dark green, shiny, alternate; lance-shaped, clasping stem; sunken midvein, toothed, to 5" long.
Blooms:	February–May.
Elevation:	1,500 to 3,500'.
Habitat:	Along washes and on rocky slopes.
Comments:	Somewhat shrubby. Has reddish stems. Twenty-four species of *Senecio* (seh-NEE-sih-oh) in Arizona. Photograph taken at King Canyon, Tucson, April 17.

GROUNDSEL   432
Senecio multicapitatus
Sunflower Family (Compositae)

Height:	To 4'.
Flowers:	Yellow rays, yellowish orange disks; narrow, floppy petals; to 1" wide; in loose clusters.
Leaves:	Dark green, smooth, very narrow; threadlike segments; to 4" long, occurring all along stem.
Blooms:	May–November.
Elevation:	5,000 to 7,000'.
Habitat:	Clearings in pine forests, mesas, and plains.

Comments: Many-stemmed. Twenty-four species of *Senecio* (seh-NEE-sih-oh) in Arizona. Photograph taken at Upper Lake Mary, September 6. Unlike **THREADLEAF GROUNDSEL** (*Senecio douglasii*), this species has smooth bracts and stems, and smooth, undivided leaves.

AXHEAD BUTTERWEED   431
Senecio multilobatus
Sunflower Family (Compositae)

Height: To 14".
Flowers: Yellow rays, orangish disk flowers, to 1" wide; numerous flowerheads in wide, flat-topped cluster, with many clusters per plant.
Leaves: Dark green, divided into sharply toothed lobes or segments; to 4" long.
Blooms: May–August.
Elevation: 6,000 to 8,000'.
Habitat: Rocky slopes.
Comments: Several varieties of this species. Twenty-four species of *Senecio* (seh-NEE-sih-oh) in Arizona. Photograph taken at North Rim of Grand Canyon National Park, May 30.

NEW MEXICO BUTTERWEED   433
New Mexico groundsel
Senecio neomexicanus
Sunflower Family (Compositae)

Height: To 32".
Flowers: Yellow rays, darker yellow disk flowers; to 7/8" wide; in terminal cluster.
Leaves: Grayish green with woolly hairs; oval to lance-shaped; sharply saw-toothed, mostly basal; to 3" long; few and smaller leaves on stem.
Blooms: April–August.
Elevation: 3,000 to 9,000'.
Habitat: Pine forest and oak chaparral.
Comments: Perennial herb. Most abundant of *Senecio* species in Arizona. Twenty-four species of *Senecio* (seh-NEE-sih-oh) in Arizona. Photograph taken at Chiricahua National Monument, April 24.

SENECIO   434
Senecio quercetorum
Sunflower Family (Compositae)

Height: To 4'.
Flowers: Yellow rays, orange disks; to 1 1/4" wide.
Leaves: Dark green, pinnately lobed, toothed; end lobe to 3" long, side lobes shorter; leaf to 8" long; upper leaves smaller and clasping stem.
Blooms: March–May.
Elevation: 3,500 to 6,000'.
Habitat: Oak woodland areas.
Comments: Reddish to purplish hollow stems. Twenty-four species of *Senecio* (seh-NEE-sih-oh) in Arizona. Photograph taken northeast of Superior, April 20.

RAGWORT   435

Groundsel
Senecio salignus
Sunflower Family (Compositae)

Height:	To 7'.
Flowers:	Yellow, ray flowers vary in number from 2 to 8; flowerhead to 7/8" wide.
Leaves:	Dark green, willowlike, narrow; tapered at both ends; to 4" long.
Blooms:	February–May.
Elevation:	2,500 to 5,000'.
Habitat:	Along streams and moist washes.
Comments:	Sprawling bush. Twenty-four species of *Senecio* (seh-NEE-sih-oh) in Arizona. Photograph taken at Harshaw, April 27.

BROOM GROUNDSEL   436

Grass-leaved ragwort, broom senecio
Senecio spartioides
Sunflower Family (Compositae)

Height:	To 2'.
Flowers:	8 yellow, slightly drooping rays, each with 2 notches; orange disks; flowerhead to 3/4" wide.
Leaves:	Dark green, alternate, very narrow; some with narrow lobes; to 3" long, along length of stem.
Blooms:	July–October.
Elevation:	6,500 to 9,000'.
Habitat:	Clearings in pine forests.
Comments:	A bushlike plant with numerous stems. Twenty-four species of *Senecio* (seh-NEE-sih-oh) in Arizona. Photograph taken in vicinity of Nelson Reservoir, August 16.

WOOTON'S BUTTERWEED   437

Senecio wootonii
Sunflower Family (Compositae)

Height:	To 2'.
Flowers:	Yellow, 8 to 10 irregularly shaped rays; darker yellow disks; to 5/8" wide; in loose, terminal clusters.
Leaves:	Grayish green, leathery, smooth; toothed or untoothed; spatula- to spoon-shaped with long, tapering, flat stalk; basal, to 10" long.
Blooms:	May–September.
Elevation:	6,000 to 9,500'.
Habitat:	Coniferous forests.
Comments:	Has leafless stem. Twenty-four species of *Senecio* (seh-NEE-sih-oh) in Arizona. Photograph taken at Carnero Lake near Greer, July 11.

MILK THISTLE   734

Lady's thistle, holy thistle
Silybum marianum
Sunflower Family (Compositae)

Height:	Flower stem to 6'.
Flowers:	Purplish red flowerhead, to 2" wide; curved spines on bracts surrounding flowerhead; to 1 1/2" long on stout, erect stem.

Leaves:	Shiny green with white blotches and veins; margins lobed and spiny; to 18" long, 12" wide.
Blooms:	May–September.
Elevation:	Below 3,000'.
Habitat:	Roadsides, wasteland, and fields.
Comments:	Annual, sometimes biennial, field weed; hard to eliminate. Native of Europe, now naturalized in parts of U.S. One species of *Silybum* (sil-LYE-bum) in Arizona. Photograph of leaves and undeveloped flowers taken at Hassayampa River Preserve, Wickenburg, May 7.

TALL GOLDENROD   474
Yellow-weed
Solidago altissima
Sunflower Family (Compositae)

Height:	To 5'.
Flowers:	Bright yellow, heads to 1/4" wide, 1/8" long; forming a pyramidal, terminal cluster with flowers mostly on one side.
Leaves:	Green and lance-shaped; to 6" long, gradually smaller on upper stem.
Blooms:	August–October.
Elevation:	2,500 to 8,500'.
Habitat:	Roadsides and clearings.
Comments:	Perennial herb. A variable species. Nine species of *Solidago* (sol-i-DAY-go) in Arizona. Photograph taken at Willow Springs Lake, August 5.

CANADA GOLDENROD   475
Meadow goldenrod, yellow-weed, rock goldenrod
Solidago canadensis
Sunflower Family (Compositae)

Height:	To 6'.
Flowers:	Bright yellow, tiny, to 1/8" long; on arching stems in a large, loose, terminal cluster.
Leaves:	Dark green, narrowly lance-shaped, with 3 prominent veins; to 5" long.
Blooms:	July–September.
Elevation:	3,000 to 8,500'.
Habitat:	Clearings in ponderosa forests, meadows, fields, and roadsides.
Comments:	Perennial herb. Nine species of *Solidago* (sol-i-DAY-go) in Arizona. Photograph taken at Dead Horse Ranch State Park, September 9.

DWARF GOLDENROD   476
Decumbent goldenrod
Solidago decumbens
Sunflower Family (Compositae)

Height:	Below 10".
Flowers:	Yellow rays, yellow disks; to 3/8" wide; in dense cylindrical, terminal cluster.
Leaves:	Dark green, alternate, smooth; often toothed at rounded tip; spatula-shaped but variable; to 3" long at base; upper leaves smaller.
Blooms:	July–August.
Elevation:	8,000 to 9,500'.
Habitat:	Clearings in coniferous forests and mountain meadows.

Comments: Has reddish stems, which often creep along the ground for a few inches before growing erect. Often grows in small patches. Nine species of *Solidago* (sol-i-DAY-go) in Arizona. Photograph taken in mountains above Greer, August 7.

MISSOURI GOLDENROD 477
Prairie goldenrod
Solidago missouriensis
Sunflower Family (Compositae)

Height: To 3'.
Flowers: Bright yellow, to 1/4" long, 1/8" wide; about 8 in each flowerhead; in tight cluster, total flowering cluster to 6" long; on slightly arching stem.
Leaves: Dark green, shiny, smooth; alternate, lance-shaped, margins curved upward; basal leaves to 7" long, 3/4" wide; shorter, narrower leaves up stem, with small clusters of tiny leaves at leaf axils.
Blooms: June–August.
Elevation: 5,000 to 9,000'.
Habitat: Along streams and clearings in pine forests.
Comments: Perennial herb; has smooth, reddish stem. Native Americans use leaves as salad greens. Nine species of *Solidago* (sol-i-DAY-go) in Arizona. Photograph taken near Christopher Creek, August 11. Recognizable by smooth leaves and stem, and by close arrangement of flowers on arching stem.

ALPINE GOLDENROD 478
Solidago multiradiata
Sunflower Family (Compositae)

Height: To 16".
Flowers: Yellow, up to 13 rays, each to 5/8" wide, 3/4" long; in tight, terminal cluster.
Leaves: Dark green, alternate, smooth; broadly spatula-shaped and tapering to stem; to 4" long. Stem leaves are stalkless.
Blooms: July–September.
Elevation: Not available. Photograph taken at 9,500'.
Habitat: Mountain meadows and clearings in moist coniferous forests.
Comments: Has erect stem. Nine species of *Solidago* (sol-i-DAY-go) in Arizona. Photograph taken in mountains above Greer, August 7.

SPARSE-FLOWERED GOLDENROD 479
Solidago sparsiflora
Sunflower Family (Compositae)

Height: To 2'.
Flowers: Bright yellow, to 1/4" wide, 1/8" long; about a dozen in each flowerhead; in clusters to 1 1/4" wide on one side of arching stem; total flowering clusters to 7" long.
Leaves: Dull grayish green, alternate, rough; lance-shaped to linear, with 3 prominent veins; to 3" long.
Blooms: June–October.
Elevation: 2,000 to 8,500'.
Habitat: Roadsides, chaparral, and clearings in pine forests.
Comments: Perennial herb. Nine species of *Solidago* (sol-i-DAY-go) in Arizona. Photograph taken near McNary, August 10. Recognizable by its rough-textured leaves and loose, sparse flowers on arching stem.

COMMON SOWTHISTLE 454

Annual sowthistle
Sonchus oleraceus
Sunflower Family (Compositae)

Height:	To 5'.
Flowers:	Yellow, dandelionlike flowerhead to 1 1/4" wide; in sparse clusters; followed by seeds ribbed lengthwise, attached to soft white hairs forming a miniature parachute.
Leaves:	Dark green, thin, deeply lobed into 1 to 3 lobes on each side; tip lobe broadly triangular; clasping stem; to 7" long.
Blooms:	February–November.
Elevation:	150 to 7,000'.
Habitat:	Waste areas, roadsides, and disturbed places.
Comments:	Fleshy annual. Naturalized from Europe. Birds feed on seeds. Two species of *Sonchus* (SOHN-kuss) in Arizona. Photograph taken near Granite Reef Dam, March 1. A similar species, **SPINY SOWTHISTLE** (*Sonchus asper*), has prickly toothed leaves.

DESERT STRAW 726

Small-flowered wire-lettuce
Stephanomeria pauciflora
Sunflower Family (Compositae)

Height:	To 2'.
Flowers:	Lavender, with deep pink stamens; all rays, toothed, to 3/4" wide; followed by fruits with brownish, feathery bristles.
Leaves:	Bluish green with whitish midrib; narrow, smooth, sharply lobed; to 3" long at base of plant; sparsely leaved on upper stems.
Blooms:	Almost throughout the year.
Elevation:	150 to 7,000'.
Habitat:	Washes and dry, sandy plains and slopes.
Comments:	Perennial herb. Many-branched with bluish green stems. Smooth stems and leaves. Seven species of *Stephanomeria* (steff-an-oh-MER-i-ah) in Arizona. Photograph taken at Fort Bowie, May 8.

THURBER'S STEPHANOMERIA 727

Thurber's wire lettuce
Stephanomeria thurberi
Sunflower Family (Compositae)

Height:	To 3'.
Flowers:	Lavender; up to 20 rays, each tipped with 6 shallow notches; purplish stamens; pointed bracts tipped with purple; flower to 5/8" wide, 3/4" long, on 1/2"-long stem, followed by bright white, feathery bristles.
Leaves:	Grayish green, mostly basal, alternate; pinnately cleft with lobes turned backward; clasping stem; leaf to 6" long. Upper leaves, few, entire, linear, short.
Blooms:	April–August.
Elevation:	4,000 to 8,000'.
Habitat:	Clearings in pinyon-juniper and ponderosa pine forests.
Comments:	Erect stem, branched above. Seven species of *Stephanomeria* (steff-an-oh-MER-i-ah) in Arizona. Photograph taken at Oak Creek Canyon, June 8.

STEVIA   236
Stevia lemmoni
Sunflower Family (Compositae)

Height: To 3'.
Flowers: White, tubular, 5-lobed, with long stamens; flower to 1/8" wide, 1/2" long; in clusters to 2" wide.
Leaves: Grayish green, very hairy, rough; linear to elliptical, opposite, to 1 1/2" long; in clusters along brownish stems.
Blooms: February–May.
Elevation: 2,500 to 5,500'.
Habitat: Rocky slopes and canyons.
Comments: Many-branched, mound-shaped shrub. Five species of *Stevia* (STEE-vi-ah) in Arizona. Photograph taken in vicinity of Kitt Peak, April 18.

COMMON DANDELION   455
"Tramp with a golden crown"
Taraxacum officinale
Sunflower Family (Compositae)

Height: Flower stalks to 15".
Flowers: Golden yellow flowerhead, straplike ray flowers toothed at tips; flowerhead to 1 1/2" wide; solitary on hollow stalk; followed by downy, globular mass with seeds attached to parachutelike hairs.
Leaves: Dark green, lance-shaped, deeply cut into triangular-shaped sections; in basal rosette; to 10" long.
Blooms: April–September.
Elevation: 100 to 9,000'.
Habitat: Roadsides, lawns, meadows, and fields.
Comments: Perennial weed, with deep taproot and milky stem juice. From Europe; now naturalized. Used for food and medicine. Three species of *Taraxacum* (ta-RACKS-a-kum) in Arizona. Photograph taken near Greer, July 4.

GRAY FELT THORN   470
Spineless horseweed, black sage, gray tetradymia, spineless horsebrush
Tetradymia canescens
Sunflower Family (Compositae)

Height: Rounded shrub to 2' tall, 5' wide.
Flowers: Yellow, petalless, 4 disk flowers per head; 4 woolly bracts surrounding head; to 5/8" long; in terminal clusters on branches; followed by tan bristles to 3/4" long.
Leaves: Grayish green, stiff, woolly, narrow; to 1/2" long; growing along entire stem.
Blooms: June–October.
Elevation: 5,000 to 8,000'.
Habitat: Rocky, sandy, dry soils in woodlands; clearings in ponderosa pine forests; and roadsides.
Comments: Has a woody base and many branches. Native Americans use plants medicinally. Safely browsed by cattle, but often fatal to sheep when consumed in large quantities. Two species of *Tetradymia* (teh-truh-DIH-mih-uh) in Arizona. Photograph taken near Aripine, August 4.

HOPI-TEA GREENTHREAD   471
Colorado greenthread, cota
Thelesperma megapotamicum
Sunflower Family (Compositae)

Height: To 3'.
Flowers: Yellow disk flowers surrounded by green bracts; rayless; to 1/2" wide, 1/2" long; terminal on long, leafless stems.
Leaves: Dark green, pinnate, linear; 3 to 7 threadlike segments; mainly basal, opposite, leaf to 4" long.
Blooms: May–October.
Elevation: 4,000 to 7,500'.
Habitat: Open woodlands and forest, plains, roadsides, and mesas.
Comments: Annual herb. Hopi Indians used flowers and young leaves for making tea. A dye extracted from plant is used for textiles and basketry. Three species of *Thelesperma* (thel-eh-SPUR-mah) in Arizona. Photograph taken at Black Canyon Lake, September 29.

STEMLESS DAISY   259
Easter daisy
Townsendia exscapa
Sunflower Family (Compositae)

Height: To 2".
Flowers: Very narrow, white to pale pink rays; pinkish on undersides; yellow disk flowers; flowerhead to 2" wide; stemless; occurring singly, or in cluster nestled among rosette of leaves.
Leaves: Dark green, narrow; linear to spatula-shaped, hairy; to 2" long, in basal rosette.
Blooms: March–August.
Elevation: 4,500 to 7,000'.
Habitat: Mesas, hillsides, and clearings in ponderosa forests and oak woodlands.
Comments: Perennial. Five species of *Townsendia* (town-ZEN-di-ah) in Arizona. Photograph taken in Sharp Creek area northeast of Christopher Creek, April 22. (Much variation in flowers in this location, from all white disk flowers to pinkish, spoon-shaped rays on other specimens.)

TOWER DAISY   258
Townsendia formosa
Sunflower Family (Compositae)

Height: To 20".
Flowers: White, with pointed rays above, purplish tinge beneath; yellow disk flowers; daisylike, solitary; to 2 1/2" wide; on tall, unbranched stem.
Leaves: Green, spatula-shaped, to 1 3/4" long; in basal rosette. Small, linear leaves along stem.
Blooms: June–September.
Elevation: 7,000 to 9,500'.
Habitat: Wet meadows and hillsides in moist coniferous forests.
Comments: Five species of *Townsendia* (town-ZEN-di-ah) in Arizona. Photograph taken south of Alpine, August 2.

YELLOW SALSIFY   456A and B

Meadow salsify, moonflower, yellow goatsbeard, goat dandelion
Tragopogon dubius
Sunflower Family (Compositae)

Height: To 3'.
Flowers: Lemon-yellow, individual ray flowers to 1/2" long; 10 to 13 bracts longer than ray
           flowers; open in morning, closed by noon; flowerhead to 2 1/2" wide; followed by a
           large, spherical seedhead resembling a giant dandelion.
Leaves: Grayish green, long, grasslike; clasping stem; to 10" long.
Blooms: June–September.
Elevation: 3,500 to 7,000'.
Habitat: Dry roadsides, fields, and vacant lots.
Comments: Perennial herb. Introduced from Europe; now naturalized. Stems release milky sap
           when broken. Native Americans used plant for food and medicine. Five species of
           Tragopogon (tra-go-POH-gon) in Arizona. Photograph in flower taken near
           Prescott, May 26. Photograph in seed taken near Show Low, July 22.

TRIXIS   472

Trixis californica
Sunflower Family (Compositae)

Height: Sprawling shrub to 3 1/2'.
Flowers: Bright yellow, rayless, surrounded by leaflike bracts; flowerheads composed
           of 9 to 15 flowers, to 3/4" wide, at branch ends; followed by seeds with straw-
           colored bristles.
Leaves: Dark green, lance-shaped, smooth-edged to fine-toothed; numerous; to 1/2" wide,
           2" long.
Blooms: February–October.
Elevation: Below 5,000'.
Habitat: Rocky slopes, along washes, among other bushes.
Comments: Browsed by cattle. One species of *Trixis* (TRIX-is) in Arizona. Photograph taken at
           Usery Mountain Recreation Area, March 1.

GOLDEN CROWNBEARD   438

Crownbeard, cow pasture-daisy, cowpen daisy, girasolillo, butter-daisy,
hierba de la bruja
Verbesina encelioides
Sunflower Family (Compositae)

Height: To 3'.
Flowers: Yellow rays, each notched into 3 lobes; yellow disk flowers; to 2" wide.
Leaves: Grayish green, triangular, with toothed margins; to 4" long.
Blooms: Early germinations, March–July; later germinations, July–December.
Elevation: Below 7,000'.
Habitat: Roadsides, waste areas, and washes.
Comments: Annual. Flattened seedhead covered with grayish brown hairs gave rise to name,
           "crownbeard." Rodents and birds eat seeds. Native Americans and early settlers
           used plant to treat skin diseases and boils. Hopi Indians use water of steeped plant
           for treating spider bites. Three species of *Verbesina* (ver-be-SY-nah) in Arizona.
           Photograph taken near Salome, March 28.

ANNUAL GOLDENEYE   439
Annual viguiera
Viguiera annua
Sunflower Family (Compositae)

Height: To 3'.
Flowers: Yellow, pointed rays, yellowish orange disks, flat at first, later cone-shaped; flowerhead to 7/8" wide; terminal, and numerous on branches.
Leaves: Dark green, very narrow, rough, opposite and alternate; with margins rolled under; to 2 1/2" long, 1/8" wide.
Blooms: May–October.
Elevation: 2,500 to 7,000'.
Habitat: Roadsides, fields, and hillsides.
Comments: In fall, turns hillsides golden yellow, especially in Yavapai County. Forage for sheep. Eight species of *Viguiera* (veh-GWARE-ah or vig-wee-AIR-ah) in Arizona. Photograph taken north of Payson, September 30. This species of *Viguiera* recognizable by its numerous small flowers and very narrow leaves with margins rolled under.

PARISH VIGUIERA   440
Viguiera deltoidea var. *parishii*
Sunflower Family (Compositae)

Height: Shrub to 4'.
Flowers: Yellow rays with lighter yellow tips; darker yellow disks; to 1 1/4" wide; solitary, on long stalks at branch tips.
Leaves: Dark green, shiny, crinkled, mostly opposite; triangular-shaped, hairy, toothed; to 1 1/2" long.
Blooms: February–June.
Elevation: 1,000 to 3,500'.
Habitat: Rocky slopes, canyons, and mesas.
Comments: Many-branched, with grayish bark. Eight species of *Viguiera* (veh-GWARE-ah or vig-wee-AIR-ah) in Arizona. Photograph taken in vicinity of Tortilla Flat, March 19.

GOLDENEYE   441
Viguiera longifolia
Sunflower Family (Compositae)

Height: To 3'.
Flowers: Yellow rays, darker yellow disks, large bracts; to 2" wide; at tips of slender stalks.
Leaves: Shiny, dark green, willowlike; lance-shaped to linear; to 2" long.
Blooms: July–October.
Elevation: 4,500 to 8,000'.
Habitat: Clearings in ponderosa pine forests.
Comments: Perennial herb. Many-branched with reddish stems. Eight species of *Viguiera* (veh-GWARE-ah or vig-wee-AIR-ah) in Arizona. Photograph taken at Upper Lake Mary, September 2.

MANY-FLOWERED VIGUIERA   442
Golden-eye, resin-weed
Viguiera multiflora
Sunflower Family (Compositae)

Height:	To 4'.
Flowers:	Yellow ray flowers, darker yellow disk flowers tinged with brown; disk is flat but as flower fades it becomes cone-shaped. Green bracts beneath flowerhead are in 3 layers: lowest are long and turn down; middle ones are short and turn down; upper ones are short and turn up. Flowerhead to 2 1/2" wide, terminal on stem.
Leaves:	Green, lance-shaped, opposite on lower stem; to 2 1/4" long, 3/8" wide.
Blooms:	May–October.
Elevation:	4,500 to 9,500'.
Habitat:	Mountain meadows, slopes, and ponderosa pine forests.
Comments:	Perennial herb, with branches. Eight species of *Viguiera* (veh-GWARE-ah or vig-wee-AIR-ah) in Arizona. Photograph taken near Willow Springs Lake, September 13. This species of *Viguiera* recognizable by its layers of bracts and larger flowers and leaves.

ARIZONA MULES EARS   443
Wyethia arizonica
Sunflower Family (Compositae)

Height:	To 2'.
Flowers:	Bright yellow, 10 to 15 rays, yellow disk flowers; to 2 1/2" wide; solitary at tip of stem.
Leaves:	Dark green, with white midstripe; hairy, with wavy margins; oblong or elliptical; basal leaves to 1 1/2' long, 3" wide; stem leaves much shorter.
Blooms:	June–August.
Elevation:	7,000 to 9,000'.
Habitat:	Slopes and canyons in ponderosa pine forests.
Comments:	Perennial herb. Two species of *Wyethia* (wy-EE-thee-ah) in Arizona. Photograph taken in Mormon Lake area, June 2.

SANDPAPER MULES EARS   444
Mule's ears
Wyethia scabra
Sunflower Family (Compositae)

Height:	To 30".
Flowers:	Yellow rays, yellowish brown disks; long, spiny bracts on flowerhead turned downward; to 3" wide.
Leaves:	Shiny, dark green, sandpapery, with whitish midvein; finely toothed, narrowly lance-shaped, mostly basal; to 20" long, shorter on stem.
Blooms:	June–October.
Elevation:	5,000 to 6,000'.
Habitat:	Dry slopes and mesas, often in very sandy conditions.
Comments:	Perennial herb. Two species of *Wyethia* (wy-EE-thee-ah) in Arizona. Photograph taken south of Kayenta, June 27.

COMMON COCKLEBUR   810
Clotbur
Xanthium strumarium (*Xanthium saccharatum*)
Sunflower Family (Compositae)

Height:	To 4'.

Flowers:	Male: tiny, in clusters at top of stem; female: spiny, oval, brown burs to 1 1/2" long in leaf axils. Bur encloses 2 female flowers covered with hundreds of stiff, hooked prickles.
Leaves:	Yellowish green, heart-shaped, coarsely toothed; rough, glandular, long-stalked; to 14" long, 8" wide.
Blooms:	June–October.
Elevation:	100 to 6,000'.
Habitat:	Waste areas, roadsides, and cultivated fields.
Comments:	Bushy annual. Spiny burs get tangled in fur and fabric; 2 seeds inside each bur. Seeds and young plants are poisonous to livestock, especially chickens and hogs. Two species of *Xanthium* (zan-THEE-uhm) in Arizona. Photograph taken north of Payson, September 2.

WILD ZINNIA   257

White zinnia, spinyleaf zinnia
Zinnia acerosa (*Zinnia pumila*)
Sunflower Family (Compositae)

Height:	To 10".
Flowers:	4 or 6 white or light yellow ray flowers; yellow disk flowers, semi-drooping, to 1" wide; on dense-growing, rounded clumps.
Leaves:	Grayish green, very narrow, stiff; to 1" long.
Blooms:	March–October.
Elevation:	2,000 to 5,000'.
Habitat:	Dry mesas and slopes.
Comments:	Perennial. Three species of *Zinnia* (ZIN-i-ah) in Arizona. Photograph taken near Why, March 30.

PRAIRIE ZINNIA   445

Wild zinnia, Rocky Mountain zinnia, plains zinnia, zacate pastor, desert zinnia, little golden zinnia
Zinnia grandiflora
Sunflower Family (Compositae)

Height:	To 1'.
Flowers:	Bright yellow, 3 to 6 ray flowers, reddish disk flowers in center; to 1 1/2" wide; occurring singly on tips of branches.
Leaves:	Grayish green, linear, very narrow; somewhat curled; to 1" long; all along stem.
Blooms:	May–October.
Elevation:	4,000 to 6,500'.
Habitat:	Mesas, dry plains, roadsides, and pinyon-juniper woodlands.
Comments:	Spreading, many-branched herb forming rounded clump. Three species of *Zinnia* (ZIN-i-ah) in Arizona. Photograph taken near Wupatki National Monument, September 8.

GLOSSARY

Acaulis, -e	Stemless.
Acerosus, -a, -um	Stiff-needled; sharp.
Achene (ah-KEEN)	A small, dry fruit that does not split open; one-seeded.
Acris	Biting or acrid.
Acuminate	Tapering to a point.
Acute	Sharp-pointed.
Aduncus, -a, -um	Hooked or bent backward.
Alatus, -a, -um	Winged.
Albicans	Whitish.
Alternate	Not opposite each other (as leaves on a stem).
Ambiguus, -a, -um	Uncertain (as in a plant's identity).
Angled	Sided (as in the shape of fruits).
Angularis, -e	Angled.
Angustifolius, -a, -um	Narrow-leaved.
Annuus, -a, -um	Annual.
Annual	A plant that completes its life cycle in one season.
Anther	The part of a stamen bearing pollen.
Arenarius, -a, -um	Growing in sand.
Areole	A raised area in a cactus from which spines develop.
Argenteus, -a, -um	Silvery.
Arvensis, -e	Of the fields.
Asper, -a, -um	Rough.
Asymmetrical	Irregular; not divided into like and equal parts.
Aureus, -a, -um	Golden.
Axil	The angle where the leafstalk or flowerstalk joins the stem.
Banner	The upper petal in a pea flower, or the three erect petals of an iris flower.
Barbatus, -a, -um	Bearded or barbed.
Barbed	With a backward-facing tip; resembling a fishhook.
Basal	At or near the base (as leaves).
Berry	A fleshy or pulpy fruit that does not usually split open and that has one or more seeds.
Biennial	A plant that completes its life cycle in two years, growing vegetation in the first year and flowers and seeds in the second, then dying.
Biflorus, -a, -um	Double-flowered.
Bifolius, -a, -um	Double-leaved.
Bipinnate	Describes compound leaves having secondary leaflets that are also pinnate.
Blade	The portion of a leaf not including the stalk.
Bloom	White, powderlike coating.
Bract	A modified leaf at base of flowerhead or fruit.
Bracteatus, -a, -um	Bearing bracts.
Brevicaulis, -e	Short-stemmed.
Brevipes	Short-stalked.

Bristle	A stiff, hairlike structure.
Bud	A developing stem, leaf, or flower.
Bur	A spiny or prickly fruit or seed.
Calyx	Collectively, the group of sepals that encircle flower parts.
Campaniflorus, -a,-um	Having bell-shaped flowers.
Canescens	Having grayish white hairs.
Capsule	A dry fruit divided into two or more seed compartments that split longitudinally or, uncommonly, around the circumference.
Cardinalis, -e	Scarlet.
Catkin	A long cluster of tiny, petalless flowers, often all one sex, also called an "ament."
Caudatus, -a, -um	Tailed.
Cell	A chamber or compartment (as in a seed).
Chaparral	An area dense with leathery-leaved, evergreen shrubs.
Chlorophyll	A green, photosynthetic substance found in plants.
Clasping leaf	A leaf with leafstalk wrapped around a stem.
Cleft	Cut about halfway (as in a leaf).
Coccineus, -a, -um	Scarlet.
Column	A center structure in a flower formed by united stamens, or stamens united with style or stigma.
Complete	Describes flowers with petals, sepals, pistils, and stamens.
Composite	A flower that is a member of the sunflower family.
Compound	Describes a leaf divided into two or more smaller leaflets.
Cone	A dry fruit with overlapping, woody scales.
Conifer	An evergreen, needled, cone-bearing tree or shrub.
Cordatus, -a, -um	Heart-shaped.
Corm	An enlarged base of a stem, resembling a bulb.
Corolla	Collectively, all the petals of a flower.
Crassifolius, -a, -um	Thick-leaved.
Cristatus, -a, -um	Crested or comblike.
Crown	The top branches, twigs, and leaves of a tree.
Deciduous	Describes a plant that sheds its leaves or other parts at a certain time or season.
Deltoides, -deus, -a, -um	Triangular.
Demissus, -a, -um	Weak or low-hanging.
Densiflorus, -a, -um	Densely flowered.
Dentation	The toothed edges of leaves or leaflets.
Dentatus, -a, -um	Toothed.
Depressus, -a, -um	Flat.
Dicot or Dicotyledon	A plant having two seed leaves (cotyledons); one of the two major divisions of flowering plants.
Digitatus, -a, -um	Fingerlike.
Dioecious (dye-EE-shus)	Describes a species with female and male flowers on separate plants.
Disk flowers	Tiny, tubular flowers, often forming the center "button" on a composite flower.
Dissected	Finely cut or divided into many, narrow segments (as in a leaf).
Diversifolius, -a, -um	With different leaf shapes.

Drupe	A fleshy fruit with a hard stone or nut in its center.
Edulis, -e	Edible.
Elatus, -a, -um	Tall.
Elegans	Elegant.
Elliptical	Wider in the center and tapering at base and tip (as in a leaf).
Entire	Without teeth or notches on margins (as leaves and petals).
Ephemeral	Describes a plant or flower that lasts a very short time.
Erectus, -a, -um	Upright.
Escapee	A plant that escaped from cultivation and now reproduces on its own.
Evergreen	A plant having green leaves all year; describing such a plant.
Fasciculatus, -a, -um	In a tight cluster.
Female flowers	Flowers with pistils but no functional stamens.
Filament	The thin stalk of a stamen supporting an anther at its tip.
Filifolius, -a, -um	Having fine or threadlike foliage.
Floret	A single, small flower.
Flower	The reproductive parts of a seed plant.
Follicle	A dry, many-seeded fruit opening along one side only.
Frond	A fern leaf.
Fruit	A mature ovary, containing one or more seeds.
Fruticosus, -a, -um	Shrubby.
Giganteus, -a, -um	Large.
Glaber, -ra, -rum	Hairless, smooth.
Glandular	Producing tiny globules of sticky or oily substance (as in a leaf or stem).
Glaucus, -a, -um	Having a white or grayish powder or bloom.
Globosus, -a, -um	Globe-shaped.
Glochids	Barbed bristles on cacti.
Gracilis, -e	Slender and graceful.
Grandiflorus, -a, -um	Large-flowered.
Habitat	The environment where a plant lives.
Herbaceous	Fleshy-stemmed; not woody.
Herbs	Fleshy, nonwoody plants.
Hip	A fleshy, berrylike fruit (as in some members of the rose family).
Hirsutus, -a, -um	Hairy.
Hispidus, -a, -um	Rough-haired.
Hooked	Curved at the tip.
Host	A plant furnishing nourishment to a parasite.
Hybrid	The offspring of cross-fertilization between two different species.
Imperfect	Describes a flower having stamens or pistils, but not both.
Inferior	Describes an ovary low in a flower, with petals and calyx lobes above.
Integer, intergra, -um	Whole, with no cut.
Involucre	A circle of bracts or leaves supporting a flowerhead.
Irregular	Describes a flower that is not radially symmetrical, with parts of unequal size or shape.
Joint	Segment of a stem (as in a cactus), or a plant node (as where leaves join the stem).

Keel	The fused lower petals of a member of the pea family, or in some species, the single lower petal; the ridge on some seeds or fruits.
Key	A dry, one-seeded fruit with a wing or wings, also called a "samara" (as in maple or ash seeds).
Lanceolatus, -a, -um	Lance-shaped.
Lanceolate	Lance-shaped, or narrow and tapering at the tip (as a leaf shape).
Latifolius, -a, -um	Having wide leaves.
Leaflet	One segment of a compound leaf.
Leafstalk	An appendage attaching a leaf to the plant's main stem.
Legume	A seed pod (as in the pea family) that splits along two sides; a member of the pea family.
Linear	Long and narrow with parallel margins (as a leaf shape).
Linearifolius, -a, -um	Having narrow, parallel-sided leaves.
Lip	The upper or lower segment of an irregular (or asymmetrical) flower.
Lobatus, -a, -um	Divided into lobes.
Lobed	Describes leaves with marginal indentations that dissect less than halfway, and their associated rounded projections.
Longiflorus, -a, -um	Long-flowered.
Longifolius, -a, -um	Long-leaved.
Luteus, -a, -um	Yellow.
Macrocarpus, -a, -um	Having large seed pods or fruits.
Macropetalus, -a, -um	Large-petaled.
Macrophyllus, -a, -um	Large-leaved.
Maculatus, -a, -um	Blotched or spotted.
Male flowers	Flowers with stamens, but no functioning pistils.
Margin	The edge of a leaf or petal.
Marginatus, -a, -um	Pertaining to margins or edges.
Micranthus, -a, -um	Small-flowered.
Microcarpus, -a, -um	Having tiny seed pods or fruits.
Micropetalus, -a, -um	Small-petaled.
Microphyllus, -a, -um	Small-leaved.
Mollis, -e	Soft-haired.
Monocot or Monocotyledon	A plant having one seed leaf (cotyledon); one of the two major divisions of flowering plants.
Monoecious (mo-NEE-shus)	Describes a species with separate male and female flowers on same plant.
Naturalized	Describes plants from another region that have established themselves with the native flora.
Needle	The long, narrow leaf of some conifers.
Nervosus, -a, -um	Having prominent nerves (veins).
Node	The point on a stem where a leaf or bud sprouts.
Nut	A hard-shelled fruit with one seed.
Nutans	Nodding.
Nutlet	A small nut.
Odorus, -a, -um	Fragrant.
Opposite	Paired or opposite each other (as leaves on a stem).
Oval	Broadly elliptical or egg-shaped.

Ovary	The base of a pistil where female germ cells develop into seeds after fertilization.
Ovatus, -a, -um	Egg-shaped.
Palmately compound	Describes leaves divided or lobed from one point (as fingers growing from palm of hand).
Palustris, -e	Growing in wet areas.
Pappus	A scale, hair, or bristle on the tip of an achene (as on seeds of a dandelion).
Parasite	An organism obtaining nourishment from a host organism.
Parviflorus, -a, -um	Small-flowered.
Patulus, -a, -um	Spreading.
Pedicel	A flowerstalk.
Perennial	A plant living more than two years.
Perfect	Describes a flower with both male and female organs.
Perianth	Collectively, the calyx and/or corolla.
Petal	One of the segments of the corolla, usually colored.
Petiole	A leaf stem.
Phyllary	One of the bracts below the flowerhead in members of the sunflower family.
Pictus, -a, -um	Painted or variegated.
Pinna	A compound leaf division or leaflet (plural: "pinnae").
Pinnatus, -a, -um	Divided or lobed.
Pinnately compound	Describes leaves divided or lobed along each side of a leafstalk, resembling a feather.
Pinnule	A subleaflet of a fern frond or other twice-compound leaf.
Pistil	The female organ of a flower, composed of an ovary, a slender style, and a stigma or stigmas at tip.
Pistillate	Describes a female flower bearing one or more pistils but no functional stamens.
Pod	A dry fruit that splits open when mature.
Pollen	Spores, borne by the anthers, that contain the male germ cells.
Pollination	The transfer of pollen from anther to stigma.
Pome	A fleshy fruit having several seeds (as an apple).
Prickle	A weak or rigid outgrowth from bark or other tissue.
Procumbens	Trailing or lying down.
Prostrate	Lying horizontally.
Pubescens	Having hairy-soft, short hairs.
Pumilus, -a, -um	Small.
Purpureus, -a, -um	Purple.
Pusillus, -a, -um	Small.
Raceme	An unbranched flower stem with stalked flowers, the newest flowers forming at its top.
Racemosus, -a, -um	Having flowers in racemes.
Rachis	That part of a fern frond stem bearing the leaflets, also called the axis; also, the main stalk of a flower cluster or of a compound leaf.
Radial spines	Spines emerging from the edges of an areole.
Radiatus, -a, -um	Raylike.
Ray flowers	Flat, straplike flowers on a member of the composite family.
Reflexus, -a, -um	Turned back on itself.

Regular	Describes a flower with petals or sepals all of equal size and shape; radially symmetrical.
Repens	Creeping.
Reticulatus, -a, -um	Netted.
Ribs	The raised rows on stems of cacti; the primary veins of leaves.
Rosette	A cluster of leaves in a circular arrangement at the base of a plant.
Rotundifolius, -a, -um	Round-leaved.
Rugosus, -a, -um	Wrinkled.
Samara	Dry fruit with wings that do not open when mature (as maple and ash seeds).
Saprophyte	A plant living off dead or decaying organic matter and usually lacking chlorophyll.
Scaber, -ra, -rum	Rough to touch.
Scale	A greatly reduced leaf or outgrowth on skin.
Seed	A mature ovule that has been fertilized.
Sepal	A calyx segment.
Sessile	Without a stalk or stem.
Shrub	A small, woody plant with several stems.
Simple	Describes a leaf with one part, not divided into leaflets.
Sori	Clusters of spore sacs on a fern frond.
Spike	A long flower cluster with each flower attached to the stalk, either directly or nearly so.
Spine	A sharp, stiff outgrowth on a plant stem.
Spinosus, -a, -um	Spiny.
Spore	The reproductive cell of a non-flowering plant.
Spur	The hollow, tubular projection from the base of a petal or sepal, often producing nectar; a short side twig on a tree.
Stamen	The male organ of a flower, composed of a slender stalk (filament) tipped with a pollen-producing anther.
Staminate	Describes a male flower having one or more stamens, but no functional pistils.
Stellatus, -a, -um	Star-shaped.
Stem	The part of the plant above ground where leaves and flowers appear.
Stigma	The tip of the pistil that receives pollen at pollination.
Stipe	That part of a fern frond stem below the rachis (below where leaflets are attached); the "leaf stem" of fern fronds.
Stipules	Small, leaflike, paired projections at the base of a leafstalk.
Style	The slender stalk of a pistil joining ovary and stigma.
Succulent	Fleshy, juicy, and thickened; a plant with those characteristics.
Superior ovary	An ovary high in a flower, above the joining of stamens, sepals, and petals.
Tendril	The coil of a modified stem or leaf, often used for support.
Terminal	At the end of branch or stem.
Thorn	A short, stiff, sharp-pointed branch.
Tomentosus, -a, -um	Covered with soft, matted, flat hairs.
Triflorus, -a, -um	Three-flowered.
Trifoliatus, -a, -um	Three-leaved.
Tripinnate	Divided three times.

Tubercle	A knoblike projection (as on a cactus joint).
Tubular	Describes a flower with united petals forming a tube.
Twining	Climbing by coiling around something.
Umbel	An umbrella-shaped flower cluster with all flowerstalks evolving from same point.
Umbellatus, -a, -um	Having flowers in umbels.
Undulatus, -a, -um	Wavy.
Uniflorus, -a, -um	One-flowered.
United	Describes petals fused together.
Variegatus, -a, -um	Having markings of a different color than the basic color.
Versicolor	Having variable colors.
Villosus, -a, -um	With long, loose hairs.
Viridiflorus, -a, -um	With green flowers.
Viscosus, -a, -um	Sticky.
Vulgaris, -e	Common.
Whorl	Three or more leaves or flower parts radiating outward from a stem node.
Wing	A thin, paperlike flap on a seed capsule, stem, or flower.
Woolly	Having soft, woollike hairs.

Parts of a Flower

Pistil = stigma, style, and ovary

Corolla = all the petals

Calyx = all the sepals

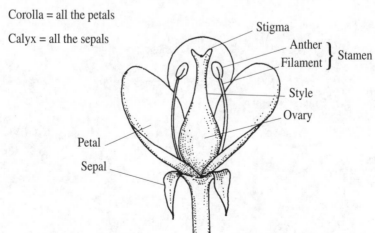

REFERENCES

Arnberger, Leslie P. *Flowers of the Southwest Mountains.* Globe, AZ: Southwestern Monuments Association, 1962.

Baerg, Harry J. *How to Know the Western Trees.* Dubuque, IA: C. Brown Company Publishers, 1973.

Benson, Lyman. *The Cacti of Arizona.* Tucson, AZ: University of Arizona Press, 1969.

Benson, Lyman, and Robert A. Darrow. *Trees and Shrubs of the Southwest Deserts.* Tucson, AZ: University of Arizona Press, 1981.

Bernard, Nelson T. *Wildflowers Along Forest and Mesa Trails.* Albuquerque, NM: University of New Mexico Press, 1925.

Bowers, Janice Emily. *100 Desert Wildflowers of the Southwest.* Tucson, AZ: Southwest Parks and Monuments Association, 1989.

————. *100 Roadside Wildflowers of Southwest Woodlands.* Tucson, AZ: Southwest Parks and Monuments Association, 1987.

Coombes, Allen J. *Dictionary of Plant Names.* Portland, OR: Timber Press, 1990.

Craighead, John J., Frank C. Craighead, Jr., and Ray J. Davis. *A Field Guide to Rocky Mountain Wildflowers.* Boston, MA: Houghton Mifflin Company, 1963.

Crittenden, Mabel. *Trees of the West.* Millbrae, CA: Celestial Arts, 1977.

Crittenden, Mabel, and Dorothy Telfer. *Wildflowers of the West,* Millbrae, CA: Celestial Arts, 1975.

Desert Botanical Garden Staff. *Arizona Highways Presents Desert Wildflowers.* Phoenix, AZ: Desert Botanical Garden, 1988.

Dodge, Natt N. *100 Desert Wildflowers in Natural Color.* Globe, AZ: Southwestern Monuments Association, 1963.

————. *Flowers of the Southwest Deserts.* Globe, AZ: Southwestern Monuments Association, 1969.

————. *100 Roadside Wildflowers of Southwest Uplands in Natural Color.* Globe, AZ: Southwestern Monuments Association, 1967.

Elias, Thomas S. *The Complete Trees of North America.* New York: Van Nostrand Reinhold, 1980.

Elmore, Francis H. *Shrubs and Trees of the Southwest Uplands.* Tucson, AZ: Southwest Parks and Monuments Association, 1976.

Florists' Publishing Company. *New Pronouncing Dictionary of Plant Names.* Chicago: Florists' Publishing Company, 1990.

Foxx, Teralene S., and Dorothy Hoard. *Flowers of the Southwestern Forests and Woodlands.* Los Alamos, NM: Los Alamos Historical Society, 1984.

Gentry, Howard Scott. *Agaves of Continental North America.* Tucson, AZ: University of Arizona Press, 1982.

Jaeger, Edmund C. *Desert Wild Flowers.* Stanford, CA: Stanford University Press, 1940.

Kearney, Thomas H., and Robert H. Peebles. *Arizona Flora.* 2nd ed. Berkeley, CA: University of California Press, 1951.

Lamb, Edgar, and Brian Lamb. *Colorful Cacti of the American Deserts.* New York: Macmillan Publishing Company, 1974.

Lamb, Samuel H. *Woody Plants of the Southwest.* Santa Fe, NM: Sunstone Press, 1977.

Lehr, J. Harry. *A Catalogue of the Flora of Arizona.* Phoenix, AZ: Desert Botanical Garden, 1978.

Little, Elbert L. *The Audubon Society Field Guide to North American Trees* (Western Region). New York: Alfred A. Knopf, 1980.

Martin, William C., and Charles R. Hutchins. *Fall Wildflowers of New Mexico.* Albuquerque, NM: University of New Mexico Press, 1988.

————. *Summer Wildflowers of New Mexico.* Albuquerque, NM: University of New Mexico Press, 1986.

McDougall, W. B. *Grand Canyon Wild Flowers.* Flagstaff, AZ: Museum of Northern Arizona, 1964.

Mickel, John T. *How To Know the Ferns and Fern Allies.* Dubuque, IA: William C. Brown Publishers, 1979.

Miller, Howard A., and Samuel H. Lamb. *Oaks of North America.* Happy Camp, CA: Naturegraph Publishers, Inc., 1985.

Mohlenbrock, Robert H. *Wildflowers: A Quick Identification Guide to the Wildflowers of North America.* New York: Macmillan Publishing Company, 1987.

Munz, Philip A. *California Desert Wildflowers.* Berkeley, CA: University of California Press, 1962.

————. *A Flora of Southern California*. Berkeley, CA: University of California Press, 1974.

Newcomb, Lawrence. *Newcomb's Wildflower Guide*. Boston, MA: Little, Brown & Company, 1977.

Niehaus, Theodore F., Charles L. Ripper, and Virginia Savage. *A Field Guide to Southwestern and Texas Wildflowers*. Boston, MA: Houghton Mifflin Company, 1984.

Orr, Robert T., and Margaret C. Orr. *Wildflowers of Western America*. New York: Alfred A. Knopf, 1974.

Parker, Kittie F. *An Illustrated Guide to Arizona Weeds*. Tucson, AZ: University of Arizona Press, 1986.

Patraw, Pauline Mead. *Flowers of the Southwest Mesas*. Globe, AZ: Southwestern Monuments Association, 1959.

Pesman, M. Walter. *Meet the Natives*. Denver, CO: Pruett Publishing, 1988.

Phillips, Arthur M. *Grand Canyon Wildflowers*. Flagstaff, AZ: Grand Canyon Natural History Association, 1979.

Rickett, Harold W. *Wild Flowers of the United States*. Vol. 4 (in 3 parts). New York: McGraw-Hill Co., 1973.

Spellenberg, Richard. *The Audubon Society Field Guide to North American Wildflowers* (Western Region). New York: Alfred A. Knopf, 1979.

Venning, Frank D. *Wildflowers of North America: A Guide to Field Identification*. New York: Golden Press, 1984.

Vines, Robert A. *Trees, Shrubs and Woody Vines of the Southwest*. Austin, TX: Texas Press, 1976.

Ward, Grace B., and Onas M. Ward. *190 Wildflowers of the Southwestern Deserts in Natural Color*. Palm Desert, CA: Best-West Publications, 1978.

INDEX

Each plate number, genus, and scientific family name appears in **BOLDFACE** type.